Metaculture

PUBLIC WORLDS

Dilip Gaonkar and Benjamin Lee, Series Editors

G R E G U R B A N

Metaculture

How Culture Moves

through the World

F O R E W O R D B Y B E N J A M I N L E E

PUBLIC WORLDS, VOLUME 8

UNIVERSITY OF MINNESOTA PRESS

MINNEAPOLIS LONDON

Published by the University of Minnesota Press
111 Third Avenue South, Suite 290
Minneapolis, MN 55401-2520
http://www.upress.umn.edu

Library of Congress Cataloging-in-Publication Data

Urban, Greg, 1949-
    Metaculture : how culture moves through the world / Greg Urban.
        p.   cm. — (Public worlds ; v. 8)
    Includes bibliographical references and index.
    ISBN 0-8166-3841-1 (hard : alk. paper) — ISBN 0-8166-3842-X (pbk. : alk. paper)
        1. Culture.   2. Social values.   3. Intercultural communication.   4. Civilization, Modern—Philosophy.   5. Tradition (Philosophy)   I. Title.   II. Series.
    HM621 .U72 2001
    306—dc21

                                                                        2001003515

Printed in the United States of America on acid-free paper

The University of Minnesota is an equal-opportunity educator and employer.

12 11 10 09 08 07 06 05 04 03 02 01   10 9 8 7 6 5 4 3 2 1

Nature cannot be ordered about, except by obeying her.
                                        —Francis Bacon, *Novum Organum* (1620),
                                                          book 1, aphorism 129
                                                      (translated by J. Spedding)

. . . we create continuously before us the road we must journey upon . . .
                                        —Thomas Pynchon, *Mason and Dixon*

Contents

Foreword

Benjamin Lee

A foreword to a book is not unlike a christening of a ship. It launches the reader into a new text at the same time, one hopes, that it accelerates the book's circulation among an ever-widening audience. Greg Urban's new book, *Metaculture*, not only partakes in these minor rituals of print capitalism, but also explicitly puts them at the heart of the investigation of culture. What are the implications of using the concept of circulation as the framework for looking at cultural processes? What are the issues and methodologies at stake in such a turn?

The lucky but probably unsuspecting reader will be led through a fascinating and, at times, mind-bending terrain of Brazilian Indian myths and rituals, nuclear discourses, movie reviews, and declarations of independence, not to mention the disciplines of linguistics, anthropology, semiotics, and sociology—all aimed at elucidating the dynamics of cultural production. Yet this is not the culture concept of E. B. Tylor, Alfred Kroeber, or even Victor Turner or Clifford Geertz. Nor is it the culture of cultural studies or poststructuralist literary analysis. Instead, it is culture as metaculture, or culture about culture, that provides ways of seeing continuities and discontinuities in all social processes.

In Urban's hands, circulation is not simply the movement of people, things, and ideas within or among societies. Instead, it is a process with its own types of abstraction and constraint produced by the semiotic nature of the circulating forms. Urban shares this insight with thinkers such as Jürgen Habermas and Benedict Anderson, who also emphasize that the public sphere and nationalism grew out of the circulation, reading, and discussion of specific textual forms (novels, journals, newspapers), but he differs in his focus. The use of any cultural form both presupposes the existence of other forms and, as an action, brings about new ones. A metacultural judgment can see the form in terms of its similarity to previous ones, or in terms of what it has brought about or "created," setting up a contrast that Urban uses to elucidate the differences between tradition and modernity that underlie the whole book. How he uses empirical analyses to illuminate rather than reify this distinction is one of the many pleasures of this book. But perhaps even more important is the turn to circulation itself, and perhaps translating some of his ideas into other vocabularies makes it easier to see the importance of the breakthrough.

Two at first glance unlikely allies, both mentioned by Urban in different breaths, demonstrate the range of issues raised by his book: the semiotician and philosopher Charles Sanders Peirce, and the literary scholar and cultural critic Walter Benjamin. From Peirce we can get an original insight about how signs, circulation, and community work together to create interpretable meanings; from Benjamin, especially in his classic article, "The Work of Art in the Age of Mechanical R·production," we see how these semiotic themes might be used to look at the problems of tradition and modernity.

Urban's account of circulation brings together three themes of Peirce into a productive synthesis: the self-reflexivity of the sign, the open-ended nature of semiosis, and the semiotic construction of community. The self-reflexivity is built into the very definition of a sign. According to Peirce, a sign consists of three parts, a sign vehicle, the object, and an interpretant or interpreting cognition, which stand in an irreducibly triadic relation to one another. The sign vehicle stands in some specified relation to the object. What we might call the internal structure of the sign determines the interpretant to stand in the same relation to the object as the sign vehicle, while its external structure brings it about that another sign stands in a similar relation to the object that its interpretant does, ad infinitum in a potentially infinite process of semiosis. The self-reflexive dimension of semiosis introduces a continuous interplay between what might be called presupposition and creativity: Each sign presupposes a relation between itself and its object that has been brought about by previous signs, yet it also creates another sign to assume a similar relation, and so on. In a passage picked up by both Jacques Derrida and Paul de Man, Peirce reanalyzes the role of rhetoric in the trivium of logic, grammar, and rhetoric that is at the heart of classical sign theory: Instead of being part of the arts of persuasion or the classification of tropes, rhetoric becomes the process by which "signs give birth to other signs."

Peirce extends his semiotic analysis by introducing various classifications of signs based upon the nature of the sign vehicle, the relation between sign vehicle and the object, and the different types of interpretants. Among his interpretants are various types of arguments, including deduction, induction (statistical inference), and abduction (hypothesis generation), that form the core of scientific inquiry. Peirce then defines reality as that which an ideal scientific community would come to agree upon as true. He believed that the self-correcting quality of scientific investigating would weed out competing theories and, eventually, hit upon what was true. Science is a special type of community built around specific semiotic processes of argument, inference, and experimentation. Some of his later writings suggest an even more radical interpretation: In order for science to function, it has to create a notion of a presupposed external reality as the end of inquiry.

The notion of a community created by specific semiotic and interpretive processes links Peirce with the contemporary discussions of interpretive communities and social imaginaries that have been developed by such thinkers as Benedict Anderson, Jürgen Habermas, Richard Rorty, Charles Taylor, and Cornelius Castoriadis. Urban combines these different strands of Peirce's thought—mediation/circulation, self-reflexivity, and community—through a notion of metaculture. Metaculture consists of judgments people make about similarities and differences, whether they judge token instances of cultural production to be manifestations of the same cultural element; they are a second-order form of semiotic self-reflexivity that helps frame first-order processes. Like Peirce's account of the scientific community, metacultural judgments form the normative core for the creation of community and the reproduction of culture. Urban extends these insights from Peirce's focus on the development of scientific inquiry into an account of the metaculture of newness, and thereby enters the terrain of Benjamin's insights into tradition and modernity.

In "The Work of Art in the Age of Mechanical Reproduction," Benjamin weaves together several themes that form the core for much of his subsequent thinking about the relations between cultural form, tradition, modernity, mass culture, and capitalism. One of the achievements of Urban's analysis is that he provides a semiotic framework that sharpens these insights by allowing us to see the connections between and among them. Benjamin argues that modern techniques of mechanical reproduction detach cultural objects from tradition by substituting a "plurality of copies for a unique existence" and displacing the artwork from a particular site of viewing in which it determines the audience to the interpretive situation of the individual beholder or listener. Traditional art is linked to ritual, to what we might now call its performative role in integrating the artwork and its context. The authenticity of the artwork is tied to its ritual location; it is a token with no classifying type. Instead, it accrues meaning through its history, through an indexical chain traceable to its originary moment and place. The authenticity and aura of authority conveyed by the object lie in its unique ability to signal something beyond itself, namely, the totality it ritually invokes; this produces a distancing between the audience and the artwork that contributes to the latter's authority.

Mechanical reproduction of the artwork produces a "plurality of images" that severs the link to unique performance and context, thereby disembedding the artwork from tradition and shattering its aura. The authentic token now becomes a token of a type that is no longer appreciated by an audience tethered to an act of ritual performance, but to a dispersed reception made up of individualized acts of appreciation. The uniqueness and permanence associated with traditional artworks are replaced in modernity with transitoriness and reproducibility.

Instead of Benjamin's focus on visual objects (paintings, sculptures, photography, film), Urban looks at discourse in its oral and print versions. His counterpart to Benjamin's artwork as the subject of ritual and cult activities is the telling of myths among a "traditional" Brazilian Indian group, the Shokleng, and various forms of contemporary genres such as movie reviews. He then draws a distinction between the replication and dissemination of culture. Culture is spread through its instantiation in things, in token manifestations. Meaning is lodged in forms that are spread by public "dissemination"; these forms are then responded to, interpreted, and re-externalized in processes of cultural "replication." A simple example of this might be the telling of a myth, the encoding of a specific set of meanings in sounds and bodily gestures; if subsequent myth tellings were judged equivalent to earlier ones (a metacultural judgment), then we would have an example of some form of replication. For culture to spread or circulate, it must be replicated through different types of social relations. In traditional societies, dissemination and replication tend to be fused. Among the Shokleng, there is a ritual occasion in which different participants alternate in reciting and repeating consecutive syllables of the origin myth, thereby foregrounding the link between replication, dissemination, and the reproduction of community.

Urban's counterpart to Benjamin's mechanical reproduction of artworks is the printed book. With the development of new technologies such as printing, dissemination and replication differentiate. As books became stabilized commodities during the spread of print capitalism, it became possible to separate the circulation of books from the labor (manual and intellectual) involved in producing them. Urban suggests that printing allows people to acquire more books more easily than before, and to compare and evaluate them. As the circulation of books expands, the possibility of local cultural replication decreases. The common basis for metacultural judgments then becomes the interest that owners have in acquiring books; demand becomes the key, and people become "driven not so much by a desire to reproduce the exact same thing, as by a desire to produce objects that, while not totally new, appear new enough to attract the interest of those who already have the old thing." What emerges is a metaculture of newness in which culture replicates itself via a striving for newness. The emphasis is upon the creation of new pathways of dissemination through the production of new objects; as Urban puts it, a metaculture of newness becomes the driving force behind the spread of capitalism. As a structuring presupposition, a metaculture of newness creates demand for future circulations.

Both Benjamin and Urban see a link between tradition and ritual performance. By the delicate semiotic calibration of objects and actions, ritual performances produce a vision of social totality that plays a crucial role in social and cultural reproduction. The artwork presents the totality it helps to invoke and create. A statue of a goddess in a Greek temple or an image of the Madonna in a medieval church is thus seen as embodying a higher reality, and it is this connection, along with their location in a particular time and space, that provides them with their aura.

The speech act counterpart to Benjamin's artwork rituals might be the baptismal rituals for proper names, which are also performances that bestow an object with "authenticity" and prepare it for an individualized and unique history. The counterpart in traditional Shokleng society (there was no traditional self-ascribed proper name for the group) is the multivoiced ritual telling of the origin myth. The emphasis on syllable-for-syllable accuracy ensures that it is the same "object" in each telling, and the organization of the participants and audience becomes a microcosm of the very social organization created in the narrated myth. For both Benjamin and Urban, mechanical reproduction frees the object from its dependence on ritual. For Urban, this leads to the development of societies organized around a metaculture of newness, while for Benjamin it leads to the development of mass audiences and participation that have transformed the nature of art and perception.

According to Benjamin, the most powerful agent in this shattering of the aura of the traditional artwork is film, which reactivates the reproduced object in the particular situation of the individual viewer (not the ritual context of the traditional artwork) and changes the very mode of perception from contemplation to distraction. Urban adds to these insights by adding another level of discursive mediation essential to mass circulation and commodification: that of metacultural commentary and review. In a series of fascinating examples, he analyzes movie reviews as metacultural commentaries that, in establishing what is new about each film, thereby accelerate the films' dissemination as commodities. Under a metaculture of newness, objects must be seen as creative responses to other objects, not merely as fixed replicas as in a metaculture of tradition. The purpose of film reviews is to give audiences who have not yet seen the film a sense of its newness. The metaculture of newness adds a self-reflexive dimension to movie reviews. In order for the review to circulate, it must be seen as an interesting response to the film; at the same time, favorable reviews present films as interesting responses to other social phenomena, whether to other films or even to the books from which they might be adapted. By attracting more readers, a successful review will increase its own circulation; it will also impart that interest to the film, thereby increasing demand for it. In this case, culture and metaculture end up reinforcing each other's circulatory potential by creating a semiotic bridge across different demand structures. The creation of such interconnections is at the heart of the expansion of capital.

These insights highlight and make explicit the metacultural dimensions of Habermas's analysis of the public sphere, which is a social imaginary that grew out of the circulation and discussion of novels, newspapers, journals, and magazines. It was this very discussion that helped to create the demand for the objects discussed. The culture of modernity depends upon the creation of social institutions organized around a metaculture of newness that directly contribute to the expansion of capitalism and democratic discourse. The public sphere develops, according to Habermas, "as the result of a felt need arising from the displacement of a metaculture of tradition by a metaculture of newness." It provides the environment for the development of a new political subject that is ideologically represented as the performative product of promises, contracts, and exchanges; and it is this subject that will become the basis for the constitutionalized people-hoods of modern nationalisms. The "voice of the people" is the tropic em-bodiment of the development and circulation of a metaculture of newness that will challenge traditional forms of political legitimation.

In a series of fascinating microanalyses in chapter 3, Urban pushes be-yond Habermas and Anderson and shows how "we, the people" emerges as the performative refiguring of the large circulatory processes of which it is a constitutive element; at the same time, it creates and names the semi-otic space through which these new forms of collective identity will circu-late, in effect creating the conditions necessary for its own circulation. Urban's account answers a question raised by Benjamin's analysis: Where does ritual go in modern society? Benjamin suggested that ritual performa-tivity plays a crucial role in the creation of the aura and authenticity as-cribed to the work of art in traditional societies, but that this is shattered with the development of mass subjectivity..Of course, one such form of mass subjectivity is that of a national people, and it is in the formation of "we, the people" that we can see how a metaculture of newness replaces ritual performativity with a performative ideology of reading that is at the heart of the public sphere and modern citizen-state. Each reading of a "nationalist" text creates a token instance of a "we" that subsumes the narrator/characters/readers in a collective agency that creates itself in every act of reading. These token "we's," when aggregated across acts of reading, become the basis for the imagined community of we-ness at the heart of nationalism. Nationalism is thus a particular example of the semi-otic constitution of community, a social imaginary created out of the semi-otic mediation of circulation.

The ritual performativity of traditional societies has been replaced by the mass performativity of nationalism. The key transformation is that the ritual performativity that creates the image of social totality in traditional societies has been relocated from a unique, indexical experience to shared, mass-mediated individual performative epiphanies that are aggregated into a social totality created by the act of reading under a metaculture of newness. The irony is that, under these specific conditions of the perfor-mative regimentation of the self-reflexivity of narration, the aura and au-thenticity that Benjamin associates with the traditional artwork reappear as properties of the newly created national subject.

In his concluding chapter, Urban shows how the circulation of meta-culture provides a unique perspective on contemporary processes of glob-alization. In a tour de force reworking of Habermas's ideas about the pub-lic sphere, Bourdieu's analysis of taste, and Gramsci's notion of hegemony, he argues that the development and circulation of a metaculture of new-ness produces not only "a greater consciousness of culture on the part of its producers," but also "a taking of control over destiny through self-consciousness or understanding." And yet it is perhaps the very sugges-tiveness of his approach that allows a darker interpretation, more in line with the concluding paragraphs of Benjamin's famous essay. Writing on the eve of the Holocaust and during the rise of fascism, Benjamin warned that combining a mass aesthetics with politics culminates in only one thing: war.

In our contemporary situation, is not the spread of a metaculture of newness leading to a backlash that creates new, essentialized nationalisms with their invented traditions of authenticity and aura, as we are now see-ing in many parts of the world? Or perhaps, as Michael Hardt and An-tonio Negri provocatively argue in their book *Empire*, are not postmodern-ism, as a metaculture of newness, and fundamentalism, as a metaculture of tradition, simply two different reactions to globalization, with the former appealing to the winners and the latter to the losers? If at the heart of globalization is the expansion of capitalism, what if a metaculture of new-ness cannot keep up with the cultural processes it helps to accelerate? Does that turn such a metaculture into an ideological formation that, in its essential falseness, is a necessary component in the expansion of capitalist inequalities and nondemocratic processes?

Although *Metaculture* may not provide definitive answers to such ques-tions, its great merit is to provide us with some of the new tools necessary to ask the right questions.

Acknowledgments

How does an amorphous idea take shape as a book? In the case of the present volume, the story began at the then Center for Psychosocial Studies (now the Center for Transcultural Studies) in the mid-1980s, when I first vaguely glimpsed what this book might become. I am grateful to all of my colleagues who were there at the time, and also to two intrepid research assistants, Matt Lawson and Janet Morford, who collected what must have seemed masses of pointless data. The Center continues to provide intellectual interactions, especially, most recently, discussions with Vincent Crapanzano, Dilip Gaonkar, Ben Lee, Michael Leff, Beth Povinelli, Michael Silverstein, and Michael Warner.

The other key matrix of interactions through which the ideas in this book were nourished is the University of Pennsylvania, and, especially, its anthropology department. The imprints of numerous colleagues and students are present, however subtly, throughout these pages. I am indebted to several outstanding research assistants, Hilary Parsons Dick, Jenny Jacobs, Kristin Smith Cahn von Seelen, and Matt Tomlinson, and to the various graduate students who provided commentary on innumerable draft versions—notably, Trevor Stack, Jeremy Wallach, and Kristina Wirtz. Other colleagues, especially Asif Agha, Nancy Farriss, Gary Tomlinson, and Stanton Wortham, contributed through conversations over the years. The University of Pennsylvania partially funded the sabbatical year during which this book was drafted.

That glorious year was spent at the Center for Advanced Study in the

Behavioral Sciences, a research institution nonpareil. My consciousness, at the time, was saturated by images of the rocky shorelines and golden hills of northern California, to be sure, but also by the gustatory impressions of those lovely meals prepared daily by Susan Beech for our delectation. I am thankful to the Center's directors Neil Smelser and Bob Scott for making this possible, as well as to the fellows during the 1998–99 academic year. Among my most constant interlocutors at the time were John Gumperz and Dan Segal, and also Don Brenneis and Wynne Furth.

Various friends and colleagues read manuscript versions and supplied invaluable comments, including Don Brenneis, Steve Feld, Aaron Fox, Laurie Graham, Webb Keane, Ben Lee, and Susan Lepselter. Adrian Cowell supplied information on the Uru-eu-wau-wau contact, as well as help with Figure 3. Fran Sarin of the University of Pennsylvania Museum of Archaeology and Anthropology's Photo Studio prepared Figures 12a and 12b from the Asch and Chagnon film. Thank you all.

I received copious feedback on excerpts of this manuscript (in varying degrees of preparation) presented as papers at the annual meetings of the American Anthropological Association in 1996, 1997, and 1999; at the University of California at Santa Cruz (anthropology), the University of Chicago (anthropology), Northwestern University (communication studies), Stanford University (both linguistics and cultural anthropology), Swarthmore College (linguistics), and Yale University (Latin American studies); and at a summer NEH Institute at Northwestern University. The influence of colleagues too numerous to mention has, as a result, found its way into my thought and writing.

Lastly, I would never have watched the movie *Babe* or had such intimate familiarity with the phenomena of cultural motion through families, not to mention motivation for writing this book, had it not been for my daughter, Jess, and her wonderful mom. They have my lasting love and appreciation.

And that's how—in part and in brief, to be sure—an idea became, through social interactions, a book.

1

The Once and Future Thing

Hic iacet Arthurus,
rex quondam rexque futurus.
Sir Thomas Malory, Le Morte d'Arthur, book 21, chapter 7

The Vector of Futurity

The answer is culture, but the riddle continues to vex, as if we have not yet
gotten it, not seen quite clearly. What moves through space and time, yet
has no Newtonian mass? What is communicated from individual to individual, group to group, yet is not a disease?[1] Our sphinx, in vaporous ap-
parition, peers down. Yes, this is the right word, but have we penetrated
the veil of mystery? For there is more. The ghost-like journey of our thing
(or is it things?) takes place along pathways, social pathways, that it itself
lays down. It creates the space that makes its movement possible. How
can it accomplish this social world-building task? The paradoxical answer
is that it must look like what has come before it, like what has already
been down that way. Its secret is in the mixture of oldness and newness
that makes the journey possible. The king is dead; long live the king!

Culture is necessarily characterized by its "onceness." It has been. But
culture is also on its way somewhere—whether or not it gets there—and,
hence, it is also characterized by its futurity. What I hope to do in this

book is follow this intrinsic vector of movement into a future. To leave it at "oneness" results in the trope that has dominated anthropology throughout the twentieth century. Culture recedes into a past, slipping away into ever murkier origins. Hence, it must be salvaged, dug up, preserved. There is the romance of discovering the thing in all of its dripping nostalgia.

But that trope misses the essential dynamism of culture, its restlessness, its itchy movement into uncharted and mysterious futures. There is something risky about the movement, but also something exciting. An appropriate figure for this riskiness, this restless seeking, is the entrepreneur, whose status as culture-bearer has been obscured by anthropology's obsessive concern with oneness and its reluctance to follow the vector of futurity. The entrepreneur takes something old into a new world, or tries something new out on an old world. The former is transparently cultural—taking the already given to new people, new places, another generation, hoping that something from the past will carry over. I propose to show, however, that the latter is no less cultural—giving something new to the same people (although I'll question what it means to be "new," and also what it means to be the "same people").

Reduced to its simplest formula, culture is whatever is socially learned, socially transmitted. It makes its way from point A (an individual or group) to point B (an individual or group). This book seeks to explore the no-man's-land between A and B. Rather than asking: What is the culture of A?—a traditional anthropological question where the fact of prior movement is read off of difference in the present—this book asks: What gets from A to B? How does it make that journey? Are some things better suited to make the journey than others? Do some travel more quickly than others? Are some more long-lived?

In the simplest case—I'll explore more complex ones later, including mass mediation of culture—if something immaterial is to get from an individual A to another individual B, it must first be lodged in a material entity—a story carried through the air in sounds, a gesture—that B can perceive. Let's call that material, perceptible entity α. α is a discrete and, possibly, unique thing. When it dies, it is gone.[2]

However, my interest is in something that lives on after α dies. α in effect undergoes a phoenix-like rebirth in other objects of the senses—another story, another gesture, another thing. The original is dead (or maybe it is not), but the original lives on in its copies. I catch a glimpse of culture, get a sense of its movement, if I find that B, subsequent to encountering α, produces a material form β, and β looks like or resembles α.

What carries over, in this case, is nonmaterial. The stuff moving through space and time is an abstract form or mold for the production of something material—a story that happens to be lodged in audible sounds, the abstract and reproducible outline of a gesture that happens to be incarnated in physical movements. The transitory home of culture is things in the world. But the stuff of culture is immaterial.

On the temporal trail of resemblances, I find myself in my outside observer's hat—my anthropologist's pith helmet, as it were—making judgments about similarities and differences between α and β. And in the case of things cultural, or so I want to argue, there is always, in some measure, a mixture of similarity and difference. Just how similar α and β have to be to be considered manifestations of the "same" cultural element is a matter of judgment, and it is a judgment that I, as an outside observer, can and must make in order to investigate culture.

However, if I as an outside observer can make this judgment, so too can participants in the ongoing set of social relations of which A and B are part. Such judgments made by natives about similarities and differences—continuity with the past and change—are part of what I will call *metaculture*, that is, culture that is about culture. A may pass to B not only the core of similarity between α and β that helps to circumscribe the cultural element; A may also pass on a judgment about the relationship of α to β. That judgment will be encoded in another material entity, another "story," so to speak, for which the written name ALPHA, the first letter of the Greek alphabet, might be appropriate to distinguish it as a metacultural form. Thus, ALPHA is metacultural in relationship to α because ALPHA is about α.

What makes ALPHA metacultural is not its physical characteristics as object—the combination of letters A + L + P + H + A—but its meaning, the fact that it is about other aspects of culture. As the abstract metacultural element gets passed on, that element could be studied by an outside observer as just another part of culture. But for the participants, the meaningfulness of one specific manifestation of the metacultural element might suffice to calibrate or define the relation of α to β—for example, the statement "β is the same as α," and, hence, that both are manifestations of the same cultural element, or "β is something new; it is not like α."

One aspect of culture, conceived in this way, is not only its inherent dynamism, its built-in propensity for change, but also its ability to generate self-interpretations or self-understandings that help to define what change or sameness is. And I am by no means unaware of the irony that I am at this very moment generating a piece of metaculture (the book you have before you), insignificant as my own offerings may be when compared with the veritable industry of metacultural production in the contemporary United States, including book and film reviews, about which I will have more to say in chapter 5. Indeed, the circulation of metaculture today reaches such remarkable proportions that nightly local news shows feature "news" (ALPHA) about fictional television shows (α). The Philadelphia channel 29 *Ten O'clock News*, for example, in its Sunday evening May 17, 1998, newscast, which directly followed the season finale of the show *The X-Files*, featured a news story on that show's leading actress, Gillian Anderson.

One question I will be asking throughout this book is: Why metaculture? What is this all about? And one answer I will be offering is this: Metaculture is significant in part, at least, because it imparts an accelerative force to culture. It aids culture in its motion through space and time. It gives a boost to the culture that it is about, helping to propel it on its journey. The interpretation of culture that is intrinsic to metaculture, immaterial as it is, focuses attention on the cultural thing, helps to make it an object of interest, and, hence, facilitates its circulation. The news story about *The X-Files* aids the circulation of the *The X-Files* itself, interesting people in it. From this perspective, metaculture is a supplement to culture.

Simultaneously, cultural expressions may also foster the circulation of the metaculture that is about them. In the case of *The X-Files*, the news story preview began:

> [Narrator's voice with logos, followed by film clips of actress Gillian Anderson]:
> Tonight, on Fox: Her TV show is a smash hit; now she has a feature film ready for the theaters. But what's life really like for *X-Files* star Gillian Anderson?
> [Cut to clip from interview with Anderson speaking]:
> "I wish I could tell you, but I'd have to kill you."
> [Cut to logo for Fox *Ten O'clock News*]:
> Find out tonight on the Fox *Ten O'clock News*.

The function of this clip was to get those who were already interested in, and, indeed, had just watched, *The X-Files* to stay tuned for the news.

The phenomenon of metacultural acceleration of culture, however, only discloses the mystery inside the enigma. We have yet to glimpse the riddle within. For the metaculture-culture relationship—wherein ALPHA means α—is itself a strange pathway of motion, the site of a magical interconversion. When it is put into place, a connection is established between two realms, one material, the other ethereal. Things in the world—objects of the senses, like ceramic pots or the flickering surface images of films projected onto a silver screen—brush up against, make contact with, ideas about those things. And the ideas come in this way to have effectiveness in the material realm.[3] Something of the world gets into the idea, and something of the idea gets into the world. Herein lies a secret about cultural motion.

I do not wish to dwell on metaculture just yet, however, central as the concept is to the mystery surrounding modern cultural motion and important as it will be as this book progresses. Instead, I want to wade further into the problem of movement itself. For I have only mentioned the simplest case of motion, where an individual A transmits something to another individual B.[4] In a perhaps more typical case, B may not have received the element from any one A, let alone from exposure to only one single concrete manifestation (α) of the element. In the case of a story understood metaculturally as "traditional"—the myth of the Giant Falcon, for example, in the Brazilian Indian community residing at Posto Indígena Ibirama—B may have heard "the story," that is, various tellings understood as manifestations of a single story, from many different individuals at many different times. We can think of all of these variant manifestations of the cultural element as α_1, α_2, and so forth.[5] The judgment made by outside observers, in this case, as well as natives, if the interpretation is based on a metaculture of tradition, is that β is essentially like or one of the set of manifestations $\{\alpha_1, \alpha_2, \ldots, \alpha_n\}$, all of which encode or reflect or manifest a single abstract cultural element. β then becomes, effectively, α_{n+1}.

But what if a given manifestation of culture is not an incarnation of a single recognizable cultural element, let alone a copy of a given specific earlier "original," after which it is fashioned? What if outside observers, as well as natives, have a hard time pinning down a temporal connection grounded in linear movement? I am now thinking, especially, of contemporary Western art and scientific productions, where a given entity—a novel, say—may be regarded as something radically, well, "novel" by the circulating metaculture. Does this mean that the entity itself is sui generis, and therefore does not participate in the general processes of motion I am seeking to characterize, that the vector of futurity ceases to operate here? I propose to argue that such an entity—let us call it ω—may still be a manifestation of the movement of culture, just not the replication of a specific antecedent. Rather, the new production makes reference to a range of prior and seemingly disparate cultural elements. Without those temporal referents, the new entity would have little prospect of further motion or future circulation. It would simply be incomprehensible.

I am arguing that the novel production, rather than becoming α_{n+1}, in effect assimilates earlier manifestations of culture unto itself. The various manifestations of a whole set of cultural elements become, in effect, just the backdrop or ground for the emergence of the figure ω. They are the context of emergence of ω, and, in some sense, ω defines the collection of prior expressions as interconnected, as forming a system, just by virtue of calling up reference to all of them. What they share in common is that the traces of them can all be seen in ω.[6]

I realize, even as I write this, how cryptic it sounds. However, I hope it is apparent—and I will take up the matter further in chapter 2—that I am talking about what culture is like under "modernity." Under modernity, it is no longer possible to study just the linear motion of an abstract underlying element—for example, the myth of the Giant Falcon—which can be traced from A to B to C. In the kind of movement I am describing in the case of ω, past expressions of culture are only lightly hinted at by ω, haunting it without being fully apparent. In effect, ω brings all of those hinted-at entities forward into it, traveling along the vector of futurity. The movement of culture takes place in ghost-like fashion, with ω incarnating various aspects of different kinds of prior expressions, yet seeming to be new. Looked at from the perspective of ω-type culture, therefore, what appears to move through space and time is a whole system of relationships.

It is crucial to my argument that temporal movement is what makes possible the recognition of a system or structure. Systematicity appears to emerge, and, therefore, does in fact emerge, because ω contains within itself traces of all the cultural elements that were the backdrop against which it took shape. That is what brings those diverse cultural expressions together, making them form a system.

Having said this, it is also important to recall that modernity itself is part of a naturally occurring metaculture. As a part of metaculture, modernity is an attempt to define relations between α's and β's, with the vector of futurity pushing the β's forward towards ω-like expressions. I propose to take care to distinguish the metaculture of modernity from the cultural processes that the metaculture seeks to define. One conclusion I will draw is that modernity propels culture in a different manner than does "tradition," but that, even under an explicit metaculture of modernity, the linear movement is still detectable through probing fine details. The kind of movement that modernity stimulates—the movement of a system of relationships through us—is crucial to the reproduction of culture in what Walter Benjamin (1969) called "the age of mechanical reproduction."

I propose to explore culture's movement through the world by taking you on a journey I have myself taken. Yet I do so with a certain trepidation, derived not only from a loathing of those pointless personal narratives that make up too much of contemporary ethnography—the merciless blather of: "There I was, under the blue sky on a sandy beach, the palm trees swaying in the breeze . . ."—but also from the humility I feel in the revelation that this journey has brought. How can it be that, even in those moments when I most fancy myself a producer of novel ω expressions, I am but a humble and unwitting conduit for prior ω (or are they α?) expressions?

It was February 1982. I recall this, but I can also reconstruct it from my field notes. On February 10, in fact, I was in São Paulo, Brazil, and at precisely 8:40 A.M. local time I boarded a plane bound for Dallas, Texas. From there I would take another plane to San Antonio to rendezvous with my wife, then a first-year medical student at the Health Sciences Center of the University of Texas. I was a fledgling assistant professor of anthropology at the University of Texas at Austin, which is located eighty miles to the north. For the past several months, I had been residing at an indigenous post near the town of Ibirama in the southern Brazilian state of Santa Catarina, immersing myself in the local culture there to which I had grown so attached that refrains from the local origin myth ran through my head and, in almost dream-like fashion, communicated to me something profound about my own life: "I descend dancing, confronting my destiny."

Now I was coming back, even if only for a short break. There is always something revelatory about a return to the States after a prolonged stay abroad. The minutiae of daily life stand out as foreign despite their utter mundaneness—conveyor belts at the airport along which luggage streams, the shape and color of taxicabs, even the reassuring lilt of central Texas English. It is as if one sees and hears it all for the first time. The experience is fleeting, but it allows a special glimpse of reality—such as phenomenologists claim for the eidetic reduction, the process of stripping away the nonessentials to reveal experience's essences. Travel provides one with ready-made eidetic reductions. In my case, I would be going back to Brazil a month later for another prolonged stay. Meanwhile, I was eager to emerge, blinking, from what seemed an isolation from the American public sphere.

The hot topic of talk was nuclear war, global thermonuclear war. Ronald Reagan was president of the United States, having taken office just a year earlier, and Leonid Brezhnev was leader of the then Union of Soviet Socialist Republics. The Berlin Wall was still standing.

How strangely familiar all of this nuclear war talk seemed, foreign though it was from my vantage point in the steamy tropics of Brazil. Yes— it reminded me of my youth. Standing on the playground of Oakview Elementary School, I recall a conversation with my childhood friend, Warren Webb. Would we see each other again? It was the autumn of 1962, with a chilling wind under gray skies adding a tangible layer of coldness to the inner chill we felt. How apt the metaphor of a cold war. If Kennedy launched a missile attack against Cuba, then—heaven forbid!—the Russians would attack us with nuclear weapons. There would be all-out nuclear war. We would lose that warmth of human companionship as we receded into our basement fallout shelters and, ultimately, as everyone secretly knew, into doom. Sociability would vanish with the traces of life itself. The term "nuclear winter" had not yet been coined, but we would have known intuitively, through synesthesia, what it meant: the perpetual coldness of death.

But twenty years later, in 1982, America was warmed by the talk of nuclear war, a talk that gradually spread, building conversations and communities around it. Even my wife, ensconced in her own cave-like isolation of the first-year medical student, had come into contact with it. It was she who told me about a set of articles in the *New Yorker* magazine. She had heard about them on National Public Radio. I should look them up, she said, and I did.

The articles were by Jonathan Schell, a staff writer for the *New Yorker*, and they were later assembled into a little book called *The Fate of the Earth*. The articles were mesmerizing, though I cannot be sure, as I write this today, precisely why. How much did their interest have to do with my odd position, having just returned from field research in Amerindian Brazil? Was I the barbarian coming to Rome, beholding its glittering spectacle of public life? Was I fascinated by the novelty of Schell's words? Or, alternatively, was there in them the echo of something familiar, feelings I had known as a child, suppressed by twenty intervening years of distraction? After all, the nuclear hysteria of the 1950s and early 1960s gave way to the Vietnam era antiwar movement, and that movement dissipated into generalized "countercultural" activity in opposition not only to the American government, but also to the middle-class way of life itself. Schell had picked up on something—a fearful and steely coldness at the prospect of nuclear devastation—that the conviviality of the late 1960s and 1970s had forgotten. But he managed to summon the latter to call attention to the former.

Here are some of the words I encountered in 1982:

> Four and a half billion years ago, the earth was formed. Perhaps a half billion years after that, life arose on the planet. For the next four billion years, life became steadily more complex, more varied, and more ingenious, until, around a million years ago, it produced *mankind*$_i$—the most complex and ingenious species of them all. Only six or seven thousand years ago—a period that is to the history of the earth as less than a minute is to a year—civilization emerged, enabling *us*$_i$ to build up a human world, and to add to the marvels of evolution marvels of *our*$_i$ own: marvels of art, of science, of social organization, of spiritual attainment. But, as *we*$_i$ built higher and higher, the evolutionary foundation beneath *our*$_i$ feet became more and more shaky, and now, in spite of all *we*$_i$ have learned and achieved—or, rather, because of it—*we*$_i$ hold this entire terrestrial creation hostage to nuclear destruction, threatening to hurl it back into the inanimate darkness from which it came. And this threat of self-destruction and planetary destruction is not something that *we*$_i$ will pose one day in the future, if *we*$_i$ fail to take certain precautions; it is here now, hanging over the heads of all of *us*$_i$ at every moment . . . It is as though life itself were one huge distraction, diverting *our*$_i$ attention from the peril to life. In its apparent durability, a world menaced with imminent doom is in a way deceptive. It is almost an illusion. Now *we*$_{i,j}$ are sitting at the breakfast table drinking *our*$_{i,j}$ coffee and reading the newspaper, but in a moment *we*$_{i,j}$ may be inside a fireball whose temperature is tens of thousands of degree. Now *we*$_{i,j}$ are on *our*$_{i,j}$ way to work, walking through the city streets, but in a moment *we*$_{i,j}$ may be standing on an empty plain under a darkened sky looking for the charred remnants of *our*$_{i,j}$ children. Now *we*$_i$ are alive, but in a moment *we*$_i$ may be dead. Now there is human life on earth, but in a moment it may be gone. (Schell 1982, 181–82; my italics and subscripts)

What to make of these words? Perhaps they seem strange to you because of my tinkering with italics and subscripts, or perhaps because they come out of a past that now seems unsettlingly distant, however familiar. If so, that is not bad, since they were also, in some measure (and even at the time), strange to me. Strange, but fascinating. I was drawn to them, like Princess Aurora, as if in a stupor, up the stairs to the sorceress Maleficent. They worked their magic on me, to the point, even, of getting me to do their bidding with regard to others.

Now I wish to conceal part of the story, however, in order that I may later reveal it. For this part was, so to speak, concealed from me when I first reconstructed it. There was a piece to the puzzle I had misplaced or overlooked—an important piece, the period from 1982 to 1984. The absence nagged at me, but my recent reconstruction had ignored it, instead picking up the story in 1985, when I was back in Brazil, this time lecturing at the University of São Paulo on the arcane subject of semiotics, with a focus on Amerindian languages and cultures. My colleague and good friend, Sylvia Caiuby Novaes, intrigued by our conversations about nuclear war, arranged for me to give a public lecture on the subject.

In Brazil, the burning issues of public debate seemed far removed from those preoccupying the U.S. public sphere. This was especially true in the case of American scenarios for high-tech nuclear war—they were just not in the public consciousness of the people of São Paulo in the mid-1980s. In my talk, I used what had come to be, on American campuses, a standard technique for illustrating nuclear devastation. On a map of São Paulo, I superimposed a grid illustrating the blast effects of a five-megaton bomb detonated over the center of the city—"ground zero." American students would be (and were, on college campuses across the United States) duly horrified by this exercise. But in São Paulo, the response was different. One person quipped: "This is a *gringo* thing. I don't know what we have to do with it; we don't have bombs." Responding to my statement that a nuclear war could destroy all of humanity, not just Americans, someone else remarked (was this a uniquely Brazilian scenario?): "Well, it's not going to happen that way. You see, the bomb that was headed for Brazil, the guy who was there was probably asleep and forgot to press the button at the right time; and besides, if he did manage to press the button, that missile wouldn't work anyway. In any case, we have absolutely no control over this, so you guys up there in North America, you worry about it. You've got all the bombs; you've got all the power. It's your problem, so deal with it."

In my conscious reconstruction of the events, this story stood out in my mind.[7] I learned from this experience—and other related ones—that the rhetoric of the U.S. antinuclear movement did not necessarily travel well. As a piece of culture, the story of nuclear devastation made its way through various parts of North America, but it could also experience resistance to its movement outside of its natural pathways. What was the source of this resistance?

That question preoccupied me, and so I decided to take a closer look at Schell's book. What was perplexing was the seemingly inclusive and encompassing character of Schell's "we." His was a "we" of the human species with which all people could (couldn't they?) identify: "It [evolution] produced *mankind*$_i$—the most complex and ingenious species of them all. Only six or seven thousand years ago . . . civilization emerged, enabling *us*$_i$ to build up a human world." The "us" here is clearly meant to have the same reference as "mankind"—"us humans." What could be more encompassing than this? And if one accepts inclusion in the category of human—aren't "we", after all, all humans?—then Schell's conclusion seems to inexorably follow: "As *we*$_i$ built higher and higher, the evolutionary foundation beneath *our*$_i$ feet became more and more shaky, and now, in spite of all *we*$_i$ have learned and achieved—or, rather, because of it—*we*$_i$ hold this entire terrestrial creation hostage to nuclear destruction, threatening to hurl it back into the inanimate darkness from which it came." Yes, we humans are responsible for this mess. How could my Brazilian audience that day not see this? Could they not identify with being human?

Inspecting Schell's pronominal usages under the microscope, the "us humans" seemed to be reshaped, remolded into something much more specific by its surrounding words: "Now *we*$_{i,j}$ are sitting at the breakfast table drinking *our*$_{i,j}$ coffee and reading the newspaper, but in a moment *we*$_{i,j}$ may be inside a fireball whose temperature is tens of thousands of degree." Well, wait a minute. Who sits at breakfast tables drinking coffee and reading newspapers? Not me, at least not in the months leading up to February 1982, when I first read these words. For me, the statement should have read: "Now we are sitting around campfires, listening to myths and scary stories about jaguars." And how about: "Now *we*$_{i,j}$ are on *our*$_{i,j}$ way to work, walking through the city streets . . ."? Again, not me. For me it should have been: "Now we are trekking through the forest, trying not to step on poisonous snakes." If Schell's words had a detectable hollowness in some measure even for me, then what about for others?

I actually undertook a detailed study of the 1,310 first-person plural pronouns I found in *The Fate of the Earth*.[8] This was not easy, as the pronominal references were not always as explicit as those in the passage I cited above. My technique was simply to go through and jot down what each "we" or "us" or "our" meant in its specific context, trying to presume nothing at the outset. However, it quickly became clear that the pronouns fell into certain broad classes over which you and I might quibble, but which give a general sense of the patterning of the first person plural pronoun in this text. The classes and their absolute numbers and frequencies are listed in Table 1.[9]

So I had some evidence here about the possible reasons for resistance to the flow of this particular bit of culture. While *The Fate of the Earth* was

Table 1. "We" Categories in Schell

CATEGORY	NUMBER	PERCENTAGE OF TOTAL
1. Human species	855	65
2. Present generation of species	185	14
3. Within quotations	94	7
4. Ambiguous	68	5
5. Author plus readers	45	4
6. Generalized individual	36	3
7. Nongovernment	13	1
8. Nonscientist	12	1
9. United States	1	0
10. United States and U.S.S.R.	1	0
Totals	1,310	100

built up around a "we" of the human species—such "we's" accounting for 79 percent of all first-person plural usages in the text—specific inflections of that species-wide "we" suggested a more provincial perspective, more restricted meanings. Those meanings could be seized upon by someone to whom they did not seem transparent—as in the case of my Brazilian audience: "This is a *gringo* thing. I don't know what *we* have to do with it." The "we" of this remark specifically excluded me, and, presumably, all other gringos, though it is a "we" that might be readily inhabited by others, not just Brazilians. Could not many Third- and Fourth-World peoples identify with the statement: "We don't have bombs"?

Thus far my story is a heroic one, the anthropologist's perspective as outsider enables him privileged access to culture—in this case, to resistance to the movement of one piece of culture. However, our hero has not told the whole story. Something is not quite right; there is a piece missing. What happened between 1982 and 1984?

During that period, I now recollect, I was voraciously reading in the nuclear war literature, and, in the spring of 1984, I wrote a paper, "Cultural Representations of Nuclear War," which circulated samizdat, but which, mercifully, I never published. Moreover, I developed an undergraduate course, "Culture and Nuclear War," which I taught several times in the middle and late 1980s, and in which the unpublished paper was among the texts students were asked to read. I remember this, alas, only after having reconstructed the heroic tale—the tale of anthropologist as over and above culture, as one able to give privileged readings of culture (a notion I now find suspect, but not entirely wrong).

Why is this bit of self-archaeology humbling? So I wrote such a paper called "Cultural Representations of Nuclear War"—so what? It occurred to me only recently to look at that paper itself under the microscope, to see what pronominal patterns might be at work there. My first thought was that they should certainly be different from Schell's, since I was, after all, an anthropologist and a scientist, not a journalist. Moreover, the central argument of the paper was different from anything I had read in Schell or elsewhere. I was producing a piece of ω culture—or so I thought. My argument was that the then current antinuclear discourse was not taking account of the significant attachments that people have to collectivities like the United States or the then Union of Soviet Socialist Republics. Such attachments had to be brought into focus if antinuclear discourse were to engage the peace-through-strength position in any meaningful way. But the attachments also had to be realigned if the world was to avoid a nuclear conflagration.

My technique in studying my own writing, fourteen years after the fact, was the same as it had been in Schell's case. For each occurrence of "we," "us," "our," or "ourselves," I jotted down what seemed to be its specific meaning in its context. I then looked for patterns. The patterns I found are summarized in Table 2.

Table 2. "We" Categories in Urban (1984)

CATEGORY	NUMBER	PERCENTAGE OF TOTAL
1. Human species	90	57
2. Present generation of species	34	21
3. United States	11	7
4. Students of anthropology	6	4
5. Author plus readers	5	3
6. Viewers of *Dr. Strangelove*	5	3
7. Within quotations	3	2
8. Those who talk about nuclear war	3	2
9. Participants in the nuclear debate	1	1
Totals	158	100

If you compare these with Table 1, you will see that some of the categories are different. Table 2 includes a students of anthropology "we," a viewers of *Dr. Strangelove* "we," a those who talk about nuclear war "we," and a participants in the nuclear debate "we" that are not found in Table 1. And these "we's" confirm my original intuition that my own "we" usage would be distinct from Schell's. There are also, of course, the kinds of "we" in Schell that have no counterpart in my own paper.

However, the stunning result is the nearly identical frequencies of the human species and present generation of the human species "we"—the combined total for the human species "we" and the present generation of the human species "we" in Schell is 79 percent; in Urban it is 78 percent. The similarity is not coincidental. Compare the following passage from my paper (as I write this, the pronoun "my" gives me pause; was that really me? Should I not refer to myself in the third person as Urban 1984?):

> The variability of "right" from one culture to the next—which anthropologists discuss in connection with the concept of "cultural relativity"—does not affect the vehemence with which warriors endeavor to protect what they consider right. Nor has this moral variability been without its benefits for the species. On the contrary, alternative moral systems, alternative ways of doing things, provide a degree of flexibility, of adaptability in *our* species, that has allowed it, in the past 40,000 years or so, to expand into niches everywhere around the globe. This variability has been a key to *our* remarkable success.
>
> However, now, or so the proponents of disarmament maintain, a dark cloud has appeared on *our* previously sunny horizon—the specter of nuclear war. (italics added)

Was I producing a piece of ω culture, or was my work but a β copy of Schell's original? For those subscribing to a metaculture of novelty, the question looms large. Is worth not measured by the distinctiveness of one's expressions? Whatever the sources of Schell's own pronominal usage, this example provides evidence of the movement of culture through space and time—from Schell as A to me as B. Schell published his work originally in 1981. Presumably, he wrote it a year or two earlier. I drafted my paper in the spring of 1984, having read Schell's work first in February and March of 1982; thus, several years had passed from the time of Schell's α to the time of the β copy. The pattern of pronominal usage, as a detectable fragment of culture, managed to travel through time and across space from A to B, from Schell to me. What passed in this remarkable journey was an abstract pattern of pronominal usage, a pattern that has no detectable Newtonian mass. As I wrote my paper in the spring of 1984, a phoenix-like rebirth of the pattern was taking shape. And it was taking shape without my having been aware of it. Such is the mystery of culture.

The Once and Future Thing

Inertial and Accelerative Culture

What makes culture move? Part of the answer, or so I am arguing in this book, is that it is already in motion. And whatever is in motion tends to remain in motion unless something else stops it. This observation has been made implicitly or explicitly by many others, notably by the diffusionists,[10] for whom invention was understood as arduous, copying as easy. However, the principle—which I will, with only mild irony, refer to as the principle of inertia—is also intuitively appealing, and this for two different reasons.

The first has to do with simple presence or prior existence. Something tends to be copied just because it is there already. This is most apparent in the case of cultural and, especially, language learning by young children, for whom the models that are present are what tend to be reproduced. Why does a child learn the language it does? The answer is that it is the language spoken by those around it. This is inertial culture. The child does not set out to create something new. In the elementary case discussed earlier, the child B produces an expression β—for example, the word "mamma"—phonetically, [mama]—that happens to look like another earlier expression α produced by A, the parent. The principal reason for this is that the α expression is already there.[11] And the word might as well have been a gesture, a bodily posture, a facial expression, an attitude toward food or music, or any one of a number of capabilities under the control of B. The cause of β is the inertial carrying over of the abstract form of α, simply because of α's prior existence. This first type of inertia might be dubbed "existential."

There is a second and related, albeit distinct, intuitive reason for accepting a principle of inertia. It is possible to think of inertia as operating even in the motion of what I have been calling ω culture. In the present context, ω culture might be more appropriately, if wryly, dubbed "accelerative culture," that is, culture on the side of futurity, looking forward rather than backward, characterized by newness and novelty, rather than oldness and familiarity. In the case of accelerative culture, the expression ω produced by A—for example, Schell's *The Fate of the Earth*—is not simply a replica of some earlier book that has come before it, pace the main character in Borges's celebrated story, "Pierre Menard, Author of *Quixote*":

> [Menard] did not want to compose another *Quixote*—which is easy—but *the Quixote itself.* Needless to say, he never contemplated a mechanical transcription of the original; he did not propose to copy it. His admirable

intention was to produce a few pages which would coincide—word for word and line for line—with those of Miguel de Cervantes. ([1944] 1962, 39)

It must, instead, be significantly new.

The force behind such accelerative culture is the interest it generates, which stems in part from its novelty. It moves because it generates interest, catches the attention. How it accomplishes this task is what we (that is, you, the reader, and I, should you continue to so graciously accompany me on this journey) must investigate. However, one way it does so is by resembling something from the past that has already generated interest. The resemblances are not (or are not necessarily) blatant. And the whole cultural object cannot be a copy of some earlier original, the way one (re)telling of a myth, in a Brazilian Indian village, can be a copy of another. At the same time, the ω object must be recognizable to those in whom it is designed to kindle interest. To be recognizable, the object must draw upon earlier models, although it may—and, if it is truly original, must— weave together bits and pieces of different models. Consequently, the ω expression demands that it be analyzed if the continuities it contains are to emerge.

Those continuities—although present only in microaspects or facets of the overall cultural object—are examples of inertial culture. The β copies are copies not of a whole, recognizable cultural element, like a myth, but of some component of it, like the statistical frequencies of types of "we" usage. The principle of inertia, in the case of accelerative or ω culture, operates on α's that are pieces of a larger whole. The cultural elements flowing through the world give rise to specific aspects of the cultural object— the film or novel, for example—but not the whole recognizable object, which appears, therefore, to be new. This is what I meant in claiming that the "novel production, rather than becoming α_{n+1}, in effect assimilates earlier manifestations of culture unto itself." It represents a new combination of those manifestations or elements even as it contributes something new to them.

I am wary of the distractions, lurking at every turn, in the use of an analogy from physics. However, I cannot resist the observation that my own copying of the term "inertia" serves to illustrate what I am talking about. The word was already available to me as a prior α expression, which I could then import via a β copy into my larger ω expression—namely, the book I am writing. Indeed, any new utterance I produce necessarily contains β replicas of prior α expressions, if for no other reason than, as

Bakhtin noted: "Our speech is filled to overflowing with other people's words" (1981, 337).

My own interest in *The Fate of the Earth*, and, specifically, in its pronominal patterning, no doubt stemmed in part from the resemblances that patterning exhibited to other expressions with which I was familiar, and, moreover, which I had myself produced. A "we" of the human species was something by no means foreign to me as an anthropologist and scholar more generally. You will find it, should you look, in numerous anthropological writings as a statement of universal identification, even at the very moment when, in those writings, the plurality of worldviews, or "cultures," is being celebrated.

Picking a book off my shelf, Clifford Geertz's *The Interpretation of Cultures*—a book published in 1973, and one I had read as a graduate student prior to encountering Schell's work—I turn to the chapter entitled "The Impact of the Concept of Culture on the Concept of Man," where Geertz argues for the crucial differentiating role of culture. Even as Geertz stresses differentiation, he saturates his prose with "we's" of the human species (italics added): "*We* are, in sum, incomplete or unfinished animals who complete or finish *ourselves* through culture . . ." (49); "Between what *our* body tells *us* and what *we* have to know in order to function, there is a vacuum *we* must fill *ourselves*, and *we* fill it with information (or misinformation) provided by *our* culture" (50); "*Our* ideas, *our* values, *our* acts, even *our* emotions, are, like *our* nervous system itself, cultural products—products manufactured, indeed, out of tendencies, capacities, and dispositions with which *we* were born . . ." (50). Picking another book off the shelf, an elementary textbook in cultural anthropology (Nanda 1994), I find similar "we" usages. The "we's" are present there, to be sure, in much lower frequencies than in *The Fate of the Earth* or "Cultural Representations of Nuclear War," but they are there nonetheless, providing an inertial conduit for future "we's."

Part of my argument is that Schell's words could be taken up most readily, and would circulate most naturally, where familiarity with a "we" of the human species is already established—among academics, physicians, writers, artists, and the like. Even if that "we" occurs in lower frequencies than in Schell, and even if it is not put to the same political uses, the fact that something like it is already being produced by B renders a copy of the specific original produced by A more likely. α can serve as a model to be copied in part, at least, because α is recognizable; it looks like other expressions B has already produced.

In pronouncing a new word in a language, one I am just learning as an adult, I use the sounds already available to me—the sound patterns of my old language. The result is the phenomenon known as "accent." Because I am used to producing certain sounds, certain α expressions, in certain ways, when I produce new sounds in β expressions, I do so in ways that resemble the α expressions I am accustomed to producing. This is the principle of inertia at work. But it is a second type of inertia, which might, in contrast with existential inertia, be dubbed "habitual."

A corollary of the principle of habitual inertia is that, where new ω expressions have little or no resonance with α expressions already being produced, there will be resistance to it. For example, where a "we" of the human species has no or little currency—I will give an example later—it will tend not to be taken up. It may actually arouse suspicion. Certainly, its movement will experience resistance. The social space through which culture moves is nonhomogeneous. It is a space configured by prior movements of culture and in which the motion of new culture is constrained, in part, by prior movements.

What reshapes social space is accelerative, rather than inertial, culture. Left to its own devices, inertial culture—the language, for example, one learns as a child—moves through those pathways for which the grooves have already been cut. Inertial culture does not reshape space, at least not by inertia alone. However, inertia can be harnessed by ω culture, which takes bits and pieces of available expressions and assembles them into new wholes. Such new wholes, therefore, have access to the different pathways of their constituent inertial elements. They can, by this means, cut across existing pathways. This is the case of culture produced by the entrepreneur. Such productions restlessly seek pathways, and they continuously refine themselves for the purpose of entering new pathways, of reshaping social space.

Cultural Caducity

The idea of an inertial culture—whether existential or habitual—implicitly underlies all arguments about culture. A child grows up speaking the language of those around it because that language—and not some other one—was there to be learned. The child adopts the mannerisms, gestures, tastes, and customs of its elders and peers because those mannerisms, gestures, tastes, and customs—not other ones—were there to be adopted. This is existential inertia. An adult, already fluent in one language, endeavors to speak another. The result is an accent in the new language. This is habitual inertia. Put the two together—existential and habitual inertia—and you have the anthropological concept of culture *sensu lato*.

What is missing from this view, however, is a conceptualization of accelerative culture. Insofar as inertial culture moves along social pathways that are described by its prior movement, its future is its past. Social organization appears as something resolutely separate or distinct from culture.[12] And it is hard to understand agency, activity, change, and development. It is hard to understand history. Social space is fixed once and for all, becoming a Newtonian space with absolute coordinates, absolute locations. However, accelerative culture opens the possibility that a new object—an ω object—can cut new pathways, can reshape social space by harnessing different strands of extant inertial culture.

Nor should the process of deceleration be ignored—the process, that is, whereby cultural elements undergo transformation in shape as they move. The original object decelerates, and, in the course of that deceleration, either dies out (caducity) or transmogrifies—eventually, over time, becoming a new thing unrecognizable to its ancestor. While inertia is at work, all things being equal, a cultural element will tend to be reproduced just because it is there. But in fact all things are not equal. There are forces that make the process of copying difficult and, hence, that render the transmission of culture problematic. Contemplating the durability of books, films, magnetic recordings, and the like—all of which are kinds of ω culture—it is easy forget what an achievement continuity is, an observation made long ago by the anthropologist A. R. Radcliffe-Brown ([1952] 1965). A given α expression may be subject to physical degradations[13]; it may not be accurately perceived or learned by B; B may be unable to produce an adequate copy of it for any one of a variety of reasons; or the original shape of α may cease to fascinate or be useful. Entropic forces such as these are summed up in the concept of "cultural drift,"[14] although they demand much closer scrutiny than has heretofore been given them.

As a consequence, accelerative characteristics—like poetic structuring, in the case of words or ritual movements, or practical utility, in the case of tools—must be built into cultural elements in order to insure their survival over time. And survival is the inherent telos of all culture: In some sense, it wants to continue on its journey through space and time. You—if you ever pass on any of the culture carried in this book—should not, therefore, imagine that culture survives just because of inertia. It survives because it is able to overcome the forces of deceleration that act upon inertia. All culture must undergo acceleration if it is to move through space and time, and if it is to maintain its shape. As I will argue, the very idea of tradition as a kind of metaculture is an attempt to overcome entropic forces of deceleration, an attempt to impart a positive accelerative force to culture.

There is a second aspect to the decelerative problem with which I shall be concerned later. If the first type of deceleration may be dubbed "entropic," the result of forces tending to degrade or transform an inertial element, there is a second type that can be characterized as "competitive" deceleration. A given ω cultural expression moves into new territory, but as it does so, it competes for attention with existing expressions and elements. Indeed, elements invariably enter into competition in the age of mechanical reproduction, since older objects can linger on sufficiently to require displacement—as when a song rises on the pop charts, peaks, and then, a new one having come to take its place, declines. However, competition also occurs without mechanical intervention; the latter merely intensifies the effect. Owing to limitations on the number of cultural objects to which an individual or group can pay attention, some expressions must give way to others. The acceleration of certain cultural objects results in the deceleration of others. Acceleration thus produces deceleration under conditions of competition.

The Concept of Acceleration in Contemporary Cultural Theory

Though perhaps not formulated in terms of inertia and acceleration, there is, in fact, considerable interest among contemporary social and cultural theorists in the phenomena these concepts describe. I take a brief look here at three such arguments: Benedict Anderson's ([1983] 1991) study of the role of print media in relation to the rise of nations; Pierre Bourdieu's ([1975] 1984) consideration of the role of the "habitus" in relation to taste; and Antonio Gramsci's notion, especially as formulated by Chantal Mouffe (1979), of "articulation" in relation to hegemony.

PRINT MEDIA AND IMAGINED COMMUNITY

A fascinating version of the inertial argument can be found in Benedict Anderson's ([1983] 1991) inventive, and now itself widely circulated, interpretation of the rise of nationalism through what he called "print capitalism." In this argument, people who share a common vernacular language are aided in their recognition of their commonality as a "people"—their imagining of themselves as a community—by the circulation of printed literature. The very fact of circulation—that is, the fact that people have access to the same printed materials—helps to give them a sense that they share something in common.

There is another side to the argument. It is not just that people share access to a printed literature that fuses them into a people. The literature to which they have access also contains within itself, in the form of its semiotic construction, an awareness or consciousness of other people as coparticipants in a single social reality. This problem of the semiotic construction of social consciousness is something I want to take up again in chapter 3, for it has bearing on the issue of acceleration, and, in particular, of how a cultural element can be designed to secure its own circulation.

Here I want to focus on another question. Why does the printed literature circulate along the pathways it does? The implicit argument in Anderson is an inertial one, in particular, an argument having to do with habitual inertia. The movement of cultural elements—in this case, the dissemination[15] of books, newspapers, and the like—is impelled, in part, by the fact that the elements are the continuation of something old. They are already familiar. The basis of their familiarity, their oldness, is the vernacular language in which they are written. Even though the books, newspapers, and the like are new—they are ω culture—an aspect of them is old, namely, the language they employ.

Anderson's argument about vernacular languages is that they help to circumscribe the limits of circulation of printed material, and hence to determine which groups of people would imagine themselves as nations. His is by no means a mechanical argument. He stresses the "interplay" between linguistic diversity, technology, and capitalism, noting that not all vernaculars become the basis for nations (Anderson [1983] 1991, 43). Furthermore, boundaries might be established despite the sharing of a vernacular language, as in the case of England and the newly emergent United States, or Spain and the Latin American nations. However, the *prior* existence of a spoken vernacular facilitates the flow of printed material written in that vernacular. The new cultural objects—the printed items—seize upon an old element or set of elements—the language of their expression. The pathways through space of the new expression are in part described by the pathways of the older elements that they continue.

There is something more here, however, from the point of view of motion. Print dissemination did not simply seize upon the existing inertia pathways of language. It also seized upon the existing inertial pathways of trade, and those two were not identical. This is the essence of the ω-like character of print. As an emergent class of cultural objects, printed discourse inserted itself into two patterns of cultural flow: commercial items passed by trade, and language passed by domestic reproduction and schooling. The motion of culture was accelerated by print, its pathways of motion changed, because the pathways of commerce could be made to intersect with those of language. The result, if you believe Anderson— and there are good reasons to do so—is the territorial parameters of at least certain modern nations.

It is not that the pathways so established were rigidly determinant. True, without modification—in this case, without translation—the printed object would be too unfamiliar to be interpretable; hence, it could not survive its journey into a new land. However, a cultural element that, because of its design features, holds interest for a broader audience, can break out of these inertial constraints. For this reason, incidentally, a theory of cultural motion is incompatible with a complete linguistic relativism. The movement of a cultural element across linguistic boundaries, though admittedly through translation, is evidence that something—even if not everything—can and does carry over. Not just any object finds its way into translation. There must be something about that object that recommends or demands its translation.

Look at one of the Greek legends—about Pygmalion, for example— written down some two thousand years ago by the Roman poet Ovid. The story tells of a sculptor and king of Cyprus named Pygmalion who sculpted his ideal woman, with whom he then fell in love. Marston retold the story in English in 1598 in his *Metamorphosis of Pigmalion's Image*. And it was even adapted and retold in W. S. Gilbert's 1871 comedy, *Pygmalion and Galatea*. Something about the story carried over in these various retellings, something powerful enough to overcome the inertia of the specific language of its tellings, something that allowed it to break out of those inertial constraints placed on its motion through space and time.

Not only can the cultural element traverse language boundaries, providing sufficient interest accrues to it for other reasons, but the language itself can move. Indeed, it would be a corollary of the principle of accelerative culture that a language will tend to spread in proportion to the number of linguistically encoded expressions within it that are of interest for speakers of other languages. When the numbers and degree of interest are low, translation suffices. But after a point, it becomes more expedient for the language itself to spread.[16] The movement of ω expressions induces the movement of the quintessential set of α expressions— language.

Social space is nonhomogeneous, and the question is: How does non-homogeneity arise? Pierre Bourdieu's landmark study, *Distinction: A Social Critique of the Judgement of Taste*, grounds the analysis of social differentiation in tastes (for art, music, food, clothing, body style, and so forth) in an inertial theory of culture. For Bourdieu, people differ in their tastes because of the differing life circumstances in which they happened to grow up. They acquired the tastes they did because those tastes were there to be acquired. This is inertial culture of the first variety I discussed earlier—existential inertia. People acquire something because it is already there.

However, Bourdieu is also concerned with acceleration and its relationship to habitual inertia. The result of acquisition of tastes through the operation of inertial culture is the creation in the individual—literally, in the individual's body—of a systematic set of dispositions, which Bourdieu, following Marcel Mauss (1979), calls the *habitus*. These dispositions condition the response an individual will have to any new cultural element with which he or she happens to come into contact. They are, therefore, analogous to the second kind of inertia discussed earlier, habitual inertia, the kind in which B's ability and/or likelihood to find interest in and reproduce some aspect of an ω expression is conditioned by the prior expressions B has produced—as in the case of the accent when one learns a second language as an adult. The habitus is the filter created by inertial culture for new expressions. The flow of new expressions follows pathways laid down by old elements.

At the same time, if only inertia were at work, people would be locked into their positions in a larger social space, condemned by the tastes they acquired as children. In fact, however, they are not so condemned. They can travel through that space, in accord with what Bourdieu calls "trajectories." What makes those trajectories possible? It is the fact that tastes—as evidence of embodied habitual inertial culture—can change. In Bourdieu's scheme, taste is part of cultural or symbolic capital, that is, forms of capital that are distinct from, but interconvertible in some measure with, economic capital. The idea of acceleration is inherent in Bourdieu's model precisely because taste is made a form of acquirable capital.

The acquisition of cultural capital, or, in present terms, the transformation of habitual inertial culture, is illustrated—to continue the earlier theme—in the twentieth century refraction of the Greek myth of Pygmalion. I am referring, of course, to George Bernard Shaw's 1916 play by that name, later turned into a popular Lerner and Loewe musical, and then into a successful 1964 film, *My Fair Lady.* The central plot of the original myth is recognized here only with difficulty, but the new plot is strikingly Bourdieuian: A cockney-speaking flower girl comes to phonetics professor Henry Higgins to learn how to "talk like a lady." Higgins makes a bet with a friend that he can, in fact, transform this woman, turning her into a lady in speech and manner so thoroughly, so convincingly that she could pass for having acquired her accent and manners in a family, the normal way in which accent and taste are understood to be acquired. As Bourdieu suggests is possible, Higgins is in fact successful. The flower girl, Eliza Doolittle, cannot, by those who make it their profession to know—in this case, another linguist—be picked out as Higgins's creation. Higgins is, so to speak, the social sculptor, and Eliza his statue. Like Pygmalion, he finds himself in love with his creation.

Such a scenario is evidence for the acceleration of culture. How else than through a change in the course of her inertially acquired culture could Eliza have come to pass for an upper-class British lady?

But if acceleration is possible at the individual level, as the culture that passes to Eliza from Higgins transforms her, can ω cultural objects themselves reshape the social space through which culture moves? This is a topic on which I will have more to say in chapter 6, but it should already be apparent, from the preceding discussion of Anderson, that I consider this conclusion inescapable. Social space is reconfigured, however incrementally or radically, by the motion associated with specific ω cultural objects. While Bourdieu himself seems to attribute considerable solidity to social space—and there is in fact considerable solidity to it—the possibilities for its transformation, whether gradual or radical, are implicit in his concern with accelerative processes.

HEGEMONY AND ARTICULATION

The work of Antonio Gramsci (1985), especially as filtered through Chantal Mouffe (1979) and Ernesto Laclau and Chantal Mouffe (1985), is intriguing in light of accelerative culture because Gramsci was explicitly concerned with how new configurations of social relations might be achieved. What is crucial for present purposes is that, according to Gramsci, reconfiguration can be *achieved.* That is, leadership is not simply determined by the inertial character of social space. While the character of that space is an important determinant, new configurations are possible, even if their newness is constrained. This kind of understanding focuses attention on the possibly shifting character of space through time.

Indispensable to the achievement of hegemony—that is, the achievement of leadership by a group—is the synthesis of prior cultural elements in new expressions—that is, ω expressions—in present terms. Mouffe (1979, 193) views this process as one of articulation. According to her, the patterning of extant cultural elements contains an implicit alignment around a hierarchy of social relationships—like the organization of iron filings in the presence of a magnet. The principle of that organization is what Gramsci called a "hegemonic principle." Mouffe considers the cultural elements to be "articulated" in relationship to one another.

To unpack this in present terms, Mouffe is talking about a social space that is constituted inertially via the movement of cultural elements through individuals. Hierarchy is a result of differential movement through a non-homogeneous space. In this regard, the model is similar to that proposed by Bourdieu. However, crucial to the Gramsci-Mouffe scheme is the idea that, for some individuals to exercise leadership, there must be active consensus. That is, there must be a shared understanding that, despite the different positions individuals are occupying, they do, in fact, occupy the *same* space. Hence, there must be cultural elements that communicate this sense of participation in a single space, and those elements themselves must be widely circulated; they must form part of the inertial culture of leaders and led, alike.

George Bernard Shaw's version of the myth of Pygmalion, for example, as a bit of Gramscian hegemonic culture, has something in it for everyone. Upper-class values—the culture carried by the leaders—are affirmed as those toward which everyone, as embodied in Eliza Doolittle, ought to aspire. Of course those values, that culture, that way of life are good ones—nay, even superior ones, the story assures us. Our leaders can rest content that their leadership, their world, is being affirmed. Yet there is something in it also for the led—the great American hope that everyone can ascend the social ladder, that they can acquire the accents, the manners—in short, the culture—of the elites. This is a dream or a myth into which they can buy. Here is a bit of hegemony at work.

A key to articulation is that the widely circulated cultural objects—Shaw's *Pygmalion*, or Lerner and Loewe's *My Fair Lady*—must contain analytically separable elements that link up with the inertial elements that are distinctive of the various isolable parts of the nonhomogeneous space.[17] In particular, they must contain subelements recognizable to both the leaders and the led. There is a difference here from the notion of a "shared culture," since any given element need not be shared by all of those who are in leadership positions, or all of those who are among the led. *My Fair Lady* may not be everyone's cup of tea. What is important, instead, is that there be elements (in the plural) whose pathways of movement link together some of the leaders with some of the led; the elements must do so by drawing together pieces of inertial culture from both leaders and led. Complete consensus—probably never obtained in fact—would be achieved when some set of elements capturing an agreed-upon participation in a single space was in fact universally shared.

Such a social space, however, could still be inertial if all of the elements in question were simply reproduced over time. The accelerative aspect of the Gramsci-Mouffe framework is to be found in the process of achieving new articulations. In Mouffe's words: "Ideological struggle in fact consists of a process of disarticulation-rearticulation of given ideological elements in a struggle between two hegemonic principles to appropriate these elements" (1979, 193). The process must depend upon the production of new expressions, and, hence, on ω culture.

At the same time, this struggle seems to have, at least for Gramsci, an end. The end is the realignment whose parameters are already set by a Marxist theory of class. In Laclau and Mouffe (1985), the process of disarticulation-rearticulation appears to become perpetual and is intimately linked to their idea of a democratic politics. In present terms, their vision is of the continual production of ω expressions. I will be arguing later that something like this is already happening under a metaculture of modernity, but that the result is not, and perhaps is necessarily not, social equality.

Boundaries

I would like to resume the journey I left off earlier, namely, the journey mapped out by my investigation of "we" usage. For the story does not end with Schell and myself. My curiosity about "we's" led me to examine other political writings—and I will be reporting some of my investigations in chapter 3. However, here I wish to pick up the story in the mid-1980s, when it occurred to me to look at the writings of someone working for the U.S. government, someone who was directly inside of it. Because Schell's focus was nuclear war and he was arguing an "antinuclear" position—do away with the weapons—I wanted someone who would espouse a "peace-through-strength" position. A logical candidate was Caspar Weinberger, then secretary of defense under Ronald Reagan. In 1986, he published an article in the journal *Foreign Affairs* entitled "U.S. Defense Strategy."

I subjected the article to the same kind of scrutiny I had applied to *The Fate of the Earth* and, much later, my own "Cultural Representations of Nuclear War." I looked at each first-person plural usage and jotted down what seemed to be its meaning in its specific context. Just as in the other studies, patterns quickly emerged. However, the patterns here were quite distinct from those I found in the other studies. I summarize the results in Table 3.

Table 3. "We" Categories in Weinberger (1986)

CATEGORY	NUMBER	PERCENTAGE OF TOTAL
1. United States	137	63
2. Reagan administration	29	13
3. Ambiguous	28	13
4. Department of Defense	8	4
5. Within quotations	7	3
6. President and I	5	2
7. United States and U.S.S.R.	3	1
8. U.S. government	2	1
9. Human species	1	0
Totals	220	100

Again, I do not expect that you, the reader, would come up with exactly the same statistical results, were you to do this study. The meaning of each "we" is a matter of interpretation. However, the interpretation is not unconstrained, and I would expect your study to confirm the pattern these results suggest.

The pattern is that Weinberger's "we" is primarily a "we" of the United States. The "we" of the human species, so prominent in Schell and in Urban 1984, is found here only in trace amounts (one occurrence out of 220), just as a "we" of the United States is found in trace amounts only in Schell (one occurrence out of 1,310), although it plays a more substantial role in Urban. What to make of this? The answer, I propose, is that such differences are characteristic of cultural boundaries. But of what are those boundaries made?

The "boundary" separating Weinberger from Schell could well be a flimsy one, a matter of the statistics of only one ω expression produced by each. Weinberger might on another day author a piece reminiscent of *The Fate of the Earth*, and Schell might produce something resembling "U.S. Defense Strategy." If my suspicion is correct, however, these different statistical patterns reflect distinct α-type cultural elements. They obey the principle of inertia, even though they can be employed as constituents within pieces of noninertial, accelerative culture—such as the actual writings produced by Schell and Weinberger.

The inertial character of these elements is in fact of the second type mentioned above—habitual inertia. B is attracted to cultural expression α because B has already produced similar expressions. The statistical patterning of "we" is analogous to the phenomenon of accent. If you try to pronounce new words in a language you are learning as an adult, you tend to pronounce them with an accent. It is not that you could not ever learn to pronounce the words as a native speaker does; it is that the path of least resistance is to do what you have always done. Inertia sets in; to change patterns requires effort.

Correspondingly, Schell could adopt the statistical patterning of "we" in Weinberger's article only with effort, just as Weinberger could adopt Schell's use of "we" only with effort. It is not that the passage cannot be made—witness Eliza Doolittle's miraculous transformation of accent and mannerisms in Shaw's *Pygmalion*. Change of inertially guided patterns is always possible. It is rather that to make the change requires effort. Eliza had to procure the aid of phonetician Henry Higgins: "I don't want to talk grammar, I want to talk like a lady." In the end, she did "talk like a lady," and she did marry a "gentleman." But it is easier to continue in the familiar pattern, to follow the grooves that have already been cut. The inertia of habituation is at work. To put it differently, the patterning of "we" in each case is not the product of a momentary whim, or so I am claiming, but reflects microstrands of cultural movement. The "we's" are part and parcel, in each case, of a more enduring habitus, as Bourdieu would call it.

To see whether my suspicion might be correct, I did follow-up studies of other writings by Weinberger, who is, fortunately, a prolific writer.[18] He resigned his post as secretary of defense in 1987, and, as of 1998, was writing a column for *Forbes* magazine, of which he was publisher. I sampled some of his commentaries in *Forbes*, and picked one out at random from June 15, 1998. The title of it is "Protecting the ABM Treaty Instead of Our People." Written twelve years after "U.S. Defense Strategy," the "we's" of this piece, if anything, exhibit an intensification of the patterns found in the earlier work. There are, in this short essay, twenty-four distinct occurrences of the first-person plural pronoun. Every one of them is, in fact, a "we" of the United States, as the anaphoric usage of the very opening sentence suggests: "I am continually struck by how few people in the audiences I address here and abroad know that the $U.S._i$ has no effective defense against missile attack, whether it be directed at our_i troops in the field, our_i cities or our_i allies."

My proposal is not that Weinberger could not construct an essay around a "we" of the human species. It is that the "we" of the United States comes naturally to him as a result of longer habituation. These "we's" are part of inertial culture. To change that pattern would require the expenditure of effort. The easier course is to continue to inhabit the "we" to which one is accustomed.[19]

There is some suggestion, as well, in Weinberger's case that the "we" of the United States was also inertial in the first sense (the existential sense)—that is, that it was simply there to be replicated when he was a child. I have no direct evidence of this, for obvious reasons. However, I ran across a fascinating interview with Weinberger that originally aired on television (C-Span) on July 15, 1990. Here is an excerpt from the interview:

BRIAN LAMB Caspar Weinberger, secretary of defense for seven years for this country and author of the new book, *Fighting for Peace.* Why do you start your book by telling us about your father's bedtime story when you were a little kid?

CASPAR WEINBERGER Well, it was such an interesting bedtime story. He told us, told my brother and me, the story of the Constitution, how the Constitution was formed and the various compromises that had to go into the creation of the House and the Senate, and this was not the sort of story that you would ordinarily think would hold the attention of anyone of fairly tender years—I guess I was maybe seven or eight, nine, something like that—and yet he told it in such a fascinating fashion. He was an attorney, but a very broad-gauge man and a great father, and I just became thoroughly fascinated with not only the Constitution and its formation, but the legislative procedure, and, indeed, everything connected with government.

LAMB You obviously remember the details of it—how, you say, it went on for weeks?

WEINBERGER Yes, it was a long story—he just took us right through the constitutional convention and all the problems in Philadelphia and how hot it was and how the delegates started to go home and the difficulty of keeping a quorum. It was . . . it was a remarkable performance in every way.

The "we" usage in this stretch of discourse—the "we" of "my brother and me"—is not what intrigues me here. What intrigues me is the suggestion that the inertial pattern may have been present in childhood. Weinberger may have begun to reproduce a "we" of the United States—which he carried on so prominently—in part, at least, because it was there in the household to be reproduced. Certainly, in his own reconstruction of his childhood, Weinberger attributes his father's story about the constitution to his burgeoning interest in "everything connected with government."

Whatever the case, the prominent identification with a "we" of the United States has persisted in Weinberger's writing for some time. This patterning of "we," as a bit of microculture, has been taken up by him, and passes through him to others. The movement through time and space of such a piece of culture defines a boundary simply because there are other patterns of "we" usage alternative to the one that Weinberger might have inhabited. In particular, there is the "we" of the human species in Schell.

One might think of such a pattern as a two-dimensional figure—let's say a circle, for simplicity's sake—that moves through time to form a cylinder or tube. The cylinder wall is a boundary of social space. It may not be a boundary that is difficult to cross, but it is one that appears more and more solid when the motion of this isolated pattern—this cultural element—is reinforced by the motion of other cultural elements. In that case, the position within social space defined by the boundaries of the element may become recognizable to people more generally, and it may be actually labeled as a position. Such labels are, of course, a part of meta-culture. They are culture—they themselves move through space and time. But they are also about culture.

It is possible to imagine the construction of a new cultural element—one, for example, in which the two "we's" are brought into harmonious relationship. If such a new ω expression were effectively constructed, it might be able to harness the inertial force of the previously separated elements, moving through both of the places within social space simultaneously. Such an ω expression would be accelerative, and it would effectively reconfigure the social space, which is, after all, a space mapped out by the movement of inertial elements over time. It comes to appear to be stable and fixed by virtue of a metaculture that labels different places within it. Even in this case, there was a clear divide between a "prostrength" and an "antinuclear" position.

As I think back on it now, that was my implicit desire—never realized—in writing the little 1984 piece, "Cultural Representations of Nuclear War." Its intended audience was of the highly educated adult variety—readers of the *New York Review of Books*, for example, to which I actually sent the piece, receiving in return a kind and encouraging note of rejection, for which I am now grateful.

At the time, I had not yet discovered the "we" patterns in either Schell or Weinberger. However, I knew that I was not wholly happy with Schell's brooding vision, impressed as I was with its cosmological scale. After all, it completely ignored the United States as an important something in the world, something to which I myself was attached. For one solution to the problem Schell posed would be for the United States to simply give up its weapons unilaterally, perhaps even to give up its commitment to a capitalist way of life in favor of Soviet-style communism. Wasn't that just as unthinkable as the possibility of nuclear annihilation of the species? What would I be if I were not an American? Isn't my life so thoroughly intertwined with the culture that is within me that I cannot distinguish the death of my culture from my biological death? As Geertz says, paradoxically using a "we" of the human species, "Our ideas, our values, our acts, even our emotions, are, like our nervous system itself, cultural products" (1973, 50).

While never as immersed in a "we" of the United States to the extent that Weinberger was, nevertheless Schell's seeming rejection of it provoked a reaction in me. I wanted to do something that would correct it, that would right this wrong. I now recognize my aborted ω expression as a failure. True, 7 percent of my "we's" in that piece were of the United States variety—as compared with only a single such instance out of 1,310 in Schell's case. This is a full one hundred–fold difference. Nevertheless, my overwhelming tendency was to follow Schell's pattern. The inertial force of my identification with a humanistic "we" was just too great. The accelerative culture I had hoped to produce fizzled. But wasn't something like it—or many such things like it—necessary if a genuine dialogue were to be established, if there were to be any bringing into alignment of these disparate positions? Wouldn't social space have to be reconfigured to solve the problem?

Structure, System, and Rationality as Derivatives of Movement

The movement of cultural elements in space and time seems to take place *through* a structure—a point of view that the anthropologist Marshall Sahlins (1976, 1981, 1985, 1995; also Kirch and Sahlins 1995), among others, has vigorously argued. From this point of view, structure is understood as a system of relationships linking diverse elements into a larger whole and constraining the movement of those elements. Isn't structure, therefore, rather than movement, the proper starting point for cultural analysis? Isn't it prior to movement? Indeed, isn't it able to be studied independent of movement—a conceit dating back to Saussure's original work on language?

What I hope to convince you of by the end of this book is that structure is in fact not prior to movement, in some absolute sense, but rather a derivative of movement. It is not that structure does not exist; it is rather that structure is a consequence of the way in which cultural elements move through space and time. In particular, structure (or system) is the result of a combination of the inertial and accelerative properties of culture, and it is something that emerges momentaneously when it is lodged in particular things—specific, unique cultural expressions, whether α or ω. Indeed, this is, I believe, a singular merit of a view of cultural motion—it is not simply an alternative to late twentieth-century concepts of culture as structure, but an idea from which what are genuine and valid insights about structure can be derived.

It is easiest to see this in the case of an ω cultural expression. By my definition, an ω expression is something new. It is accelerative in the sense that it takes old cultural elements—which can be microelements such as patterns of pronominal usage—and fuses them into new wholes. In bringing those elements together into a single thing, like a book, it simultaneously makes those elements part of a larger whole. That larger whole—the unique cultural expression, such as Schell's *The Fate of the Earth*—gives the impression that those elements were always interrelated, even before the whole was produced in the unique expression. Acceleration therefore produces the illusion of prior structure—real as the constraints of past motion may be when only inertial motion is involved. Something that is the property of a thing in the world appears to be a property of a system that is thingless.

Of course, the system may have been created for the first time in that thing in the world. This was my own conceit in my youthful work, "Cultural Representations of Nuclear War." I thought I could bring together different parts of social space by articulating them in a single essay. But, while my attempt was a failure, such articulations can and do occur. Different strands of local culture come together in things—ω expressions. Moreover, because the ω expressions have a circulation of their own, as they move through space and time—a circulation that draws upon the parts of space inertially constituted by the movements of their constituent elements—the parts so brought together can become a single thing. Culture can be structured.

The structure is not totalizing, unless every strand of local culture can be synthesized into a single thing-in-the-world—a difficult task, indeed. But the emergence of partial structures, drawing upon certain elements and their trajectories, produces the idea that a complete structure is possible. This is the presupposition of a metaculture of modernity, such as I will examine in chapter 2 and throughout this book. And, if it is possible to articulate all cultural elements in a single thing, then that possibility can be held up as a goal, an ideal towards which individual transmitters and producers of culture can aspire. A premium is thus placed on the purposeful attempt to articulate structure, the rational or consciously calculated attempt to weave interconnections.

If culture is that which is socially transmitted, why place emphasis on the purposeful attempt to articulate structure? Why prod individuals in the direction of rationality? For this is, after all, what a metacultural emphasis on creating new cultural objects does. But what is in it for culture? This is a mystery to which I have devoted considerable attention, and to which this book offers one solution.

It is possible for individuals to be regarded as mere transmitters of culture, as the conduits through which culture flows. Such is the essence of a metaculture of tradition—an idea about individuals as conduits. Yet the view from tradition—as a kind of objective characterization of culture, disregarding for the moment the role of this metacultural idea in producing motion—focuses only on the inertial side of culture, and, even so, fails to comprehend the decelerative forces acting on that inertial culture. It is a view that comprehends onceness, but fails miserably at futurity. Any cultural element, to survive, requires that some measure of accelerative force be added to it. Otherwise, it deforms and disintegrates or evolves into something else. Yet culture has a telos: It wants to be carried on, and this means resisting entropic deceleration.

There is more. If I am right, it is the telos of certain kinds of culture, at least, to spread—although spread, through globalization, may be a way of trying to achieve temporal continuity.[20] This is the itchy, restless side of culture. That restlessness is the mother of rationality—of the urge to get culture from A to B. It is a side of culture that induces missionary zeal. It is a side of culture that motivates entrepreneurs. It may even be a side of culture that stokes the ambitions of would-be conquerors. Without this restlessness, culture is content to move along pathways whose grooves it has already cut, content to perpetuate itself through time along routes with which it is already familiar. With it, culture is propelled into a lateral motion whose end is to encircle the globe, and from there, perhaps, to move elsewhere.

The Paradox of Observation

What could be more straightforward than the contrast between α and ω culture? A cultural object—a word, a myth-telling, a ceramic pot, for example—can be understood as a replica of what has come before it, or, alternatively, as something new and distinct, something that draws on the past, but changes it in significant ways. Yet, from the point of view of empiricism, there is something unsettling about the contrast. Scratch its surface, and the outlines of something quite different begin to emerge.

The simple contrast appears empirical enough. It makes reference to the perceptible world, for sure. The senses, or instruments that are extensions of the senses, must be used to detect the similarities and differences. Two ceramics pots, for example, can be closely examined for techniques of painting, coiling, and firing. Is one so similar to the other as to suggest that both are replicas of some prior originals, or, perhaps, that one is a copy of the other? Or, alternatively, is one so different from its predecessors as to suggest that it constitutes something new—an innovation over older patterns? Empirical observation is crucial to answering these questions, but does it suffice?

Here one can view the cultural investigator as scientist, studiously documenting perceptible things in the world, examining their objective characteristics. In the first half of the twentieth century, anthropology was this kind of positive science. Researchers collected cultural objects from around the world, catalogued them, studied their properties, mapped their distributions around the globe. They even detected patterns of motion of cultural elements, which they described in terms of processes of diffusion or independent invention or, perhaps, even brain structures.

But something unsettled this sunny paradigm of normal science. Since the cultural objects were produced by people who had their own understandings of the world, what role should be accorded the native's judgments in relation to the anthropologist's? In a profound article, "The Psychological Reality of Phonemes," Edward Sapir ([1933] 1968) proposed that his own observations of phonetic differences in Native American languages did not always or perfectly correspond to those of the Native Americans from whom he collected the linguistic information. To take an English example, which Sapir used, the seemingly unitary sound "p"—as in the words "pin" and "spin"—appears under close observation to consist of at least two distinguishable sounds, a "p" (writable as [pʰ]) with a little puff of air after it, which can be detected by saying the word while holding a small strip of paper in front of one's mouth, and a "p" (writable as [p] or [p=]), with little or no corresponding puff of air. Yet the distinction is difficult for native speakers of American English to bring into conscious focus, easy though it may be for them to reproduce in words. Should the two sounds be regarded as distinctive by the anthropologist?

The problem is compounded by the fact that there are some languages—Urdu, for example, a language of Pakistan—within which native speakers readily recognize the difference. As a young assistant professor, I recall using the "p" example in a large introductory undergraduate cultural anthropology class. I spoke the words "pin" and "spin" and asked whether anyone detected a difference between the two "p's." A hand from the back of the room shot up. "'Tis perfectly obvious," the student said, and proceeded to describe the puff of air after the "p" in "pin." I asked him whether he had learned about this distinction in another class—linguistics, perhaps—but he said no, he had not learned about it anywhere. It then occurred to me to ask him what his native language was, and, sure enough, he responded: "Urdu."

Sapir's study led to one of the great insights of twentieth-century linguistics, namely, that there were two kinds of sounds in language: those that the outside observer, through careful observation, can detect, and those that are salient in the consciousness of native speakers. Study of the former became known as "phonetics" and of the latter as "phonemics." Within cultural anthropology, the contrast was generalized to one between "etics"—culture as objectively describable by an outside observer— and "emics"—culture as construed by the native inhabitants of that culture themselves.

The distinction has been, in considerable measure, the raison d'être of cultural anthropology, and, perhaps, of studies of culture more generally in the latter twentieth century. If there are emic perspectives, is the cultural scientist's own perspective one of them? If so, how can one be sure that one's view of the world is "objective"? Perhaps the scientist of culture is just another native with a quirky emic perspective. How can one be certain of making contact with the world in reporting empirical observations of it? A cloud of radical self-doubt descended upon the sunny paradigm of positive research.

One solution for language was propounded by Roman Jakobson (Jakobson and Waugh 1987). It can be summed up in the dictum "phonetics is a comparative phonemics," and generalized as "an etics is a comparative emics." In other words, to understand what linguistic sounds human beings are capable of perceiving or cognizing, we need to compare the different phonemic systems around the globe. Phonetics, within this method, takes as its object the repertoire of all sounds produced by all such phonemic contrasts. Hence, there is an implicit call to researchers to go out into the world and study the different phonemic systems through which sound is rendered intelligible.

By analogy—and this comes close to describing the project mapped out by the great anthropologist Claude Lévi-Strauss in his *Mythologiques* series—human beings cannot directly grasp the world as it is simply by reflecting upon their sensory observations. Since emic perspectives intervene between the individual and the world, the best hope of grasping the world, insofar as a human is able to, is by studying and comparing the different emic systems through which the world is rendered understandable by people. This philosophical vision of the relationship between understanding and the perceptible world motivated a generation of scholars—I was one of them—to embark upon journeys to the remote corners of the earth in search of alternative emic frameworks, the systematic comparison of which would shed light on great philosophical questions about reality and the ability of humans to comprehend it.

If the goal of research is to determine the range of sounds that have been empirically used for purposes of phonemic contrast in languages around the globe, or if the goal is to map the human cognitive apparatus through which reality has been processed, then the etics-as-comparative-emics model works well. But what if one's goal is to understand culture itself—not just the human cognitive apparatus—as a phenomenon in the world, as an object of scientific interest? What if one's goal is to study the motion of culture through the world, especially its trajectory into a future? Can one be sure that the past history of phonemic contrasts exhausts its future history? And if a future phonemic system generates consciousness of a new sound, was that sound already there, waiting to be discovered by the future system, or was the sound itself something new, something whose existence could not have been comprehended within an etics-as-comparative-emics framework?

The problem is one of the relationship between ALPHA and α, or between OMEGA and ω, that is, the metacultural characterization by natives (or by the observer, for that matter) and the cultural object. But that relationship—which is characterized in Figure 1—leads to two radically opposed and at least partially unsatisfactory alternatives, though both also capture elements of truth.

One interpretation is empiricist: The metacultural characterization of the object is ALPHA (or OMEGA) because the object really is an α (or ω), that is, because it really is sufficiently similar to (or different from) its predecessors to warrant being called ALPHA (or OMEGA). The qualities of perceptible cultural objects determine metacultural characterizations of them. The world of cultural things discloses itself directly to metacultural understanding, finds its way into or is reflected in that understanding.

ALPHA   OMEGA

α   ω

Figure 1. Empiricist (up arrow) and relativist (down arrow) interpretations of culture-metaculture relations.

The other interpretation is the relativistic one: The object is only α (or ω) because it is construed by metaculture as ALPHA (or OMEGA). The perceptible world does not work its way into the metacultural construal. Any perceptible cultural object might be construed in either way. Metacultural construal is part of an arbitrarily imposed understanding of the world, a way of cutting up reality—in the cookie-cutter image—that is only one among several or many—perhaps, even, infinitely many—possible ways. This is the solution for which some contemporary cultural analyses have opted.

While the two possibilities seem irreconcilably at odds, in fact they come together in a third possibility inherent in the paradox of observation—in the seeming paradox, namely, that observation affects the thing observed. What if the idea contained in and carried by metaculture is not only about the thing in some passive sense, a detached representation of the thing's past characteristics or of its relationship to the past? What if the idea is interested also in the thing's future? Then the idea will want to make contact with the perceptible object, will want to contain a truth about it, a truth that must include the object's relationship to the past, but a truth that wants to direct the object toward a future that it envisions. This is, of course, what the sculptor Pygmalion does in contemplating the slab of marble. He sees it for what it is. But he also sees it for what it can become.

If something of the cultural object finds its way into the metacultural interpretation—that is, if the interpretation is not arbitrary relative to the object—does the metacultural interpretation find its way into the object? Might not the metacultural interpretation actually influence the cultural object and fashion it, at least in some measure, after its own image? Construed in this way, metacultural interpretation is a force in the world of perceptible things, not just an arbitrary conscious representation of things construed as indifferent to their representation. This active, though ethereal, force might then be responsible for the acceleration of culture, whether via an emphasis on maintaining tradition—and, hence, on over-coming the forces of dissipation to which culture, moving through the world, is subject—or, alternatively, via an emphasis on newness, which propels culture in directions that the ideas in some measure, at least, foresee.

Figure 2 is an attempt to graphically represent this dynamic linkage where both metaculture and culture are moving through the world, circulating among people, not as two wholly independent forms of motion taking place on unconnected planes, but rather as forms or planes of motion that are dynamically interconnected through representation. The proposal is that culture is not just something that can be represented in metaculture, but something whose very nature—whose existence as thing in the world—is positively affected by that representation.

This proposal is confined to a limited range of phenomena, namely, those involving the interaction between cultural objects and metacultural representations.[21] Can it have broader implications for understanding reality? This is where future trajectories surface as important. What, precisely, is a cultural object, and what might become one? So long as cultural objects are confined to a few ceramic pots here and there, to some ephemeral words passed on over the generations, it is easy to imagine a reality independent of culture, a reality that, unlike the cultural object, does not require culture for its perpetuation. There is a fixed, timeless quality to it, just as there is to tradition; this is ironic, or perhaps not so ironic, since the concept of an immutable reality itself may be one of the last bastions of traditionalism.

Yet culture has shown itself to be a formidable shaper of reality. Can land be reclaimed from the sea? Yes, with the help of cultural learning. Can rivers be diverted from their course of flow? Yes, with the help of cultural knowledge. Can lush forests be turned into deserts or deserts into lush forests? Yes, thanks to culture. What are the limits of control over reality by this mysterious thing?

A noteworthy irony of the late twentieth and now early twenty-first

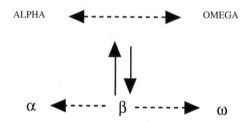

Figure 2. Dynamic interconnection between culture and metaculture.

century has been talk about biological determination of human life, talk growing out of the human genome project, as well as out of attempts to locate medical disorders and human propensities in genes. I find no irony in the research agenda underlying these claims, nor in any specific result. What strikes me as ironic,[22] rather, is that this talk has been occurring at the precise moment in history when biogenetic engineering—cumulated cultural learning—is making possible the achievement by culture of an unprecedented degree of control over the genetic apparatus, control enabling the creation of new life forms and the alteration of old ones, of a God-like control. True, culture has been gaining control over biology for hundreds and thousands of years through domestication and breeding of plants and animals and through regulation of biological reproduction among humans. But cumulated learning—that is, culture—has made possible control of biological reproduction on a new scale. Where is that control lodged? It can only be in metacultural ideas about cultural processes, and, in particular, about the cultural practices surrounding biological manipulation.

Who can foresee the limits to the capacity of culture to reshape reality after its own image? Do those limits lie at the edge of the ocean, with the tides studied by Isaac Newton as evidence for gravity? Or will culture find ways to harness and even affect those great forces of nature? What about the glacial movement of tectonic plates on the earth's surface that give rise to earthquakes and reshape the face of the planet? Will we forever be able to make observations in this area without those observations, paradoxically, reshaping the world we observe? Perhaps the line will be drawn there as to what is immutable and what outside the control of culture. Or perhaps the safe place to draw the line, once and for all, will be with the orbital motion of heavenly bodies, since we can at least imagine an age in which culture might achieve complete terrestrial domination. Surely, though, planetary motion will never succumb to the control of culture, will never be subject to reshaping from the ethereal realm of ideas— unless, of course, one subscribes to something like the Biblical view: "And the earth was without form, and void; and darkness was upon the face of the deep. And the Spirit of God moved upon the face of the waters" (Genesis 1:2).

It is just too hard presently to foresee the limitations on culture, and hence on the metacultural shaping of reality, especially given the equally awesome capacity of culture—is this not, after all, our sphinx?—to strike us down, destroy humanity, hurl it back into a dark age, as in Schell's nightmare vision. But even the humble and seemingly insignificant processes investigated in this book—the role of metacultures of newness and tradition in maintaining or reshaping such cultural objects as myths and films—reveal something of epistemological significance. The metacultural plane cracks open, and the great chisel of Pygmalion descends towards the marble of an unformed world, imparting the ethereal force of ideas to perceptible things. Yes, something immaterial is in our midst, something whose elusiveness and riddles perplex us, but must not stop us from continuing with research. After all, the sphinx is guardian of a passage—a wondrous, if strange, passage into an unforeseen future. This is one trip we will not want to miss. Yet, the sphinx waylays travelers on their journey, prompting them, upon pain of death, to correctly solve the riddle. Can we be sure that our own sphinx will not kill us, should we fail to answer its questions? What more powerful incentive could there be for future generations of researchers? Yes, the motion of culture is the central mystery of our time, the last frontier for an older science, and the first test of a newer one, yet unborn.

2

In Modern Time

> The moving finger writes; and, having writ,
> Moves on: nor all thy piety nor wit
> Shall lure it back to cancel half a line,
> Nor all thy tears wash out a word of it.
>   Edward Fitzgerald, *The Rubáiyát of Omar Khayyám* (1859), stanza 51

Surface Textures

The sleek curves and shiny surfaces of stainless steel cooking pots from the 1950s and 1960s—the period of my youth—seemed to me so natural, as if they were an expression of the scientific, rational surface texture of my then lived world, the same kind of smooth curvature found in the close-cropped, oiled hair of men or the bun hairstyle of women or the girdles women wore to smooth out their surface appearance. My memory is jogged by the visual signatures of Hitchcock movies from that period. When did I detect the change? Probably before I went off to college in the late 1960s, but it was in college that it really hit home (perhaps my first anthropological epiphany): The style of my youth wasn't "natural," part of some immutable order of the universe; it was socially learned, socially transmitted, moving through the world and changing, part of that mysterious phenomenon of motion called culture.

What made the revelation—the denaturalization—of my youthful life world possible were the changes in the surface texture of material things that became apparent in the late 1960s and early 1970s: long, unkempt hair that replaced the oiled hair and bun, loose floral dresses on women who had jettisoned their girdles, a crazy proliferation of colors. Here is the lived experience of transhistorical difference, something akin to the ethnographic sensitization to cross-cultural difference achieved through prolonged immersion in another locale. How ironic that an earlier generation of scholars conceptualized cultures as primordial, seemingly changeless things.

The movement of culture through the world is possible only because it becomes lodged, however fleetingly or enduringly, in material, perceptible things—stainless steel pots, girdled bodies, and even words as physical objects, as sounds or shapes. These are things that humans have fashioned, and hence that make tangible or manifest accumulated social learning. It is from such physical manifestations, and only from such physical manifestations, that culture is able to journey through the world, making its way from individual to individual, group to group.

Yet, if culture finds a transient home in the material world, it itself is profoundly immaterial—not this or that pot, but the more general, aestheticized form that is reflected in the specific thing. What is the connection between it—the immaterial, ghostlike form of culture—and things? The thing is a vehicle for the *dissemination* of culture. When an Amerindian Brazilian myth-teller tells a story, the story is placed in things—sounds and gestures—that are publicly accessible to others. The others may require many exposures to the things; they may have to listen to and watch the storyteller on numerous occasions. Eventually, however, they acquire the ability to tell the myth to someone else. Their (re)telling of it is an act of *replication*—the creation of a new thing that shares the abstract form of an older one.

The distinction between replication and dissemination is crucial for the project mapped out in this book, and, I believe, is closely linked to the rise of a metaculture of modernity,[1] as I propose to show. The movement of culture requires, so to speak, externalization, internalization, and re-externalization. Externalization, or making public or intersubjectively accessible, is what I am calling "dissemination." Its counterpart is the internalization of the abstract form, the extraction of the abstract entity from its surface manifestations in things such as stainless steel pots.

The connection between these two processes—externalization and internalization—is that the public evidence for the internalization by another is the reexternalization of the entity by that other, the re-embodiment of the abstract form in another physical thing. Consequently, dissemination and replication exist in a dynamic interrelation. The movement of culture through the world—as the movement of something abstract and ungraspably immaterial—is dependent on both processes, and hence on its transitory but recurrent habitation in the material world of things.

Why is this distinction important? The answer, I believe, has to do with the relative separability of the two phases or moments of the motion of culture. In the canonical movement of culture studied by classical anthropologists—including myself—the distinction is not apparent. This is so because the two phases are inextricably bound up: Making the cultural element public (that is, disseminating it) is only possible through replication.

My paradigm case is the movement of myth in a non-mass-mediated context, such as the Brazilian Indian communities in which I have worked. An individual learns myths by listening to others tell them. The individual internalizes them, but that internalization is made apparent only when the individual in turn retells the myth, that is, reexternalizes it in concrete, audible sounds and bodily gestures understandable as (more or less) equivalent to the earlier tellings. The reexternalization provides the occasion for a public check on internalization. Proof of internalization is the ability to reexternalize.

That public check on internalization depends on metaculture, that is, on some kind of formulation or acknowledgment by people that the two tellings are equivalent. This will become a key issue in my subsequent argument. Does the circulating metaculture emphasize cross-temporal equivalence of tellings (a metaculture of tradition)? Or does it emphasize the uniqueness of the discrete telling as a thing (a metaculture of modernity)? For the time being, however, I want to bracket this metacultural problem and focus on the nature of the movement itself.

What emerges as significant about myth is the space-time constraint on the relationship between dissemination and replication. In the Amerindian Brazilian communities I mentioned earlier, dissemination and replication are inextricably bound up with one another. Without replication, the temporal span of the myth might be confined to the life of the original teller(s), if not actually to the one instance of telling. And spatial dissemination would be confined to the audience that teller (or those tellers) might reach. For culture to achieve greater longevity, and wider spatial spread, for it to move from person to person, group to group, it must be replicated.

Imagine social life flourishing through this kind of cultural motion. The conduits through which culture moves—social relations—are based upon replication. The paradigm case of such a conduit is the parent-child bond, which is critical to the motion of culture across time. The parent-child bond is the locus for the kind of inertial culture—like a "mother tongue"—which is acquired by the child simply because it is there to be acquired. Social situations in which the movement of culture is largely based on the inseparability of dissemination from replication form the classical material for cultural anthropology—so-called kinship-based societies. There is good reason for this: It is through kinship relations that much of culture, as studied by anthropology, is passed.

However, if the parent-child conduit insures the movement of culture across time, it does not necessarily insure its movement across space. For such lateral movement across space, the parent-child conduit by itself is woefully inadequate. Other pathways of motion are needed. The most obvious device that can be added onto the parent-child bond to produce spatial motion is a culturally transmitted pattern of marriage or set of marriage rules that bring about exogamy, such as those documented by Claude Lévi-Strauss ([1949] 1969) in his *Elementary Structures of Kinship*. Here is culture engaged in its mysterious world-building efforts. The marriage rules are socially transmitted, and hence are culture; but they also help to create the pathways through which culture moves.

Marriage rules bring into physical proximity and interaction people who might otherwise participate in the evolution of separate lines of culture, conjoining those separate lines in the same individuals in the succeeding generation. This strategy is important where replication and dissemination cannot be separated or teased apart. The physical proximity in space and time of disseminator (parent) and future replicator (child) is the principal basis for cultural motion. No wonder Fortes regarded filiation as "the nodal mechanism and crucial relationship of intergenerational continuity and social reproduction . . . , the meeting point of synchronic order and diachronic extension at the core of social structure" (1969, 256). Filiation, coupled with marriage regulation, makes possible the development of a "shared culture" at the level of a community or set of interrelated communities as residential units.

But even in these kinship-based societies, the motion of culture presents a more complex picture. This is due to the presence of types of cultural elements that diverge from myth. I refer here specifically to ceramic pots and figures and other more durable types of "material culture." Like the sounds and bodily gestures produced by a myth-teller, ceramic pots are material manifestations (or externalizations) of cultural learning—not only about the materials and methods of manufacture of the pottery, but also about aesthetic forms and shapes, as in my opening examples from 1950s and 1960s American culture. This immaterial culture is carried in the pots as things.

What is different, however, is that the pots do not show the same kind of space-time constraints found in myth. Once manufactured, a pot can travel independently of its manufacturer. It can be carried great distances, coming into the realm of sensory accessibility of numerous people. Moreover, the pot has temporal longevity. It can last for tens, hundreds, thousands of years, bringing future generations into contact with the immaterial forms that previous generations have materialized in things.

Dissemination, in the case of ceramic pots, is, in some measure, at least, uncoupled from replication. I say "in some measure" because the physical things carry only a portion of the immaterial culture—the accumulated social learning—that is actually embodied in the material object as finished product. Transmission of the fullest measure of immaterial culture contained in the thing can only be had by close observation and interaction with the actual producer(s) of the thing—of the ceramic pot, for example—during the course of its production. What gets transmitted in the latter case is not unlike what gets transmitted in the case of myth—the embodied ability to produce a physical example of the cultural element. Even with those cultural products that are readily disseminable as physical things, therefore, the greatest quantity of immaterial culture is transmitted through propinquity, that is, through spatio-temporal proximity of the producer (or externalizer) and the internalizer (or future replicator).

From this it follows that, for the maximal amount of social learning that an individual A has acquired to be transmitted to B, B should be exposed to as much as possible of the process and product of externalization by A. In practical terms, living together and interacting with A furnish the optimal conditions for B to extract the immaterial culture from the physical manifestations of that culture in A's actions and the products of those actions.

What is gained for culture, in this case, is the greatest possible volume of flow over time. What is lost is lateral movement in a present world. For the greatest volume of culture to move across time, we would imagine a long string of individuals, with the elder A passing to the younger B, who then, on A's death, would pass to a new younger C, and so on. But this would render difficult the lateral spread of that culture, or some of it, to other individuals of the same generation. Hence, maximal transmission over time would inhibit the motion of culture across space.

The answer to the problem is to open up interactions laterally, which occurs, for example, in the case of the exogamous marriages discussed earlier. The far-flung motion of durable physical objects—like ceramic pots—represents another solution. Culture here finds its way through space (and also through time). But its far-flung dissemination through the physical movement of the pots themselves has its costs. Only a limited amount of culture can be internalized through exposure to the pots. By looking at a pot in the museum, I am not therefore able to produce a similar pot. Still, I might be able to extract something from it—characteristic shapes, patterns, colors—and I might be able to reproduce these in other forms.

Traveling through the western United States in the summer of 1998, I was struck by the proliferation of the Anasazi figure known as Kokopelli. It was everywhere—in art shops in Taos, appearing in the form of little statues, on billboards along the superhighways in Arizona, even on some potholders I purchased at Rocky Mountain National Park in Colorado. The culturally constructed form of a previous people—the so-called Anasazi, who flourished from about A.D. 900 to 1200 in the Four Corners area of the southwestern United States—continues to move through the world, stripped as it is of other aspects of immaterial culture that were, at one time, deposited in it.

The Culture of the Pathway

In the film *The Gods Must Be Crazy*, an airplane pilot flying over the Kalahari Desert in southwestern Africa carelessly tosses an empty Coca-Cola bottle out of the cockpit. The bottle falls through the air and strikes one of the Bushmen people, for whom it is a wondrous new object, presumably sent down by the gods. Here is an example of the dissemination of culture—whatever culture is embodied in a single Coca-Cola bottle—maximally uncoupled from replication. The movement of the thing through the world is purely physical, detached from social relations.

If I were to conceptualize the historical patterns of the split between dissemination and replication in this way, I would be hopelessly wrong. The physical things that are carriers of culture move through social relations that themselves depend on cultural learning. The social relations are learned patterns of interaction and are a part of culture. They depend on replication.

But what is distinctive is that the social relations that go to make up a pathway of dissemination of physical things do not depend on the same kind of replication that the production of those things depends on. This, I believe, is crucial. In the case of myth, the social relations that constitute the pathways of motion for the myths are themselves bound up with the replication of the myth. Replication lays down the very pathways through which the replicated culture moves. The pathways of dissemination are the pathways of replication of culture.

It is entirely possible for the movement of the culture embodied in ceramic pots to occur in the very same way. Indeed, in many kinship-based societies described by anthropologists, the movement of ceramic pots has been primarily of this mythological type, where replication and dissemination are inseparably linked. The split between the two begins to take shape when distinct types of replication emerge—a replication whose purpose is to transmit the very culture that is replicated (myth), and a replication whose purpose is to create social pathways for the physical movement of culturally-created objects through the world.

A film, for example, is lodged in a concrete thing—a roll of celluloid tape with images imprinted on it. Think of the enormous amount of social learning that has gone into the production of the celluloid tape itself, minus the images. Add to it the additional social learning behind the scripting, staging, and shooting of the film. The product, in some sense, carries all of that learning inside it. But the learning is not readily recoverable by the casual viewer of the film. The transmission of this learning, however, is essential if new films are ever to be made. If only those who actually produced films or wanted to produce films viewed them, the situation would be roughly analogous to myth. Replication and dissemination would co-occur along the same pathways.

However, films are designed also for viewers who will never replicate them by making their own films and who have no interest in doing so. True, in the case of myth, some people may be better storytellers than others. Some who hear the stories may never tell them at all. But in principle, everyone could be a replicator of the disseminated culture. This is because listening to the myths, observing the behavior of the myth-teller, allows one to internalize the cultural form of production. One could, in principle, reexternalize that form on a subsequent occasion.

This is not true in the case of films. Repeated viewing of a film does not allow you to make a film yourself. It does not allow you to know how to use projection equipment to show the film. It does not even allow you to know how to obtain the film from someone else so that you might show it.

All of those abilities require social learning that the film itself does not render accessible to you.

It is true that viewing the film allows you to replicate something. For example, you can narrate the plot of the film to someone else; you can use lines from a film in your discourse; you can imitate the clothing or hairstyles or mannerisms of the actors; and more. Something immaterial from the film gets out of the film and into you as a viewer, just by virtue of viewing, and you can, in turn, pass that something—albeit in different material form—onto someone else. So it is not that your viewing of the film does not result in the movement of culture. It does. But the culture that gets across to you does not exhaust—or even begin to tap—all of the culture embodied in the film as a thing or set of things in the world.

What makes this possible is a culture of dissemination—social learning that enables the movement of physical things between people. And, note, it may be possible for someone to learn how to procure films and how to project them, even though they themselves have no interest in viewing the films. This may not be typical—people may be attracted to distribution of films as an activity because of their interest in viewing films—but it is possible. The pathways of culture that enable dissemination are not necessarily identical to the pathways of replication of the culture that is disseminated.

The historical appearance of pathways of dissemination, relatively uncoupled from replication, makes it appear as if culture were a mind in the world, calculating how best to facilitate its own movement. The problem with the culture of myth—where replication and dissemination are inextricably bound up—is that the lateral movement of culture is limited. Because replication almost always results in changes, however minute, culture that is dependent on replication for movement in space is circumscribed in its scope of movement. By the time it has gone from point a to point n, via points b, c, d, etc., it is no longer the same thing. But, when dissemination can be, relatively speaking, freed of replication—that is, where the replication of the pathway can be distinguished from the replication of the culture carried along that pathway—then the lateral movement of culture can be greatly expanded. The pathways through which elements flow can evolve through the microprocesses of social transmission of the culture necessary to maintain those pathways, but the cultural elements that flow along those pathways need not themselves be affected.

Let me quickly head off a possible misinterpretation. I am not making a technologically determinist argument. I am not saying that it is the technological development of film as a medium, for example, that enables the far-flung dissemination of culture. The latter statement is true in present-day terms. Film does enable dissemination of culture. But the prior condition of this is the long development of cultures of dissemination—of the social pathways along which culture flows without being reproduced. I will even be making the argument, subsequently, that it is the presence of cultures of dissemination that drives technological innovation. I believe that the presence of such a culture is intimately linked to the rise of a meta-culture of modernity, and that the latter impels technological change.

It's the Economy, Stupid!

In his haunting documentary film, "The Decade of Destruction," which records the convulsive transformation of the Amazonian rainforest during the 1980s, director Adrian Cowell follows a Brazilian government team on an expedition to contact[2] one of the last remaining isolated indigenous populations in the world, the Uru-eu-wau-wau. This population lived, in the early 1980s, in a vast and uncharted forest in the western Brazilian state of Rondônia. But it was also in the crosshairs of theodolites that were being used to survey the path of a proposed highway designed to open up the Amazon region to settlement and commerce.

We follow the government team—over the course of months, turning into years, of frustration—as they attempt to make "contact," that is, enter into peaceful social relations with these elusive people. Prominently, the team leaves "gifts" for the Indians—steel machetes and pots and other manufactured items. The gifts are hung from wooden cross-supports in places the Indians are known to inhabit. We see the metal objects dangling and clanking in the breeze. But the Indians reject the gifts—perhaps because they understand intuitively Marcel Mauss's (1967) dictum: A gift freely given demands a gift in return.

I find myself musing about the motion of culture in this instance. Are these gifts for the people in question analogous to the Coca-Cola bottle falling out of the sky? Yet the dissemination of culture here is purposive. The agents do want something. They want to bring these Indians into the orbit of Brazilian national culture, and they do so by bringing pieces of that culture to them.

How far have the pots and machetes traveled? How did they get to this remote headwaters region? As to the first, they may have been—indeed, likely were—made in São Paulo, the manufacturing center for Brazil, a couple of thousand miles to the south and east. The culture of replication of these artifacts has its locus in São Paulo, and, while that culture is deposited in those pots and machetes as material manifestations of social learning, it cannot readily be extracted from them by one not engaged with the local process of production. If some of the culture deposited in these items can be extracted by anyone who sees them or uses them, other aspects of culture remain locked up in the things, awaiting a future archaeologist to extract their meaning, if no current ethnographer documents them.

As to how the items made the journey, the important point is that, unlike myth—transported thousands of miles only through numerous tellings and retellings—the underlying form of the items (of the pot, for example) would not have to be remanufactured by each adjacent population in a long chain extending out to Rondônia, resulting in a pot that resembled the original thousands of miles away. Of course not. The pot could just be loaded onto a truck and shipped across the country to a nearby town, where the government team could pick it up. But this process of being able to transport the thing without replicating it depends on the replication of another kind of culture—the culture of dissemination.

The Brazilian government contact team is itself part of a culture of dissemination—government-trained members of the Indian service agency who carry on years of accumulated learning about how to peacefully contact isolated indigenous groups. The team's leader, Apoena Mereiles, is himself the son of a government Indian agent who established contact with another isolated population—the Xavante—some thirty years before. Apoena was actually named after the Xavante chief with whom his father had entered into contact—social learning about dissemination, evidently, here passing through the parent-child bond, the classic conduit of cultural replication.

Indeed, the methods employed by the government team—including the leaving of "gifts" such as metal pots and machetes—were themselves part of a long tradition in Brazil, going back at least to the founding of the first government Service for the Protection of Indians (SPI), formed in 1911. I myself documented, through oral and written accounts, the use of similar techniques in settling a different population. The techniques were part of a tried-and-true method for the dissemination of Brazilian culture. They were not the result of the rational scheming of this particular team, but an abstract method, socially learned and transmitted and reimplemented by generations of frontiersmen. They were thus part of a replicated culture of dissemination.

What is especially interesting about the case of contact is that the isolated population—the Uru-eu-wau-wau, in this case—did not itself, at that time, participate in the same culture of dissemination. Bringing metal pots and machetes to this population was thus quite a different matter from bringing them to a population—such as settlers who have migrated from the northeast of Brazil—that already shared some aspects of this culture of dissemination. We who participate in the culture of capitalism forget how much cultural learning we have acquired about dissemination, about "buying" objects, about trading. The knowledge and skills we have are not the product of an independently arrived-at calculation, nor are they part of the natural order of the universe. Rather, they are the result of a long process of social accumulation; they are a precious inheritance from our ancestors.

A dramatic moment occurs in the Cowell documentary: After more than a year of frustration for government team and camera crew alike— not to mention for the indigenous population—the first contact is about to occur. The filming takes place from inside a hut, unbeknownst to the Indians. Through the camera lens, we see a Brazilian Indian agent hold out a machete; the machete is grasped by an Indian man clad in the characteristic Uru-eu-wau-wau belt (see Figure 3). The Indian man is smiling, but offers nothing in return. After a few moments, he hears the crackling of the government short-wave radio inside the attraction hut. We see him peer suspiciously into the hut, through the hole out of which the camera is filming.

What has happened here? My contention is that a social pathway of dissemination has been opened. The Indians have had to learn, through experience, that they can trust these particular white men not to do them physical harm, and, moreover, that they can receive material items from them. And they have had to learn how to behave in these transactions. They learn embodied forms of greeting and of signaling nonaggression as well as how to comport themselves in order to receive the "gifts." All of these are part of the socially learned patterns that make up a pathway of cultural dissemination. And the government agents have had to learn, as well. Such socially transmitted patterns are acquired gradually over years.

There are setbacks—conflicting signals are given. Clashes occur with other white men who are not part of the government team and who move into the area: settlers, prospectors, illegal ocelot trappers. What is distinctive about the government team? What kinds of behaviors are appropriate in dealing with them, as opposed to with the others? The Indians make mistakes. They shoot one of the government agents—apparently, an edgy response attributable to conflicts with other white men in the region. Gradually, however, over years, the dissemination network takes hold.

Figure 3. Cultural objects find their way to new sites of local uptake and flow through social relations; simultaneously, the social relations are themselves constituted by the motion of culture. Here, the Uru-eu-wau-wau Indians of western Brazil are shown in the early days of contact with a Brazilian government representative, and the cultural object of interest is a machete. From the "Decade of Destruction" series, part I, "In the Ashes of the Forest." Courtesy of Adrian Cowell.

The Uru-eu-wau-wau have entered the orbit of the Brazilian nation. The pathways of dissemination of Brazilian culture have been laid down, paving the way for a dramatic transformation in the patterns of replication that had previously made up Uru-eu-wau-wau life.

Pathways of trade and commerce—the basis for the dissemination of culture in Europe—have ancient roots.[3] Consequently, it is truly difficult, if not impossible, for someone currently inside of Western culture to appreciate how much accumulated social learning had to go into the laying down of pathways, how much cultural replication is at the basis of even knowing how to lay down pathways. This is culture that has accrued over thousands of years. We need to ask: What has culture been up to all that time in laying down such pathways? Why has it done so?

Of course, the case I have considered is inadequate for addressing these questions. A huge asymmetry is involved.[4] One side of the contact—the Brazilian government side—is the heir to thousands of years of accumulated experience with cultures of dissemination. The government team itself is the heir to decades of experience in contacting isolated indigenous populations. I cannot here come close to finding the fumbling beginnings of experimentation with a culture of dissemination and its effects, how people had to learn how to make and maintain pathways of dissemination that did not require the replication of the material that was disseminated.

This last point is important. By acquiring metal pots and machetes, the Uru-eu-wau-wau did not automatically acquire the ability to reproduce metal pots and machetes—to make new embodiments of culture that would look like the ones they had received. They might well have been able to replicate other aspects of the culture embodied in these things—the aesthetic shapes and patterns of use, for example—but not the ability to reproduce the items themselves. With the disseminated cultural artifacts does not automatically come the culture of replication that produced them.

The relative severing of dissemination from replication results in what Durkheim ([1893] 1933) and others have called the "division of labor." But attention to the motion of culture offers a different perspective on the problem. What the relative severing of dissemination from replication allows is the greater accumulation, in quantitative terms, of social learning within a population as a whole. If the parent-child bond is optimal for maximizing the volume of transmission of culture between two individuals, A and B, it is not optimal for maximizing the total amount of culture deposited in a population at any given moment. If every member of a population were only a B receiving culture from an A, the population would be the conduit for unconnected strands of culture, each one similar to the next, although the strands would diverge over time. This is the scenario Durkheim might imagine—were he to adopt a perspective of cultural motion—under his concept of "mechanical solidarity," with each of the constituent parts of society essentially like the others, at least insofar as their role as conduit is concerned.

Where dissemination is (again, relatively speaking) severed from replication, however, certain individuals need not be the recipients of all of the culture that is required to replicate a completed object such as a pot, but they could still replicate some of the culture that has gone into making that pot. Through dissemination, a broader population comes to consist of pockets of replication brought into relationship through pathways of dissemination.

The Uru-eu-wau-wau had been stealing metal pots and machetes from

Brazilian settlers before the government team arrived on the scene (Adrian Cowell, personal communication). They initially rejected the "gifts." Yet a dependency of sorts did arise after the fact. Having come to accept metal pots and to use them in place of ceramic ones—for which internal patterns of replication could supply an infinite number of replacements—the metal pots would, over time, result in the loss of the autochthonous patterns of replication. The survival of the population, in the style to which it had been accustomed, would come to depend on the dissemination of cultural artifacts reproduced elsewhere.

With greater reliance on cultural items produced elsewhere, the local population—in this case, the Uru-eu-wau-wau, but I could be talking about any village or community in a modern nation—comes to be less the site of replication of culture, in the classic sense where dissemination depends on replication, and more the site of penetration of culture originating elsewhere. This is not to say that culture does not continue, in some measure, to be reproduced within the family through the conduit of the parent-child bond. However, Fortes's idea that filiation is "the nodal mechanism . . . of intergenerational continuity" (1969, 256) becomes less true the more culture enters the family from the outside through pathways of dissemination.

Of course, I do not believe that the Uru-eu-wau-wau family was the exclusive conduit for the flow of culture prior to the arrival of the government team in the early 1980s. A great deal of the culture was, undoubtedly, carried at the communal plane, and passed on through public rituals. But I do imagine that the culture passing through the community was, relatively speaking, publicly accessible. The externalizations of culture were there, in the community, and available for reinternalization. Consequently, the culture of the community could, in principle, at least, be replicated by anyone.

I recall a quip by one of my own teachers, the anthropologist David Schneider. He said that an ethnographer required only one good informant—provided that the informant didn't lisp. The partial truth of this statement is to be found in the nature of cultural motion in an isolated community, though even there the anthropologist finds differential access to the externalizations of culture. But if this single-informant method has some plausibility for studying the kind of culture where dissemination is inextricably tied to replication, it is woefully inadequate where dissemination becomes relatively detached from replication—that is, where cultures of dissemination become distinguished from cultures of replication.

If the sites of cultural replication are concentrated in pockets linked together by pathways of dissemination, then the study of "representative" villages—as in W. Lloyd Warner's (1941, 1942, 1945, 1947, 1959) Yankee City series or the Lynds's (1929, 1937) Middletown research—cannot be a wholly adequate method of investigating "American culture"[5] or, at least, the significance of the community study is distinct from the study of a pre-1980s Uru-eu-wau-wau village. The latter research would have the greater claim to illuminating the culture of the Uru-eu-wau-wau more generally because cultural replication and dissemination are inextricably linked. But the study of a community in the contemporary United States would shed little light on the cultures of replication that produce the disseminable cultural artifacts coming into the community from without.

To get at the cultures of replication within the larger population, anthropology needs ethnographies of sites of replication.[6] The corporation (the film studio, the publishing house, the manufacturing firm) rather than (or in addition to) the village would be the proper object for ethnography. How are steel pots replicated, anyway? Of course, the corporation itself is not an isolated community, but rather complexly intercalated in a broader population even as regards its processes of replication. Still, to look at the motion of culture through the world as it is replicated, corporations are excellent sites. What knowledge has to be passed on, what embodied practices have to be replicated within the corporation, in order for the replication of disseminable culture to take place? For an anthropologist, the corporation ought to be a wondrous phenomenon—a set of social relations built up around the replication and dissemination of culture. In this sense, its role with respect to contemporary culture is reminiscent of the role of the family in situations—such as that of the pre-1980s Uru-eu-wau-wau—where dissemination of culture is inextricably bound up with its replication.

Correspondingly, the role of the family and kinship ought to be dramatically different in situations where the parent-child bond is not the crucial relationship of intergenerational continuity, but only one of many such relationships. Indeed, David Schneider's method in *American Kinship: A Cultural Account* (1980) cannot really provide a true cultural account in this kind of situation. Schneider used the method of interviewing in depth a small number of people, asking them questions about their understanding of kinship and kinsmen.[7] In a society where the family is the locus of replication and dissemination of culture, this method has some claim to validity. But in contemporary America, the workshop of kinship is often not the family but the film studio—or the sites for other disseminated culture, such as the music recording studio or the publishing house—where images of the family and kinship begin their journey on a wider dissemination. Such representations enter the family from the outside, and become the basis for secondary replications off of the disseminated form (Dick 1999).

In relation to the replication and dissemination of culture in contemporary America, ethnographers are truly like the blind men and the elephant. Each one explores but a small patch of the larger beast. Yet with enough ethnographers empirically documenting sites of cultural replication—and here I would add replication of the pathways of dissemination, as well—a broader picture of the beast can emerge—indeed, is emerging—even as I write.

Valuing Dissemination over Replication

The entrepreneur is often thought of—by some perhaps cynical academics, at least—as a crass materialist interested only in the accumulation of wealth, this despite Max Weber's ([1958] 1976) attempts to link the rise of modern capitalism in Europe to religious origins—namely, to the Protestant Reformation. Weber traced the spirit or ethos of capitalism to the attitudes of Calvinism. A disregard for the earthly pleasures of profit—coupled with uncertainty about one's own salvation, which results in attempts to allay one's anxieties through the manifestation of grace—led the Calvinist to reinvest profit in more efficient means of production. Such reinvestment of profit Weber saw, in turn, as the cornerstone of the modern capitalist system.

But it is interesting to approach the problem of the rise of modern capitalism from the perspective of the differentiation of cultures of replication from cultures of dissemination. Here I note that a key question about culture—one I have not yet addressed—is embedded in the Uru-eu-wau-wau contact: Why did the Indians finally accept the gifts? In the case of the metal pots, in particular, if the Uru-eu-wau-wau could already manufacture ceramic pots, why take on the metal ones?

I have already proposed that a certain amount of cultural replication takes place off of the disseminated item—the pot, in this instance. The dissemination does not result in the ability to produce another item like the received one; that is, the Uru-eu-wau-wau cannot automatically produce their own metal pots. But it does result in the replication of some of the culture contained in the item. So one can appreciate—from the point of view of Brazilian national culture—why it would be desirable for the

Indians to take up the pots. They would be accepting some small measure of Brazilian culture. But why is it desirable for the Indians to do so?

I do not want to make the answer to this question too simple. Undoubtedly, the decisions involved were complex. The Uru-eu-wau-wau originally rejected the offerings. Perhaps, recognizing the "gifts" as expressions of peaceful or friendly intentions, the Indians accepted them because of their perception that these white men might be allies against the others—the settlers, prospectors, ocelot trappers—with whom the Indians were clashing. But while this might be a reason for accepting the items, it would not be a reason for continuing to use them, and hence for the dependency on outside cultural production that results. Indeed, recall the the Uru-eu-wau-wau had already been stealing metal items from settler camps. In this case, I believe, the items come to be evaluated, over time, through processes of internal dialogue and debate, as new and better—yes, better—with respect to the cultural elements they come to replace.

Of course, there is also a laziness factor here. It is easier to simply take the items from the government agents rather than manufacture analogous items oneself. However, metal is superior for certain purposes—and, as I say this, I am making a metacultural judgment, a judgment such as I believe is essential for the dissemination of culture. For certain purposes, metal is superior. Like the Uru-eu-wau-wau, the Indians at P. I. Ibirama, in the southern Brazilian state of Santa Catarina, stole metal from the settlers moving into their region during the first decade of the twentieth century. They hammered it with stones, laboriously shaping it into lance and arrow points, using it to replace the wood and stone they had used previously. Why did they do so? The metal was harder to fashion than wood, but it made for a superior lance point, one that could withstand the attacks of jaguars—who would, it is said, impale themselves on lances while trying to jump hunters.

The important point here is the metacultural judgment about the new material received through dissemination over the older material it comes to replace. What if the government team contacting the Uru-eu-wau-wau had left crude pots that cracked easily and could not hold water or other liquids? The Uru-eu-wau-wau still might have taken them up, but there would have to have been reasons—metacultural evaluations of the differential significance of the native and imported pots. While the metacultural reasoning is not simply a reflex of cultural facts—for example, about the superiority of metal over ceramics—neither is the metaculture indifferent to the culture. The metaculture, in this case, is a gate keeper that can keep the new elements out or let them in. But it is not a whimsical gatekeeper. It must take into account the realities of the culture whose movement it fosters or hinders.

Why might the Uru-eu-wau-wau, even at some later time down the road, opt to reject the metal pots? One reason, so prominent in many indigenous communities in the 1980s and 1990s, is the metacultural value placed on the replication of traditional indigenous culture, which accepting the metal pots might subvert. That is not an unreasonable position. But in the 1980s and 1990s that metacultural valuation has not simply arisen autochthonously within native communities. It has also been part of a larger transnational circulation of images and ideas about traditional indigenous cultures—images and ideas that are part of a globally circulating metaculture, like the Adrian Cowell documentary. What is the basis, after all, of the interest that Western audiences have in isolated Amazonian Indian populations? Evidently, such populations or, rather, the images of them, play a role in processes of local Western cultural reproduction. The reassertion of traditional ceramics, therefore, coupled with the rejection of imported metal pots, might be one outgrowth of a reassertion of the metacultural valuation of tradition over the new.

My point here is not about indigenous responses, per se, but about the general problem. Dissemination relatively uncoupled from replication, as occurs in the "contact" situation, depends on a metacultural valuation of the new (i.e., disseminated) culture over the older (i.e., replicated) culture. There is thus spun out of the contact encounter a necessary clash between a metaculture of modernity (valuing the new over the old) and a metaculture of tradition (valuing the old over the new). Traces of a metaculture of modernity, therefore, far from being an invention of Europe of the last few hundred years, are a necessary component of the cultural motion resulting from dissemination relatively decoupled from replication. The metaculture of modernity (or of the new) is what enables or facilitates the motion of the new disseminated cultural element into previously uncharted territory. Dissemination and modernity (as metaculture) are two sides of the same coin.

Alas, however, it is not that simple. If a trace of the metaculture of modernity is a sine qua non of the initial movement of a new cultural element into uncharted territory, it is certainly possible for that movement to be reassimilated into a metaculture of tradition. The disseminated element—even though not replicated locally—can come over time to seem part of an old pattern. The metaculture of modernity, spun off of the initial movement of culture into new terrain, is a cusp phenomenon and can recede in significance as the pathway of dissemination becomes established as a necessary conduit of old culture.

In the Kula ring described by Bronislaw Malinowski ([1922] 1961), the native islanders living east of New Guinea exchange items—red spondyllus shell necklaces known as *soulava* and *Conus millepunctatus* arm shells known as *mwali*. The items move in great circles between the islands, the *soulava* necklaces moving clockwise, and the *mwali* arm shells moving counterclockwise. If one imagines that this trade must have once been stimulated by the novelty of an initial dissemination, it had, by Malinowski's time, at least, long since lost that function. Indeed, the novelty had been thoroughly reabsorbed into a metaculture of tradition, where exchange of the same kinds of items was merely the way things had been done. It was tradition.

In this sense, the fifteenth and sixteenth centuries in Europe loom large—though I make no pretense to historical expertise and do not really much care to assign a precise date to the phenomenon about which I am talking, namely, the emergence of a widespread metaculture of modernity. If traces of a metaculture of modernity are part and parcel of—indeed, are a necessary initial moving force behind—dissemination uncoupled from replication, their establishment as a dominant form of metaculture that reshapes the motion of culture through time is not the inevitable outcome of dissemination uncoupled from replication. Moreover, the ascendancy of newness is likely something that takes shape gradually over several generations, with the thirteenth through fifteenth centuries showing a growth, albeit gradual, in demand for manuscript copies (Thomas [1958] 1976). Yet the fifteenth century was particularly notable as the "Age of Discovery," especially of the "New World," a term first circulated, evidently, by the Italian historian Peter Martyr in *De Rebus Oceanicis et Novo Orbe* (1511–30). I note the idea of newness here: *novo orbe*. It is tempting to wonder about the relationship between dissemination and metaculture that grew out of that period.

The very idea of cultural motion prods me—as if it were an independent agent, peering over my shoulder—to concede that metacultures of newness have likely surfaced to dominate metacultures of tradition at different places and in different times—ancient Greece being one possibility, with the Heraclitean doctrine of change circa 500 B.C. suggesting a burgeoning concern with newness, and the subsequent mathematical, philosophical, and artistic developments indicating a competition over the production of new culture as well as a suspicion of received culture. This was also, of course, an age of flourishing trade, the *agora*, or marketplace, having proliferated during the immediately preceding period.

The fifteenth and sixteenth centuries in Europe were not unprecedent-ed, in this regard. Still, between the fifteenth and eighteenth centuries, dissemination, rather than being reabsorbed into a metaculture of tradi-tion, mushroomed in significance, with a metaculture of newness coming to occupy a prominent and even dominant position—Francis Bacon's *Novum Organum* appeared already in 1620. Or, looking at it the other way around, the spread of a metaculture of newness resulted in the reevaluation of the significance of dissemination. Dissemination came to seem an expression of the highest value of culture, with the entrepreneur as culture hero. Why? What is the significance of this for the motion of culture through space and time?

I will propose a specific response to this question in the next section. But already here I want to suggest—with Weber and others, though from the perspective of cultural motion—that the crass materialism of the en-trepreneur needs to be rethought. The entrepreneur is interested in the surface of culture—its externalization in things. But what interest does culture—as social learning moving through space and time—have in the entrepreneur? Should not the interest of culture be better served by the continuing valuation of the replicator over the disseminator, of the old over the new?

To set these questions in context, it is useful to think about dissemina-tion in relationship to the four great mechanisms for the lateral spread of culture through space—mechanisms that go beyond elementary diffusion resulting from unstable and intermittent contact and beyond migration or relocation. The four are: marriage, wars of conquest, conversion religion, and trade. I would add education, but for the purposes of this overview, it is essentially like conversion religion.

I have already mentioned marriage, grounded in filiation, and, corre-spondingly, in processes of motion where dissemination is inextricably bound up with replication. Marriage moves culture laterally, bringing to-gether into the same conduits of transmission what might otherwise be distinct lines, tending over time—through the gradual changes associated with replication—to diverge from one another.

It is intriguing that wars of conquest and conversion religions pick up where marriage leaves off, as if culture were searching to find new avenues for lateral motion, restlessly seeking new pathways through the physical world. Both mechanisms, like marriage, are based ultimately upon a form of cultural motion in which dissemination is inseparably bound up with replication. In the case of military conquest, the movement of culture takes place through the setting up of an administrative apparatus through which culture flows. In the absence of mass media, the flow is from person to person, group to group, and hence subject to the forces of dissipation associated with replication. But the ultimate interest of the conqueror is in the behavioral manifestations of the conquered, and, therefore, in the replication of a specific form of culture.

In the case of conversion religion, similarly, the proof is in the behavioral evidence that some social learning has passed to the converted. For Catholicism, for example, the proof of motion is the learning of the catechism and the ability to properly reexternalize or replicate teaching.

I hesitate to lump conversion religions together, since there is something intriguingly different in certain forms of Protestantism—notably, the Wycliffe Bible translators, whose overt goal is to translate the Bible into every language on earth, and thus to make the word of God publicly accessible. This idea bears a striking resemblance to the form of dissemination associated with trade and commerce, as I will argue. Simply having the Bible available is sufficient to bring its culture to those who have not previously had it. Yet even Protestant sects rely upon baptism or other manifestations of commitment for entrance into a particular religious community.

The case of trade is distinct, however. Trade zeroes in on the motion of the physical things in which culture its deposited. It concentrates on the externalizations of cultural learning themselves, with no apparent regard for replication. Traders do not involve themselves in questions of how the material items they transmit are to be used—or, at least, this is not the essence of trade as a social phenomenon. Its essence is the dissemination of the material things in and of themselves.

I am especially interested in this phenomenon: the development of a metaculture that values dissemination over all else, including the replication of culture. My hunch is that the development of such a metaculture goes hand in hand with the ascendance of a metaculture of newness. It is easy to see why the other great mechanisms of lateral motion of culture are tied to metacultures of tradition, which emphasize replication. A metaculture of tradition seeks to see each new externalization as essentially like ones that have preceded it, with β collapsing into α. Such a metaculture seeks not only to describe that temporal folding back or reabsorption of the present into a past, but also to bring it about—to get people to actually carry on a strand of culture, to replicate a cultural element. In this way, a metaculture of tradition can be understood as a mechanism for propelling culture through time, and, hence, for insuring continuity.

It is more difficult to see a connection between the emphasis on dissemination (with apparent disregard for replication) and a metaculture of newness. Since emphasis on dissemination appears as crass materialism, how can a metaculture that values it be linked to the propulsion of culture—as a profoundly immaterial thing—through the material world?

Here it is interesting to reflect on the phenomenon of price, or on the idea of the equivalence of objects in trade more generally, as an aspect of cultural motion. The phenomenon has been well studied and admirably described by economics. What has not been so well studied, however, is the relationship of price, as a metacultural phenomenon, to the motion of culture, or, rather, to the motion of the things in which culture is carried. Price appears, from this perspective, as a measure of the force that impels an object along social pathways—what economists call "demand." If the price goes up for an object—admittedly, in an ideal marketplace—this is because demand exceeds supply.

But for the cultural theorist, the question is: What is the force impelling that motion? What is demand? And here it is relevant to return to the Coca-Cola bottle tossed out of the cockpit and landing on a Bushman in the Kalahari Desert in *The Gods Must Be Crazy*. The Bushman had no demand for the bottle; the pilot was not satisfying a Bushman need. And, more generally, demand is not related only to the scarcity of the object. The object must have—again, in the economist's language—"value." The object must be something the Bushman actually wants.

How do the metal pots and machetes come to have value for the Uru-eu-wau-wau in the far west of Brazil? They come to acquire value by virtue of their role in the replication of culture within the community. They come to substitute for other containers that the Uru-eu-wau-wau were already able to produce themselves through their socially transmitted learning. From the point of view of Uru-eu-wau-wau metaculture, the obviously "new" items come to seem as superior, for the purposes for which they are employed, to the traditional containers. Consequently, they become something the Uru-eu-wau-wau seek to acquire. Demand is created because of the role the new items play in local processes of cultural replication. Demand—measured through price or in some other way—is itself a function of the role of the item within the replication of culture.

Many anthropologists—in recent decades, in any case—have tended to be at odds with economists, viewing them as supporters and propagators of a capitalist culture that—as in the case of the Uru-eu-wau-wau—subverts traditional processes of cultural replication among the people with whom they work. Yet, there is room for cooperation, all the more so because the cultures carried by the populations with whom anthropologists work have "value"—yes, in this economic sense—for those who are the bearers of capitalist culture. The "Decade of Destruction" itself has as its principal source of demand people in the West who take up the film for their own local purposes. What about the Kokopelli figure of the mysterious Anasazi? These images have value in the economic sense. They are objects in demand.[8]

Great as the contribution of economists may be to understanding the motion of material items through social pathways, however, what is missing from their analyses, and what makes cultural researchers so uniquely positioned to contribute through ethnographic work, is an understanding of what attributes of the physical thing, relative to its metacultural construal, make it desirable, make it something that is in demand. Since demand depends upon local processes of cultural replication, who better to fathom those local processes than the ethnographer?

I still have not answered my main question, though now I am getting closer. It is beginning to become apparent what interest culture—as a mind in the world, seeking its own lateral motion—might have in a metaculture that values dissemination over replication. In capitalist forms of dissemination, at least—that is, those grounded in and regulated by price rather than by other social values—dissemination is linked to replication. But it is only indirectly linked to those processes. Demand for an object is an indication that the object is playing a role in local processes of replication—whatever those are—and hence in local patterns of cultural motion.

Here is the rub for culture, understood not as physical thing, but as the underlying and exquisitely nonmaterial form or abstract learning that goes into the thing: Without a test of replication, there is no way to know for sure that culture has, indeed, been carried along with the material object that moves through the world. Has it, or hasn't it? This is why conversion religions and conquest administrations demand evidence of replication. From the point of view of the bearers of culture who bring the "new" culture to the unconverted or unconquered, how else can they know that the new culture has actually reached these people?

Something fundamentally different, however, is involved in the cultures of dissemination that developed in Europe. The disseminator gives up on knowing whether the culture has passed. There is an implicit faith here in the surface of things as bearers of something far less scrutable. When a Brazilian Indian man tells a myth he has heard his father or father-in-law tell, there is prima facie evidence that the immaterial underlying form of culture has been passed on. When a woman fashions a new ceramic pot like the one she has helped her mother to make, there is prima facie evidence that social learning has worked its way yet another step through the world. But when an American child watches a movie, or an adult buys a cooking pot at the store, who can be certain that some specific cultural learning has been passed on?

To add insult to injury, a metaculture of modernity decrys the simple act of replication. If a filmmaker makes a film too much like ones that have come before it, critics label the film "more of the same," a "dull remake." When a new year comes around, auto manufacturers unveil their "new" line of cars. The new models are berated by critics if they are not "improvements" over older models. The emphasis here is not on the replication of the same thing—that is, on continuity—though some customers profess to prefer this. A metaculture of newness suggests that the test of replication itself is ho-hum—not of interest in the contemporary world. How can such a metaculture facilitate the movement of underlying, abstract patterns of social learning through the world?

My questions are not rhetorical. I do think there are answers. Indeed, I think that culture—as accumulated social learning—stumbled upon something of monumental significance when it developed a metaculture valuing dissemination over replication, and newness over oldness. It discovered that culture was carried through the world in things, and, moreover, that exposure to those things was sufficient for its movement through the world, without evidence of replication, provided that the things themselves were of interest to people—provided, that is, that they were in demand.

In an earlier book, I proposed that "culture is localized in concrete, publicly accessible signs, the most important of which are actually occurring instances of discourse" (Urban 1991, 1). The idea of public accessibility of signs is closely akin to the faith in the material in which cultural learning is deposited. One acquires culture only through sensory encounter with the externalizations of culture created by others—in the case of language, with the sounds uttered or the signs produced by those around one. Correspondingly, the greatest possibility of cultural sharing occurs when people have the same kinds of access to the same sensory experiences of the materials in which culture is deposited—whether sounds or written documents or films or ceramic pots.

What a remarkable step it is for culture to place all of its faith in those things—independently of the evidence of their replication. This is, in effect, what happens when a metaculture of dissemination rises to ascendancy. Such a metaculture focuses only on the demand for the things, not on the replication of those things, which would be evidence that cultural learning has passed between people. Why should this be the case? Because, implicitly, the metaculture acknowledges that the immaterial social learning will pass along with the material.

The isolated Coca-Cola bottle falling into a community or the scattering of metal pots and machetes left by a government attraction team and taken up by an indigenous community will not result in the spread of all of the culture that went into the making of those material things. But repeated exposure to numerous objects emanating from a different cultural tradition—if those objects are of interest to people for their own local reasons—will result in the transmission of something. Moreover, over time, it will result—and this is, again, the implicit faith attached to this kind of motion—in the desire not only for the objects themselves, but for the ability to produce those objects.[9]

This goes to the heart of the issue: The metaculture of dissemination that took shape in Europe—perhaps in the fifteenth and sixteenth centuries, but undoubtedly with older roots—is based upon this implicit faith. If people take up objects that are the embodiment of cultural learning and the result of cultural replication, one can have faith that some culture will pass to those people, even without regard to specific evidence of replication. The price system provides evidence that people have interest in objects, but it provides no evidence of the specific role those objects play in cultural replication. Therefore, it provides no basis for the faith in the transmission that is occurring. The essence of the development of a culture of dissemination is an implicit faith in the association between physical objects in which culture is deposited and the process of transmission of that culture.

To be sure, I, as a student of culture, subscribe to that same faith. As I have argued, for culture—as abstract form or accumulated social learning—to move through the world, it must be located in sensorily accessible evidence: sounds, gestures, physical objects. But this necessity is not sufficient for movement to take place. It might be sufficient under the operation of existential inertia, where one acquires culture simply because it is there to be acquired and nothing else rises up to compete with it. However, habitual inertia—inertia resulting from the prior acquisition of patterns, as of pronunciation—acts as an inhibitor to the taking up of the culture embodied in things, insofar as those things don't resemble traditional ones. This is, of course, why the test of replication developed. A metaculture of tradition emerges as a way to insure that the flow of culture has actually occurred, a way to erase doubt. When it comes to cultures of dissemination, there is a test, namely, that the physical objects in which culture has been deposited attract interest. This is the test of price. And interest is evidence that the objects are being taken up in local cultural processes.[10] What is lacking, however, and, from the point of view of cultural flow, must be taken on faith, is that some of the culture deposited in those objects is actually finding its way out of them and into the people who are their users.

Why Newness?

It is obvious why a growing culture of dissemination is incompatible with a metaculture of tradition. Valuing dissemination means valuing the lateral motion of the material items in which culture is embodied, even if that motion occurs without the aid of replication of those items themselves. The motion occurs thanks to the establishment and maintenance of pathways, and it is the maintenance of those pathways, rather than the replication of the items, that should rightly be valued if one wants lateral motion. Were the metaculture to emphasize the replication of the items carried along the pathways, the idea of dissemination itself would diminish in significance. Dissemination would, effectively, be reabsorbed back into tradition. Consequently, a metaculture of dissemination cannot emphasize tradition—at least, not as its key test—and in this respect, it is fundamentally unlike conversion religion or conquest. To celebrate dissemination, and hence to encourage the development of pathways of lateral motion, a metaculture of tradition simply will not do.

This much said, it is by no means obvious that the denial of a metaculture of tradition as the basis for a culture of dissemination requires a metaculture of modernity or newness. Under newness, what is valued is the novelty of a cultural expression—for which previous cultural elements are seen as mere precursors leading up to the new element. Prior α's become the backdrop for ω. But does this not completely undercut the very purpose of lateral dissemination in the first place, namely, to get culture to spread spatially and not just temporally? Can culture spread if the material form in which it is embodied is constantly changing?

Of course, a metaculture of modernity—important as it may be today—is, even today, not the only metaculture operative in Europe or America. Conversion religions continue to play a prominent role, and while higher education, especially post-baccalaureate study in U.S. universities, places a premium on the newness of scholarly or scientific contributions, basic education still relies largely on tests of replication—how well students have internalized the culture of their teachers. The metaculture of modernity competes with metacultures of tradition, this being a key theme of our time. Why should newness win out?

A clue can be found in the Uru-eu-wau-wau case. Accepting metal pots and knives for the first time, introducing them into normal daily activities, requires an assessment, and hence a metacultural judgment, that the "new" items are in some respects better or more appropriate for the tasks for which they are employed than the old items. And with this, I am closer to making a case for the correlation between cultures of dissemination and metacultures of modernity. To get a new social pathway of dissemination into operation, the recipients of the disseminated item must in some way argue—that is, represent to themselves metaculturally—that the "new" item is better than the old one and that the old item was a precursor to the new one. The new item does what the old one did (continuity) but does it better (newness).

Let me stress this: The purpose of a metaculture of modernity is to assist in the establishment of *new* social pathways of dissemination. This is crucial to my present argument. Its purpose is not (or, rather, not only) to maintain an existing pathway of dissemination. The latter task can be accomplished by a metaculture of tradition, once a regular pathway of dissemination is up and running. This is a crucial point: A metaculture of tradition can be used to keep open an existing avenue for the lateral dissemination of culture. Consequently, for the thousands of years of development of the division of labor and of organic solidarity, as imagined by Durkheim ([1893] 1933), an emphasis on replication suffices.

It more than suffices. It actually explains oddities of the cultural organization of replication where replication is, relatively speaking, distinct from dissemination, that is, where there is division of labor. A metaculture of tradition regards the organization of cultural reproduction—for example, the specialized production of ceramics or, for that matter, of agriculture—as like the reproduction of culture in situations where replication and dissemination are indistinguishable. In the latter cases, the core processes of replication and dissemination take place through the parent-child bond. No wonder the social unit of specialized craft production has so regularly been understood as a kinship unit. The ability to reproduce the specialized objects is passed through families, and hence obeys the same principles of movement as myth, with the exception that the objects so produced move outward from these groups to other locales. Indeed, under an idea of tradition, even the pathways of dissemination themselves are tradition-bound, with the social class of merchants or traders or disseminators being construed as a kinship group—confirming the emphasis on oldness over newness.

You may rightly wonder: If a metaculture of tradition dominates even in cases of the ancient division of labor, how does change come about? My answer is that the problem for cultural motion historically has not been how to produce something new. On the contrary, the problem of culture has been—until the last few hundred years, at least—how to maintain something old. Culture had to be concerned with reigning in or containing incessant, ceaseless, change—the kind associated with entropic decelera-tion. When a myth is retold, the new telling is, in actuality, a new thing. Inherent in this newness is the ever-present possibility—nay, certainty— that the abstract form of the earlier culture will not carry over precisely. The concern has been that culture will not move, but rather dissipate. Where movement necessarily results in difference, the key question is how to produce sameness, how to tame newness, how to insure that enough of the original is carried over in the copy.

When something new arises, whether randomly or by design, it pro-vokes a confrontation between the metacultures of tradition and moder-nity. If the new thing is not remarkably new, it can be reassimilated into the past. But as local traditions passed through the domestic group under-go microchanges, changes that are imperceptible to the replicators, those changes accumulate over time. When that local tradition comes into con-tact with another, similarly experiencing its own processes of micro-change, the differences stand out prominently. Does the one local group, as a carrier of its local tradition, want to acquire the shape of the culture it encounters in the other? If the two traditions are sufficiently similar, this can be handled by elementary diffusion. The one group simply copies what it finds in the other.

However, where major difference is involved—the steel pots and ma-chetes, for instance, as they must have appeared to the Uru-eu-wau-wau— another possibility opens up: Acquire the new cultural objects from those who are its producers, without oneself having to produce them—perhaps take them, or perhaps give something in return. We must imagine a long history of stumbling confrontations with newness for pathways of dissem-ination uncoupled from replication to develop. One outcome of the con-frontations is the establishment of pathways, which themselves become traditionalized. Maintenance of the pathways of dissemination, as well as production itself, are lodged in kinship-based groupings, with their focus on the family as the conduit of traditional culture.

It is not, therefore, that organic solidarity or the division of labor are dependent on a metaculture of newness for their survival. It is that the establishment of a new social pathway of dissemination depends on a confrontation between newness and oldness. Correspondingly, a metaculture of newness necessarily provokes the continuous, restless attempt to establish new pathways. It is this kind of metaculture that, I believe, comes to assume a dominant position in Europe between the fifteenth and eighteenth centuries, even if something like it may have emerged before in ancient Greece or elsewhere.

Words in Things

Until now, I have been treating all cultural objects as essentially the same, at least as regards their relationship to metaculture. But in fact, the metaculture of tradition has been, first and foremost, concerned with the culture passing through words rather than with the culture passing through nonlinguistic things, such as pots and machetes. And it is the culture contained in spoken words that is the most mercurial, most in need of a metaculture of tradition for its stabilization or containment. This is because of the relatively unstable character of the physical object—the sounds in which words are encoded, in the case of myth—through which dissemination takes place.

Writing, in some measure, fixes the disseminated object.[11] This partially frees it from the constraints upon the movement of culture associated with oral transmission, namely, that dissemination must take place through replication, so that motion exhibits a gradual characteristic outward radiation through space, mutatis mutandis, such as was defined by the diffusionists and reified in the "culture area" (see Wissler 1938). A written document can travel through space and time with less help from replication. I say "less" rather than "without" because cultural movement is dependent on the ability to read, and, more specifically, the ability to read in a particular language, and that ability itself passes primarily through replication. Some culture can be extracted from an indecipherable text—this was the task, for example, of the early Mayan epigraphers and the decoders of other written languages whose oral language had long since undergone transformation or disappeared, such as ancient Sumerian. Through casual exposure to the objects, the forms of the characters could be imitated. But a flow of culture analogous to that of oral transmission depends upon reading, which in turn depends upon cultural transmission through replication, even if scholars, through protracted study, are able to crack ancient codes.

Yet writing itself does not automatically give rise to a metaculture of newness. Indeed, as the case of medieval European universities illustrates, writing can be subordinated to replication—the purpose of the lecture (derived from the Latin *lēctus*, past participle of *legere*, "to read"), for example, having been to facilitate the copying into written form by students of a text that was read by the professor.

If writing is not directly a cause of the metaculture of newness, it raises questions about the nature of cultural motion whose answers bring us closer to an understanding of the social significance of a metaculture of newness. For the written document transforms a stretch of discourse into a physical object with properties unlike those of the sounds that bring about dissemination in the case of orally transmitted myth. The written document has properties reminiscent of the ceramic pot, with spatial portability and temporal durability. The medieval lecture was designed to give students their own "ceramicized" discourse, so to speak, which could then be carried around and consulted at later dates. Replication is crucial to the movement of such "ceramicized" objects precisely because the objects were coming to be a form of personal property, on a par with pots and pans.

I am not denying the historical significance of writing per se for the development of a metaculture of newness. Historically, writing emerged in the ancient Near East several thousand years ago in conjunction with the development of trade and markets, albeit not trade based on a price system, which did not come into being, evidently, until ancient Greece.[12] But I am pointing out that writing as handwriting is only one step in the process of uncoupling dissemination from replication. The handwritten text could—in principle, at least—be viewed and read by many different people, but they could have possession of that object, for purposes of their own local processes of cultural replication, only if they themselves hand-copied it or had someone else hand-copy it.[13]

What hinges upon individuals having direct and long-term access to written documents, such as would be had by possessing copies of those documents? In asking this question, I am addressing the difference, as regards the motion of culture, between writing, per se—as a durable medium for the circulation of words—and print. For writing, in the form of handwriting, can and did (in medieval European history, at least) fit into patterns where dissemination depended upon replication.

When large-scale printing developed in fifteenth-century Europe, it drove a wedge between dissemination and replication, or, rather, imparted a hearty blow to a wedge already in place, making it possible for people to own more written discourse, despite the fact that they themselves had not produced that discourse through processes of replication. This is a matter of degree, since earlier scribes could be employed to copy documents that ended up in another individual's possession without the latter individual having engaged in the process of replication at all. With large-scale printing, people could more easily have direct and long-term access to the same physical-discursive object, the same α or ω.

From the point of view of metaculture, a key difference associated with print is the ability of the possessor to acquire more such objects more readily, and therefore to compare the objects one with another, using comparison as the basis for metacultural judgments. If an object—a book, for example—has been disseminated from elsewhere and is not a product of local processes of replication, what hinges on such comparisons is the interest possessors might have in acquiring the object. Hence, what hinges on comparison is demand for objects. Such demand is, ultimately, responsible for keeping open pathways of dissemination. Once individuals own a particular discursive object, their need to acquire additional identical objects is lessened.

Demand for objects—at least for "ceramicized" objects like printed books—arises out of metacultural concern for their newness. If a discursive object is sufficiently distinct from one already in one's possession, then possibly, just possibly, one might want to acquire it. My suspicion is that a direct relationship exists between the rise in Europe of a metaculture of modernity or newness and the print circulation of discourse. This development is part and parcel of a new type of cultural motion.

Lucien Febvre and Henri-Jean Martin ([1958] 1976, 248) estimate that by 1500, a half-century after the invention of the printing press, twenty million books had been printed in Europe. That amounted to one book for every five people, as Anderson ([1983] 1991, 37) has observed. By 1600, this number had increased ten-fold (Febvre and Martin [1958] 1976, 262). Printed discourse, as durable object, had become possessible as never before.

From the point of view of cultural motion, however, an explosion in the number of books in Europe is not immediately equatable with the lateral spread of the culture contained in those books. As physical objects acting as repositories of cultural learning, books are like metal pots and machetes for the Uru-eu-wau-wau—available, yes, but to what local use can they be put? As objects, one can extract little from them except the shapes of printed characters or the aesthetic forms of figures or graphics. If the pots could be insinuated into local process of cultural replication, in the case of the Uru-eu-wau-wau, only because of the analogy with existing cultural artifacts, printed books could be assimilated into patterns of European cultural replication only with analogy to handwritten books. This means that they would have entered, initially at least, the existing pathways of writing and literacy—the church, the aristocracy, and the bourgeoisie. This seems to have been the case, according to Febvre and Martin, though throughout the seventeenth century "churchmen were declining in relative importance as purchasers of books," with lawyers becoming "steadily more important" ([1958] 1976, 263).

Lateral dissemination of culture does not increase instantaneously with print because the extraction of culture from the printed materials depends on literacy, which in turn moves primarily by processes in which dissemination depends on replication. From this point of view, Anderson's ([1983] 1991, 43–46) understanding of print as circulating within the existing oral languages in which the printed material is written is only partially adequate. Oral languages, as inertial culture of the habitual type—in this case, the habit being that of speaking in a particular vernacular—would have conditioned the flow of literacy through the population only insofar as literacy, in alphabetically written languages, is more readily acquired where oral fluency in the same language has already been achieved. However, acquisition of literacy would presumably have obeyed the laws of motion characteristic of myth, where interactions between transmitter and receiver of the literacy are based on spatial contiguity. Hence, print would not immediately result in the large-scale lateral dissemination of culture, but would—like language itself, as mother tongue—result initially, at least, in the spread of culture based on propinquity.

One conclusion I draw from this is that, initially, books should have accumulated in the hands of those who had already achieved literacy, though the growing popularity of books would have simultaneously stimulated the acquisition of literacy. The significance of this is that a metaculture of newness, facilitated by the ability to carefully compare written documents with one another, would have first originated in those segments of the population where accumulation of books or other written documents was taking place.

According to Habermas ([1962] 1989, 31–43), the institutionalization of metacultural practices of close comparison that formed the basis of the "bourgeois public sphere" arose within a century and a half or two centuries after the initial proliferation of books. The first coffee house in England opened in the middle of the seventeenth century; fifty years later there were three thousand of them. The salon tradition in France came into full flower in the eighteenth century, but grew out of the earlier aristocratic court of the seventeenth century. Social organization—as viewed through the lens of cultural motion—seemed to take shape around the movement of culture, and, in particular, around the rise of a metaculture of comparison.

Why newness? As I have indicated, demand for a printed document would be significantly greater if the individuals who could demand it did not already possess "it," that is, an identical copy of it.[14] The interest in a document that underlies demand therefore correlates, in some measure, with the perceived newness of the document itself. How unlike the situation in Amerindian Brazil, which is under the domination of oral transmission of culture. There, "demand" for the telling of a myth works in the opposite way: It is based upon the interest in a potential future audience that a prior telling has kindled. Retelling makes possible the reexperiencing of emotional involvement one has had in a prior telling. Such reexperiencing is possible only if the "same" myth is retold. The metaculture in that case, therefore appropriately, is one of oldness. What is valued is the perpetuation of the experiences attached to earlier tellings through "retellings."

Replication of myth, in Amerindian Brazil, is driven by a desire to reexperience. But reexperiencing a printed document is possible without driving the demand for new writing. Curiously, therefore, under a metaculture of tradition, the reproduction of cultural learning that is required to "write" is accorded no value. Reexperiencing is possible by simply rereading the existing book in one's possession. If a metaculture of tradition is a way of propelling the movement of discourse (as culture) over time such that the forces of dissipation inherent in oral transmission are overcome, a metaculture of newness is a way to insure the continuing ability to produce discourse where that ability might otherwise die out. Oddly enough, a metaculture of newness is actually a way of guaranteeing the perpetuation of a certain kind of culture—the ability to "write" books.

If you read a book you yourself have not written, culture carries over to you. If you watch a film, to be sure, culture carries over. However, what carries over is not, at least not directly, the ability to write a new book or make a new film. As in the case of film, print is a medium of dissemination of culture. The dissemination is split off from replication, at least from the ability to replicate or reproduce a similar kind of physical entity—another book or another film. The transmission of that ability, curiously, depends integrally on the spread of a metaculture of newness or modernity in which the past is seen, not as something to be recreated in the present, but merely as backdrop for a new present. The valued experience under a metaculture of modernity is the experience of newness, which, paradoxically, drives the motion of culture over time—that is, it motivates the ability to produce mass-disseminated "ceramicized" discourse objects.

As I have argued, it is possible and inevitable for multiple metacultural discourses to circulate at the same time. Certainly, the Uru-eu-wau-wau must have employed a metacultural discourse of newness—in regard to the metal pots and machetes, at least—even though their metacultural discourse about myths almost certainly placed highest value on oldness. If I am correct, however, while metacultural discourses may compete, some of them tend to predominate, at any given moment, over others. Metacultural discourse about discursive replication—myth-telling, for example—tends, at certain moments, to dominate metacultural discourse about nondiscursive material items such as pots and knives. Hence, the oldness associated with myths can exercise an effect on the processes of lateral dissemination of material items. Where such a metaculture is operative, dissemination folds back into tradition—as in the phenomenon of craft specialization lodged in kinship groups.

Correspondingly, however, where metacultural understanding of discourse is dominated by the valuation of novelty—as I am suggesting began to take off in Europe about five hundred years ago—dissemination itself surges to the fore; a striving for newness becomes the motor behind the replication of culture. Metacultural newness emphasizes the keeping open of pathways of dissemination by their constant recharging with "new" objects. The positive valuation of newness also promotes the entrepreneur, as discoverer or opener of new pathways of dissemination. Hence, those pockets of the population wherein the replication of disseminable items takes place—corporations, movie studios, publishing houses—are driven not so much by a desire to reproduce the exact same thing as by a desire to produce objects that, while not totally new, appear new enough to attract the interest of those who already have the old thing. In short, capitalism as we know it is a product of the movement of culture driven by a metaculture of newness.

Dissemination and Domestic Groups

From an ethnographic perspective, domestic groups appear to play distinct roles as regards the motion of culture; this is so in the cases of Amerindian Brazil and the contemporary United States. Two ethnographic vignettes illustrate this.

The year is 1982; the month May. I am sitting on a dirt floor in the house of my friend Wãñpõ, an elder member of the indigenous community at P. I. Ibirama. Other people are there, as well, among them Wãñpõ's wife and another elder, Kañā'ĩ, highly respected for his storytelling ability. It is a rainy day. People take up sundry domestic chores—the preparation of arrows, the mending of clothes. A young man addresses Kañā'ĩ: *yug, nèn ci ẽñ yò wãmèn* ("Father, tell me stories, old things"). And Kañā'ĩ begins his tales. As I look around, I observe the physical items present—including metal pots and plastic basins. Writing these words today, I can visualize the room. And although I did not remark it at the time—indeed, it would have been odd to do so—I see in my mind's eye no books or written materials of any kind.

Switch now to December of 1998. I am in Menlo Park, California, on a sabbatical year at the Center for Advanced Study in the Behavioral Sciences at Stanford University, where I am drafting the book you have before you. Around my living room, I see children's books. They are everywhere—forty-nine of them from the library alone, my wife tells me, one short of the library's limit. Scattered around are other books we have purchased, not to mention magazines and newspapers, and a sizable collection of videos. My nearly three-year-old daughter says to her mother in her adorable, albeit insistent, style: "Mom, read me a story." Her mother says: "Okay, pick a book." She does, and the mother begins to read.

Obviously, books and other printed materials are involved in the contemporary U.S. case, while orally recollected and retold tales are involved in the Brazilian case, but what to make of this? In each, the domestic group functions as cultural workshop, as Fortes contended, with culture passing in some measure from elders to youngers. Both vignettes highlight storytelling. But in the American case, storytelling is mediated by print. The site of production of the original discourse—here, read aloud—was far removed in space and time from the reading that took place. Indeed, as my wife and I reflect on it, we cannot think of a single children's story that has passed orally through our families across the generations. We pass on some stories about family members or ancestors, but nothing on the order of myths or historical narratives such as pass orally through the Brazilian Indian family. In the American context, to be sure, we make up stories, and tell them to our daughter. However, these are not stories we have heard from our own parents. More than likely, our daughter will not pass them on to her children. At the same time, some of the books we read to our daughter were also read to us.

In the contemporary American case, dissemination insinuates itself into processes of local replication of culture—so much so, indeed, that replication is no longer the principal mechanism for dissemination. In

Amerindian Brazil, the stories would not be disseminated—they would simply die out—were it not for replication in the form of retelling. In this regard, significantly, the narratives themselves are called, in the native language, nèn ci ("old things"). Individuals tell stories about contemporary events. Some of those stories do, over time, achieve a broader circulation, becoming "old things." But the stories only move through time by becoming old, that is, by virtue of retelling.

What is significant is that cultural change occurs through microprocesses of entropic deceleration in the Amerindian case. The stories evolve and adapt to local situations.[15] Consequently, myths and other locally transmitted discourse come to be, over time, expressions of their locales. They appear to grow organically out of those locales. What happens in the contemporary U.S. case? The stories are fixed, though parents may tinker with them in the course of readings—substituting a feminine pronoun for a masculine one to change the gender implications of a story, or substituting one word for another. However, microchanges in literary sensibilities—which, in the Brazilian Indian case, are incorporated immediately into retellings—in the contemporary U.S. case work their way back to the site of primary replication only through the mechanism of demand. Local difference manifests itself through differences in demand for cultural objects. Why select this book rather than another? Because something about it appeals to the local sensibilities of the selectors. Those sensibilities are linked (as in Bourdieu's concept of the habitus) to processes of local cultural motion through replication.

Imparting the Force of Ideas to Things

If books—or other mass-disseminated, "ceramicized" forms of discourse—infiltrate the domestic arena of cultural reproduction, is the culture they carry, as physical objects, in any way distinct from the culture transmitted through processes of oral dissemination? More specifically, since mass dissemination is linked to a metaculture of newness in our present world, does that metaculture itself shape the discourse that circulates in a population? Or is the metaculture merely a way of understanding discursive processes, floating about them so to speak, without making contact? In attempting to investigate these questions empirically—and, obviously, I am committed, in some measure at least, to the position I outlined in chapter 1—I compared discourse that is replicated in the Amerindian Brazilian case to the discourse that circulates in the contemporary U.S. case.

My questions were: How different are tellings of the "same" story in the Amerindian case? Correspondingly, how "new" are different stories—keeping in mind the image of piles of books—in the contemporary American case? These are problems I have been investigating for a decade and a half now. In the course of that investigation, I found something roughly analogous, in the Amerindian Brazilian case, to the reduplicative processes of print. This is verbatim memorization. During my stay at P. I. Ibirama, the origin myth—known as *wãñĕklèn*—had been learned verbatim. In one form of retelling, the story was narrated by means of a ceremonialized dialogue, with one of the two interlocutors shouting one syllable, the other interlocutor then repeating that syllable, the first then shouting the second syllable, and so forth. This leads to a relatively precise retelling, and, hence, a "virtually ceramicized" myth. In comparing subsequent tellings, six years later, it became clear that the myth exhibited a high degree of stability over time (Urban 1991, 89 ff.).

The similarity over time was not only at the level of words, but also sounds, including intonation, voice quality, and rhythm. Different copies of the origin myth recorded over a six-year period cannot match, for precision, the similarity between duplicates of the same tape recording; neither can they match the similarity found in different copies of the same printed book. The maximally distinct versions showed word similarities of between 84 percent and 93 percent—something I will discuss further in chapter 6. The origin myth was the closest approximation I found to the near-identity between different copies of the same printed document.

For my present study, however, I wanted to learn just how different two narrations could be and still count as retellings of the "same" myth. Similarly, I wanted to find out, for the contemporary U.S. case, just how similar two different stories could be and still count as "different." My materials for the Brazilian case were limited. I chose the story of an owl spirit who wreaked havoc among humans. I had recorded a version of this myth in 1975, and I found another collected and transcribed by Paul Mullen (n.d.), a missionary working with the Summer Institute of Linguistics during the early 1980s. I will call the two versions or stories Owl I and Owl II.

The two stories contain, at several points, identical phrasing. No doubt, such word-for-word similarities signaled to the audience that the two were, indeed, tellings of the "same" story.[16] Yet both were free-form, with no serious effort directed at precise replication. And there were crucial differences between the two, as regards plot. If I am correct, however, if culture, as abstract form, is indeed working its way between individuals through the replication of material form, then I should be able to detect a similarity between the two tellings not only as regards plot, but also as regards sensible material appearance. That is, there ought to be a noticeable similarity in the actual words employed. After all, it is through physical replication, or so I have contended, that the public test of cultural motion—that is, of tradition—occurs.

The general principle of motion for myth is as follows: The more widely a narrative circulates, the more likely the material form of its expression is to become fixed. The perhaps obvious reason for this is that, if the myth does not become fixed through "virtual ceramicization," then dissipative forces gnaw at it, threatening its spatial and temporal motion. It tends, as it moves, to become something different.

The principle leads to a possible method for exploring continuity where the tellings are free-form. Since a story represents a selection of words from a total lexicon, two stories, insofar as they are continuous with one another—that is, insofar as they embody the movement of culture over time and space—ought to be materially similar in the words they use. This meant to me that I should be able to inventory words in each story and compare those inventories, determining thereby the extent to which the two tellers actually had replicated the same material form—in other words, the extent to which the same culture, as reflected in sensible things-in-the-world, was passing through the storytellers.

With this in mind, I set out to compare Owl I and Owl II. I entered into the computer the texts of the stories in the native language. I then broke each story into its constituent words. There were 807 physically distinct word tokens in the case of Owl I, and 1,184 in the case of Owl II. This suggested that the two tellings were, indeed, distinct. And I have already remarked that there was scant evidence of verbatim repetition. So I moved to the next step, sorting the words alphabetically, so that all of the occurrences of a word having the same physical, sensible shape would be lumped together. This allowed me to determine what word types were present in each telling.

Let me explain this, in case you are not already familiar with the linguistic concepts of "type" and "token." Each word—as an abstract sound or graphic form—can be realized many times within a single narrative. Each of those occurrences is a token of the word type. Therefore, while a given telling of the Owl myth may contain one thousand word tokens, there will be many fewer word types. Those types are the abstract, reproducible form of the thing. Indeed, the relationship of type to token is really that of cultural element (that is, abstract form passing through the world) to cultural object (the embodiment of that abstract form in sensible things). In some sense, therefore, the movement of culture, such as occurs between tellings of a single myth, also occurs, on a microscale, within a given telling. I will return to this issue in the next section, as text-internal micro-replication provides significant evidence about the impact of immaterial (metacultural) ideas on sensible things.

In any case, I found that Owl I—which contained, recall, 807 word tokens—consisted of just 152 distinct word types. Correspondingly, Owl II, with its 1,184 tokens, contained 163 types. How many of those types were shared in common between the tellings? My study[17] came up with 92, that is, 60.53 percent of the words in Owl I were also found in Owl II, and 56.44 percent of the words in Owl II were also found in Owl I. Was this a lot or a little?

If these two versions were materially similar—if culture as abstract form were passing through individual tellers—then these two versions ought to be substantially more like one another than either was like a third, unrelated, myth. To determine whether this was the case, I selected another story, which I will call Animals, and determined the number of word types it contained. Sure enough, I found that Owl I shared only 36.18 percent of its words with Animals, and Owl II shared 35.58 percent with Animals. So the two stories—or versions of the same story—really were detectably more similar to one another in terms of their sensible, perceptible shapes than either was to a third myth.

At the same time, the idea of inertial habituation suggested that there might be individual effects in this regard. Just how similar would two distinct myths told by the same individual be? If you think of storytelling as a kind of habit (as in Bourdieu's *habitus*), then might not storytellers have a propensity to use the same words in their tellings of different myths? The motion of the myth—as abstract form—through the teller would be deflected by that habitual inertia. How great would that effect be? If material similarity were a reflection of the motion of culture, then under a meta-culture of tradition one would expect the two tellings of the same myth by different individuals to be more similar to each other than two different myths told by the same individual. The motion of culture ought to dominate. But there might still be an effect of habitual inertia as distinct cultural elements pass through the same individual.

To study this problem, I needed a fourth myth (or, rather, telling). Since Owl I and Owl II were told by different individuals, and Animals was told by yet another individual unrelated to the first two, what I needed was an example a different myth told by the narrator of Owl I. If there were individual effects, then Owl I ought to be more similar to the fourth myth than was Owl II. However, that similarity should be much less than that between Owl I and Owl II themselves.

In fact, this turned out to be the case. The fourth myth—which I will call Newo—shared 43.42 percent of its vocabulary with Owl I, but only 36.81 percent of its vocabulary with Owl II. The latter percentage was very similar to those for the relationship between Owl I and II, on the one hand, and Animals—whose narrator was unrelated to the first two. The figures in the latter cases were 36.18 percent and 35.58 percent. The individual effect in this study was small. Perhaps follow-up studies would show it to be a statistical aberration. Still, the effect does make sense. Habituation resulting from the production of one narrative could conceivably exercise an inertial effect on the production of another narrative, deflecting that other narrative in its direction.

However, this effect was dwarfed by the phenomenon of cultural motion. The different tellings of the "same" myth by different individuals showed dramatically greater similarity to one another than did the tellings of two distinct myths by the same narrator. The myth—as abstract form moving through the world—has a detectable material presence. The abstract form passes through individuals, resulting in the production of things in the world that are demonstrably similar in material terms. Such similarities are, after all, what makes possible a public test of replication in the first place. The folding back of β onto α, which is both described and prescribed by a metaculture of tradition, has a detectable material basis.

With this conclusion in mind, my attention turned to the Euro-American case. The question was this: Under a metaculture of newness, would two obviously and recognizably similar stories by different authors—stories that were nevertheless considered to be "different"—show greater similarity to one another than to a third, unrelated narrative? Moreover, would they be as similar to one another as two variants of the "same" story in the Amerindian case? If the latter were true, then a metaculture of tradition or newness would be a kind of false consciousness, floating above the material surface of culture, so to speak, without brushing up against it. Metacultures could be understood, in a purely relativistic way, as furnishing arbitrarily distinct construals of what is effectively the same thing. However, if two stories that were obviously similar but construed as different were unlike each other, then perhaps the metaculture might be accurately capturing differences at the cultural plane. Furthermore, perhaps, just perhaps, the metaculture might actually be inducing those differences—the chisel of Pygmalion here descending to the material realm.

In order to investigate this question, I chose two nuclear war action-thriller novels: *Red Alert*, by Peter Bryant (1958) (also published in England with the title *Two Hours to Doom* under the name of Peter Bryan George), and *Fail-Safe*, by Eugene Burdick and Harvey Wheeler (1962). Both were transformed into major motion pictures that appeared in 1964: the former into *Dr. Strangelove, or How I Learned To Stop Worrying and Love the Bomb*, directed by Stanley Kubrick, and the latter into *Fail Safe*, directed by Sidney Lumet. (The name of the latter film differs from that of the book only by virtue of its elimination of the hyphen.)

Why this choice? The answer: A lawsuit developed around the books. What I had, in this lawsuit, was evidence of the recognition of similarity between these two cultural objects. The makers of the film version of *Red Alert* were accusing the authors of *Fail-Safe* of plagiarism. The filmmakers were concerned about the immanent release of *Fail Safe*, which they thought might undercut the box office receipts of *Dr. Strangelove*. As it happened, the case was settled out of court; Columbia Pictures picked up and agreed to distribute both films. Nevertheless, I had my metacultural evidence of similarity.

The film *Dr. Strangelove*, albeit based on *Red Alert*, was also subsequently turned into a novel that was officially authored by Peter George, the author of *Red Alert*. However, the movie and the subsequent book are both markedly different from the earlier novel. The original book is a serious thriller, while the movie and subsequent book are black comedies. Indeed, Richard Gid Powers, who wrote the introduction to the book version of the movie, contends that "the combination of seriousness and slapstick in *Dr. Strangelove* [the novel] is so deft, and the writing is on such a high level, as to make it most unlikely that the novelization was actually written by the author of record, Peter Bryan George" (1979, vii). Powers concludes that the real author must have been the key script writer for the film, Terry Southern (1979, xv).

The comparison posed methodological problems. The books were too long to study in their entirety, so I had to sample comparable passages. And I had to make selections that were of relatively the same length as the myths.[18] Moreover, I had to find other unrelated stories with which to compare these two, and I ended up testing a range of them.

The basic conclusion I reached, however, seemed sound: The two stories (*Fail-Safe* and *Red Alert*) were not significantly more similar to each other, as regards their material form, than were either of them to a third, unrelated story. It is not that there was no detectable similarity at all between the two; rather, it is that the relatively greater similarity was so small that it might be explained by any of a number of factors. The selection I chose from *Fail-Safe* contained 614 distinct words; that from *Red Alert* contained 476 distinct words. Of those, 217 were shared in common. This amounts to 35.34 percent of the words contained in *Fail-Safe*, a figure comparable to the similarity between the two unrelated Indian myths. When thinking about these figures, recall the 56.44 percent to 60.53 percent similarity between the versions of the same myth.

I then compared the excerpts from *Fail-Safe* and *Red Alert* to randomly chosen passages from other novels, some related by genre (the action-thriller *Patriot Games* [Clancy 1987], for example), and some wholly unrelated (the science fiction novel *Patternmaster* [Butler 1976], for example). The selection from *Patriot Games* contained 595 words, 215 of which were shared in common with *Fail-Safe*, or 35.12 percent, and 206 with *Red Alert* or 34.62 percent. The selection from *Patternmaster* contained 505 words, of which 195 were shared with *Fail-Safe*, or 38.61 percent, and 177 with *Red Alert*, or 35.05 percent. Evidently, despite the lawsuit alleging plagiarism—a metacultural recognition of similarity—*Fail-Safe* and *Red Alert* proved to be no more like one another, in terms of the physical words in which they are embodied, than either is to any other generically related or unrelated novel.

I did further studies to determine whether there was an individual effect due to habituation here. I looked at a selection from another novel *(Commander-1)* by Peter George, the author of *Red Alert*. No significant similarity emerged. Lastly, I studied the book version of *Dr. Strangelove*, nominally authored by Peter George, although perhaps actually written, as Powers suggests, in significant measure by Terry Southern. This last is of interest as a method for determining how physically similar different tellings of the "same" story would appear under a metaculture of newness, since the film *Dr. Strangelove* was based on the earlier novel *Red Alert*, and the book *Dr. Strangelove* was based on the film. In fact, I found no significant similarity in word choice. I selected a passage in the latter work that was roughly equivalent to the former, including a few verbatim repetitions. The passage in *Dr. Strangelove* contained 621 word types. Of these, 225, or 36.23 percent were shared with *Red Alert*. This is comparable to the figures for unrelated novels. Moreover, 229 words, or 36.88 percent, were shared with the parallel passage in *Fail-Safe*. The book *Dr. Strangelove*, therefore, was curiously no more closely related in terms of word choice to the book on which it was based *(Red Alert)* than it was to a distinct book.

My conclusion: The metaculture of newness seems to accurately reflect cultural realities. (Am I right to suspect also that it brings about those realities?) Stories that are considered to be similar, but distinct, are in fact distinct as regards their physical shapes, at least as investigable through words. If culture carries over between stories, it carries over in a different way than in the case of myth. The movement of culture through the world, under a metaculture of newness, appears to be distinct from that which occurs under a metaculture of tradition. Indeed, a puzzling question—and one to which I propose to return in chapters 5 and 6—is how culture does move under newness if the physical forms in which it is embodied are so distinct. In some ways, the movement here is more mysterious than under tradition. How can its passage through the world be effected, if not through the replication of physical form? I think there is an answer.

The Linearization Effect

In the course of investigating the similarities and differences between α and β, I made another discovery, which I put forth here tentatively as one meriting further research: Where a myth (or other similar cultural element) is widely replicated, the internal organization of the element tends to involve repetition. Since a metaculture of tradition fosters dissemination through replication, it also fosters a repetitive pattern on the linear unfolding of the narrative, as if the pattern of relations between cultural objects were reflected in the internal structure of the object itself.

This conclusion will make immediate sense to students of oral literature.[19] It has been recognized, at least since the pathfinding work of Dell Hymes (1981), Milman Parry (1954, 1971), and Albert Bates Lord (1960, 1991), that oral forms have internal poetic structure and that "formulaic" components tend to be repeated within them—as evidenced in "the early born, rosy-fingered dawn" and the "wine-dark sea" of Homeric epic. They are built up around patterns of repetition, and there is a reason for this. The ability to repeat a unit within a larger cultural element—a line, for example, or a dance step—is correlated with the ability to replicate that larger element over time. The public test of learning—that the element can be repeated—applies internally to the cultural unit (the myth, for example) as well as to the relationship between units.

In the Amerindian case, replication and dissemination are simultaneous moments of the process whereby culture moves through the world, through space and time. Replication is a form of repetition across tellings. And repetition across tellings is tradition. Consequently, if a metaculture of tradition were to have a definite, specifiable effect on the organization of a linear stretch of discourse, that effect ought to be detectable through measures of the internal repetition within that linear stretch. The effect of a metaculture of tradition ought to be to highlight repetition within the units of discourse (in this case, myths) themselves.

The interesting question—if this earlier proposition holds, as I think it does—is whether a metaculture of newness tends to promote nonrepetitive or "linearized" forms of narrative. If the idea of oldness tends to promote the unfolding of discourse in such a way that the momentaneously unfolding words tend to resemble those that have come before them, would the idea of newness tend to promote an unfolding in which the new words tend to be different from those that came before?

My method was this: Having counted the number of occurrences of words and the number of distinct words—understood as underlying and abstract forms—I then calculated the ratio between the two. This would be a measure of the average degree of repetition of a given word within the narrative. The results for the Amerindian myths are given in Table 4.

Table 4. Frequency of Repetition of Words in Amerindian Myths

MYTH	OCCURRENCES	WORDS	REPETITIONS PER WORD
Owl I	807	152	5.31
Owl II	1,184	163	7.26
Newo	930	153	6.08
Animals	502	133	3.77
Total	3,423	601	5.70

When I did the corresponding study of the contemporary U.S. narratives, as in Table 5, it became immediately apparent that there was a striking difference. Words tended to be repeated much more frequently (nearly twice as frequently) in the Amerindian narratives as in the contemporary U.S. narratives.[20]

Table 5. Frequency of Repetition of Words in Contemporary Novels

NOVEL	OCCURRENCES	WORDS	REPETITIONS PER WORD
Red Alert	1,597	476	3.36
Fail-Safe	2,070	614	3.37
Commander-1	1,711	610	2.80
Patriot Games	1,803	595	3.03
Patternmaster	1,768	505	3.50
Total	8,949	2,800	3.20

To explore this difference further, I broke up the linear narratives into one-hundred-word (token) segments. If the discourse itself was shaped by ideas of tradition or newness, the degrees of similarity among the parts— even as so arbitrarily defined—ought to reveal some tendency towards similarity or difference in the linear unfolding. One measure I chose was the degree to which the words in the first segment were carried over in subsequent segments—a measure of something like "internal continuity" within the micro-space-time frame of the specific myth-telling or novel reading. The results are given for one Amerindian myth (Owl I) and for one U.S. novel in Figure 4. Here the relation between the parts, as regards continuity with the first segment, is consistent. In Owl 1, all segments show a 39–56 percent similarity with the first one, the average being 46 percent. In *Fail-Safe*, all segments show a similarity between 19 percent and 32 percent with the first one, the average being 25 percent. Consequently, the words in the first segment of the myth tend be repeated in subsequent segments with almost twice the frequency with which the words in the first segment of the novels tend to be repeated in subsequent segments.

Another related but distinct test concerns the similarity between adjacent one hundred–word token segments. If there is a force driving the novelistic discourse to become different from preceding novels, and if that force is applied constantly through the writing of the novel itself—"the moving finger"—then segments of the novel ought to be consistently more distinct (and hence less similar) to their adjacent segments than in the case of myth. As indicated in Figure 5, this is indeed what I found. In *Fail-Safe*, one hundred–word token segments have a similarity, as regards their word types, of between of between 22 percent and 34 percent with their adjacent segments. The average is 28 percent. In the case of Owl I, the similarities range between 35 percent and 56 percent, with an average of 48 percent.

This much said, there is more than meets the eye here. The simple assumption is that oldness promotes repetition, newness linearization— period. But this correlation elides a more complex process of circulation. Recall that a metaculture of tradition promotes the replication of cultural objects, such that β tends to resemble an α that has come before it. The effect of a metaculture of tradition on cultural objects is imparted to the circulation of those objects. It just so happens that the cultural objects that lend themselves to replication are those that are built around an internal architecture of repetition. The conclusion here is not that one cannot find linearized narration under a metaculture of tradition. It is, rather, that

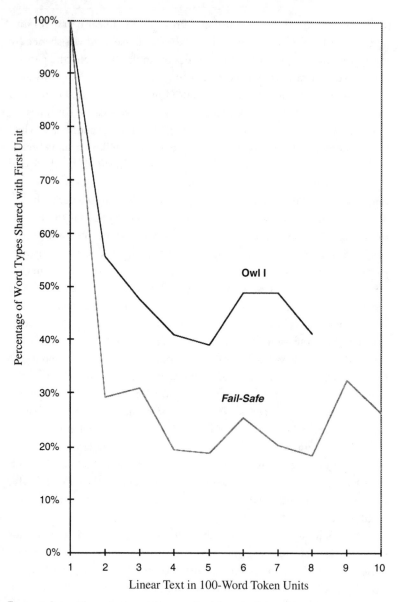

Figure 4. Internal continuity within a replicable unit of discourse.

those narratives which tend most closely to conform to a metaculture of tradition—because they have been replicated in the past—are also those that exhibit patterns of internal repetition. Internal repetition within objects promotes external replication between them.

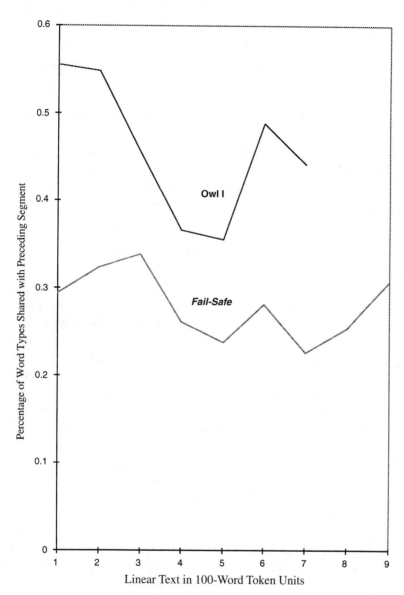

Figure 5. Internal similarity of adjacent segments within a replicable unit of discourse.

Yes, linearized narratives can be—indeed, are—produced in situations where a metaculture of tradition dominates. However, those narratives will not tend to circulate widely, or, if they do circulate, they will come, over time, to acquire patterns of internal repetition. If a narrative has already widely circulated, odds are that it will reveal a pattern of internal repetition. Of course, not all narratives written down by ethnographers have in fact already achieved wide circulation. Some may be novel expressions.

Here is a key difference when writing and, especially, print is introduced. Writing and print facilitate the dissemination of narratives that might not otherwise circulate, were they dependent on replication for their dissemination. In other words, writing and print make possible the dissemination of linearized narratives because dissemination can occur without replication taking place. The possibility of "ceramicizing" discourse means that a given narrative—which might otherwise have had no social life, or which might have been transformed in the course of its movement through space and time—is plucked from its processes of replication (or dying out) and cast about through space and time—albeit without necessarily undergoing replication.

A metaculture of newness does not, therefore, directly promote the linearization of narrative, at least not initially. Rather, the conditions of motion put into place by a metaculture of newness render the dissemination of linearized narratives feasible. Some of the discourse that is circulated under newness can be internally repetitive, just as some of the discourse created—but not circulated—under an idea of tradition can be linearized. Newness does not dictate linearization in a knee-jerk way. But newness does enable the dissemination of linearized discourse—just as does writing, though the question there is what gets written down. Hence, newness promotes linearization indirectly. Newness, so to speak, latches onto linearization as its best expression, thereby, over time, promoting linearization as a valued characteristic of cultural objects. Linearized narratives, precisely because of their surface textures, come to be the objects that an idea of newness finds as its best expression.

One caveat in taking up these preliminary results: Internal word repetition is correlated (in both the Amerindian Brazilian and contemporary U.S. cases) with the length of the discourse. If you study this problem in cumulative terms, breaking up the narrative into one hundred–word token segments, you find that words tend to be repeated on average, let's say, twice. If you take the first two hundred words, the frequency of repetition goes up. And it goes up further if you take the first three hundred words, and so forth. This is linked to probabilities, given that vocabularies are finite. The empirical patterns for two narratives—Owl I and *Fail-Safe*—are given in Figure 6.

Obviously, if you sample stretches of discourse of unequal length, the

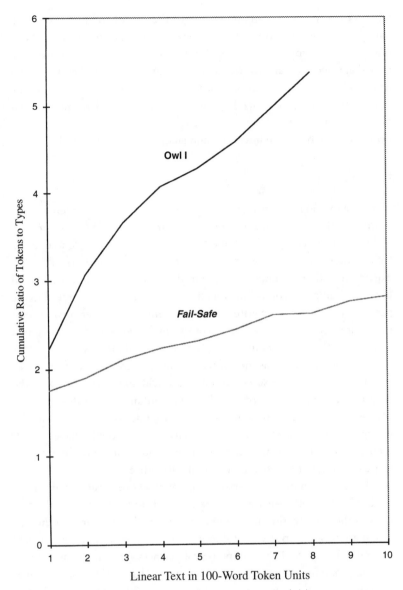

Figure 6. Cumulative token/type ratios in unfolding narrative.

ratios will not accurately reflect similarities or differences between those stretches, as regards their overall degrees of redundancy or linearization. A one thousand–word stretch of *Fail-Safe* has a greater degree of internal repetition than a one hundred–word stretch of Owl I. One wonders whether this correlates in any way with the rise of the modern novel, namely, as the longer book-length stories we know as "novels" today. Such novels contain typically around eighty thousand word tokens, as opposed to perhaps one thousand to two thousand words for a typical myth. Eighty thousand words—measured in word types—interestingly is roughly the size of the vocabulary of an educated adult. Could it be that, with the emphasis on linearization, the greater length (measured in word tokens) is necessary to achieve the internal redundancy of the shorter myths?

Story Time

"The moving finger writes; and, having writ, moves on." Fitzgerald's line represents the idea of newness played out in the flow of words, present and future haunted by a past, but unable to return to it, unable to undo it. Cosmological time, historical time—the time of a world postulated as existing "out there"—finds its way into the writer's body, into hands and fingers, guiding and controlling their motion, inhibiting their return to the past, to correct, erase, rewrite—instead pushing them ever forward into the future, into new words, new expressions. A world in flux becomes a finger in motion. A finger in motion becomes a world in flux.

I have argued that this idea of temporality in narration conforms—for complex reasons, to be sure—to the ideals held up by newness, as if the very linear stretch of words, at their momentaneous unfolding in the course of narration, were scrutinized under a microscopic lens, thereby giving rise to a surface texture of modernity in the aesthetic shapes of cultural objects. Here is the Pygmalion effect—ideas shaping the material world—through the mediation of circulatory processes.

The world comes to appear as natural precisely because it conforms to an idea of the world—narrative linearization is in harmony with the textures of the lived world, the feel of a universe in flux, captured in the surface markings of narrative unfolding. Sound shapes and graphic figures present to the senses images of perpetual newness as the storyline unfolds. How appropriate. Obviously, for something to "happen" in a story so materially conceived, new words must be introduced—new sound shapes, new graphic figures. With this as one's lived world, no wonder the surface feel of narrative understood through the lens of tradition[21] seems so ludicrous, so laughable, so artificial.

Recall the aspirations of Pierre Menard not to make a "mechanical transcription" of Quixote, but to "produce a few pages which would coincide—word for word and line for line—with those of Miguel de Cervantes"

(Borges [1944] 1962, 39). The notion is hilarious viewed from a meta-culture of newness, and this is the brilliance of Borges's insight: to unmask metacultural presupposition. Yet Menard's goal is within the myth-teller's reach: the production of words which "coincide—word for word and line for line—with those" of the ancestors. The surface sensibility clashes with what is understood as natural within a framework of newness. Yet one can begin to experience, in this clash, the texture of traditional narrative.

The year is 1975. Nil of the *macuco*—then elder and ritual specialist at P. I. Ibirama, since deceased—tells the origin myth. While doing so, he appears to grow distant, perhaps slipping into trance, yet not fully. He is here, but also elsewhere. Where? Inside the myth? Transported back—in search of lost time—to some earlier world? Has he reinhabited that world, grasped its generative core, produced the words as if they were his own creation?

Something he does strikes me as odd. He employs the "I" of his character as if it were his own, as if the character were speaking through his body: "Relative Zàgpope Patè arrived in front of *me*." I scratch my head. That "me," that "I" must have existed at the very dawn of time, when the first ancestors emerged from a hole in the ground. How can he deploy it now, as if telling this story for the first time? Is it possible for him to produce—not copy—those old words, inhabiting them so thoroughly that the abstract culture (the spirit of the time) carried along with them passes through him and recreates them? He is not simply copying the words in a rote way, but rather extracting from them some secret they contain, their life and vitality, which he, in turn, employs to produce them, in an act of creation.

How does the cosmos feel to him, I wonder, as I inspect the surface of his words. After all, those words are not truly his, but only passing through him, temporarily resident in him on their journey in time, drifting through the universe. The words circle back. I have heard them before, in this very narration. Is he saying the same thing again, repeating himself? No, there is something new, but the new sounds old. I have heard it before. None of Fitzgerald's regret here, no sense of loss. Nil of the *macuco* has gone back to the past, retrieved it, and plunked it down in the present, making it accessible to a future—to me, to us—creating a bridge across time. Perhaps he will even, in some measure, correct, erase, rewrite that past. We will never know.

For now I am back in modern time, mindful of a past, yet with an eye always to possible futures. My course is charted: head for parts unknown, but with a sure compass—the microtemporality of unfolding discourse. I am

on the trail of a mysterious force, one manifested in the connection between the surface textures of words—in particular, consciousness of those
words as momentaneously unfolding discourse—and grand historical
events: revolution, the founding of a nation, the abolition of slavery. My
hunch is that changes in surface texture, such as I have described here, are
linked to changes in the self-understanding of discourse, including such
innocuous triflings as pronouns. Who are "we," anyway? That consciousness, in turn, accelerates culture, propelling it through space and time,
shaping the course of civilization as its moves ever onward—into the fog.

3

This Nation Will Rise Up

> He has plundered *our* seas,
> ravaged *our* Coasts,
> burnt *our* towns,
> and destroyed the lives of *our* people.
>
> The Declaration of Independence of the United States
> of America (italics added)

A Tiny Pronoun

A pronoun—a single instance of the word "our" written on a page, for example—seems hardly an object in motion, as if it were a particle cutting a trail in a cloud chamber. Yet the cloud chamber analogy is not so far-fetched, or so I propose to argue. Even in the microtime of a given stretch of discourse, one instance of "our" looks back to another. A tiny trail leads through the vapors, as the reader's or listener's attention engages a present. In the above snippet, the "our" of "ravaged our Coasts" looks back on an earlier "our"—that of "He has plundered our seas." At the same time, the trail winds off into the future, looking forward to subsequent "our's," including that of "our people." Something is carried across from one instance to the next. But what?

It is tempting to solve this problem by reference to an extradiscursive object—a people that possesses, in this case, seas, coasts, and towns. But is such a people already there? Of course, the answer to this question depends in part on answers to other questions such as: When and for whom is such a people already there? My concern here is not with details of historical fact, however, so much as with the conceptual problems pertaining to culture in relation to social groupings that this case raises. When, in principle, can a social grouping be said to exist as thing-in-the-world? In the American case, what if the revolution had been unsuccessful? What if the rebellion had been quelled?

Examples of misfired (or still unresolved) rebellions abound, a case in point being the "Republic of Texas" movement, whose goal has been secession from the United States. The "ambassador" of the restored republic, Richard L. McLaren, engaged in a standoff with Texas state officials in April and May of 1997. The secessionists constituted themselves as a government, analogously to the self-appointment by the Continental Congress of the United States of America on July 4, 1776. The new "Republic of Texas" even issued checks, which it claimed were backed by the "full faith and credit of the people of Texas" (Verhovek 1997).

On July 4, 1776, the outcome of the American declaration of independence was itself uncertain. Would it not be anachronistic to imagine that it was simply the prior existence of the object—"the people of the United States," as it is called in the subsequent constitution—that was the something that was carried over between the various occurrences of the "our" in the above snippet? Jacques Derrida dismissed the idea: ". . . this people does not exist . . . before this declaration, not as such" (1986, 10).

Derrida gives instead a performative account of the foundational paradox. The American "people" only came into existence after the signing of the Declaration of Independence. It was created by the act of signing. As Derrida puts it: "The signature invents the signer. This signer can only authorize him- or herself to sign once he or she has come to the end, if one can say, of his or her own signature, in a sort of fabulous retroactivity" (1986, 10).

The fallacy of Derrida's argument, it seems to me, is the apparent assumption that the "people" of the United States of America came into existence at the moment of signature. No more did it come into existence then than did a new "Republic of Texas" upon the occasion of its "official call" on the steps of the capitol building in Austin, Texas, on January 16, 1996 (Republic of Texas Web Site, "Official Call," 16 Jan. 1996).[1] It may be that the United States achieved an existence for the signers of the Declaration, based on their faith in the magic of performative constitution, a belief growing out of a historical pattern of performative constitution in Western discourse, as Benjamin Lee (1997, 323–41) has so aptly argued. But so too did (and does) exist the new "Republic of Texas" for Richard L. McLaren and other followers of the movement.

What is crucially missing from the performativity account is an understanding of cultural motion, of the circulation of discourse that is necessary for a significant number of individuals to come to articulate their membership in a group, of a "we." The articulators (Thomas Jefferson and the other signatories) produced a piece of writing that, by virtue of its semantic and pragmatic meanings, defined a group of individuals in the world as a free and independent "people," with the declarers as their rightful representatives. So too did "President" Van Kirk of the "Republic of Texas" claim in his January 16, 1996, speech: "We represent millions of Texans." (I use quotations around the titles and name of the "Republic of Texas" to emphasize that these social entities exist at the time of this writing only, or primarily as discursive entities.)

What is lacking in the "Republic of Texas" case is replication. Not only must the officials of this discursive entity produce a discourse that defines millions of people as citizens of the "Republic of Texas," but those millions of people (or some significant fraction of them) must produce discourse that defines themselves as part of the "Republic of Texas"—and even that would be insufficient to constitute the "Republic of Texas" as a sovereign nation, independent of the United States. Officials of some other, already recognized independent nation would also have to recognize the new republic, and, ultimately, the United States itself would have to recognize the new republic, if only tacitly by ceasing to employ force to stop the new republic from engaging in self-government outside the union.

What is hard to see is that the processes whereby this happens—whereby a "people" comes to exist as a recognized social entity—are processes of replication, of the movement of culture through the world. What is being replicated are patterns of discourse—in particular, patterns in the usage of pronouns such as "we" and "they" and in the use of proper names such as "Republic of Texas."

This leads me back to the question from the opening paragraph: What carries over between the discrete instances of "our" in the Declaration of Independence? What forms the trace of cultural movement within the cloud chamber? The answer has to be a pattern (or set of patterns) of usage of the pronouns themselves. The pattern, in particular, is an "our" or "us" or "we" that stands in opposition to a specific "he"—the "King of Great Britain"—but also, and, perhaps, more importantly, as the discourse proceeds, a "they"—which in the Declaration refers back to "our British brethren":

> We have warned *them* from time to time . . .
> We have reminded *them* . . .
> We have appealed to *their* native justice . . .
> We have conjured *them* by the ties of our common kindred . . . (italics added)

Colonial American subjects would have to have been reproducing in their discourse at the time patterns of usage in the pronouns "we" and "our" that resembled those of the Declaration. The key discourse pattern to emerge out of this process, of which the Declaration of Independence was only one moment, would have to have been a kind of "we"—analogous to the "we" of the human species from Jonathan Schell's *Fate of the Earth*, but circumscribing a population in certain of the British colonial states of North America. This replicated "we" would have to set its articulators, collectively, in opposition to various "they's," but particularly to a "they" of the British.

I expect historians to scrutinize the proposition that a "we" of the American colonies was already in circulation long before the Declaration of Independence, that it grew through replication over time, having broad currency on the eve of the Declaration. A key question is when and how that "we" became opposed to a "they" of "the British." In the "Declaration of Arms" (July 6, 1775), "Parliament" and the "legislature" are opposed to an "us" of the American colonies, but the opposition is not extended to a "they" of the British more generally, as in the Declaration. Yet surely that opposition was already in place in less official discourses of the times.

As to a "we" of the British colonies of North America more generally, certainly that was in circulation at least two decades prior to the revolution—as a few passages from Nathaniel Ames II, writer and publisher of *The Astronomical Diary and Almanack* (1758), suggest. An interesting "we" of the inhabitants of colonial North America is the following passage:

> O! Ye unborn Inhabitants of America! Should this Page escape its destin'd Conflagration at the Year's End, and these Alphabetical Letters remain legible,—when your Eyes behold the Sun after he has rolled the Seasons round for two or three Centuries more, you will know that in Anno Domini 1758, *we* dream'd of your Times. (Jehlen and Warner 1997, 718; italics added)

More extensive use of the colonial American "we" occurs earlier in this same piece:

Our Numbers will not avail till the Colonies are united; for whilst divided, the strength of the Inhabitants is broken like the petty Kingdoms in *Africa.*—If *we* do not join Heart and Hand in the common Cause against *our* exulting Foes, but fall to disputing among *ourselves,* it may really happen as the Governour of *Pennsylvania* told his Assembly, "*We* shall have no Priviledge to dispute about, nor Country to dispute in." (1997, 717; italics added)

This "we" is even oppositional—witness "our exulting Foes." But when and how did this British colonial America "we" come, in the course of its replication and movement through people, to be opposed to "the British," in particular?

The Declaration of Independence of the United States of America played upon the discontents of its population, and, undoubtedly, in some measure, replicated already circulating discourse of discontent: "He has plundered *our* seas, ravaged *our* Coasts, burnt *our* towns, and destroyed the lives of *our* people." Just so does the discourse of the "Republic of Texas" play upon already circulating discontents of the people it claims to represent.

We represent millions of Texans that have loved ones in Federal prisons for alleged revenue crimes, created out of a hole [sic] cloth, by a government. Or were the result of a failed, bogus war on drugs, that is not a war at all but a government-perpetuated enterprise.
We represent all who are tired of a government, any government, that when it cannot go swashbuckling around the world to fight someone else's war, it declares war on its own people!
We represent all the people who want to restore common sense in the courts, and laws under which they can live, and live well. The people who yearn for a system of justice where you do not have to hire someone, at exorbitant hourly rates, to explain to them their alleged rights and responsibilities, non-existent in a military, statutory setting, framed by a gold-fringed military flag, and run by tiny men who think they are God! (Republic of Texas Web Site, "Official Call," 16 Jan. 1996, italics added).

Nor is it entirely unimaginable that a discourse of secession for a new "Republic of Texas" could achieve wider circulation beyond the handful of its current followers—in January of 1997 estimated at "perhaps a few hundred people with varying degrees of commitment" (Verhovek 1997). The Official Call appeals to "the people who yearn for a system of justice where you do not have to hire someone, at exorbitant hourly rates, to explain to them their alleged rights. . . ." To recognize the discourse of discontent on which this statement builds, just think of how many lawyer jokes and stories now circulate in the broader population. Indeed, one resident of Fort Davis, Texas, T. Houston, who was not a part of the movement, remarked: "Actually, it would tickle me pink if we left the United States, but this guy [Richard L. McLaren] is going at it all the wrong way" (Verhovek 1997).

Micromotion and Macrocirculation

What is it that gets a pattern of "we" usage to circulate? I have already suggested that it is, in part, that the pattern replicates what is already in circulation. This is the principle of inertia. The Declaration of Independence drew on the colonists' already circulating discourse of discontent. Similarly, the "Republic of Texas" movement employs rhetoric that draws upon already existing discontents—already circulating patterns of discourse—among the people it seeks to enlist.

But that cannot be the end of the story. If only inertia were at work, nothing new would emerge except by the action of forces of dissipation on the inertial culture. The "United States of America," at one time a discursive entity analogous to the "Republic of Texas," did emerge as a recognizable social entity. It was an outgrowth—and represented the continuation of—older circulating discourse patterns. But something decidedly new did come into existence, whether one dates the birth of that new thing July 4, 1776, or 1787 (when the Constitution of the United States was drafted in Philadelphia) or 1788 (when the Constitution was ratified) or 1789 (when the Constitution was put into effect) or even 1865 (when the Civil War ended). How can such a new thing come about?

According to the theory I have been developing here, the transformation of discourse necessary to bring a new pattern into existence requires the application of accelerative force. Some of this force comes, I propose, from the peculiarities of key pieces of discourse—like the Declaration of Independence. The key piece of discourse has properties that attract attention to it. We are familiar with this phenomenon from the pop charts on the radio, where certain songs, because of their intrinsic properties relative to other contemporary music, work their way up the charts as people listen to them. But it is hard to recognize that this process is operative in the case of discourse more generally. Some bits of talk or writing, because of their internal organization, achieve greater circulatory prominence.

Not only is the discourse in question prominent in consciousness, but that prominence impels its reproduction. In the case of music, one hums or whistles or sings a tune one has heard or attempts to play it on a musical instrument. In the case of discourse, a similar copying takes place. Patterns of word usage circulate, sometimes through conscious acts of memorization and reproduction, as in lines from the Declaration: "When in the Course of human events . . ." or "We hold these truths to be self-evident, that all men are created equal. . . ." More typically, however, replication occurs through unreflective imitation, as one takes words or patterns of words one has heard and reproduces them. The words enter into the rhetorical unconscious and find their way out again in expression.

The Declaration is a highly poeticized text—and it is its poetic structure, at least in part, that, following Jakobson (1960a), makes the text stand out. Here I do not want to analyze the general rhetorical structure of the text, which has been the subject of earlier studies. Instead, I want to focus specifically on the poetics of the first person plural pronominal usage, since it is this pattern, I believe, that is crucial to the formation of a new social entity. Members of that emergent collectivity (or a significant fraction of the members) must come to think of themselves as a "we," and coming to think of themselves as a "we" is inextricably bound up with the patterns of deployment of actual pronouns in specific ways.

There are, by my count, forty-seven occurrences of the first person plural pronoun—including the forms "we" (eleven), "us" (ten), and "our" (twenty-six). Only one of these pronouns occurs in the first half of the Declaration—in the famous phrase: "We hold these truths to be self-evident. . . ." What is the discourse meaning of this "we"? On the one hand, it might look forward to the signers. But on the other hand, it occurs in the context of a discussion of universal rights and humankind, and thus bears a resemblance to Schell's "we" of the human species—this is a "we" of rational (human) beings. My inclination is to regard the latter as the correct interpretation, but, in any case, no other first-person forms occur for some time in the unfolding discourse.

When they do occur, however, they occur hot and heavy, and they appear in the grievances section. The first of these occurs in the line:

> He has erected a multitude of New Offices, and sent hither swarms of Officers to harass *our* people, and eat out their substance. (italics added)

The "our" of this line gains its specific meaning through its reference back to an earlier noun phrase, "the population of these States," which, like "our people," occurs in the object position, with "He"—referring back to the "present King of Great Britain"—occurring as subject. The pattern of "He" versus "us" is poetically salient. Repeatedly throughout the grievance section, "He" occurs in agentive subject position. Correspondingly, "us" or "our"—referring back to "the population of these States"—occurs in direct object, indirect object, or object of preposition position. Here are the occurrences from this section, in their immediate discourse contexts:

He has . . . sent hither swarms of Officers to harass *our* people . . .
He has kept among *us* . . . Standing Armies, without the consent of *our* legislatures
He has combined with others to subject *us* to a jurisdiction foreign to *our* constitution
and unacknowledged by *our* laws
He has abdicated Government here by declaring *us* out of his Protection and waging War against *us.*
He has plundered *our* seas,
ravaged *our* Coasts,
burnt *our* towns,
and destroyed the lives of *our* people.
He has constrained *our* fellow Citizens taken Captive on the high Seas to bear Arms against their Country
He has excited domestic insurrections amongst *us,*
and has endeavoured to bring on the inhabitants of *our* frontiers, the merciless Indian Savages. (italics added)

There is a palpable rhythm to these passages. Readers or listeners have the pattern drummed into them, so to speak, so that the reality of the discourse object is felt as well as cognized.

There is a section in the middle of these grievances, as well, in which a related parallelism is established in a series of "for" clauses, with the "King of Great Britain" being accused of giving his assent to measures that prejudice the "population of these states." Below, I excerpt just the ones with first-person plural pronouns in them:

For cutting off *our* Trade with all parts of the world:
For imposing Taxes on *us* without *our* Consent:
For depriving *us* in many cases of the benefits of Trial by Jury:
For transporting *us* beyond Seas to be tried for pretended offences:
For taking away *our* Charters,
abolishing *our* most valuable Laws
and altering fundamentally the Forms of *our* Governments:
For suspending *our* own Legislatures,

and declaring themselves invested with power
to legislate for *us* in all cases whatsoever. (italics added)

Again, it is the palpable quality of repetition that lends reality to the discursive object. Clause after clause follows a single pattern: "For [verb]-ing ___ us (our) ___," where a series of verbs supplies the key variation: "depriving," "transporting," "taking away," "abolishing," "altering fundamentally," "suspending," "declaring." A temporal reality emerges in the discourse through the repetition of physical words "for," "us," and "our" in their appropriate grammatical positions.

What I wish to contend is that this micromovement, based upon intratextual replication, bears a relationship to the macro- and intertextual movement of a pattern of discourse in the broader population. If one looks only at a single line—"He has plundered *our* seas . . . ," for example, that movement is not apparent. The line projects a discursive image of a collectivity, of an "our" whose referent would be traceable back to "the population of these states." And, by virtue of being a first-person plural pronoun, it would invite readers or listeners to ask of themselves—Am I part of that group? But the repeated occurrence of the first-person plural forms in grammatical positions in which they are acted upon by an external "He" or "they" does something more. It creates a movement—however microscopic—of that collectivity through time, the time of the textual reading or listening. The pattern appears as a temporal trace, with each subsequent occurrence building upon its predecessor and reconfirming the existence of that trace. The collectivity assumes an existence in time, if only the microtime of the text. But it clearly becomes something more than the projected image off of one isolated occurrence of the pronoun. That projected image could be shrugged off. But the palpable durability of the discourse pattern within the text suggests the durability of the thing that that pattern purports to represent.

I want to argue that this making palpable of the temporal durability of the collectivity is one component, perhaps even an important component, of the accelerative force that helps to bring a collectivity into existence in the first place. The poetic characteristics are not simply a device for foregrounding the text, thereby making possible its circulation in the broader world—although they surely are that, as well. Additionally, the text, as built around an architecture of repetition, contains within itself a miniature version of the movement of a discourse pattern through time. That miniature version lends experiential temporal reality to the object in the world—the collectivity—that each isolated line represents. The feel of reality of movement of the pattern within the text in turn impels the replication of that pattern in those who read or listen to the text.

I do not want to make light of the significant content of this pattern—an aggrieved "we." On the contrary, grievance—complaint about an other or others hurting oneself or one's group—may be among the most effective ways of kindling a sense of group identity. Indeed, it is possible to build a discourse primarily around a "they," with the "we" being largely implicit, as in anti-Semitic rhetoric, or the recent right-wing antigovernment rhetoric. Moreover, the discourse of aggrievement in the Declaration is critical to building upon an already circulating discourse of aggrievement in the broader Anglo population of coastal North America. I have been at pains to say that this Declaration did not create something ex nihilo. It took the existing movement of culture—the existing circulating discourse of complaint—and sharpened and focused it, making explicit its connection to a "we" that was aggrieved. What I am pointing out here is that the pattern is given a temporal existence (and, hence, reality) through repetition that is present within the text. The poetic repetition adds incremental accelerative force to culture that is already in motion.

It is intriguing that, after the grievance section, in which the putative collectivity is aggrieved, the first person plural is then reincarnated as an actor, an agent bringing about events in the world, making them happen. No longer is it simply a patient—the inert thing to which something is done. The grievance section is highly patient-centric. But, immediately after it, an agentive "we" is born:

> *We* have warned them from time to time . . .
> *We* have reminded them . . .
> *We* have appealed to their native justice . . .
> *we* have conjured them by the ties of our common kindred . . .
> *We* must, therefore . . . hold them, as
> *we* hold the rest of mankind, Enemies in War, in Peace Friends. (italics added)

I want to make it clear that these "we's" circumscribe the same collectivity as the "our's" that came before them—and I will note, shortly, that they are different from the "we's" in the resolution section that follows. Each "we" here refers back to the preceding first-person plural forms, and, ultimately, back to "the population of these states." These are "we's" of the collectivity.

But there is a difference. These are not the phlegmatic and passive "our's" and "us'es" of the earlier section. The collectivity here begins to stir, as if the repeated, unprovoked proddings finally awaken the beast from its groggy slumber; it here begins to lurch into action, warning, reminding, appealing, conjuring, and, finally, holding them "Enemies in War, in Peace Friends." Those who could identify with the aggrieved "us" of the earlier section are now invited to identify with the active "we" of a collectivity at war with another.

Once again, however, this active "we" gains palpability by the movement of the discourse pattern through the microtime of the text. The "we's" occur in rapid succession, each building upon the other, each reaffirming the temporal trace of the pattern, and hence also of the entity that the "we" purports to represent—a collectivity capable of agency in the world, of doing things and making things happen rather than simply responding to them.

The performative magic of this text, with which both Derrida (1986) and Lee (1997) are concerned, does not occur until the next section. The "we" of this section is distinctive; it is the third type of "we" in this text, if the first type—the "we" of "we hold these truths to be self-evident"—is a universal "we," akin to Schell's "we" of the human species. The second type, which dominates the text, is the "we" of the American collectivity, and the third type is the representative "we," circumscribing the signers of the Declaration. The shift to it is explicitly announced: "*We*, therefore, the Representatives of the United States of America. . . ."

I think Lee (1997) is right to argue that the validity of this discourse tactic, in the eyes and ears of potential readers and listeners, derives from prior discourse—specifically, from the history of performative usage in Western cultures. The self-constitutive acts make sense or become intelligible for people for whom the performative creation of things in the world—social relations through marriage, names through christening, admission into religious communities through baptism—is already understandable.

At the same time, this kind of self-creation or self-constitution as representatives makes no sense if there does not already exist the social body whose people the representatives are to represent. The precondition of self-constitution is the prior existence of a collectivity. This is reflected in the linear unfolding of the text. Self-appointment as representatives occurs only after the collectivity achieves palpable existence as a discourse trace. Microtemporality parallels the macrotemporality of broader discourse circulation, at least as I have been depicting it. The resolution section follows upon a long section of grievances and then a shorter section in which the aggrieved collectivity becomes agentive.

What I am suggesting, therefore, is that the microflows of discourse in textual time parallel or model the macroflow of historical time. The collectivity takes shape in the text the way it was actually taking shape in the world. The Declaration is a discourse image, written in miniature, of the broader historical flow of discourse patterns through the people who occupy the east coast of North America.

But, at the same time, the text is not simply a microcosmic image of these macrocirculatory processes. It also represents an intervention in those processes. It is designed to be persuasive, to have an effect, to pull people into an incipient collectivity, and thereby to solidify that collectivity. The practical means by which it is able to do this is its stimulation of discourse patterns. It adds an incremental force to the movement of those patterns by persuading people to take them on in their own speech, in the way they narrate their own lives. And in taking on those patterns, people are encouraged to organize their own behavior in the world so that their behavior might be narrativizable in accord with the patterns. In short, the discourse contributes to the historical movement of culture through which a collectivity is constituted.

If the Declaration contributes to the movement of discourse patterns by modeling that movement and intensifying it on the microplane, it follows that the general textual trend ought to be toward an increase in the frequency of first-person forms as the text unfolds. Figure 7 demonstrates

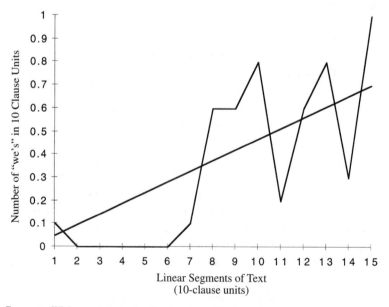

Figure 7. "We" over time in the Declaration of Independence.

that this pattern holds true for the Declaration; I have charted the occurrence of the first-person plural forms ("we," "our," "us") as a function of the linear unfolding of the text. In this case, I have divided the text in units of ten clauses[2] each. I have then calculated the average number of first-person pronouns per clause within each ten-clause unit. Although there are ups and downs, with some parts of the text more densely populated with "we's" than other parts, the general trend is toward an increase in the frequency of the first-person plural form.

The increase in frequency of "we's" in the broader population of coastal North America—"we's" identifying with an American collectivity—is, of course, also the goal of the text itself. If one could construct an analogous figure for the frequency of the "we" usage of British colonial America over historical time—for example, over the eighteenth century—one would expect to see a similar increasing trend. The statistical pattern of "we" usage over the microtime of the Declaration itself, as a piece of linearly unfolding discourse, would then appear as a miniature model of the broader historical replication of the pattern over time within British colonial North America.

I have argued, however, perhaps even too tediously, that the Declaration, as circulating discourse, does not simply encode or reflect the historical replication of that discourse pattern in the broader population; it also itself plays a role in shaping the historical course of replication, in deflecting the discourse pattern from its inertial trajectory. The Declaration is agentive, though not in the way Derrida (1986) imagined—namely, as the instantaneous and magical creation of a social entity that had not before existed. The Declaration is instead a rhetorical entity, shaping and accelerating a pattern of "we" usage, and, thereby, helping to bring a social entity into existence. But that entity depends on the broader circulation of the pattern of "we" usage within the American population and elsewhere. That circulation takes time—historical time—and is not instantaneously achieved. The Declaration may have come at a key moment, may have constituted a key rhetorical intervention, but the groundwork of circulation was laid long in advance and the circulatory processes continued long after, as I will argue below. At the time of the Civil War, and, in particular, of Abraham Lincoln's Gettysburg Address, the "we" of the United States of America was all but unutterable.

The statistical trend of intensification of "we" usage in the Declaration is not, by any means, a unique characteristic of that text. The intensification is actually found in much politically persuasive discourse in America. It is a way of building emotional involvement in the discourse, and is, in this regard, analogous to other techniques, such as the increase in frequency of shot changes in film that goes along with points of peak excitement in the narrative.

In the case of "we" usage, however, what the author or speaker is trying to do is build emotional interest in a specific pattern of that usage. You will recall, from the first chapter, that Jonathan Schell's *The Fate of the Earth* and Caspar Weinberger's "U.S. Defense Strategy" both contain multiple types of "we's." In each, a particular "we" was dominant: in Schell, the "we" of the human species, and in Weinberger, the "we" of the United States—which, incidentally, is evidence of the continuing replication of the Declaration's "we." If the purpose of statistically increasing the frequency of "we" usage is to cause others to take up that usage, and hence to get it to spread in a broader population, it would follow that the statistical increase ought to apply to the basic "we"—the one that is most prevalent in the text—but not necessarily to the other ancillary "we's."

To determine whether this is actually so, I have charted the patterns of "we" usage over textual time for the basic and nonbasic types of "we" in both Schell and Weinberger. The results for the distribution of the basic "we's" are shown in Figures 8 and 9. The pattern is similar in each case to that observed for the Declaration.

Regarding the nonbasic "we's," some of them occur too infrequently to draw any solid conclusions. The remainder, however, can be studied. Of the nonbasic "we's" in Schell, the author plus reader "we" shows an upward trend—with readers being drawn into the author's point of view. The present-generation "we" shows a nearly flat trend, with only a slight upward incline. The rest show a downward trend. For Weinberger, the nonbasic "we's" include the Reagan administration, ambiguous, Department of Defense, within quotations, and President and I "we's." The trend in each of these cases in downward.

My conclusion is that what matters in these texts are the basic forms of first-person plural usage that the authors are attempting—whether consciously or not—to stimulate in their readers. Writers or speakers can sense patterns, just as their readers or listeners do, without fully recognizing those patterns in a conscious way. The texts, as interventions in the historical replication of discourse, are designed to promote a particular pattern of "we" usage. In this, they are like the Declaration. But, unlike the Declaration, no social entity came into existence as a result of them, or as what can be seen retrospectively to be a result of them. In the case of Schell, there is evidence that *The Fate of the Earth* exerted some accelerative force in stimulating a "we" of the human species—witness my own un-

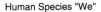

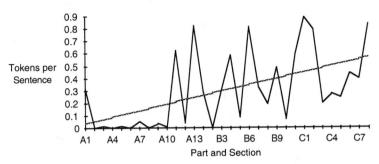

Figure 8. "We" over time in Schell (1982).

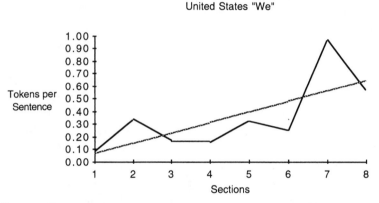

Figure 9. "We" over time in Weinberger (1986).

witting replication of its patterns discussed in chapter 1. But if a social entity like "the human species" is to become readily recognizable in human discourse, the processes of circulation still have far to go—pace the establishment of a "League of Nations" and a "United Nations" during the twentieth century.

The En-Chanting of "We"

There is more to this pronominal story. True, micromotion and macrocirculation gave birth to another social entity; but such births must have happened numerous times in the planet's history. With a "we, the people of the United States,"[3] however, something else emerged, something of epochal significance. It is as if tectonic pressures built up over time by the

This Nation Will Rise Up

spread of a metaculture of newness produced a gigantic snap in the crust of society, causing fundamental realignments. If I am correct, what was born on the eastern coast of North America was not simply a new social entity, but a new kind of social entity—one conceived in the context of a novel interpretation and deployment of the pronoun "we." The pronoun—and its nominal counterpart, "the people"—perfectly captured the metacultural idea of newness, and, as a consequence, the American "we" became a world-transforming element. An idea of newness undoubtedly stimulated its birth, perhaps even sired it. However, once born, the new "we" appeared to metaculture as its perfect incarnation, a child conceived after its own image.

What precisely is this new "we"? How can it be detected? To answer these questions, I propose to turn to the first-person singular pronoun ("I"), since the same transformation took place here. Moreover, since the meaning of "I" seems—intuitively, at least—so much more stable, so much less susceptible to metacultural influence, than that of the mercurial "we,"[4] its transformation stands out all the more starkly.

In the theory of motion articulated in the preceding two chapters, metacultural understanding crucially affects the nature of cultural movement. A metaculture of tradition values the replication of the cultural objects themselves—the transmission of the whole elements—with the valued reproducers being those who have mastered the elements and demonstrated their ability to recreate them, thereby contributing to their passage through time. In contrast, a metaculture of newness values cultural objects that are not simply replicas of ones that have come before them, but instead are "new" in important ways.

One consequence of the idea of newness is that specific, concrete individuals come to seem to be the controllers or "authors" of their own narratives.[5] It is not narratives—myths, for example, as culture moving through time—that control individuals, but the other way around. In novelistic discourse, an author constructs an "I" of a character or even of a narrator. The "I" is narrativized in such a way that author and audience alike recognize it as pointing to an imaginary character. What is significant, however, is that the imagined character or narrator is thought of, under an idea of newness, as the product of a concrete, in-this-world individual (the author). The "I" has an extrasomatic referent that points to a fictive character, but that referent, that imaginary entity, is a product of the here-and-now body of the author. There is an individual, material, biological agent behind that "I," even if one step removed from it.

"I's" that point to fictive characters, even in a narratorial role, are present under an idea of tradition, as well, as discussed at the end of the last chapter. Such narratorial or projective "I's" are by now well documented.[6] In my own research, what is interesting is that the trance-like "I" was not present in every instance of origin myth-telling. When it did occur, however, as I have recounted, the myth-teller seemed to grow distant and his eyes glazed over. It was as if he were possessed by some other controlling force that animated his body.

This particular myth, at the time of my research, was memorized verbatim. Consequently, I was able to record analogous passages from different tellings in which one made use of the third-person narratorial style (referring to the character as "he") and the other made use of the first person (the character was referred to as "I," as if narrator and character were one and the same):

Relative Zàgpope Pate arrived in front of *him.*

↓

Relative Zàgpope Pate arrived in front of *me.*

Why this assumption of the first person?

The characteristic of the "I" used in such cases—as opposed to the imagined "I's" produced by contemporary American authors—is that the mythical "I" is not thought of as an imaginary construct of a real, flesh-and-blood speaker of the "I." Instead, the "I" is understood as the product—as being under the control of—an immaterial being. The immaterial entity seizes the utterer's body and speaks through the utterer. The distinction is crucial. An imagined "I" is just that—the product of an individual imagination. A mythical "I" (or the "I" of trance) is the product not of imagination, but of control over the individual by extrasomatic forces or beings.

Perhaps I should quickly dispel a possible misinterpretation of what I am saying. I am not suggesting that Brazilian Indians (and others) are mistaken—that in their cases, as in the novel, individuals really are "in control," that they only pretend not to be. How reassuring such an interpretation would be for contemporary westerners. Something far more significant is at work, something meriting closer scrutiny, if we are to understand the world out there and its "hard, scientific" reality.

From the point of view of motion through space and time, Amerindian (and other) claims regarding extrasomatic forces capture an unsettling truth. Culture is something that moves through the world. It is something that controls individual bodies. The phonology of a language—not something an individual has created or controls, in an agentive sense—nevertheless shapes, through habituation, the vocal apparatus of that individual as it passes through that individual on its way elsewhere. It is the phonology, or phonological pattern, moving through time and space between individuals that is in control. Any given individual has relatively little influence over it. In the origin myth examples discussed above, the individual tellers have not created or produced the myth. The words they utter are words that have been uttered by those who came before them, and they are words that will be uttered by those who come after them. The present utterers are merely conduits for those words, for that culture, as it wends its way through a physical world.

No, this claim does not mean that the view from a metaculture of modernity is false. Even in the case of myth narration, individuals make a difference, as I have so laboriously tried to show in the previous chapter. The question is: On what does metacultural awareness focus? Does it focus on aspects of the narration for which the individual is responsible (modernity)? Or does it focus on aspects for which the culture, as cumulated learning moving over time, is responsible (tradition)? Correspondingly, what is the effect on culture of that focus? How is culture reshaped by critical observation of it and reflection on it?

Bakhtin mentions "a series of statements that accompanied the emergence of a new novel-type in the eighteenth century" (1981, 9). Among the characteristics of this "new novel-type" are that "the hero of a novel should not be 'heroic' in either the epic or the tragic sense of the word: he should combine in himself negative as well as positive features, low as well as lofty, ridiculous as well as serious" (10). Furthermore, "the hero should not be portrayed as an already completed and unchanging person but as one who is evolving and developing, a person who learns from life" (10). These characteristics, and others Bakhtin develops, reflect the emergence of imagined "I"s that are under the control of real individuals. The characters are made to seem more like ordinary individuals, and hence more likely to be the imagined constructs of ordinary individuals—the authors. The "I's" employed look like the "I's" used by here-and-now people.

The imagined "I" is something peculiar in this regard: It is an "I" designed to appear to be under the control of a flesh-and-blood author—the one who produced it. The fictive characters portrayed by that "I" are fictive, but they are fictive in a way that makes them suspiciously human, the kind of beings any ordinary individual might imagine. They are, in other words, adapted to a metaculture of newness, which focuses attention on the act of creation of the linguistic form by an individual rather than on the passage of a linguistic form over time through that individual. Under a metaculture of tradition, correspondingly, one would expect to find a different kind of character, one less scrutable to ordinary humans, one embodying the power of culture over its human transmitters.

Such an analysis of the first-person singular pronoun could be taken much further, though I can only point out the path here. If newness emphasizes control by a physical person (the author) over the construction of a represented person (the character), so also does the narrator come to be depicted as a kind of human with human-like control over the characters. That narratorial voice comes to look like a voice emanating from a real, concrete person. This, in turn, paves the way for the deflation of the narrator, from a position of omnipresence and omniscience, to—in the present period—just another voice among the many within the novel. The unreliable narrators are proof of humanness, and hence of construction by humans rather than by some mysterious force that passes through humans on its way elsewhere.

You may be wondering by now what all of this has to do with the first-person plural pronoun. The answer is that the same transition is at work in the case of "we." An imagined "I" of a novelistic character—understandable metaculturally as the creation (and under the control) of a real flesh-and-blood author—has a counterpart in "we." If an imagined "I"—unlike the mythical "I"—represents itself as the product of an individual, so does a metaculture of modernity represent "we" as a product of a collection of individuals, a group of "I's." The "we" is under the control of those individuals.

The latter is an especially odd phenomenon, whose oddness deserves to be underscored. Monty Python's film *The Life of Brian* plays up the ironies of such agentive control. The main character—a Christ figure—is pursued by throngs of supporters. He takes refuge from his admirers in a building. Throwing open the shutters, he shouts to his followers: "Go away! . . . You are all individuals." And they begin to chant in unison: "We are all individuals. We are all individuals." One voice from the back of the crowd says: "I'm not."

The peculiarity of a "we" is that it can be the expression of one individual—if we focus on individual control—as in the case of Jefferson's drafting of the Declaration of Independence. (Here I will ignore the history of words and discourse on which Jefferson drew and on the contributions made by other members of the Continental Congress in the course of rewriting Jefferson's draft [see Maier 1997]—central factors, if one were to examine the Declaration from the perspective of tradition.) By focusing on the creative moment, what appears odd is that words that originated elsewhere (with Jefferson) come to seem to be the expression of those through whom they are merely passing (a broader population endorsing the Declaration). Since agency comes from individuals—under this kind of metacultural interpretation—each reutterer of an expression containing a "we" comes to seem to be the creator and controller of that expression, even though they themselves have made no contribution to its actual formulation. Such a "we" really is culture moving through them, but it is made to seem (by metaculture) as something under their control, as expressions of them.

The image of a crowd chanting in unison a "we" slogan—so pervasive in contemporary social movements—captures this irony, as in the Vietnam war era chant:

Hell no, we won't go!
Hell no, we won't go!

Or in chants at political rallies:

We want Bush!
We want Bush!

Or in chants at sports events:

We're number one!
We're number one!

In each case, the words are circulating words. They have come from elsewhere. But they are taken up by individuals as if they were the expressions of those individuals.

In this regard, it is noteworthy that the Declaration of Independence was signed by fifty-six individuals. Why did they do so? They were not only engaging in dissimulation, or even, as Derrida suggested, in a "fabulous retroactivity" (1986, 10). They were, instead, signaling their own agency, and with it their interpretation of the agency behind a "we" as that of a collection of individual agents who have a collective "voice."

What makes a community "imagined," from this perspective, is not only that individuals can imagine others whom they "will never meet, or even know" as essentially like themselves, pace Benedict Anderson ([1983] 1991). It is also, and perhaps more importantly, that individuals can understand or interpret—thanks to a metaculture of modernity—an expression containing the first-person plural pronoun as one emanating from themselves, even though they have not created it. The metacultural understanding obscures the circulatory process that brought that "we" to them and that is passing through them on its way elsewhere. In doing so, it gives agency to a group or collectivity.

Physical Thing, Spiritual Meaning

As I sit here, I thumb through a slim fourteen-by-ten inch booklet entitled the "Liberty Collection." Its front cover bears a tiny copyright: 1963, the year I acquired it as an eighth-grade student in Oak View Elementary School. This is a booklet I have carried around for thirty-five years. Through the peregrinations of my life, it has maintained a strangely special quality, something to which I am attached by unconscious ties. Never once have I seriously considered jettisoning it, despite geographical displacements that have forced me to dispose of other childhood treasures. Why did this one maintain a hold on me?

It now seems so hokey, with a label pasted inside bearing the name "Polk Bros.," a department store of little note long since forgotten, that used this giveaway—no doubt as a promotional. (Or could it have been for genuinely patriotic reasons?) The pages were made to look old, like parchment (see Figures 10 a–c), and the very first one contains lines deeply etched in my individual memory—and, I believe, in the collective memory of the nation: "We hold these truths to be self-evident, that all men are created equal, that they are endowed by their creator with certain unalienable Rights, that among those are Life, Liberty, and the pursuit of Happiness."

These are dusty words, and, as I dust them off, I find myself asking what they meant to that thirteen-year-old boy. Why had he so carefully guarded them? Pauline Maier describes the relative disregard in which the now enshrined parchment was held: "In 1776 the Declaration of Independence was not even copied onto a particularly good sheet of parchment, just an ordinary type of colonial manufacture that could be easily found on sale in Philadelphia and was perhaps 'improvidently selected, being improperly cured and sized'" (1997, xi). It was then dragged around and battered, the inky signatures at the bottom fading. In 1841, it was put on display in the State Department, and then later exhibited in Philadelphia at the centennial, when concern for its longevity began to set in: "The documents [the Declaration, Constitution, and Bill of Rights] were finally placed in their current airtight thermopane containers with an electronic device to detect helium loss in September 1952" (Maier 1997, xiii).

Looking back on it today, as an anthropologist, it is clear that the documents, as physical things, had, by the time of my childhood, if not long

Figure 10a. Small section of the original (now badly faded) 1776 Declaration of Independence. Note the physical appearance of not only the titles, but also the first word of the text (*when*).

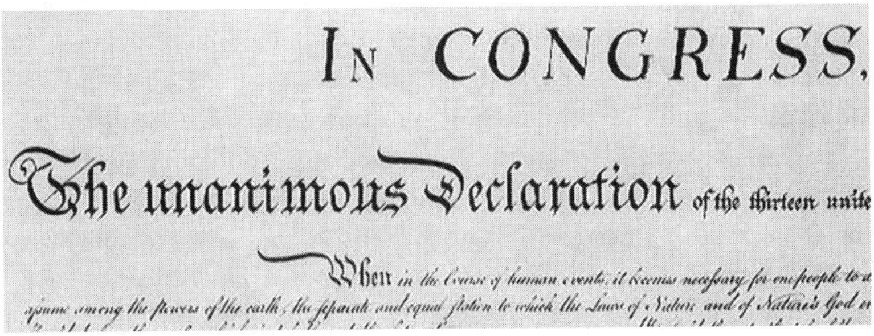

Figure 10b. Analogous section from a print made of the 1823 William J. Stone engraving, the most widely reproduced image of the Declaration of Independence. The physical form of the text, not just its semantic meaning, is replicated here in great detail; the word *when* appears in identical form to the original.

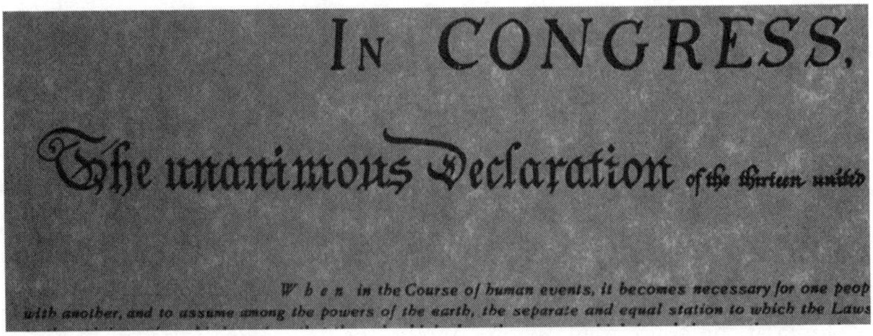

Figure 10c. Analogous section of the 1963 reproduction of the Declaration of Independence, contained in the "Liberty Collection" and distributed gratis by Polk Bros. The physical form of the title is reproduced, but note the distinct script employed in the body of the text, beginning with the word *when*. The new script is designed to render the text more readable by a modern audience. Transmission of meaning begins to take precedence over the transmission of physical form of the object, although insofar as its words are concerned, the text is identical to the original.

before, become symbols of my collectivity. They were the analogs of *churingas*, strange pieces of wood or stone fashioned by Australian aborigines that Emile Durkheim, in his work *The Elementary Forms of the Religious Life* ([1912] 1969), described as material entities thought to embody the immaterial, but nevertheless effective-in-this-world, essence of the group. They were physical things that had taken on spiritual significance as the concrete representation of that intangible social entity that perdures over time called "The United States of America."

This led to me to recognize that, as an anthropologist, I was on familiar terrain. Here was something fundamental about my culture, and yet part of a class of phenomena I had been studying in my researches abroad. In my Brazilian work, indeed, I had documented a process much like that I have just described—words, valued initially for their meanings, that over time came to assume value as physical things. In the Brazilian Indian case, the process involved dreams that were narrated, and which, over time— a century and a half, by my estimates—came to lose their connection to the realm of dream narrative and enter the realm of myth. As the stories circulated more widely, their form of expression—the actual words and the physical nuances of their pronunciation—came to be fixed. And those words, as physical things being replicated over time through oral transmission, became unglued from their original meanings. At the farthest pole of migration toward fixity, they became ritualized in their telling, the actual performance of the origin myth—done in dyadic syllable-by-syllable fashion—coming to be a collective rite.

Of course, in my childhood, growing up in the Midwest, I was steeped in anticommunism. In the same drawer in which I kept the "Liberty Collection" as a boy, I also stored various political pamphlets I had received. One, I recall vividly, told me how to recognize a communist and had sketches of dangerous-looking red men hiding under beds and in closets. And I was genuinely worried about communists. At the age of nine or ten, as I recall, I thought up a scheme: We could build a tunnel underneath the Kremlin and place a bomb there; its detonation would end the threat from communism once and for all. Maier writes that the shrine in the National Archives in which the Declaration was held came to seem "an assertion of American values . . . against fascist and communist enemies" (1997, xv).

True though this was in my case, yet there was more. The "Liberty Collection" remained in my possession long after the anticommunist political materials from my boyhood drawer had disappeared. I entered college during the tumultuous period of the late 1960s, when the country was wracked by an antiwar movement with protesters burning the American flag. My hair grew long, so much so that I was unrecognizable to Mr. Kennedy, our local policeman and father of one of my schoolmates. And yet I kept hold of the "Liberty Collection." In the 1970s and 1980s, I found myself in Brazil for extended periods, living in Indian villages. During my travels abroad, I kept the "Liberty Collection" in storage; now it became part of my "history books." I recall looking at it in 1994, while packing up to move from Austin, Texas, to Philadelphia. My thought then was: "Well, I might actually use this in my research."

The general point is that, despite my personal situation, and whatever changing relations to the booklet I have had, somehow the "Liberty Collection" (consisting, incidentally, of facsimiles of the Declaration of Independence, the Constitution, the Bill of Rights, the Monroe Doctrine, the Gettysburg Address, and "The Star-Spangled Banner," eight pages in all) has remained with me, almost as if it were a part of me. So, in some ways I am not at all surprised that many hard-bitten westerners who reside in rural Nevada keep, according to Susan Lepselter's research (personal communication), copies of the Constitution and Bill of Rights in their homes—and respect those documents over and against a government which, they believe, has come to betray them. Are not the documents, more than the incumbent government, the embodiment of the collectivity?

But if the totemic quality of the Declaration is familiar to me from my anthropological research abroad, how to think about other aspects of the role of the Declaration, which seem in important respects distinct? Could they be related? My Brazilian research suggested a lead. There I detected two types of cultural motion. One type, pertaining to "news," involved the carrying over of meaning between specific instances of discourse, despite divergences between the words (or formal expressions) used to capture those meanings. The most extreme case is the dictionary definition of a word: one word, as a physically recognizable thing, is conveyed in terms of other words. The word to be defined is not repeated in the definition. Thus, the meaning of the word *document* could be replicated as "a written or printed paper that bears the original, official, or legal form of something and can be used to furnish decisive evidence or information" without the replication of the initial word. Yet something immaterial—a meaning—is carried over between the two.

The other type of cultural motion involved the replication of physical form, with the presumption, apparently, that the (or, perhaps, a) meaning will thereby carry over, as well. In the Brazilian Indian case, such replication is found in myth-telling, where an entire origin myth may be recited in virtually word-for-word fashion. A young boy who learns this myth learns it through memorization of the words. The retelling is verbatim.

If the first type of cultural motion is "paraphrase," the second type is "repetition." In the one, meaning is transmitted; in the other, material form. My general thesis on the Brazilian case was that dream narratives, when they first began to circulate, fell closer to the side of paraphrase. What was of interest to people, initially, was the carrying over of meanings from an "original" to a "copy"—"What is the dream all about?" However, as the motion proceeds, the forms of expression—the actual words—tended to become fixed. This is not a uniform process, and some words, like those of reported speech, fix more readily than others, like background descriptions. But the important point is that, as words become the property of a larger community and are handed down over time, their physical characteristics become important. One wishes to experience the words because of their effects, which are tied to their material qualities and relations as well as to their meanings: "Tell it again. Tell the story about___." But why would one want to hear "the story about___" again? The paraphraseable meaning has already been transmitted. Isn't the process then complete? Why retransmit it? The listener must be interested in the experience of hearing itself as well as or more than the paraphraseable meaning.

A corollary of this is that, insofar as culture is carried in publicly occurring signs, such as the origin myth in this Amerindian community, then the persistence of the culture depends upon transmission of the ability to produce the signs. What distinguishes a group as a social entity is the fact that it carries along, over time, a particular set of public signs. At the same time, the reproduction of those signs over time can involve subtle shifts, as the signs are reproduced. The culture moves along but simultaneously changes in the course of that movement, readapting to new circumstances of the putative group.

But what about the Declaration of Independence? The editorial work on Thomas Jefferson's initial draft is a case of microchange over time. Maier mentions also some differences between the signed Declaration and the excerpt that appears on the Jefferson Memorial on the mall in Washington, D.C.: "The punctuation was changed; 'unalienable' went back to 'inalienable,' a 'that' was removed so that the last statement became a separate sentence, and the final phrase of what was in the original a linked sequence . . . was eliminated altogether" (1997, 210). Still, the Declaration generally fails to participate in the gradual, subtle changes undergone by myth. A textbook author can explicate and paraphrase the Declaration, but there are limits placed on the evolution of that paraphrase itself. Any paraphrase ultimately looks back to the signed copy kept in Washington as its authority.[7]

In the case of myth, the authority shifts over time. Each new telling becomes potentially authoritative, if it generates other tellings. The impression is that one is dealing with the same myth, even though an objective recording of variations over time shows significant differences. This may be true even of the Christian Bible, which has had many translations, no one of them (apparently) absolutely authoritative.[8] The Bible appears, from this point of view, to be an immaterial thing that runs through its various incarnations.

But in the case of the Declaration, one physical object, the signed copy kept in Washington, D.C., is absolutely authoritative. One can argue over its interpretation, and power becomes lodged in the metadiscursive struggle over interpretation—although plain-speaking Nevadans might reject those interpretations (which are crucial to the functioning of government) in favor the "transparent" meaning of the text. But there is still a text as a physical thing that cannot evolve discursively—that is, as culture—even if it can evolve metadiscursively. The culture that might, as in the case of myth, evolve through the reincarnations or reproductions of the public signs in which it is carried, is, so to speak, locked in the physical thing.

The only way for culture to get out of the Declaration in which it is locked, and to move through historical time—and this is part of the modern character of the Declaration—is for the original whole cultural object to be disassembled into its constituent strands and for some of those strands to be used for the purpose of constructing a new object—such as the Gettysburg Address, produced by Abraham Lincoln in 1863. Even the "Official Call" of the "Republic of Texas" in 1996 is such a putatively "new" cultural expression, under a metaculture of modernity, and here also one might include Vine Deloria's book, subtitled *An Indian Declaration of Independence* (1974). But the ones with which I will start are the Declarations of Causes, which initiated the secession of several southern States from the United States of America in 1860 and 1861.

Litanies of Complaint

What can it mean to disassemble a cultural element "into its constituent strands"? What strands are in the Declaration that might be used in "new" cultural elements? One is the pattern I'll dub the "litany of complaint." I have already described it for the first-person plural pronoun, and I think it is most rhetorically effective when employed in this way. However, the key discursive characteristic of this pattern is that it consists in a series of distinct complaints against some single other—"the King of Great Britain" or "the British" in the Declaration—and the complaints are expressed in no more than a sentence or two each, and perhaps as little as a clause or a verbal phrase. Here is a short excerpt from a longer litany in the Declaration that I gave earlier:

> He has abdicated Government here by declaring *us* out of his Protection
>   and waging War against *us.*
> He has plundered *our* seas,
>   ravaged *our* Coasts,
>   burnt *our* towns,
>   and destroyed the lives of *our* people.
> He has constrained *our* fellow Citizens taken Captive on the high Seas to
>   bear Arms against their Country. (italics added)

My claim is that this pattern—the "litany of complaint"—is a strand of culture that has found its way out of the Declaration and into new cultural elements as it moved through space and time. However, this pattern may not have originated with the Declaration. A discourse of complaint was widespread in the colonies prior to the Declaration, and even the Declaration of Arms, from just about a year earlier (July 6, 1775) includes its own litanies. Here is an example from that document:

> His [General Gage's] troops have butchered *our* countrymen,
> have wantonly burnt Charlestown, besides a considerable number of
>   houses in other places;
> *our* ships and vessels are seized;
> the necessary supplies of provisions are intercepted,
> and he is exerting his utmost power to spread destruction and devastation
>   around him. (italics added)

Still, the bulk of this document is written more in the form of a continuous narrative of events, not of a chant-like litany. One characteristic of the Declaration's litany, and of the strand of American culture I am trying to describe more generally, is that the specific grievances, in their chant-like unfolding, do not represent a historical sequence so much as a juxtaposition of complaints having no definable timeline. Moreover, even in the above excerpt, the grammatical parallelism found in the Declaration's litany is not maintained. The first few clauses have General Gage—

referenced through an anaphoric "he" that looks back to an earlier noun phrase—as the grammatical subject. The next two clauses, however, are in the passive voice, and then "he" reemerges as grammatical subject in the last one.

There can be little doubt that, as Maier (1997: 50–57) has argued, the Declaration of Independence, and other similar documents hark back to the English Bill of Rights of 1689. The litany of complaint has precedent there, with the charges against the King organized in a similar unfolding of clauses. Here is the relevant section:

> Whereas the late King James the Second, by the assistance of divers evil counselors, judges, and ministers employed by him, did endeavour to subvert and extirpate the protestant religion, and the laws and liberties of this kingdom.
>
> - By assuming and exercising a power of dispensing with and suspending of laws, and the execution of laws, without consent of parliament.
> - By committing and prosecuting divers worthy prelates, for humbly petitioning to be excused concurring to the said assumed power.
> - By issuing and causing to be executed a commission under the great seal for erecting a court called, The court of commissioners for ecclesiastical causes.
> - By levying money for and to the use of the crown, by pretence of prerogative, for other time, and in other manner, than the same was granted by parliament.
> - By raising and keeping a standing army within this kingdom in time of peace, without consent of parliament, and quartering soldiers contrary to law.
> - By causing several good subjects, being protestants, to be disarmed, at the same time when papists were both armed and employed, contrary to law.
> - By violating the freedom of election of members to serve in parliament.
> - By prosecutions in the court of King's Bench, for matters and causes cognizable only in parliament; and by divers other arbitrary and illegal courses.
> - And whereas of late years, partial, corrupt, and unqualified persons have been returned and served on juries in trials and particularly divers jurors in trials for high treason, which were not freeholders.
> - And excessive bail hath been required of persons committed in criminal cases, to elude the benefit of the laws made for the liberty of the subject.

- And excessive fines have been imposed; and illegal and cruel punishments inflicted.
- And several grants and promises made of fines and forfeitures, before any conviction or judgment against the persons, upon whom the same were to be levied.

So my argument is not that the litany of complaints originated with the Declaration of Independence, but rather that it constitutes a strand of culture that has moved through time and gradually been shaped into a specific form.

But the Declaration undoubtedly had an accelerative effect on that strand of culture, helping to make it a more general part of the discourse of America. Moreover, it and related discourses of the times—though this might have been part of the accelerative force of the Declaration itself—added a twist to the litany, or, perhaps, combined the form of the litany with another cultural strand, namely, the parallelism around a first-person plural pronoun. Furthermore, that first-person plural pronoun itself was of a peculiarly modern type, one which anyone subscribing to it could see as an expression of themselves, as being under their control—which it is, of course, since those individuals exercise the control of rearticulating it or not, and hence contributing to further circulation or not.

A brief inspection of the English Bill of Rights of 1689 reveals that its complaints section contained no first-person plural pronouns at all. The litany of complaint that, as I am arguing, has come to be an American form is built around an aggrieved first person, an "us" or "our" to whom various bad things have been done, and one, consequently, that makes its articulators feel justified in taking (as well as empowered to take) collective action. The result of this mixture is a particularly gripping discursive form. The litany of complaint, coupled with an aggrieved "we," accelerates the circulation of "we," and that circulation itself constitutes a de facto social entity.

A modern example—just one of many I've collected—concerns an African American "we." I dubbed this particular example from a National Public Radio show that aired on March 31, 1998, on "All Things Considered" at 5:40 P.M. EST, about reactions among African American college students in the United States to then President Clinton's trip to Africa at the time. The tape-recorded words were attributed, in the report, to a nineteen-year-old student named Adonna Smith, who was responding to Clinton's not-quite apology for slavery:

And I would have liked it more if he would have continued that apology, because *we* need to be apologized to.

I mean, *we* went through Hell for like four hundred years.
We went through Hell.
We got killed.
We got tortured.
I mean, it's like racism is like so prevalent here in *our* society still. (italics added)

An important characteristic of this piece of oral discourse is the shift in emotional intensity that occurs as the litany begins—in the second line, right after the "because"—and the intensity diminishes markedly immediately with the last line, once the litany is over. The intonation contours in the middle section are steep, the volume of the voice increases, and there are noticeable changes in tempo as compared with the opening and closing lines. My contention is that the emotional intensity is kindled by the litany of complaint when that complaint concerns wrongs done to a "we." The emotional intensity, in turn, stimulates interest in the discourse, and impels its circulation among those who can identify with that "we."

I am not arguing that this particular example is a direct outgrowth of the Declaration's litany of complaint, but I do think that the prevalence of this discursive form in America is a legacy of the general culture of complaint that goes back to at least 1776. There is something central about the circulation of an aggrieved "we" in the litany form. The discourse is powerful, capable of rallying people around it. Possibly because the limits of circulation of this kind of "we" coincide with the referential value of that "we"—the group that the "we" picks out—the litany of complaint found in the Declaration is a particularly effective device for creating new social entities.

If this example is not a direct outgrowth of the Declaration, other key examples can be found that more clearly grow out of the Declaration, that provide evidence that strands of culture did break out of the Declaration and furnish material for new cultural elements. Some of the obvious examples come from the "Declaration of Causes" that, in 1860 and 1861, explained the reasons for the secession of several southern states from the United States of America. The references back to the Declaration (or to other documents related to the Declaration) are made obvious. Here is the opening of the Declaration:

When in the Course of human events, it becomes necessary for one people to dissolve the political bands which have connected them with another . . . a decent respect to the opinions of mankind requires that they should declare the causes which impel them to the separation.

And here are the analogous sections of the secession documents for Georgia, Mississippi, and South Carolina:

The people of Georgia having dissolved their political connection with the Government of the United States of America, present to their confederates and the world the causes which have led to the separation. (Georgia)

In the momentous step which our State has taken of dissolving its connection with the government of which we so long formed a part, it is but just that we should declare the prominent reasons which have induced our course. (Mississippi)

And now the State of South Carolina having resumed her separate and equal place among nations, deems it due to herself, to the remaining United States of America, and to the nations of the world, that she should declare the immediate causes which have led to this act. (South Carolina)

To be sure, none of these is a word-for-word copy. If the emphasis is on creating something "new," one would not expect such a copy. Where semantic replication is concerned—the pole of "news" I discussed earlier—one would expect the new encoding of the old meaning to be paraphrasal rather then repetitive. At the same time, the wording is, in certain parts, at least, strikingly similar, as shown in Figure 11.

Partly, the carrying over of wording is a way of invoking the authority of the Declaration. The separation from Great Britain had its analog in the separations of the southern states from the union. The replication of wording indicates the similarity without making a focus of the explicit semantic meaning of the text. But the question is: What other discursive elements of the Declaration carry over into the secession documents? In particular, do the secession documents reveal the litany of complaint pattern built around a southern "we" as opposed to a northern "they"?

Of the three secession documents I have studied—the South Carolina, Mississippi, and Georgia declarations—the South Carolina document,

declare	the		causes	which	impel them	to	the separation	United States July 4, 1776
declare	the	immediate	causes	which	have led	to	this act	South Carolina Dec. 24, 1860
declare	the	prominent	reasons	which	have	induced	our course	Mississippi Jan. 9, 1861
present	the		causes	which	have led	to	the separation	Georgia Jan. 29, 1861

Figure 11. Microdiscursive replication of a sentence from the Declaration of Independence in secession documents.

which is also the earliest, makes the most explicit reference to the Dec-
laration of Independence, but it carries over least the rhetorical patterns.
That document, in particular, uses the historical facts surrounding the
U.S. independence, and the principles articulated in the Declaration of
Independence, to make its case.

> A struggle for the right of self-government ensued, which resulted, on the
> 4th of July, 1776, in a Declaration, by the Colonies, "that they are, and of
> right ought to be, FREE AND INDEPENDENT STATES; and that, as free and inde-
> pendent States, they have full power to levy war, conclude peace, contract
> alliances, establish commerce, and to do all other acts and things which in-
> dependent States may of right do."
>
> They further solemnly declared that whenever any "form of government
> becomes destructive of the ends for which it was established, it is the right
> of the people to alter or abolish it, and to institute a new government."
> Deeming the Government of Great Britain to have become destructive of
> these ends, they declared that the Colonies "are absolved from all allegiance
> to the British Crown, and that all political connection between them and
> the State of Great Britain is, and ought to be, totally dissolved."

The document subsequently asserts: "*We* hold that the Government thus
established is subject to the two great principles asserted in the Declaration of Independence." In contrast, the Georgia and Mississippi documents make no direct reference to the Declaration.

At the same time, the South Carolina document shows the least evidence of the litany of complaint style. The following passage is the best
exemplar in the South Carolina document of that style:

> Those [non–slave holding] States have assumed the right of deciding upon
> the propriety of *our* domestic institutions . . .
> *they* have denounced as sinful the institution of slavery;
> *they* have permitted open establishment among *them* of societies,
> whose avowed object is to disturb the peace
> and to eloign the property of the citizens of other States.
> *They* have encouraged and assisted thousands of *our* slaves to leave their
> homes;
> and those who remain, have been incited by emissaries, books and
> pictures to servile insurrection. (italics added)

The emotional intensity is built here by a pattern of repetition analogous
to that in the Declaration, but the pattern is not sustained and the invoca-
tion of a "we" as opposed to a "they" occurs only twice.

Compare this to the Mississippi document, which makes no overt mention of the Declaration of Independence other than through similarities of wording, but which employs a directly analogous litany, each unit beginning with an agentive "It" (which refers to the abolitionist movement) aggressively opposed to an aggrieved first-person plural:

> *It* has invaded a State,
>> and invested with the honors of martyrdom the wretch whose purpose was
>> to apply flames to *our* dwellings,
>> and the weapons of destruction to *our* lives.
> *It* has broken every compact into which *it* has entered for *our* security.
> *It* has given indubitable evidence of its design
>> to ruin *our* agriculture,
>> to prostrate *our* industrial pursuits and
>> to destroy *our* social system.
> *It* knows no relenting or hesitation in its purposes;
> *It* stops not in its march of aggression,
>> and leaves *us* no room to hope for cessation or for pause.
> *It* has recently obtained control of the Government, by the prosecution of its unhallowed schemes,
>> and destroyed the last expectation of living together in friendship and brotherhood. (italics added)

The Georgia document is less pronounced in its deployment of the Declaration's litany of complaint style, but one can see there as well the opposition of a "they" to an "us" or an "our":

> *They* have endeavored to weaken *our* security,
>> to disturb *our* domestic peace and tranquillity,
>> and persistently refused to comply with their express constitutional obligations to *us* in reference to that property,
>> and by the use of their power in the Federal Government have striven to deprive *us* of an equal enjoyment of the common Territories of the Republic. (italics added)

If my analysis is correct, if the Mississippi litany of complaint is a strand of culture contained in the Declaration of Independence that found its way out of that document and into the secession document, what has carried over? On the one hand, what carries over is a matter of discursive form—a pattern of atemporally listing complaints against someone, with each complaint at most a few clauses in length and with the aggressor as grammatical subject and agent; the aggrieved party expressed as a first-person plural pronoun; and the grammatical object an indirect object, object of a prepositional phrase, or possessor of one of those objects. With this kind of description, one could mechanically construct a litany of complaint or program a computer to do so. In this case, what carries over from original to copy is a discourse pattern.

On the other hand, what carries over with this pattern is a feeling—perhaps the inspiration or spirit behind the original. The formal pattern invites listeners or readers to identify with the aggrieved "we," and the list kindles a sense of outrage in those who can identify with that "we." That sense of anger over wrongs that have been done to a collectivity of which one feels oneself to be part is, or so I am arguing, central to the solidification of a collectivity as a socially recognizable entity. If the feeling carries over from the Declaration to the secession documents, it is because that feeling is the basis for accomplishing the social goal that the two texts, as cultural elements, share—separation, and the establishment of a new social grouping.

At the same time, the South Carolina document—the earliest of the secession documents—while carrying some of the feeling of outrage, has that feeling (and, indeed, the litany of complaint as discursive pattern) in only muted form. What seems to have carried over here, in much greater measure, are the ideas contained in the Declaration understood as semantically intelligible discourse. The explicit quotations from the Declaration are part of this self-conscious reflection on that document.

My sample is minuscule—three secession documents in relation to the Declaration—but the pattern is intriguing. The attempt to liberate ideas from an original cultural element results in a new element that refigures those ideas, but loses the emotional force behind the original. Correspondingly, the attempt to liberate the feelings from an original cultural element results in a new element that communicates those feelings, but loses track of the ideas originally associated with them. In both cases, the movement of culture reveals its modern character—the secession documents are all "new" cultural objects, not reproductions of older objects. Is it also a fact of modernity that feelings and ideas cannot move together, but get separated into distinct strands?

Seneca Falls: The Declaration As Traditional Culture?

In contrasting the South Carolina and Mississippi secession documents from the point of view of the modern movement of culture through time, I have suggested that the one carries forward the ideas of the Declaration, the other the discursive form. In this, I have made the two appear to resemble the different phases involved in the circulation of dream narratives in Amerindian Brazil as the narratives migrate from the pole of "news"—where paraphrase is an acceptable method of carrying over the semantic meaning or "news"—to the pole of "myth"—where word-for-word repetition is the method of carrying the myth through time. But I have crucially mischaracterized the secession documents, if I leave it at that.

Most importantly, the South Carolina document does not just work by paraphrase of the Declaration. In the passages I have reproduced above, it quotes the Declaration word for word. This has analogies to the circulation of dream narratives, since a kind of quotation device frames the dream narrative: "Wãñpõ dreamed this" or "this was Wãñpõ's dream," after which a third-person narrative begins. But the quotes from the Declaration are used to make a new argument, unlike the dream narrative. In the latter case, A narrates the dream to B, and the dream is made known to B—and, hence, socially transmitted—via the narrative. The movement of news involves the making known of information to persons who previously did not possess that information. Hence, paraphrase becomes an acceptable way to facilitate that movement through space and time.

In the case of the South Carolina document, however, something very different is going on. In that case, A (the authors of the document) are not making known to B (the readers) some "news," that is, something they did not know before. On the contrary, the assumption is that B is already familiar with the Declaration. The Declaration is not "news" to B. But if A is not communicating the content of the Declaration to B, then in what way is A facilitating the movement over time and space of the semantic content of the Declaration, as I have suggested? The process of movement must be distinct from that of the spread of "news."

The solution to the problem goes back to the central mystery of the movement of culture under a metaculture of modernity. In the case of the South Carolina document, A is not a conduit for the transmission of traditional culture. A (the document's authors) is creating a putatively "new" cultural element. But a new cultural element is never created ex nihilo. Rather, the new element is constructed out of already available materials. The author is a *bricoleur*, in the sense coined by Claude Lévi-Strauss ([1949] 1966), who was, ironically enough, attempting to characterize "savage" or "primitive" thought. My suggestion, however, is that this kind of *bricolage*, where one takes pieces of priorly existing cultural elements, and synthesizes them into a new expression, is actually the hallmark of the movement of culture under modernity. *Bricolage* is a modern form of cultural motion.

Granted that the South Carolina secession document is a new piece of culture, why should it make explicit reference to the Declaration rather than simply paraphrasing it? Quotation does more than carry forth ideas from the Declaration into a new piece of discourse. It is a device, or so I want to argue, for enhancing the circulation of that new discourse. Especially when ideas—such as the idea of secession—are hotly contested, their movement in the world meets resistance from opposing ideas. To get those ideas to circulate more widely, it is necessary to apply accelerative force to them. My claim is that quotation is one way of adding accelerative force to discourse.

One might say that the quotation allows the new document to draw on the circulation of the old document. It says, in effect: "If you liked the Declaration of Independence, you will like what we are saying here." The quote is a device that defines the lineage of a given new stretch of discourse, that tells the reader or listener how to situate that new discourse relative to other discourse. It thus plays a metadiscursive role, positioning the new document with respect to discourse that has come before it.

Here I come back to the image of traces left in the cloud chamber. The quotation, like the citation in a scholarly publication,[9] is an attempt to draw conscious attention to the trace. It does so not by simply proclaiming its connection to the original, but by demonstrating that connection, making it palpable, through the use of words that come from the original. By manifesting a connection to the Declaration, the South Carolina secession document hoped to capitalize on the circulation of that other piece of discourse. The accelerative force is imparted by drawing conscious attention to a linkage with already accepted culture. The force behind the acceleration is the force of consciousness.

In this regard, the movement of culture reflected in direct quotation is distinct from the movement that occurs through the litany of complaint. There, because the same words are not used, a reader or listener is less aware of the temporal trace connecting the secession document to the Declaration. True, the connection is hinted at in the similarity of wording in the sentence I analyzed earlier. But most readers or listeners would be blissfully unaware of the continuity embodied in the litany form itself. What is relevant in the latter case is the effect of the form. The litany of complaint stirs up feelings about a "we" and its aggrievement. The form moves through the world as a true piece of culture, being replicated for what it does. Accelerative force is not supplied to the discourse because of the conscious attention the litany of complaint draws to the Declaration; rather, accelerative force is supplied because of the efficacy of that litany in stirring people up.

However, the operation of the quotation as a device for imparting accelerative force is, so to speak, metacultural. If you can make another see that your argument is really the same as an argument which the other already accepts, then you have hopes that the other will accept your argument.

Of course, if you took this position to its logical extreme, you could never make a truly new argument. If your argument is really just the same as one that came before it, then there is no point in making the "new" argument, since it is not new. The strategy of quotation, taken to its logical extreme, becomes antimodern, and this antimodernism is a form of tradition. In the latter case, one represents oneself as never doing anything new, but merely carrying on venerable traditions. For this reason, one is always telling the "same" myths. But just where does one draw the line?

A fascinating case, in this regard, is Elizabeth Cady Stanton's "Declaration of Sentiments," issued at the woman's rights convention in Seneca Falls, New York, in July of 1848, which subsequently "became the rallying cry for generations of women as they campaigned for their enfranchisement" (Lutz 1971, 343). Because of its historical boundary-marking function as initiating the "woman movement," it is fitting that the Seneca Falls declaration should have been based on the Declaration of Independence of the United States itself.

What is remarkable about the document, however, is that, unlike the South Carolina secession document, the Declaration of Sentiments does not quote from the Declaration of Independence. It rather *is* the Declaration of Independence—it uses the same words as the Declaration—but with key passages changed. The Seneca Falls declaration does not try to define itself as something "new." Rather, it buries its radical newness in something that by then was already old. In this regard, it is an attempt to do something new, but to do that new thing in an old way, that is, traditionally. Here is a side-by-side comparison of the opening paragraphs in each:

DECLARATION OF INDEPENDENCE JULY 1776	DECLARATION OF SENTIMENTS JULY 1848
When in the Course of human events, it becomes necessary for one *people*	When, in the course of human events, it becomes necessary for one *portion of the family of man*
to dissolve the political bands *which have connected them with another,* *and* to assume among the *powers* of the earth, *the separate and equal station*	to assume among the *people* of the earth
	a position different from that *which they have hitherto* *occupied, but one*
to which the Laws of Nature and of Nature's God entitle them, a decent respect to the opinions of mankind requires that they should declare the causes *which* impel them to *the separation.*	to which the laws of nature and of nature's God entitle them, a decent respect to the opinions of mankind requires that they should declare the causes *that* impel them to *such a course.*
We hold these truths to be self-evident, that all men are created equal,	We hold these truths to be self-evident: that all men *and women* are created equal;
that they are endowed by their Creator with certain unalienable Rights, that among these are Life, Liberty, and the pursuit of Happiness. That to secure these rights, Governments are instituted *among Men,* deriving their just powers from the consent of the governed. *That* whenever any Form of Government becomes destructive of these ends, it is the Right of *the People* to *alter or to abolish it,* and to *institute new* Government,	that they are endowed by their Creator with certain inalienable rights that among these are life, liberty and the pursuit of happiness; that to secure these rights governments are instituted, deriving their just powers from the consent of the governed. Whenever any form of government becomes destructive of these ends, it is the right of *those who suffer from it* to *refuse allegiance to it,* and to *insist upon* *the institution of a* government,

laying its foundation on such principles	laying its foundation on such principles,
and organizing its powers in such form,	and organizing its powers in such form,
as to them shall seem most likely	as to them shall seem most likely
to effect their Safety and Happiness.	to effect their safety and happiness.
(italics added)	(italics added)

The similarities between the original and the replica are here not a matter of quotation. The Seneca Falls document does not stand in the same relationship to the Declaration of Indepence that the South Carolina secession document does. What is distinctive here is that the Seneca Falls declaration does not attempt to identity itself, overtly, as something new. Its appeal is through a metaculture of tradition rather than modernity. It says, in effect: "I am just what we have been saying all along." In this regard, it is more like an Amerindian Brazilian myth, which undergoes only small changes in the form of linguistic expression as it is retold, and hence which makes an inertial appeal for circulation—it purports to merely embody something that has already been in circulation. Perhaps this, in part, explains the troubles this document had in its initial reception in newspapers, where an expectation of newness was already firmly rooted.

Another respect in which the Declaration of Sentiments is mythical in character is that it purports to replicate a whole cultural element. Elizabeth Cady Stanton did not take a piece of the Declaration of Independence and fuse it together with other materials from other sources. She took the document as a whole entity and rewrote parts of it—including, note, making changes in grammar and punctuation here and there (e.g., a comma after the initial "when," and a "that" instead of a "which"). These changes are presumably not part of the new assertion of rights that document was meant to proclaim. Rather, they reflect the kind of microtinkering that we find in the retelling of myth. It is true that the document diverges in wording from the Declaration of Independence more and more as one proceeds through the text, and it has a lengthy "resolutions" section which is unlike the performative section of its model. Still, the document—right down to the litany of complaints—is made to look like the Declaration of Independence.

When Is "We" Inappropriate?

Having noted that the Declaration of Sentiments represents itself as a replica, I now draw attention to a crucial difference. The use of the first-person plural is attenuated in the new document. Whereas the Declaration of Independence contains, by my count, forty-seven occurrences of the first-person plural form (eleven "we's," ten "us'es," and twenty-six "our's"), the Declaration of Sentiments—which is actually a *longer* document— contains only eleven occurrences (six "we's," one "us," and four "our's").

Most importantly, in the litany of complaints, where the Declaration of Independence builds a sense of an aggrieved "we" through repeated usage of the first person plural form, the Declaration of Sentiments contains not one single occurrence of the "we" pronoun. As in the Declaration, each complaint clause begins with an agentive "he," though here the "he" is not "the King of Great Britain," but rather "man." Crucially, however, the grammatical object is not "us" or a possessive "our," but rather "her":

> He has never permitted *her* to exercise *her* inalienable right to the elective franchise.
> He has compelled *her* to submit to law in the formation of which *she* had no voice.
> He has withheld from *her* rights which are given to the most ignorant and degraded men, both natives and foreigners.
> Having deprived *her* of this first right as a citizen, the elective franchise, thereby leaving *her* without representation in the halls of legislation, he has oppressed *her* on all sides.
> He has made *her*, if married, in the eye of the law, civilly dead.
> He has taken from *her* all right in property, even to the wages *she* earns. (italics added)

Nancy Cott observes that "nineteenth-century women's consistent usage of the singular *woman* symbolized, in a word, the unity of the female sex. It proposed that all women have one cause, one movement. But to twentieth-century ears the singular generic *woman* sounds awkward, *the woman movement* ungrammatical" (1987, 3). This usage of the term "woman" is certainly consistent with the choice of "she" and "her" in the litany of complaint section. Cott also reminds us of Simone de Beauvoir's assertion, in *The Second Sex*, that "'women do not say 'We,' except at some congresses of feminists or similar formal demonstrations; men say 'women,' and women use the same word in referring to themselves. They do not assume authentically a subjective attitude" (1987, 5).

It is not that the Seneca Falls document makes no use of the first-person plural pronoun. There is the same "we" of reasoning beings in the line "We hold these truths to be self-evident." The majority of first-person forms occur in the paragraph before the resolutions section:

In entering upon the great work before *us, we* anticipate no small amount of misconception, misrepresentation, and ridicule; but *we* shall use every instrumentality within *our* power to effect *our* object. *We* shall employ agents, circulate tracts, petition the state and national legislatures, and endeavor to enlist the pulpit and the press in *our* behalf. *We* hope this Convention will be followed by a series of conventions embracing every part of the country. (italics added)

However, this "we" does not refer to all women, or even to all women in the United States, but rather to the task-oriented "we" of those at the convention and/or those subscribing to the document. Unlike the Declaration of Independence, moreover, those at the convention do not performatively constitute themselves as representatives—as in "We, therefore, the Representatives of the United States of America." The scope of the Seneca Falls "we" would seem to be coextensive with the scope of the newly constituted "woman movement."

How to understand this absence? Here are a few of the complaints with a first-person plural form substituted for the third-person female:

He has never permitted *us* to exercise *our* inalienable right to the
elective franchise.
He has compelled *us* to submit to law in the formation of which
we had no voice.
He has withheld from *us* rights which are given to the most
ignorant and degraded men, both natives and foreigners. (italics added)

Rhetorically, the use of such a "we" appears to be a more effective device— or so the comparative evidence with the Declaration and other documents would tend to suggest—in kindling strong feelings, a sense of outrage, capable of marking a sharp boundary for a social entity. Why was it not used in this document?

This question goes to the heart of the difference between the Seneca Falls document and the Declaration or the secession documents. The social entities they were attempting to create are radically distinct, and, in this sense, the Seneca Falls document does call for radical change. By way of comparison, the task of the secession documents was essentially similar to that of the original Declaration of Independence. Both deal with transformations that resemble mitotic cell reproduction. Daughter cells arise from the alignment of materials internal to a single parent cell, and then those materials pull apart spatially, with the original boundary rupturing and two new boundaries taking its place. The two new cells are functionally independent. Just so did the United States of America emerge from something internal to Great Britain, with a new boundary being formed between them, and just so did the southern states imagine their separation from the Union.

But there is no analogy here to the principle put forth by Elizabeth Cady Stanton. Her idea is not to construct a new social entity, distinct from another entity—as if women and men would become separate socio-political groupings, each self-organizing and independent. Because the attractive forces of difference continued to be seen as the social glue of a single collectivity in which both men and women would participate, with the family as the core institution of social reproduction, the proper biological analogy here is to meiotic cell reproduction, where the process of cell division leads to gametes—spermatozoa or ova—that are mutually dependent on each other for any future reproduction. The Stanton proposal is to change the internal structure of the social organism itself. Hers, in these respects, is thus the more radical proposal.

The question is: Who is to take up her proposal? Is it only women to whom Stanton is appealing? I think the answer is: No. To be successful, the proposal for a change in structure would have to be taken up by men, as well. This means designing a discourse so as to insure its circulation not only among women, but also among men. The pronouns would have to be those that men could take on as their own, as well.

The problem with the rhetorical force of a "we" of women is that it is out of keeping with this kind of circulatory process. "We," so to speak, envisions the boundary within which it is to circulate. Its content, as a referring linguistic sign, is foreseen as the population in which it is to move. Insofar as the specific discursive construction of that "we" matches the extant discourse in the population to which it refers, in that measure it does have a ready-made basis for circulation within that population. But its internal success is inversely correlated with its external success. That is, if the "we" truly picks out an extant pattern of circulation—ventriloquates the voices of that population—then in that measure is it unsuccessful outside those boundaries.

While a first-person plural rendition of the Seneca Falls litany of complaint sounds more rousing, that measure might also defeat its purpose. Since the discourses to which it is designed to give rise would have to have currency among men as well as women, a "we" of women would slow the discourse down, creating resistance to its movement outside its boundaries. Paradoxically, the emotional intensity necessary for movement would undermine movement.

For the discourse to take hold, therefore, a more distanced, seemingly more rational approach would have to be adopted. A "he" versus "she" approach places the reader/listener in the position of judge, outside the point of view of one of the participants in the discourse. Indeed, the image of a discourse designed for inspection by a judge (male or female) is not a bad characterization of the Seneca Falls text. The beginning of the "resolutions" section reads: "Whereas, the great precept of nature is conceded to be that 'man shall pursue his own true and substantial happiness.' Blackstone in his Commentaries remarks that this law of nature, being coeval with mankind and dictated by God himself, is, of course, superior in obligation to any other. . . ." The reference is to the eminent eighteenth-century legal theorist and codifier of the English common law. These passages read like a legal argument before a judge. Perhaps it is not coincidental that Elizabeth Cady Stanton's father was himself a judge on the New York State Supreme Court.

As I remarked earlier, however, it is not that the Declaration of Sentiments lacks a first-person plural pronoun. In the paragraph quoted above, there is a "we," but it is of a specific type. Indeed, all of the "we's" of this document, except that of "We hold these truths to be self-evident," are of the same type. They are "we's" of the movement: the "woman movement." To effect the kinds of changes it seeks to effect, this "we" must look forward in its circulation to a "we" of the United States. This is a "we" of the radical reimagining of the collectivity spawned by the Declaration of Independence, and the circulation of broader discourse patterns out of which it arose.

Obviously, the "we" of the movement must include men as well as women, and hence could not be only a "we" of women. One need only realize that the chair of the Seneca Falls convention was a man—James Mott—and that the demand for women's suffrage put forth by Elizabeth Cady Stanton "was eloquently defended by Frederick Douglass," ardent abolitionist and escaped slave (Lutz 1971, 343). The "we" of the woman movement, unlike the "we" of the Declaration or the various "we's" of secession, had to be a forward-looking "we" imagined as one day articulable by every American, male or female.

Indeed, this is perhaps the essence of any internal movement "we" within a broader "we" that seeks structural change rather than simple secession. While a "we" of women is certainly articulable, when its intended circulation is only through and among women, a "we" that purports to change the role of women without separating women from men altogether must project itself as a possible "we" of the nation. The "we" of an internal movement represents a claim on the "we" of a nation. It looks forward to that date when it can reshape the "we" of the nation.[10]

A Once and Future "We"

The "we" of an internal movement, such as the woman movement, is a peculiar entity—not the "we" of a nation or a would-be nation about to bud. The internal movement "we," as if gazing into a crystal ball, attempts to imagine its own future and foresees, amidst the smoke and haze and however dimly, a time when it will grow and become coextensive with the "we" of a nation or other larger grouping. If all "we's" imagine the audience in which they hope to circulate, the "we" of a movement is a realistic "we," one that imagines its present audience on a modest scale. It is not grandiose, assuming itself already acceptable to a larger population. Yet, at the same time, it does not hunker down in a narrow present, seeing itself as under siege from that larger population. Rather, it is determined and hopeful. The "we" of an internal movement, echoing Nathaniel Ames, says to a future population, "we dream'd of your Times."

Just so does the "we" of the Seneca Falls Declaration set its gaze upon the future. Each occurrence of a first-person plural form in that document—with exception of the initial "We hold these truths to be self-evident"—in some way, typically through association with a grammatical future, looks forward to something on the temporal horizon:

> *we* insist that they have immediate admission . . .
>
> the great work before *us*
>
> *we* anticipate no small amount of misconception . . .
>
> *we* shall use every instrumentality within *our* power to effect *our* object
>
> *We* shall employ agents . . .
>
> and endeavor to enlist the pulpit and the press in *our* behalf
>
> *We* hope this Convention will be followed by . . .
>
> the speedy success of *our* cause depends upon . . . (italics added)

The goal of an internal movement "we" is the acceleration of culture over a longer span of historical time. It is distinct from the litany of complaint "we" in this regard. The litany "we" is interested in securing the circulation of the discourse of which it forms a part, but it does not, at least not intrinsically, shape a trajectory for other discourse in a more remote future. The only outlet for such a "we," taken in and of itself, is thus secession.

The "we" of an internal movement, however, is bound up with a future and with imperatives—with the transformation of the social world. It thus attempts to change and reshape the social world in such a way that a new kind of "we," based on the movement "we," is able to circulate in a larger population. The movement "we" looks forward to its transformation, one day, into a "we" of the United States of America that no longer anticipates "misconception, misrepresentation, and ridicule," but that now takes the transformations to which it is committed as already accomplished, as historical fact.

In the case of the abolitionist movement, the projected future came together with the retrospective "we" in Lincoln's Gettysburg Address—the document itself now as much an American *churinga*, or totem, as the Declaration of Independence; indeed, it forms part of the "Liberty Collection" of my youth. There can be little doubt about the inspiration behind the Gettysburg Address. The document looks back to the Declaration of Independence.[11] Here is prime evidence of how the culture or social learning locked up in the Declaration—the inspiration that motivated the Declaration—was able to find its way out of there and into a new, yet equally inspiring, cultural element. The reference back to the Declaration occurs in the famous opening line:

Four score and seven years ago *our* fathers brought forth on this continent a new nation, conceived in liberty and dedicated to the proposition that all men are created equal. (italics added)

In the widely memorized and recited opening line of the Gettysburg Address, Lincoln refers back to 1776, the date of the Declaration, but he also appropriates the specific words of the Declaration: "that all men are created equal." This is significant because the idea encapsulated in those words was already in circulation prior to July 1776 in both Europe and in the United States. Maier (1997, 166 and elsewhere) points to the June 1776 draft of the Virginia Declaration of Rights drawn up by George Mason on which Jefferson drew. That document contained the line "that all men are born equally free and independent." Important as the Mason wording may have been for various state bills of rights in the late eighteenth century (Maier 1997, 165), it was not that line, but rather the Declaration's, that Lincoln picked up. The Declaration reshaped extant culture and extant discourse, but it did so in such a way as to produce a new cultural element that had inspirational force. It is that inspirational force that reemerges in the Gettysburg Address.

Jefferson's words here, however, are not simply repeated; they are taken and placed in a new context, such that the resultant cultural element appears as a wholly new entity. Readers of the Gettysburg Address hardly notice that Lincoln's words were also Jefferson's words. For Jefferson, "that all men are created equal" was a "self-evident" truth. For Lincoln, by contrast, it was a historical proposition on which "our fathers" founded a nation.

What is especially intriguing is the change that the first-person plural pronoun undergoes in the Gettysburg document. The phrase "our fathers" means, evidently, "the fathers of the United States of America"; hence, the "our" is meant to encompass the United States as a social entity. In this sense, it carries over one meaning—the referential meaning—from the Declaration. But what I find fascinating is that the "our," as part of a discourse pattern within the text—as a trace within the cloud chamber—is actually a new "our" that only appears to be identical with the "our" of the Declaration's litany of complaint section. The latter is defined by its opposition to a "He" of "the King of Great Britain," and later, to a "they" of "the British." But who is the "they" or "he" or "it" to which the address's "our" stands in opposition?

The initial "our" hints at an answer: "[O]ur fathers brought forth on this continent. . . ." The "our" is backward looking. But the hint is only subsequently developed. The next sentence adds clarity to the trace: "Now we are engaged in a great civil war." If the first sentence looks back to the founding of the United States, with "our fathers" suggesting possession by a present-day collectivity of a past, the second sentence focuses on that present-day "we"—those "engaged in a great civil war." In the third sentence, the scope of the "we" narrows: "We are met on a great battlefield of that war." This "we" refers—does it not?—to the present listening audience. Witness the following sentence: "We have come to dedicate a portion of that field as a final resting-place for those who here gave their lives that that nation might live."

Now it is true that, because of the linear unfolding of the text, the initial "we" of the present-day United States of America lingers on, in ghostlike fashion, through a kind of metaphor, in this narrow "we." But what is significant also, from the point of view of a discourse trace, is that this "we" comes to be contrasted with a "they," namely, "those who here gave their lives." The initially only hinted-at present-day "we" becomes clarified, as it moves through the text, as a present-day "we" set against a backdrop of those who have died. The contrast becomes even sharper as the text proceeds: "[W]e cannot dedicate, we cannot consecrate, we cannot hallow this ground." While "ground" becomes, again through metaphorical extension, the land occupied by the United States, the "we" attempting to consecrate, dedicate, and hallow it is a "we" of the living occupants of that American soil as opposed to the "they" who died on that soil.

What defines the positive quality of the Gettysburg "we" is the special relationship the people it names have to those who have died—their cultural, if not also biological, ancestors. Lincoln makes the opposition apparent in the second-to-last sentence: "It is for *us* the living," he writes, "rather to be dedicated here to the unfinished work which they who fought here have thus far so nobly advanced"—"us the living," that is, the present generation of Americans.

There is a melancholic quality to the chant-like deployment of the first-person pronoun in this text—and, to be sure, the pronoun is prominent, occurring fifteen times in this short document. The "we" looks back on the strewn bodies of the dead, not only at Gettysburg, but across the battlefields of the Civil War. Metaphorically, it also looks back on the aging face of America, no longer flush with youth.

At the same time, this melancholic, backward-looking "us" or "we" here begins to turn, however sluggishly, toward a future, a metamorphosis that the final sentence—in which the "we" of an abolitionist movement has fused with a "we" of the nation—brings to completion: "It is rather for *us* to be here dedicated to the great task remaining before *us*"—the "us" here becoming aligned with a future, with crystal gazing—"that from these honored dead *we* take increased devotion to that cause for which they gave the last full measure of devotion"—the "we" resembling the movement "we" of Elizabeth Cady Stanton—"that *we* here highly resolve that these dead shall not have died in vain, that this nation under God shall have a new birth of freedom, and that government of the people, by the people, for the people shall not perish from the earth." The "we" that initially looked back on a once here turns to confront a future and to shape that future. It is, truly, a once and future "we."

Over broader historical time, the Gettysburg "we" continues the "we" of the Declaration of Independence. Both have, in some sense, the same referential scope, picking out a people of the United States of America. Here is the mysterious movement of culture revealed in the microscopic matter of pronominal shapes maintaining a referential value. But at the same time, we see here the modern character of that movement. The replicated "we" has a distinct discursive shape; it is the same "we" referentially, but it is distinct discursively. The Declaration's "we" was opposed to an aggressor. But there is no aggressor in the Gettysburg "we," only an opposition to a "they" who have come before "us." This is a "we" of the living who now have a history because of those who are now dead. The dead are backdrop to that "we" in the way that α is backdrop to ω.

How different this is from Adonna Smith's projection of an African

American "we" across time: "I mean *we* went through Hell for like four hundred years." Paraphrased into the discourse of Gettysburg, this might read: "I mean, *they* went through Hell for like four hundred years, so that *we* might live." Why the Gettysburg's presentistic "we" poised between a past and a future?

Strangely, this "we," the living, was familiar to me; indeed, in an ethnography I wrote about a Brazilian Indian community (Urban 1996b, 28–65), those very words formed the title of one chapter. A "we" of the living was the principal form of the first-person plural in currency in that community. Why was it there?[12] The answer is to be found in circulation. Because of the thoroughgoing factionalization of everyday life, no particular individual could formulate a political past for the community. Because political actions are justified by stories about the past, as in the litany of complaint, any explicit statement defining who "we" are in terms of a past would be contested. Contentiousness bred a caution in discourse. To have a story about the past accepted by others, the more distant third-person form had to be used. The ancestors were always a "they." The proximity of a "we" to the utterer would lead to its rejection by those who considered themselves opposed to the utterer. The only "we" that could be widely circulated was a "we" of the living.

Just so do I think that the "we" of the Gettysburg address functioned—and continues to function. It asserts a "we" of succession or continuity as a basis for a collectivity. If we cannot agree on anything else, can we not agree that we are the descendants of people who called themselves "we"?

But if the Gettysburg "we" represents a minimal assertion of collectivity—expressible primarily, if not exclusively, through metaphor—it also represented the merging of a "we" of the abolitionist movement with a "we" of the nation. In this sense, it was the inheritor not just of the Declaration's "we," but also of a smaller, yet ambitious "we" that realized its projected future at Gettysburg. The movement "we" was forward-looking, seeking through its own replication to accelerate American culture across historical time. Foreseeing in the crystal ball an end to slavery, it found a voice at Gettysburg that could elevate it from a referentially modest but ambitious "we" to a "we" coterminous with "the people of the United States of America."

Whither the "We"?

What is transportable about nationalism, as it emerged in the United States? If anything, it is the form of semiotic self-representation of the nation—as a "we" expressing the "voice" of a "people."[13] Jefferson's words were passed on to others who signed their name to them as if those words were, in some sense, created by each of those individuals. The prior history of the words is erased by the act of signing or affirming or rearticulating. The characteristic of the modern form of "we" is its appropriation by individuals as their own creation, their own personal expression, despite the fact that it, and the words traveling together with it, have come from elsewhere. The individual articulators of the "we" represent themselves as in control of it, as its creators.

This distinctly modern characteristic of "we" derives from a metacultural focus on "newness." The words coming out of the mouth of the utterer or off the pen of the writer are a personal expression of the utterer or writer, despite the fact that the words may have been already in circulation, part of the flow of culture across time. Metaculture zeroes in on the control articulators have over words rather than the control words have over articulators. From the point of view of tradition, words are merely passing through the utterer. From the point of view of modernity, the utterer is producing those words as if they were unique and individual expressions. The voice of the people is the additive sum of n number of expressions—identical to one another as they may be—articulated by n distinct "I's." "Hell no, we won't go!" = "Hell no, $I_1 + I_2, + \ldots + I_n$ won't go."

From the point of view of the nation as a transportable concept, this modern "we" is a cultural element in circulation. It can be taken up by a ruling elite for their own local purposes, and it can pass from one elite to the next. However, this does not mean that the "we" instantaneously spreads throughout a population whose leaders have adopted it. The leaders of a population may be merely representing the "we" of their articulations as an inclusive collection of "I's," without the rest of the population assimilating that "we." The appearance is given, thereby, that the population over which the rulers rule is really a collection of consenting "I's," each articulating the "we," when in fact the "we" is the product of those elites, and under their control.

Yet at the same time, there is a telos to the modern first-person plural form. Representing utterances as if they emanated from a collection of "I's" leads to nonelite claims to participation in the "we." This is particularly clear in the American case, which began with a "we" represented as modern—as the expression of all those to whom it referred—even though it was, in fact, the property of a ruling elite. The "we" became a collective expression to which others could lay claim. The historical movement of "we" has been democratizing, as new articulators come to see themselves as controllers of it on a par with its initial articulators. That is the pattern of spread that I have endeavored to explicate here. The process continues to churn in the United States, where it has perhaps gone furthest, but it is at work also elsewhere.

Where will the movement of "we" lead over historical time? One can imagine a wearing thin of the metaculture of newness, with its spread slowed by recognition of tradition, of the movement of culture through individuals rather than, or in addition to, its creation by individuals. There is some evidence of this in the rise of postmodernism as a metacultural ideology.[14] Further evidence might be sought in patterns of "I" usage in literature and other expressive genres as well as in the usage of the plural pronoun itself. But assuming that the modern "we"—the voice of a people—continues to spread, what kinds of social entities are likely to emerge from it? Three kinds of circulatory processes seem to me to be relevant to that question.

One process grows directly out of the discourse of aggrievement that spawned the American "we" in the first place. The litany of complaint is a powerful discursive form whose circulation is insured by the discontents into which it taps. This circulation gives rise to secessionist impulses. The United States of America, obviously, is itself—at least, in part—a product of these impulses. And the secessionist processes continued in the United States after the revolution, leading to the Civil War. Nor have they disappeared, as witnessed by the "Republic of Texas" and other contemporary secessionist movements.

If culture is a form of motion that results from social learning and social transmission, discontent can be harnessed to set culture in motion. The secessionist "we" is a prime example. Utterances of discontent are replicated because of the feelings into which they tap. But correspondingly, secession limits the movement of culture—at least of the "we" that is at its heart. It circumscribes a smaller population than the "we" from which it came. This narrowing of circulatory scope runs counter to another circulatory process, namely, the tendency for culture to spread ever further, unless it is checked by forces opposing it.

A consequence of this process is that other new "we's" tend to be spawned that create larger imagined groupings, larger bases of circulation. I refer back, in this regard, to the global "we's" of the human species that have popped up, achieving greater frequency in discourse during the 1980s around the antinuclear and ecology movements.[15] These tend to be based not directly on the litany of complaint, but on a closely related pattern—the discourse of danger, danger that a "we" might be destroyed by some "it" or "they." The feeling provoked is that "we" must be protected; it is in harm's way. Here is an example of the discourse of endangerment, one of many, from Jonathan Schell:

> Now *we* are sitting at the breakfast table drinking *our* coffee . . .
>> but in a moment *we* may be inside a fireball whose temperature
>> is tens of thousands of degrees.
> Now *we* are on our way to work, walking through the city streets,
>> but in a moment *we* may be standing on an empty plain under a darkened
>> sky looking for the charred remains of *our* children.
> Now *we* are alive,
>> but in a moment *we* may be dead.
> Now there is human life on earth,
>> but in a moment it may be gone. (1982, 182; italics added)

The poetics of this passage are obvious—a "Now_____, but in a moment_____" pattern is repeated, and the pattern is used to build up a sense of endangerment for a "we" of the human species. As in the case of the Declaration of Independence, by making that "we" palpable as physical form (the actual pronoun) that is repeated, *The Fate of the Earth* contributes to the reader's sense that the human species is something real, that it is a meaningful social entity. Readers come to see themselves as articulators of these words.

National "we's" represent an equilibrium formation between these two opposed tendencies. Indeed, in some measure left-right politics in the contemporary United States arrays asymmetrically around "we" usage, with a "we, the people of United States" defining the very broad center, secessionist "we's" appearing with greater frequency on the right, and global "we's" on the left.

These two opposed tendencies of movement find themselves up against a third process—the tendency of culture (in this case, of a referentially-defined "we") to stay in motion, over historical time, not just through inertia, but by inspiring people to actively perpetuate it in the face of possible dissipation. While secessionist movements continue to this day, and while global "we's" continue to spring up, the "we, the people" that emerged with independence has endured as a referential entity. It has endured in the United States, in part, because of its relationship to internal movement "we's"—the "we's" of the future of cultural motion. The "we" of the United States took on at Gettysburg a once and future quality—it could look back on a past history of circulation of that pronominal form, but also peer into a hazy future at its possible reconfiguration, its mergers with other future-oriented movement "we's."

From this point of view, it is interesting to look at the international communist movement, which spawned its own global "we's" of the "workers of the world"—witness the Internationale, the communist hymn inspired by the Paris Commune of 1871:

> So comrades, come rally
> And the last fight let *us* face
> The Internationale unites the human race. (italics added)

In the *Communist Manifesto*, by Karl Marx and Frederick Engels, however, there is not a single first-person plural pronoun in the original 1848 edition that circumscribes "the workers of the world." By my count, there are in that work thirty-eight first person plural forms ("we's" = twenty-one; "our's" = nine; "us'es" = eight). Most of them (perhaps twenty-two, with allowance for ambiguity) are of the author-plus-reader type that one would expect of a scholarly publication. The remainder are of the "we communists" type, with two being something more like "we of the new communist society about to be born." These are internal movement "we's," analogous to the "we's" of the Seneca Falls declaration and that of the abolitionist movement. No wonder that when Communist revolutions did occur, the "we's" looked forward to merger with other "we's" of particular nations.[16]

The "we" of the modern nation is peculiarly tenacious, indeed, not just because, once established, it tends to inspire its own loyalties, its own perpetuation. The latter is true of culture more generally. Perhaps, more importantly, national "we's," because of their relationship to internal movement "we's," are forward-looking, as in the Gettysburg Address. While a glance backwards produces melancholy, a nostalgia for a past that has slipped away from "us," the "we" of a nation also peers forward in time, envisioning its own new, even more dazzling future—its city upon a hill. It draws on images of things to come, grand things. This is part of the continuing social life of the Declaration of Independence and of the cultural learning that inspired it. On the steps of the Lincoln Memorial in Washington, D.C., on August 23, 1963, in what was still another inspiring redeployment of the original linguistic material, Martin Luther King said: "I have a dream that one day this nation will rise up and live out the true meaning of its creed: 'We hold these truths to be self-evident: that all men are created equal.'"

4

This Is Ridiculous

Quintessential Metaculture

From an early twentieth-century logical positivist perspective, the imperative was an ugly duckling. It was measured against the yardstick of pure representation, uncontaminated by the observer's paradox, unproblematized by the motion of language—as part of culture—through the world. And it was found to be . . . well, odd. It didn't look like the other ducklings that made the custodians of language so proud.[1] Consequently, it languished.

It later found something of a place in ordinary language philosophy, thanks to John Austin's (1962) distinction between "constative" and "performative" utterances—that is, between saying something and doing an action by means of words. The best exemplars of performatives are those of the explicit variety, such as "I now pronounce you man and wife," where the utterance of the sentence under the right conditions is world-making or world-transforming. As a result of such utterances, new social relationships are created; people and things are moved from one category to another. Imperatives could be construed as a kind of doing. But doing with words appeared as a sort of magical process. How do imperatives or other sorts of utterances accomplish their doing? By what secret do they work? The imperative is recognized as "not a duckling." But what kind of creature is it?

The imperative[2] is not truth-functional in any direct way. It does not passively reflect a world that is already out there, a world preformed and existing independently of the words through which it is described. If it did so, its orientation would be to the past. But, instead, it peers into the future, envisioning a possible world or state of affairs not yet in existence. "Get that pig out of here!"—the utterance foresees a time in which that pig is "out of here." Moreover, as in ordinary language accounts, the utterance contributes to the bringing about of that time. It helps to make the world conform to its own representation of it, as when the sculptor, Pygmalion, foresees the image of a beautiful woman in a block of marble and then chisels her image into existence.

But how does the imperative accomplish this task? My answer: via the transmission of culture. The imperative is a conduit for the movement of culture between people. But it is a conduit of a special sort. Through it, a strange transformation or transubstantiation takes place. Meaning becomes thing-in-the-world. The semantic content of the utterance gives rise to a world that looks like that semantic content. To find out how imperatives accomplish their world-making task, how transubstantiation takes place, we have to ask how and why culture flows through them.

In the ordinary flow of culture under a metaculture of tradition, A produces a_1, a physical thing—an utterance or a gesture or a ceramic pot. Movement occurs when B imitates A, producing a_2, another physical thing that sounds or looks or feels like a_1. The motion of culture occurs through replication.

With imperatives, the movement that takes place is dramatically different. The utterance produced by A has a meaning—let's call that meaning ALPHA (or, if it is regarded as something decidedly new, then OMEGA). B produces a copy of what A has already produced. However, it is a copy of a peculiar sort. B does not produce another utterance whose meaning is ALPHA (or OMEGA). That is, B does not utter: "Get that pig out of here!" Rather, B carries out a set of actions that results in a state of affairs—the pig is out of here—whose characteristics match those described by ALPHA (or OMEGA). The acts or states are a's (or w's). And the movement of culture takes place by the conversion of ALPHA (or OMEGA) into α (or ω).

Because of this conversion or transubstantiation—in which word becomes flesh—it is difficult to see the acts performed by B, or their results, as culture. However, they are precisely that. They are something that has been socially transmitted from A to B, even though B has not imitated A's behavior, but rather has carried out actions described and prescribed by the meaning of A's behavior. Imperatives are, therefore, conduits for the transmission of culture, but they are conduits of a special sort, in which movement takes place via transubstantiation, the conversion of meaning into thing-in-the-world.

If imperatives are conduits for the transmission of culture, they are also—albeit in perhaps not so obvious a way—about culture. The thing that results from the imperative—the acts performed by B and the results of those acts—is culture because it has been socially transmitted, as I have just argued. But the thing that results from the imperative is also the thing described by the imperative, the future world foreseen within it. Since the imperative is about that future world, and that future world is cultural, the imperative is about culture.

With this we come, finally, to recognize this creature in our midst for what it is. The imperative is metaculture. Indeed, it is a kind of archetypal, quintessential metaculture. Imperatives do not just describe culture, they also shape it and the world, more generally. And they shape it after their own image.

Newness: An Essential Ingredient of Imperatives?

If movement takes place via transubstantiation (meaning into thing) in the case of imperatives, then in some measure imperatives are responsible for a kind of newness, at least insofar as meaning and acts (or their effects) are distinct kinds of things. Imperatives make possible the precipitation of tangible things out of vaporous meanings. Hence they are, at least in some measure, accelerative. But the matter is not so straightforward, and, in fact, the extent to which imperatives do precipitate something new (OMEGA → ω) needs to be empirically investigated. Can transubstantiated motion be explained by replication and the force of inertia?

In fact, it is possible to imagine imperatives with little or no effect on the world, as when you order someone to do something they would automatically do anyway, for example, if you order a living, normally functioning human being to breathe. A doctor might issue such a command during a checkup in order to more precisely regulate breathing process. Or a parent might issue the command to breathe to a child holding its breath in order to get it to start breathing again. In each case, there is some detectable measure of acceleration. However, if you are standing on a street corner and issuing the command to random passersby, their apparent compliance may have nothing to do with the command you issued. For any traditional cultural object, the accelerative role of imperatives must be carefully investigated. It may be negligible. The role of imperatives diminishes to zero when the cultural object would have been produced in precisely the same way at precisely the same time without them.

It is vastly more difficult to imagine imperatives capable of creating a radically new cultural object, one never before experienced. Perhaps the Pharaonic order to produce the first Egyptian pyramid some 4,700 years ago was of this sort. Perhaps President Franklin Roosevelt's 1939 order authorizing an attempt to develop an atom bomb, which led, eventually, to detonation of the first nuclear weapon in Alamogordo, New Mexico, on July 16, 1945, was of this sort. However, the situation in each case was undoubtedly more complex. The idea of building an atom bomb had been circulating previously; it was not Roosevelt who came up with it. No doubt the idea for grand pyramids had been present earlier in Egypt. However, pharaonic and presidential orders undoubtedly initiated or unleashed the social activities that led to the construction of the first pyramids and the building of the first atom bomb. The results in each case are that something new appeared in the world.

Yet pure newness is difficult to imagine. Perhaps that difficulty is what so regularly prompts people to fantasize a primal period before something came into existence—as in origin myths that posit a time when there was no death, imagining how death might have come to be; or a time when there was no corn and no game, imagining how corn and game might have first appeared; or a time when there was no fire, imagining how fire might have come to humans. The very difficulty in contemplating pure newness suggests that some or even much of the apparent work of imperatives can be explained by tradition and inertia. Just how new is the thing produced by an imperative?

Transubstantiation vs. Replication

In addition to asking how new the thing produced by an imperative is, we have to ask also whether that thing is actually a result of transubstantiation? Granted that A is able to get B to do something B might not otherwise have done, is what B does a result of the meaning communicated by A in the imperative? Or might B be picking up on something else about A? This is the "do as I say, not as I do" issue. Is B doing what he or she is doing because of what A says? Or is it also linked to what A does?

In the limiting case of tradition, A may already be doing what the imperative orders B to do. Hence, it is possible to argue that the transmission of culture is occurring via B's replication of A's conduct. This is ordinary replication, for which the utterance of the imperative may be superfluous.

Again, you and I will have to look at how much of apparent transubstan-tiation is actually replication. Only in that way can we gauge how much ac-celerative force imperatives impart to the flow of culture over time and space in any given instance.

Imperatives in the Service of Tradition: An Example

Examples can be found—indeed, they abound in many Amerindian com-munities in Brazil and adjacent countries—in which imperatives are so much a part of inertial culture that it is difficult to see what newness their issuance produces or even to be sure that transubstantiation has taken place. In a brief segment of a film by Timothy Asch and Napoleon Chagnon called *The Feast* (1970), shot in the Yanomamö village of Patanowä-teri on March 3, 1968, we see a Yanomamö man squatting on his haunches, wield-ing a machete in his right hand, scraping and cleaning the ground around him (Figure 12a). He gesticulates and calls out in a language we infer to be Yanomamö. The line is repeated, the English translation on the screen (Figure 12b) appearing as:

All of you there. Come help clean the plaza.

In an earlier explication of this segment, the narrator tells us that, though the man we see on the screen is a headman, and "sponsor of the feast," he "cannot order people to work. He leads by example both in cleaning the village and in providing the largest share of the food."

What is going on in this situation? By our inference, the headman's im-ploring is successful, and we imagine others coming to clean the plaza. From the point of view of the flow of culture over time, the act of plaza cleaning itself is a traditional behavior—socially learned and socially passed on. Presumably, all adults in the village are familiar with it, and adult men have probably engaged in it on numerous prior occasions. If the headman is A and another villager who heeds the command is B, it is ap-parent that A and B, through their behavior, are carrying on extant tradi-tions. The acts they perform are traditional acts, not new ones. This is far removed from the extreme of pure newness. What we see here is not new-ness, but the perpetuation of oldness.

What about transubstantiation—the "do as I say, not as I do" issue? In the ideal case of transubstantiation, B does not imitate A's utterance of words, which would constitute replication. Instead, B engages in the ac-tivity described by A's words. B realizes the future-oriented meaning that A has articulated. In the Yanomamö example, transubstantiation takes

Figure 12a. Yanomamö headman squatting on his haunches, wielding a machete in his right hand, scrapes and cleans the ground around him, the very actions he is about to order others to do. From *The Feast*, by Timothy Asch and Napoleon Chagnon (1970).

Figure 12b. Yanomamö headman, continuing to work, issues a call to his fellows: "Come help clean the plaza." The command adds an accelerative force to the movement of culture that would otherwise take place only through inertial replication and be subject to the vagaries attendant upon that motion. From *The Feast*, by Timothy Asch and Napoleon Chagnon (1970).

place if B does not go around saying: "All of you there. Come help clean the plaza." Instead, B cleans the plaza, his actions conforming to the semantic description contained in the imperative. Meaning is converted into action. The semantically understandable utterance gets enacted as conduct characterizable by that semantic meaning—for example, by the sentence "He is cleaning the plaza." In the ideal of transubstantiation, something that is abstract (a meaning) gets converted into something concrete (a behavior). The word takes shape in the world as the thing described by it.

Yet the Yanomamö example diverges from the ideal case: B's production of behavior is not exclusively—or need not be exclusively interpreted as—a response to the semantic content of A's utterance. Instead, B may be, in part or in whole, copying A's behavior, doing what A does, which just happens to correspond to what A says. Doing what A does is a classic case of replication, where transubstantiation is arguably of minimal significance. Since the acts performed by A and B alike—cleaning the plaza—are traditional, the Yanomamö example reveals imperatives maximally in the service of tradition.

At the same time, it would be incorrect to conclude that no acceleration takes place, that the imperatives, even here, are fully explicable in terms of inertia. For without the imperatives, B might construe A's cleaning of the plaza as an idiosyncratic act. B could rationalize A's conduct in any one of a number of ways, even imagining it to be A's job alone to clean the plaza. However, the imperative makes it absolutely clear that A expects or wants B to engage in similar behavior—to help out. The imperative brings to consciousness A's expectation that B will activate the cultural patterns he has already acquired. The imperative summons B's behavior by drawing B's consciousness to A's desire: "Come help clean the plaza." Therefore, A's words—the imperatives A utters—arguably have accelerative effect. They activate the passage of culture through B at a precise moment. They therefore impart an incremental force to a culture that is already there, but that might not otherwise take shape in the world at that exact time. A's words act as a catalyst to precipitate those actions in the world by their ability to focus those actions in consciousness.

The efficacy of A's utterance is aided by his status as headman. But that status itself appears, from Chagnon's descriptions, to be, in considerable measure, a result of past leadership effectiveness. Take the following example:

... a group of men from Patanowä-teri arrived [in Upper Bisaasi-teri] to explore with Kãobawä [the Upper Bisaasi-teri headman] the possibility of peace between their two villages. They were brothers-in-law to him and were fairly certain that he would protect them from the village hotheads. One of the ambitious men in Kãobawä's group saw in this an opportunity to enhance his prestige and made plans to murder the three visitors. This man, Hontonawä, was a very cunning, treacherous fellow and quite jealous of Kãobawä's position as headman. He wanted to be their village leader and privately told me to address him as the headman. (Chagnon [1968] 1992, 134)

According to Chagnon, Hontonawä wanted to be addressed as if he were the headman—hoping, apparently, to achieve the status by having people call him by the title. However, and critically, he also attempted, as the story unfolds, to orchestrate a murder that would have undermined Kãobawä's current leadership. His issuance of imperatives in the latter case would precipitate actions designed to demonstrate his own leadership and the incompetence of Kãobawä. So past evidence of having imperatives obeyed is one basis for expecting that future imperatives will be obeyed. There is a key element of traditionality here. The position of headman is part of an inertial culture, but one that can and must be incrementally accelerated by each successful instance of current leadership.

Centralized Authority: A Way to Maintain Tradition?

Judging from the Yanomamö example, tradition itself requires acceleration. Inertia alone is not sufficient to carry cultural elements indefinitely into the future. Forces of various sorts—forgetting, competition from other cultural elements, physical quirks of persons or the environment, and more—are at work to dissipate tradition. This is especially true in oral transmission—the basis for the movement of myths through space and time. The forces of dissipation must be counteracted, if culture is to continue on its journey. In the Yanomamö example, it is apparent that the imperative issued by the headman is part of an attempt to carry on a tradition, where that tradition—cleaning the plaza in preparation for the feast—might otherwise dissipate. The imperative supplies an incremental force that counteracts the dissipative forces at work on traditional culture.

If imperatives help to maintain tradition, is their centralization in the hands of a single leader also crucial to the maintenance of tradition? The Yanomamö example is instructive in this regard. One person—the headman—takes responsibility for encouraging others to, in effect, carry on the tradition. Here timing and collective coordination are crucial. But this should not obscure a crucial fact: The headman is using imperatives to maintain a common culture, and hence to counteract the tendency of different familial lines of culture to diverge and, potentially, come into conflict with one another.

The broader implication is that the headman's traditional authority is deployed to effect the lateral uniformity of culture. It is not effecting an increase in the lateral spread of culture, unlike the four great mechanisms discussed in chapter 2: marriage, conquest, conversion, and trade. Rather, it serves to prevent the diminution of lateral spread—its contraction, so to speak—as diverse familial lines go about their own business, one common culture thereby diverging into so many distinct lines.

Centralized authority benefits traditional culture in a specific way. The transubstantiation it effects, or purports to effect, imparts an accelerative force to an existing culture that is spatially distributed; that force synchronizes and coordinates the flow of culture within a population.

For Thomas Hobbes, whose view carried over into Parsonian sociology, the monarch was essential to maintaining peace, to putting an end to the war of all against all. By giving up a right of self-regulation, by vesting authority in a central absolute power, individuals in a collectivity acquired for themselves a different kind of right: the right to peace throughout their land. From the perspective of cultural motion, the Hobbes-Parsons view is peculiarly modern, inasmuch as it is based upon the notion of individual control or self-regulation. At the same time, it is not entirely wrong. If a war of conquest is a way to bring about the lateral spread of culture, its consolidation in a central authority is a way to maintain that culture across a population, against its tendency to fray into so many distinct lines.

This suggests why culture—as self-perpetuating force—might have an interest in central authority. The gradual change over time of cultural objects, as they undergo replication, can be kept in check and coordinated by the application of accelerative force through imperatives. Having a single central leader is one way, perhaps even the best way, to do this, since the divergent strands of culture that arise, and that potentially come into conflict, can be reconciled in their passage through a single individual.

We have an idea of how culture—at least, traditional culture—benefits from imperatives and centralized authority, yet we still do not have a picture of why the imperative ought to be obeyed by individuals, if it really does effect some measure of newness through transubstantiation. Much of the efficacy of imperatives can be accounted for by inertia. Culture flows through both A and B thanks to existential and habitual inertia. People carry on traditions simply because they are there to be carried on, as with "mother tongues." And they also reproduce patterns because of habituation when new objects appear, as in the phenomenon of accent when trying to speak another language. The authority figure, A, is only apparently efficacious, since A's imperatives instruct B to do what B would be doing anyway by virtue of inertia.

That cannot, however, be the whole story. If A's authority is important for culture, it is not because A gets B to do what B would have done anyway—as in the command: "Breathe!" It is because A gets B to do something that is not quite what B would have done, anyway. There is some novelty here, some transubstantiation. B has to be deflected or nudged, in however small a degree, from a course of action that B otherwise would have pursued.

Why does B participate in this deflection process? What force impels culture to pass through transubstantiation rather than through ordinary replication? In asking such questions, I am assuming that transubstantiation necessarily involves a kind of resistance, and that the resistance must be overcome. I have already argued that resistance—in the form of entropic deceleration—is at work as well on the motion of culture through replication. But I am suggesting that the resistance to motion through transubstantiation is greater than the resistance in replication, per se.

If B copies A, if B is simply doing what B sees or hears or feels A is doing, the only forces at work—other than inertia—are those that deform or refigure cultural elements in the course of replication. Yet, when an imperative is issued, the assumption is that in bringing A's expectations to B's conscious attention, A is doing so because B would otherwise, for whatever reason, not conform to those expectations. A perceives some added resistance on B's part. That added resistance may not be great; indeed, if I am correct, in the case of successful leadership, rarely is great. Nevertheless, it is added resistance, and A attempts to overcome it by drawing B's conscious attention to A's expectation. The question then is: Why does B comply? I think there is an answer to this question, and that answer is to be found in the narrativization of conduct, as well as in a metaculture of tradition.

Imperatives Are a Part of Circulating Culture

I have been talking about imperatives as metaculture, but they are also, of course, part of culture. Notably in the case of traditional culture, they form part of myths. What is especially intriguing is that myths, although a part of culture that moves through processes of replication, are themselves about newness, about the transformation of the world. They explain how the world came to be as it is today. We are dealing here with monumental, life-altering changes that, once effected, leave the world in a new equilibrium. The myths, therefore, are explicitly about what I have been calling acceleration, simultaneously as they themselves—as cultural elements—confront the problem of their own perpetuation or dissipation.

Correspondingly, or so I want to argue, the accelerative function of imperatives is construed in myths as stabilizing or restorative. The imperatives help to harness a world in flux, to produce a new equilibrium that in some important respects resembles the older equilibrium that the changes disrupted. The imperatives are, therefore, at the service of the maintenance of tradition.[3] This is acceleration, but acceleration designed to overcome the dissipative forces at work on inertial culture.

A corollary of this is that imperatives are to be obeyed—with obeyance being evidence that the original command was understood, and hence that meaning and culture have passed between the individuals in question. I say "corollary" because, were the imperatives to be represented as deliberately disobeyed, then their accelerative force in effecting the transmission of traditional culture would be compromised. If one can't expect imperatives to be obeyed, one can't expect culture to move—at least not through transubstantiation. Therefore, to facilitate the oral transmission of traditional culture, it is crucial that imperatives be represented as something to be complied with and that noncompliance be represented as the result of misunderstanding as opposed to defiance. Furthermore, the noncompliance must be the source of negative rather than positive consequences.

I will later show that the opposite is true in the case of dissemination under a metaculture of newness. There movement through space and time is rendered easier, thanks to mass dissemination, but the replication of culture is rendered harder, since replication requires the production of new cultural forms—new films or videos or books or CDs—not simply the watching or reading or listening to older cultural forms. In that case, imperatives are questioned rather than simply obeyed. Because individuals are represented as in control of their actions, control by others becomes problematic. Attempts at control are to be responded to rather than complied with.

In many Amerindian traditions, obeyance is simply taken as a matter of course. There is no question of compliance or noncompliance. This can be seen in the case of the first of the imperatives in the myth fragment I quote below. But where the question of compliance is raised within the narratives, the noncompliance is represented as negligence rather than disobedience. It is the result of a failure to fully understand the imperative in all of its details, a failure to grasp the significance of those details. The person commanded endeavors to do as he or she is told, but for whatever reason bungles the task. The result of the bungling is change. Because the imperatives are restorative, when they are not faithfully followed, irreversible change takes place.

Let's look now at a fragment of a Cherokee Indian myth. This fragment—a self-contained episode in its own right—is one part of the longer myth: "Kana'ti and Selu: The Origin of Game and Corn," as rendered in James Mooney's *Myths of the Cherokee* (1900, 242–49).

> Every day when Selu got ready to cook the dinner she would go out to the storehouse with a basket and bring it back full of corn and beans. The boys [her two sons—the Wild Boy and his younger brother] had never been inside the storehouse, so wondered where all the corn and beans could come from, as the house was not a very large one; so as soon as Selu went out of the door the Wild Boy said to his brother, "Let's go and see what she does." They ran around and climbed up at the back of the storehouse and pulled out a piece of clay from between the logs, so that they could look in. There they saw Selu standing in the middle of the room with the basket in front of her on the floor. Leaning over the basket, she rubbed her stomach—*so*—and the basket was half full of corn. Then she rubbed under her armpits—*so*—and the basket was full to the top with beans. The boys looked at each other and said, "This will never do; our mother is a witch. If we eat any of that it will poison us. We must kill her."
>
> When the boys came back into the house, she knew their thoughts before they spoke. "So you are going to kill me?" said Selu. "Yes," said the boys, "you are a witch." "Well," said their mother, "when you have killed me, clear a large piece of ground in front of the house and drag my body seven times around the circle. Then drag me seven times over the ground inside the circle, and stay up all night and watch, and in the morning you will have plenty of corn." The boys killed her with their clubs, and cut off her head and put it up on the roof of the house with her face turned to the west, and told her to look for her husband. Then they set to work to clear the ground in front of the house, but instead of clearing the whole piece they cleared only seven little spots. This is why corn now grows only in a few places instead of over the whole world. They dragged the body of Selu around the circle, and wherever her blood fell on the ground the corn sprang up. But instead of dragging her body seven times across the ground they dragged it over only twice, which is the reason the Indians still work

their crop but twice. The two brothers sat up and watched their corn all night, and in the morning it was full grown and ripe.

A first point: The imperatives, in which the mother tells her sons what to do, conform to the ideal of newness and transubstantiation discussed earlier: A (the mother) orders B (the children) to do something that she will not herself do. The situation thus differs from that in the Yanomamö example, where the headman "orders" others to do what he himself is already doing. In this narrative, B's behavior is characterizable (more or less) by the semantic description contained in A's words. A conversion thus takes place—at least as it is represented in the narrative. The meaning of A's words takes shape in the form of the behavior performed by B.

Since this is a narrative, it is crucial that the "behaviors" of B are actually, and obviously, descriptions of the behaviors encoded in words. The "conversion," in this case, is thus between quoted speech and framing speech.[4] If you compare the Cherokee myth fragment above with the Yanomamö case discussed earlier, you see that the narrative takes the place of the ethnographer/observer's description of the nonlinguistic event in which the imperative is embedded. Here is an excerpt of that description again:

> [W]e see a Yanomamö man squatting on his haunches, wielding a machete in his right hand, scraping and cleaning the ground around him (Figure 12a). He gesticulates and calls out in a language we infer to be Yanomamö. The line is repeated, the English translation on the screen (Figure 12b) appearing as:
> All of you there. Come help clean the plaza.

In this case, I—an external observer of the film—have quoted the translated imperative, described the behaviors on screen, and made some inferences from these observations. In the myth, the narrator plays the same role.

The interconversion process between meaning and behavior is thus analogous to the relationship between quoted speech and quoting speech. And, indeed, one hypothesis about the cultural organization of conduct I have advanced, and advance again here, is that people act so as to have their behavior be narrativized or narrativizable (by themselves or others) in certain ways. Those ways correspond to the available circulating narratives in the community of which the individual is part.

A second point about the Cherokee example: The behavior expected of B by A is *new*. The behavior is not part of a culturally acquired pattern already available to B. Hence, the imperatives issued by A affect the inertial flow of culture. They are accelerative, in this sense. The kind of culture produced by them that flows from A to B is a new culture. Its shape is different from that of the inertial culture out of which they grew. The imperatives participate in a process of change.

At the same time, what is intriguing is that the "newness"—the planting of corn, in this case—is an attempt to carry on an older pattern. The narrator is at pains to tell us that the boys had always had corn when growing up: "[they] wondered where all the corn and beans could come from." The mother's act, when the boys decide to kill her, is far from a retributive one. She wants the boys to continue to have corn, as they always have. And so she instructs them how to make it from her dead body. From the point of view of the inertial flow of culture over time, therefore, while effecting something new, the imperative is also (and simultaneously) endeavoring to restore something old. It is working at the behest of tradition, attempting to preserve it as it moves over time in the face of tumultuous and irreversible changes.

A third point: According to the narrative, the boys do not willfully resist their mother. Instead, they attempt to carry out her commands. This is shown in the linguistic parallelism. Parts of the imperative are matched by parts of the behavior that is subsequently described. However, they fail to carry out what is really a complex set of commands in all of their detail. From the point of view of the transmission of culture, therefore, the conversion of A's initial command into B's behavior is described as improperly executed. B fails to precisely reproduce the behavior that A is transmitting to B through the semantic meaning of her words. Cultural transmission is only partially successful here. Moreover, the failed part of transmission leads to a consequence, and that consequence is negative for B, who has to work harder or get less corn. There is an admonition here: Had B replicated A's semantic meaning in his behavior, life would be better for B. Alas, transmission is difficult. Reproduction of the semantically coded material in actual behavior involves inaccuracies of transmission.

In the following schematization of the relevant portions of this narrative, you will observe the elegant structure, which, I submit, is part of what makes this myth aesthetically interesting and hence keeps it circulating. Imperatives 1 and 3 involve mistakes, from which negative consequences follow, while imperatives 2 and 4 involve simple compliance, from which positive consequences follow:

Imperative 1: "[W]hen you have killed me, clear a large piece of ground in front of the house.

Behavior 1: The boys killed her with their clubs. . . . Then they set to work to clear the ground in front of the house.

Mistake: [B]ut instead of clearing the whole piece they cleared only seven little spots.

Bad consequence: This is why corn now grows only in a few places instead of over the whole world.

Imperative 2: "[D]rag my body seven times around the circle."

Behavior: They dragged the body of Selu around the circle.

Good consequence: [W]herever her blood fell on the ground the corn sprang up.

Imperative 3: "Then drag me seven times over the ground inside the circle."

Behavior: [T]hey dragged it over.

Mistake: [O]nly twice.

Bad consequence: which is the reason the Indians still work their crop but twice.

Imperative 4: "[S]tay up all night and watch."

Behavior: The two brothers sat up and watched their corn all night.

Good consequence: [I]n the morning it was full grown and ripe.

Transubstantiation Appears As Replication When It Is Narrativized

If we ratchet up our microscope one notch further, zooming in on these fragments of discourse, an interesting pattern emerges. The transubstantiation referred to earlier—that is, the conversion of the meaning of an imperative into a behavior in the world—reappears here as the replication of microstrings of discourse. Figure 13 highlights this for Imperative 1 above. In this figure, the upper line contains the actual words from the imperative. The bottom line consists of the words from the description of the behavior that followed from the imperative. I have drawn boxes around the

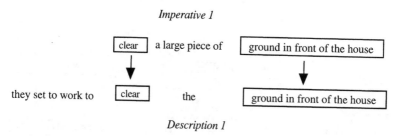

Imperative 1

Description 1

Figure 13. One example of transubstantiation as replication.

words that are physically replicated between the command utterance and the description of the resultant behavior, and drawn arrows to trace the replication process.

What is interesting is that the description of the behavior, as a collection of words, appears as at least a partial replication of the imperative, as a collection of words. The mystery of transubstantiation, wherein meanings transmitted through language take shape as objects in the world—behaviors or sequences of behaviors—is thus resolved at the level of narrative, where transubstantiation appears as discourse replication. This discourse replication involves the simultaneous reproduction of meaning and material form. Moreover, the reproduction is itself an actual instance of the movement of culture over time, however microscopic that movement may be. Because the narrative unfolds in time, whether reading time or spoken time, the subsequent stretch of discourse occurs after the initial imperative. At the microlevels of discourse, therefore, the problem of commands in relation to the movement of culture is resolved as the micro-replication of discourse fragments.

Lest this one example appear as anomalous, I have also diagrammed two others, which I give in Figures 14 and 15. Taken together, these examples make clear that imperatives, in the case of the Amerindian myths I have

Imperative 2:

| drag | my | body | seven times | around the circle |

| they | dragged | the | body | of Selu | around the circle |

Description 2:

Figure 14. Another example of transubstantiation as replication.

Imperative 4

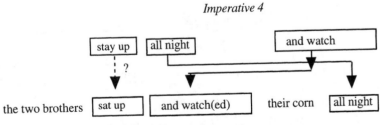

| the two brothers | sat up | and watch(ed) | their corn | all night |

Figure 15. Complexities in transubstantiation as replication.

been studying, are akin in their efficacy to the retelling of myths. Material replication is taking place, but that replication involves the relationship between linguistic materials inside of quotes and those outside of them.

I want now, however, to call your attention to a different fact: The replication here is only partial. We see evidence of change, as well. The wording of the imperative is distinct from the wording of the description. Part of the difference is a matter of linguistic design. In the case of imperatives, replication crosses the line between metadiscourse and discourse (or reporting speech and reported speech). This kind of crossing introduces regular changes (see Lee 1997, and also the papers in Lucy 1993). For example, "my body," a phrase in the first person, becomes "the body of Selu," a third-person phrase; "watch," a verb in the present tense, becomes "watched," a verb in the past; and so forth. Systematic projections transform the reported imperative into the described action.

But there is more to change than systematic projection. There is also, first of all, random alteration, part of the entropic forces of the universe at work on culture as it moves through the world. A possible example is in Figure 15—the transformation of "stay up" into "sit up." In a more perfect replication, we would expect either "stay up" or "sit up" to occur in both the imperative and the description. Instead, we find one in the former, the other in the latter. Someone who did not know the significance of the internal replication—such as an anthropologist recording or translating the myth, or even a Cherokee youth learning it—might easily introduce a random change of this sort.[5] Such random alterations constitute errors in the replication process across tellings, and they reshape the myth over time. But they are simultaneously errors within a single telling, affecting the relationship between imperatives and descriptions. Copying errors of this sort—assuming this is, indeed, a copying error—must be counteracted by accelerative force if the cultural element is to conserve its shape over time.

In addition to random alteration, there is also change that holds significance for the plot. Aesthetic tension and interest build around such change, where the fulfillment of the original command is shown to be incomplete. Such a change occurs in Figure 13, where the phrase "a large piece of" is dropped from the description of the behavior. We learn that this change has profound significance. The boys made a mistake. Instead of clearing a "single large piece of" ground, they cleared "only seven little spots." The change is of aesthetic interest because the audience, like the character, could not have readily foreseen its significance. The audience overlooks it just as the character does. How could the boys have known that clearing "only seven little spots" would produce the consequence that "corn now grows only in a few places instead of over the whole world"? The lesson to be learned here is that one must pay careful attention to the command, carrying it out in all of its details and as precisely as possible, even if one does not know its significance. The slightest deviation could have monumental consequences.

What, finally, is this pattern of inept or inexact compliance all about? My contention is that, as a piece of traditional Cherokee culture, the pattern focuses attention on the need for carefully listening to and following commands. The myth, in effect, argues for imperatives as a force that can be used to counteract the dissipation of inertial culture.

Intriguingly, in the case of the "Origin of Game and Corn" myth, the pattern may have accomplished its goal. The evidence suggests that, for a considerable portion of the nineteenth century, at least, the myth was successfully transmitted across the generations. Witness Mooney's claim that the "story was obtained in nearly the same form from Swimmer and John Ax (east) and from Wafford (west)" (1900, 431), the Eastern and Western Cherokee having been separated since the removal in 1838, and Mooney's field research having taken place between 1887 and 1890.[6]

The myth, while dealing with cosmological problems of change and continuity in its overt plot line, and while focusing on the difficulties of replication within its microaesthetic detail, of course had its own problems of historical reproduction. The forces of random change that gnaw away at culture more generally gnaw away at this myth, as well. The myth's success in propagating itself may have been due in part to its microdesign features, which reinforce its overt topic. The microfeatures focus conscious attention on the need for precise copying, and, in doing so, they supply an accelerative force to the copying of the whole myth itself over time, hence impelling its physical circulation in the world. They act like a lens, concentrating different spectral lines on a single point—the need for precise replication. In doing so, they help to bring about that replication and they help to propel the myth through time.

At the same time, myths form a model for the narrativization of one's own behavior. How do you know how to respond to a command? The answer is, in part, that you know how to respond through your knowledge (i.e., your narratively derived knowledge) of how others generally respond. You fit the original command and your response into your own narrative. And what better model for your own narrative than those with which you are already familiar—narratives that are out there, in the world, part of circulating culture. Curiously, therefore, insofar as myths insure their own circulation, they help to shape responses to imperatives. And insofar as their

own circulation is insured by emphasizing the precise obeying of imperatives, in that measure they serve to make compliance expectable—that is,
to guide the transubstantiated motion of culture through imperatives.

Imperatives Are Also Objects of Metaculture

I have described imperatives as quintessential metaculture and also, as
themselves, parts of circulating culture. I now want to complete the loop
by looking at them as the objects of metaculture—in particular, as things
that appear differently under metacultures of oldness and newness. There
is a direct analogy to the first person pronouns discussed in the preceding
chapter here. Just as "I" and "we" receive different interpretation and hence
are deployed differently, under metacultures of tradition and modernity
so, too, do imperatives receive different interpretations and get deployed
differently in these two cases.

Under tradition, the imperative is thought of not as the direct expression of the individual utterer, nor as a manifestation of his or her "will," but
rather as a traditional object moving through its articulator on its journey
through the world. An imperative is something that controls its articulator
and the person who is its intended recipient, just as the mythical "I," or the
"I" of trance, controls its narrator, rather than the other way around. Thus,
one reason for complying with an imperative is that the imperative is not
closely bound up with control by one individual (A) over another (B), but
rather with the control exercised over both of them (A and B) by tradition,
by culture.

In this regard, how appropriate that the mythologization of imperatives shows them to be inscrutable. The character who receives a command does not know its full significance. How could the Cherokee boys
have known the true meaning of "clear a large piece of ground in front of
the house"? How could they have foreseen that, had they cleared one
single large piece of ground, corn would grow everywhere, not just in a
few places? The inscrutability of the command is the inscrutability of the
force that moves through them, through us, exercising its influence over
them and us. It is the inscrutability of culture. Curiously, you or I—as ones
listening to the myth or reading it—could not know the full meaning of
the imperatives the first time around. Our discovery of their significance
occurs only once we have heard or read the myth. We could foresee the
portentous significance the next time around only because the myth—
and, therefore, any imperative it contains—by then had become traditional culture.

Looked at through the lens of newness, however, imperatives appear as under the control of their articulators. They are expressions of the articulator's "will," to use the Weberian terminology. They are not part of a culture in motion that controls both articulator and addressee. For this reason, imperatives become problematic for the motion of culture under a metaculture of newness. If they are expressions of the articulator's will, and if they are simultaneously conduits from the movement of that will through the world, from A to B, then obeying commands means subordinating oneself to the will of an other. Moreover, it means replicating—through transubstantiation—something that is not one's own expression. What is B to do when confronted with A's command?

If the idea of newness is that B should not simply copy A, but should instead come up with a new cultural object that is his or her own expression, it follows that the recipient of a command ought not to follow the command in some knee-jerk fashion, but should instead respond to it, producing a new cultural object that takes A's original expression as a backdrop. My argument is that this is in fact what we find in the narrativization of commands in the contemporary Euro-American analogs to myths—films and novels.

Resisting Commands Is Appropriate to a Metaculture of Newness

Examples of the response or "resistance" pattern in contemporary films and novels abound. I'll pick one for closer inspection here: the children's movie *Babe*. The storyline centers around a pig named Babe, who, early in life, is orphaned and sold to a farmer named Arthur Hoggett—his human master. Babe is befriended by Fly, a female sheepdog whose children are being taken away from her to be sold. Fly becomes a mother figure for Babe, who refers to her as "Mom." Hoggett, the farmer, gets the idea that the pig can play the role of sheepdog, and so, in the excerpt below, orders Babe to round up the sheep, seeing whether the pig can handle the task. The pig does, and is eventually entered in the sheepdog competition. He not only wins, but gets the highest marks ever recorded. Babe thus becomes a historic or world-transforming figure. Here is the transcript of the excerpt:

1 FARMER HOGGETT: *Get 'em up, pig!*
2 FLY (the sheepdog mother): He wants you to drive them out of the yard.
3 FARMER HOGGETT: *Away to me, pig!*

4 FLY: Remember, you have to dominate them. Do that, and they'll do anything you want. *Go! Go!*

[The pig runs out to the sheep.]

5 BABE: Woof, ruff, ruff, ruff (with baaas in the background). . . . Woof, ruff, . . . , ruff, ruff, ruff, woof (laughter in background, continuous) ruff, ruff, ruff, woof [Laughter.]

[The pig returns to the sheepdog.]

6 BABE: This is ridiculous, mom.

7 FLY: Nonsense. It's only your first try. But you're treating them like equals. They're sheep. They're inferior.

8 BABE: Oh, no, they're not!

9 FLY: Of course they are. We are their masters, Babe. Let them doubt it for a second, and they'll walk all over you.

10 REX (the sheepdog father): *Fly! Get that pig out of there.*

11 FLY: *Make them feel inferior!*

12   *Abuse them!*

13   *Insult them!*

14 REX: Fly!

15 BABE: They'll laugh at me.

16 FLY: *Then bite them!*

17   *Be ruthless!*

18   *Whatever it takes, bend them to your will!*

19 REX: Enough!

20 FLY: *Go on! Go!*

[The pig goes back out to the sheep.]

21 BABE: *Move along there ya, ya . . . uh . . . big buttheads!*

22 SHEEP: [Laughter.]

[The pig bites one of the sheep on the leg.]

23 FEMALE SHEEP: *Young one, stop this nonsense!* What's got into you all of a sudden? I just got finished tellin' what a nice young pig you been.

24 BABE: Ma, I was just trying to be a sheepdog.

25 FEMALE SHEEP: Huh! Enough wolves in the world already, without a nice lad like you turnin' nasty. Ya haven't got it in ya, young'un.

27 REX: You and I are descended from the great sheepdogs. We carry the bloodline of an ancient bahu. We stand for something. And today I watched in shame as all that was betrayed.

28 FLY: Rex, dear. He's just a little pig.

29 REX: All the greater the insult!

31 BABE: I'm sorry I bit you. Are you all right?

32 FEMALE SHEEP: Well, I wouldn't call that a bite, myself. You got teeth in that floppy mouth of yours, or just gums?

33 BABE AND SHEEP: [Laughter.]

34 FEMALE SHEEP: Ya see, ladies—a heart of gold.

35 CHORUS OF SHEEP: A heart of gold.

36 FEMALE SHEEP: No need for all this wolf nonsense, young'un. All a nice little pig like you need do is ask.

37 BABE: Thanks very much. It was very kind of you.

38 FEMALE SHEEP: A pleasure.

39 ANOTHER SHEEP: What a nice little pig!

41 FLY: All right, how did you do it?

42 BABE: I asked them and they did it. I just asked them nicely.

43 FLY: Now, we don't ask sheep, dear; we tell them what to do.

44 BABE: But I did, mom. They were really friendly. Maybe Rex might, ya know, be a little more friendly if I had a talk with him.

45 FLY: No, no, no. I think you better leave that to me.

This little excerpt is complicated from the point of view of its commands. We have the human master issuing commands to the pig (lines 1 and 3), the mother sheepdog commanding the pig (lines 4, 11–13, 16–18, 20), the father sheepdog commanding the mother sheepdog (line 10), the pig commanding the sheep (line 21), and the sheep issuing a command back to the pig (line 23).

There are interesting parallels to the "Origin of Corn and Game" myth. Both focus on an adopted child—the Wild Boy, in the Cherokee myth, and the orphaned pig in the case of *Babe*. In each, the mother-child relation figures centrally. Moreover, in each there are key transformations in the nature of social relationships.

However, there is a salient difference as regards replication. Whereas the boys in the Cherokee myth follow their mother's commands without any explicitly narrativized evidence of resistance, the pig exhibits conflict over the imperatives issued by the mother. It is not that the pig does not attempt to fulfill the commands. He does. In what is a turning point of this episode, the mother tells the pig: "Abuse them! Insult them!" And the pig later says to the sheep: "Move along there ya, ya ... uh ... big buttheads!" The mother tells the pig: "Bite them!" And we later see the pig biting a sheep on the leg.

Yet there is something importantly different here. The pig's obeyance is reluctant and conflicted, and that reluctance is narrativized. After Babe's initial attempt to comply with his mother's command, he tells her (Figures 16a and 16b): "This is ridiculous, mom," calling her authority into question.

Figure 16a. After she has ordered him to round up the sheep, the little pig (Babe) says to his surrogate mother (the sheepdog, Fly): "This is ridiculous, Mom." He responds to Fly's command in typically modern fashion rather than replicating it in his own behavior. From *Babe* (Universal Pictures, 1995).

Figure 16b. The surrogate mother, Fly, engages Babe in further discussion to get him to do what she (and, in turn, the master) wants: "Nonsense," she says. "It's only your first try." From *Babe* (Universal Pictures, 1995).

She reasserts the correctness of her position, saying: "Nonsense. It's only your first try. But you're treating them like equals. They're sheep. They're inferior." The pig argues back, in dialogic fashion: "Oh, no, they're not!" This kind of back-and-forth argument is completely absent from the myth, where commands are executed matter-of-factly, even if the execution is bungled.

A good example of this difference—which produces an entirely distinct feel to the narrative—can be found in two different tellings of the story of Abraham from the Old Testament (Genesis 22). The first is from the King James Bible:

1 And it came to pass after these things, that God did tempt Abraham, and said unto him, Abraham: and he said, Behold, [here] I [am].

2 And he said, Take now thy son, thine only [son] Isaac, whom thou lovest, and get thee into the land of Moriah; and offer him there for a burnt offering upon one of the mountains which I will tell thee of.

3 And Abraham rose up early in the morning, and saddled his ass, and took two of his young men with him, and Isaac his son, and clave the wood for the burnt offering, and rose up, and went unto the place of which God had told him.

Here Abraham complies unhesitatingly with God's command. Compare this with Bob Dylan's version of this passage in the song "Highway 61 Revisited":

Oh, God said to Abraham, "Kill me a son."
Abe says, "Man, you must be puttin' me on!"
God say, "No." Abe say, "What?"
God say, "You can do what you want Abe, but
the next time you see me comin', you better run."
Well Abe says, "Where do you want this killin' done?"
God says, "Out on Highway 61."

What to make of this difference? I want to argue that the resistance, apparent in both Babe, in "Highway 61 Revisited" and in numerous other contemporary cultural expressions in which imperatives become the aesthetic focus of narration, has to do with the transmission of culture. However, this is a distinctive version of the transmission of culture—one associated with modernity and with the mass mediation of culture through print, magnetic recordings, television, and similar vectors of culture. The resistance exhibited here is really a manifestation of how cultural replication works in the contemporary United States and, perhaps increasingly, elsewhere.

This may seem paradoxical. On the surface, resistance to commands would appear to be resistance to the transmission of culture, if my earlier observations about the Cherokee myth are correct. In that case, I argued that the myth contained an implicit moral: You should follow the semantic content of commands as precisely as possible; if you do, good consequences will follow; if you do not, the results will be negative. If there were an analogous moral in the case of *Babe*, it would be: If you do what you know inside of you to be right rather than just listening to others, then good consequences will follow. Finding the right inside of oneself is a hallmark of the "modern" individual. Correspondingly, blindly obeying the commands of others is anathema. Hence, Dylan's Abe strikes a contemporary listener as more real than the biblical Abraham. He acts the way a modern individual would and should—with horror at the thought of sacrificing his own son. Initially, at least, he resists God's command.

The problem is: How can this finding of right inside of oneself be cultural transmission? It seems the opposite of transmission. The idea of an internal moral compass is opposed to the idea of commands that come from without. You cannot blindly obey the commands of others, but rather must carefully weigh them and decide what is right. Your conduct is determined by your decision, not by the imperatives issued by another. Babe resists his mother, Fly. Fly resists her husband, Rex. The sheep resist Babe. Where is the cultural transmission in this?

A first observation is that Babe, while resisting the details of Fly's command, in fact endeavors to do what Fly and Hoggett, the human master, want: He gets the sheep to file in orderly fashion out of the yard. Moreover, in the long run, Babe effectively exerts more control over the sheep than Fly or Rex had. Indeed, as the story approaches its climax, we learn that Hoggett has entered Babe in the sheepdog competition, and we later see how, through cooperation, Babe not only wins the sheepdog contest, but receives the only perfect score in the history of the competition. Babe—a little pig—becomes, in effect, the best "sheepdog" that ever lived.

On the one hand, Babe resists the culture that Fly endeavors to transmit to him. On the other hand, he grasps the purpose or objective of that culture and comes up with a better way of achieving the end. Babe is thus a reshaper or accelerator of culture. It is not that Babe, as an individual, does something that falls outside the orbit of culture in some kind of naturalistic realm. What he does is take an existing piece of culture and refashion it into something new, something better. Culture flows through him, but it is shaped by him in the course of that flow.

Babe works not only with the culture that was transmitted to him by his mother, Fly. He also works with the culture that has been passed down among the sheep and which he has acquired by virtue of his friendship with one of the sheep, Ma. This is the one who, in line 23, tells him: "[S]top this nonsense! What's got into you all of a sudden? I just got finished tellin' what a nice young pig you been." Babe explains (line 24) that he was trying to acquire the culture of the sheepdogs: "Ma, I was just trying to be a sheep-dog." Ma—apparently a second mother figure for Babe—then attempts to summon the culture of the sheep that Babe has gotten, presumably, from her: "Huh! Enough wolves in the world already, without a nice lad like you turnin' nasty. Ya haven't got it in ya, young'un."

Babe's achievement, therefore, depends upon the synthesis of two different lines of culture, two different ways of doing things in the world: the culture of the sheepdog, and the culture of the sheep themselves. As if to drive home this point, we later see that Babe's success at the sheepdog competition depends on something he acquires from the sheep—a secret password. The sheep at the competition are not the same ones that Babe has been dealing with on the farm. Consequently, they act indifferently to him, despite his attempts to be friendly. Initially, at least, they pay attention only to Fly. Realizing the problem, Fly sends Rex back to the farm to learn the password from the sheep there. Rex then tells it to Babe, who uses it to get the sheep to comply with his commands—which are stated as requests rather than overt imperatives. Hence, Babe acquires a specific piece of sheep culture that makes his sheepdog-like control possible. The secret of his success is his fusing of distinct strands of culture. The fusion results in the acceleration or change of the culture itself. The result is a new and improved culture—a better system of control.

Of course, it is true also that the sheepdog culture and the sheep culture are both deflected from their normal course when they are transmitted to Babe, who synthesizes them. And it is not Babe who is solely responsible for this deflection. The farmer Hoggett, Babe's human master, is the one who originally gets the idea that Babe might be able to perform the work of a sheepdog. He says to Babe (line 1): "Get 'em up, pig!" But the deflection would not be possible, either, without Fly's encouragement. She translates the initial command to Babe, and encourages him to carry it out. This deflection is one of the key precipitating factors behind the synthesis. Nor would the synthesis be possible without the firm assertion of sheep culture that Ma issues. While Babe is a conduit for these two strands of culture, both deflected from their normal course, and while the synthesis takes place through him, one can hardly say that his distinctive "achievement" is the result of characteristics that he uniquely possesses as an individual. The power that Babe ultimately wields is a power that results from the flow of different strands of culture through him—indeed, it is the power of those strands as they came into conflict in specific social situations. The power, in this sense, emanates from the movement of culture, and is nothing other than the movement of distinct strands of that culture that come into conflict and then, as a result of that conflict, fuse into a new kind of culture. To make this claim baldly: Modernity is the celebration of such fusions.

Resistance Can Occur in Oral Narrative

In the previous section, I suggested that the resistance pattern may be linked to a "modern" idea of cultural transmission in which the ideal is not precise replication of a prior element (such as a myth), taken as a unit of culture, but rather the synthesis of distinct strands resulting from the challenging of prior elements or the attempt to produce elements that are "better." I have linked this to the phenomenon of mass mediation, where durable physical materials—books, videos, CDs—make it possible for discourse to be disseminated without necessarily being replicated. This is fundamentally unlike oral transmission, where dissemination—getting the message out—depends upon replication. In order for other people to get exposure to a myth, the myth must be retold, recreated—in short, replicated. In order for other people to get exposure to a video, however, it is not necessary for one to redo the entire video. On the other hand, for the social learning that went into the making of that video to be passed on—that is, replicated—dissemination is not sufficient. The test of replication of a video is the production of a "new" video. This pattern of cultural movement—based on the production of something putatively "new"—is analogous to the pattern of resistance in narrative, where the straightforward replication of the imperative is called into question in the description.

One question this raises: Is the resistance pattern a direct function of the channel of transmission—oral versus electronic, for example? As evidence, I present the narrativization of an actual incident that involved me and one of my mentors, Ray Fogelson. I began sharing this narrative with others almost immediately after the event it describes occurred, somewhere back in the late 1970s. I have told the story orally to generations of graduate students, who perhaps now carry it on—though this is something I have not documented. I finally wrote up the narrative in 1996, in preparation for an American Anthropological Association meeting. It is thus not unsullied by mass media, since I did commit it to writing, but this version was meant to be heard, and is as close to the previous oral versions as I could make it. Here is the narrative:

> I was a graduate student at the University of Chicago, just back from the field, looking for a job, and giving my first talk at a professional meeting. I had the good fortune to have Ray Fogelson as my adviser, and he actually let me stay in his hotel room so that I wouldn't have to pay for a hotel room.
>
> Well, Ray was at that time a party animal—I'm not sure, of course, that there was ever a time when he wasn't a party animal. In any case, he was out until about 4:00 or 4:30 A.M., and I had to deliver my paper at an 8:00 A.M. session. So I got up at 6:30 A.M., showered, and was about to walk out the door when I heard this voice say: *"Read me your paper!"*
>
> I said, *"Shhh, Ray—go back to sleep."* But he insisted: *"Read me your paper!"* I thought, "This is ridiculous." But he was my professor, after all. So I got my paper out of my briefcase, turned on the light, and started to read. Then I heard this voice from the bed say: "That's terrible."
>
> Ray switched on the light by his bed, put on his glasses, picked up a newspaper, and started to read the first thing he saw. "This is what you sound like," and he read in a boring monotone: "Apples are fifty cents, but oranges are forty cents. Now here's what it should sound like: APPles are FIFTY cents, BUT, ORANGes are FORTY cents."
>
> Well, I started in on my paper again, and Ray said, "That's a little better." Before you know it, he was snoring, but when I tried to sneak out, he said: *"Finish it!"* And I did. And my paper went infinitely better as a result.

I don't know how many times I've told this story. However, it was a "new story." As such, it was not the retelling of an ancient tradition.

The pattern of resistance is patent: "I heard this voice say: 'Read me your paper!'" This could be Dylan: "Oh, God said to Abraham, 'Kill me a son.'" Indeed, my response: "Shhh, Ray—go back to sleep!" parallels Abe's: "Man, you must be puttin' me on." Ray persists—as, note, did Fly after Babe's initial resistance. He reiterates his command, in response to which I think, but don't say: "This is ridiculous." These are the same words actually spoken by Babe, who, however, appended a kinship address term: "This is ridiculous, mom."

My point is not that this narrative instantiates the film *Babe*, or even the vignette from "Highway 61 Revisited." It is that the pattern of resistance found in these mass-mediated narratives also occurs in what was an oral narrative. Of course, it is an oral narrative spun out in a community saturated with mass-mediated narratives, and such narratives may have been the originals from which my specific production was copied—that is, from which the resistance pattern was copied. But the point is that the relationship between medium and rhetorical pattern is not direct and simple. We are dealing with a cultural pattern, or metacultural pattern—resistance to commands—that is compatible with mass-mediated cultural replication and its attendant idea of "modernity," but not a simple reflex of those media themselves.

Resistance to Commands May Be "Rational"

In his paradigm-fixing account of legitimate domination or authority, Max Weber distinguished three bases on which persons might be granted authority by others: the charisma of the commander, tradition, and rationality. The pattern of inept compliance, discussed earlier, obviously correlates, in some measure, with Weber's traditional grounds: "an established belief in the sanctity of immemorial traditions and the legitimacy of those exercising authority under them" ([1925] 1968, 215). But the connection between the resistance pattern and Weber's rational grounds ("a belief in the legality of enacted rules and the right of those elevated to authority under such rules to issue commands") is not obvious. Indeed, a microdiscursive account of resistance suggests a different way of thinking about the relationship between rationality and command.

An important point to note in regard to the aesthetically foregrounded resistance pattern is that resistance does not equal rejection of the command. Indeed, in each of the examples discussed in this chapter, the addressee of the imperative attempts to carry out the command. This is obviously true of the boys in the Cherokee myth, but it is also true of Babe, who, indeed, succeeds in complying with farmer Hoggett's initial command beyond Hoggett's wildest dreams. It is even true of Dylan's rendition of the story of Abraham, and also of the Fogelson story. These are stories about complying with commands. Resistance may involve rejecting a command, but this is not its essence: It is only a possible consequence of its nature.

From a microdiscursive point of view, resistance is manifested first and foremost by a questioning of the initial command. The questioning can be overtly stated in the narrative by the person commanded, or it can be revealed to the audience by the narrator. When Fly, the mother sheepdog, says to Babe: "Remember, you have to dominate them. Do that, and they'll do anything you want. Go! Go!", Babe, after his initial failed effort, says: "This is ridiculous, Mom." When Dylan's God says to Abraham: "Kill me a son," Abraham responds: "Man, you must be puttin' me on!" When Ray Fogelson says to me: "Read me your paper!", I respond: "Shhh, Ray—go back to sleep!" and I think (thereby revealing to my audience): "This is ridiculous."

What is happening here is that the imperative, rather than being simply replicated in the description of the subsequent action, is *responded* to. The response pattern makes compliance something other than a knee-jerk reaction. It makes it the negotiated outcome of a dialogical interaction. It is this dialogical negotiation of the initial command—where the response could be internal (to the audience) rather than external—that is the hallmark, or so I want to claim, of a rational grounding of authority. Dialogical response to imperatives is as, or more, important than a belief in the legality of enacted rules, although legality is, no doubt, as Habermas argues ([1962] 1989, 57–88), a consequence of the negotiation of imperatives.

At the same time, I believe that the microdiscursive pattern does reflect what Weber had in mind in dubbing this form of authority "rational."[7] From a microdiscursive perspective, the response to the imperative is narratively problematized. The initial command is subjected to doubt, but is not rejected. The person commanded appreciates the authority of the command-giver, but cannot, for various reasons, simply carry out the command. The doubt places the initial command in a discursive relationship to other factors, including other imperatives. The persons commanded may, after scrutiny of the command, simply comply with it. Or their behavior may constitute partial compliance. Or, again, it may signal their rejection of the command. What is important to the phenomenon, understood as a pattern within narratives, is that the discursive pathway to the behavior is complicated, and that the initial imperative is, along the way, subjected to scrutiny. Compliance is rational because discursive ratiocination intervenes between the imperative and the description of the subsequent behavior.

From the point of view of a theory of cultural motion under modernity, the accordioning out of the relationship between imperative and description makes sense. If the inept compliance pattern brings into crisp focus the need for careful replication, the resistance pattern zooms in on the need for contextualizing and scrutinizing the initial cultural element, with the behavior then produced being something new—the output of that scrutiny or weighing. Even where the ensuing behavior is, apparently, straightforward compliance with the initial command, the description of the compliance is only distantly related, via complex transformations, to the initial imperative. In the case of Dylan's Abraham, the only trace of "Kill me a son" is the recurrence of *"kill"* in the second-to-last line: "Well Abe says, 'Where do you want this *killin'* done?'" Note that "kill" here appears not as a description of behavior, but as part of reported speech: These are Abe's words. Furthermore, the reported speech is in the form of a question back to God, and hence is part of a continuing negotiation of the original imperative. It is not a description of the actual behavior.

The biblical story of Abraham is intriguing in this regard. It does not show the pattern of inept compliance found in the Cherokee case. But at the same time, we do see there evidence of a similar, almost word-for-word replication of the imperative in its description, as shown in Figure 17.

A new factor that is prominent here, however, is paraphrase. Parts of the initial command are fulfilled, in the narrative, not by a simple replication of the words taken from the imperative, but by an elaborate paraphrase. Thus, the command: "[G]et thee into the land of Moriah" is followed by the description "[W]ent unto the place of which God had told him." "Moriah" becomes "the place of which God had told him"—and, indeed, the name Moriah is never repeated in this entire story. In such paraphrase, we do not find the simultaneous copying of meaning and linguistic material that is characteristic of replication in the Cherokee case. A chasm opens here between meaning and behavior that is not resolved at the level of narrative by word-for-word replication. Hence, the narrative does not allow us to see imperatives as part of the replication of culture. Perhaps paraphrase, in this regard, is closer to response, and represents an incipient form of analysis of the initial imperative, along the lines that Voloshinov ([1929] 1973, 115–23; see also Bakhtin 1984) has suggested for discourse more generally. Imperatives in this case appear to partake of that mysterious transubstantiation process with which this chapter began. Even at the level of narrative, the words of the imperative become something else: the words of the paraphrase.

In any case, the response pattern more generally problematizes the

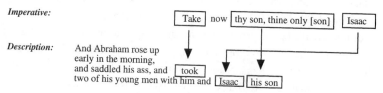

Figure 17. Replication in the biblical story of Abraham.

relationship between imperatives and the motion of culture, suggesting that in this case, cultural replication may be an inadequate way to think of cultural movement. Instead, we are forced to construe cultural elements as decomposable into parts or strands. Confronted with a cultural element, modern recipients of culture do not (or, do not in this ideal world of narratives) simply replicate the element. Instead, they place it in relation to other elements, take strands from one and intertwine them with strands from others, thereby weaving something that, while a continuation of what has come before, is also arguably something new and different, as in the case of Babe's transformation of the form of leadership among sheep. The sheep are still being led, but they are being led now in a new way—a way judged as better.

Can Cultural Objects Effect Their Own Circulation?

By now it is obvious that, from the point of view of a theory of cultural movement, tradition is far from simply inertial. It requires the infusion of accelerative force to propel it forward in time and overcome dissipative forces at work on it. Perhaps it is not as obvious that the kind of movement I have just described—movement under modernity, connected with a pattern of resistance to imperatives within narrative, and an emphasis on the production of new cultural elements—generates its own problems of movement which require accelerative force.

What kinds of problems? To answer that question, we need to look at what is peculiar about the motion of culture in modernity, namely, that the processes of dissemination and replication have become, relatively speaking, disentangled. In the case of oral transmission, the dissemination of culture depends upon its replication. For a cultural element such as a myth to get from one individual (or group) A to B, and from B to C, A must tell the myth to B (dissemination), but then B must retell it to C (replication). The movement from A to C depends upon replication in a direct way.

In the case of modern mass-mediated culture, however, A could get a book or video or CD to C without the intermediation of B as replicator. Mass media offer the possibility of broader dissemination and of greater temporal durability of the element. But at the same time—and this is one problem created by the nature of modern cultural movement—the production, and hence also reproduction, of social learning has become more difficult. If someone has already written a book, there is no need for another individual to write that same identical book—pace the Borges story. Hence, there is no need for precise word-for-word replication. The fact that the book has already been written and is publicly accessible obviates this need.

Correspondingly, the replication of the social learning that went into writing that book becomes difficult. True, great effort must be expended to learn something in word-for-word fashion. But one does not have to invent a new combination of words that has the grabbing power of the old one. The benefit of the word-for-word replication is that small changes can be made over years and even centuries so that there is gradual accretion of artistic input. In writing a new book, one must create a new and different combination that is equally as compelling as the old one, that contains within it all the artifice of generations, without precisely duplicating that artifice. How can culture stimulate its own reproduction under these circumstances?

Culture's answer to this challenge is a metacultural emphasis on modernity, on the new. Such an emphasis counteracts the tendency of social learning to fade out because of the ease of dissemination. In some sense, this is the opposite of the case of myth. There, dissemination depends upon replication; hence, to insure dissemination of culture, one must insure its precise replication. In the case of modern mass mediation, dissemination is easy—at least, it is easy to insure that the cultural element as a physical thing has such durability in the world as would allow it to be inspected by others after its producer is gone. But the reproduction of the social learning deposited in mass-mediated cultural elements is difficult. Because that reproduction depends on the production of a putatively "new" element—a new book or new video or new CD—to insure the transmission of the old social learning, one must place a premium on newness. The metacultural ideology of newness thus itself imparts an accelerative force to culture, insuring replication where that replication might not otherwise take place.

The pattern of resistance to imperatives embodies this metacultural privileging of newness. The imperatives, like the whole cultural elements of which they form a part, are not simply reproduced in the ensuing behavior. Instead, they are scrutinized, weighed against other factors, dialogically engaged. The outcome may be—indeed, typically is—compatible with the initial imperative, but that outcome does not appear as the simple reflex of the initial imperative. Just so does the "new" cultural element, under modernity, not appear as the simple copy of any one earlier element. Various elements, various factors have gone into it.

Increased difficulty of replication is not the only problem engendered by the nature of modern cultural movement. There is also a problem of competition among elements, which makes dissemination itself, at least in one sense, problematic. Because the elements are durable and because they are constantly being produced, it becomes difficult for any one element to gain the attention of individuals who would view it or listen to it or touch it. The element is out there in the perceptible world as a thing that could be paid attention to. But if the attention of individuals is otherwise occupied, how can the element surface?

Two answers to this question suggest themselves. One view gives priority to the social pathways of dissemination. The ability of an element to surface into the attention of individuals is based on its social positioning. An established film producer makes an uninteresting film which nevertheless gets out there. It circulates. This happens because of the producer's access to the pathways and networks of circulation. Correspondingly, an unestablished filmmaker produces what may be an interesting film, but cannot get it disseminated.

This view tends to construe the social networks as independent of the elements that circulate within them. But the problem of attention cannot be purely a mechanical one, since individuals could, presumably, opt out of a given network and into another. Even if they were presented with a cultural element by virtue of their participation in a network, that element would not necessarily grab or hold their attention, and if only elements of that nature were disseminated, the network itself would break down. Some uninteresting elements can pass by, living off the reputation of the others, but there cannot be only uninteresting elements in circulation.

This would suggest that one look for the motive or attractive force within the elements themselves. Roman Jakobson (1960a), following on the work of members of the Prague School, has argued that parallelism in discourse—the formal basis of the poetic function—serves to make the discourse of which it is part salient. Parallelism calls attention to itself, and hence also to the broader discourse of which it is part. It says, in effect: "Look at me." Might not this aspect of the cultural element be responsible for effecting its own dissemination? Indeed, the replication I have demonstrated in the inept compliance pattern conforms to this expectation. The description of the compliance behavior looks like the imperative from which it stems.

However, and in contrast, the resistance pattern is not grounded so much in this kind of direct, highly salient reprising. There is a key difference here with respect to inept compliance, where the characters unthinkingly and unhesitatingly try to carry out the command, but bungle the task. In the resistance pattern, the imperatives—just as for the whole cultural elements themselves—must be scrutinized, weighed against other factors, dialogically engaged. The description of the outcome bears traces of the initial imperative, in greater or lesser measure, and hence does contain parallelism, but the parallelism is not nearly as salient as in the other case.

Given the considerable differences between the two patterns, can it be the pattern alone—apart from the social network in which the pattern circulates—that supplies the motivating force, effecting dissemination by a kind of boot-strapping? The empirical question might be posed this way: Could the resistance pattern be plucked from its social context, plopped down in a new social context in which the pattern has not before appeared, and then immediately attract attention—as does the Coca-Cola bottle that falls from the sky in the film *The Gods Must Be Crazy?*

What is critical about this pattern, or so it seems to me, is that it models the processes of cultural movement within the very context of which it is part. There is a recognition of aptness to the immediate social situation of which the element forms a part. The Dylan version of the story of Abraham sounds contemporary. Dylan's Abe fits into the social networks in which the song circulates. In this sense, self-reflexive modeling of the social processes of circulation in which the cultural element itself moves is one key to the success of the pattern.

If I am correct, the two patterns of imperative usage I have described are really instructions: They tell those who behold them what to do with the discourse of which they are a part. In the case of inept compliance, the pattern instructs a listener to precisely replicate the myth. In the case of resistance, the admonition is: Produce a new piece of discourse that takes into account, in some fashion, the existing one.

But granted that such instructions are embedded in discourse, why should people follow them? The analogous question arises (and arose earlier in this chapter) in connection with imperatives themselves: Why do people respond to imperatives in the way they do? Imperatives work, or so I have argued, because of the models of how to respond to them that are contained in prior discourse. The resistance pattern cannot work immediately, if it is plopped into a social context where that pattern has not previously existed. The cultural element may be interesting to the people who behold it, but the instruction does not take hold as efficacious—reshaping the expectations about proper responses to imperatives—until a sufficient history of occurrences of the pattern has developed. That history, of course, is a strand of culture. The efficacy of the instruction depends upon its position within such a strand, its relation to prior instances of the pattern. In order for an implicit or explicit instruction about cultural replication to be efficacious in one instance, the instruction must resonate with prior instances. But then, how can such instructions—or how can imperatives, for that matter—really accomplish anything genuinely new?

My answer is that neither the instruction nor the imperative is ever wholly new; it is not something created ex nihilo. The accelerative forces I have been describing are changing or modifying or deflecting forces. They reshape an existing cultural element or course of movement, but they do not create something that bears no traces of what has come before it. This is obvious in the Cherokee pattern, where the instruction is at the service of maintaining a tradition in the face of dissipation—newness here means overcoming the decay of something old, and hence of preserving that old thing. However, and less obviously, it is also true in the case of the resistance pattern, where the instruction is to produce something new, but something that simultaneously reprises the old. The pattern is compatible with mass-mediated cultural circulation, where cultural elements have temporal longevity but are difficult to replicate. The instruction gives a boost to the replication process, and thus actually preserves old cultural learning.

If, following the resistance pattern, I dialogically engage the view of power as first and foremost about social relations, my retort—recall Babe's: "This is ridiculous, mom"—is that power is first and foremost about the mysteries of the motion of culture. Indeed, power is nothing other than that which accounts for extrainertial cultural movement: the acceleration, reshaping, and deflecting of culture as it passes through individuals, making its way across space and over time. Such a view allows the study of culture to take its proper place alongside the study of motion more generally, from the awe-inspiring spectacle of heavenly bodies in cosmic motion to the microscopic reduplication of DNA molecules, whose accumulated information thereby makes its way through the universe.

5

The Public Eye

Double-Layered Circulation

Consciousness in motion—what a strange idea![1] Can consciousness, rather than being an inherent property of us as biological organisms, move through us, as individuals, much the way culture more generally moves through us? This seemingly nonsensical proposition accrues plausibility with the realization that consciousness is, in some measure, at least, lodged in the overt meanings carried by circulating signs—especially publicly occurring discourse. When we are dealing with an awareness inscribed in metaculture, we are dealing with the explicit meanings of circulating talk and writing. The consciousness of motion—cultural motion—is also itself in motion, as if it were a second plane or layer of circulation superimposed upon the first.

And so we gallop headlong into the epistemological thicket. For, surely, if consciousness moves through "us" as individuals, it moves also through me as a researcher and student of culture. But then my awareness of culture—indeed, the very awareness sallying forth into the world by means of these words, this book—has itself come to me from elsewhere. Am I not thereby pulled into the past, under the control of the ancestors— Max Weber, Emile Durkheim, A. R. Radcliffe-Brown, Franz Boas, and others—whose ghostly presence haunts these pages?

The answer to such self-doubt can be found in the very conceptual framework for studying cultural motion I am here describing. Yes, my words are influenced by those of other scholars—not only past ones, but present ones, as well.[2] The influence is culture, and, if I focus on the influence of the past, I am looking at culture through the lens of tradition. At the same time, cultural motion can also be understood in terms of newness. What is the source of that newness insofar as circulating consciousness is concerned? Where does consciousness that is distinguishable from its past come from?

My proposal is that it comes, in part, from the world it is endeavoring to understand. Something makes its way out of that world and into consciousness, even if consciousness is also, to a significant degree, a historical residue, determined by the flow of signs over time. But just as that historical consciousness taps into the world—and, indeed, the wide circulation it enjoys is due to the fact that it does tap into the world for so many people—so also does innovated consciousness. It extracts something from the world, even if only for the one who proposes the innovation. The innovator is an intersection point, so to speak, between two lines of motion: the historical motion of consciousness from person to person over time and space, and the movement of something from the world into the consciousness that beholds it.

I cannot say precisely what directed my attention to the metaculture of film reviews as a way of investigating this problem. Perhaps it is, after all, the work of that shadowy force that I am here endeavoring to understand. Whatever the case, the choice seems, in retrospect, apt. Film reviews, as metaculture, move through space and time somewhat independently of the films they describe. And they carry a consciousness of the world—in particular, of films—with them. They create a secondary layer of circulation, laid on top of and loosely coordinated with the circulation of films as cultural objects, but themselves are distinct objects. What is the content of this secondary layer or circulating consciousness? And what is its purpose or significance with respect to the primary layer of cultural circulation? These questions seem to me empirically investigable.

What intrigues me is that the motion of film reviews is of the same type as that of the films—they represent culture whose dissemination (unlike the dissemination of myths) has been largely uncoupled from its replication. They should—even though they are quintessential metaculture—thus conform to the characteristics of cultural elements produced under a metaculture of modernity. That is, while they zero in on the newness of the films they discuss, they should also themselves display novelty. And they should do so even though they give rise to secondary replication in the form oral retellings, and even though they interact with orally circulating film commentary more generally.

I confess that I have been a long time studying a relatively small number of reviews—twenty-six different reviews in all, thirteen each of the films *Fail Safe* and *Dr. Strangelove*.[3] My interest in them goes back more than a dozen years. My original concern was to map the location of "voices"— represented by the distinct periodicals—within a Bourdieuian social space with the hope of understanding film review content as a function of location. That is, I wished to study how reviews in the *New York Times*, for example, differed from those in the *New York Post*. Were those differences correlated with the tastes and preferences of the newspapers' targeted audiences? This attempt met with only partial success, and I abandoned it upon realization of the shifting quality of the social space itself. I came to appreciate that the social space—about which I will have more to say later—is, in fact, also a product of this double-layered circulation, as it intersects with the inertial culture moving through families and other loci of social reproduction.

Recognizing this possibility, about eight years ago I began to focus on two central questions: What, exactly, is the content of the circulating consciousness contained in film reviews? What is the relationship of that content to the motion of the culture at the primary plane? To address these questions, I focused in a fine-grained way on the reviews themselves as discourse with explicit topics and overt meanings.

My procedure was to code each sentence of each review for its topic. I asked myself: What is this sentence about? Surprisingly, an answer readily suggested itself, although often two or more answers suggested themselves for the same sentence. In the latter case, I coded the sentence for more than one topic. So, for example, the sentence: "Between him [Henry Fonda] and the Albert Brenner sets . . . there is a kind of surface tension to the film" ("Unthinkable Unthought" 1964, 114) was coded for both the "actor" and "settings" topics. Little by little, it became apparent that the same topics were repeated over and over again. Their number was finite— my initial analysis turned up seventeen—and the topics cut across the film reviews. All of the film reviewers seemed to be dealing with the same kinds of issues. There was, insofar as topic is concerned, a shared consciousness of the films, even if the specific evaluations bestowed by that consciousness differed.

This surprised me. With the notion of distinct "voices," I had anticipated major differences among the reviews, and, to be sure, there were some interesting ones. Undeniably, different reviewers had different opinions or evaluations of the same film, even of the same aspects of the film. Take two different views of the performance given by one actor—one from *Films in Review*: "Dan O'Herlihy is convincing as the soft-spoken general who obeys the terrifying order to bomb New York" (Davis 1964, 506–7), and one from *The New Republic*: "O'Herlihy, as a top general, has a rich voice and posy manner that surrealistically suggest an articulate bowl of fruit" (Kauffmann 1964b, 26). These opinions cannot be reduced to an underlying commonality. How might they be related to the differential motion of culture at the level of the films themselves?

Despite the differences in evaluation, however, nearly all of the reviews included discussion of actors and acting. My question: Why? To which a typical American might reply: Duh! But I wanted to know why circulating consciousness should focus on this aspect of the films. Why actors and acting? Not only do most reviews discuss this topic—indeed, it comprises 12 percent of all the words found in these reviews—but seven of the thirteen reviews of *Fail Safe* include mention of O'Herlihy, who was not the central character.

Looking at the crystalline metaculture embodied in these film reviews as consciousness, I wondered about the source of this consciousness. Where did it come from? Part of it, no doubt, originates in a subculture of film reviewers, who read other film reviews and thus replicate the culture of film reviewing—along with the consciousness of films—in their own productions. Many of my own friends and relatives, as well as interviewees, imitate that subculture, giving films their own "three and a half stars" or "two thumbs up" ratings.

However, some of the content of that circulating consciousness—as I intend to show—comes from the films themselves. The metaculture of film reviewing is one way the culture locked up in films, as cultural objects, gets out of those objects and into other people. Film reviews are evidence for the movement of the culture contained in the films—from the original makers of the film to the reviewers, and from there outward to a broader public.

A vertical passage of something takes place between the two planes or layers of circulation—culture (films) and metaculture (film reviews)—which is also a passage between thing-in-the-world and consciousness of it as encoded in thing. The planes are loosely coordinated through such passages. However, the nature of the motion or interchange between planes is unlike the motion I have described for myths—or, rather, it is like the motion of myth in some ways, but unlike it in others. Where it is unlike it, the movement conforms—in greater or lesser measure, depending on the review—to the principle of motion central to a metaculture of newness.

Soothsayers of Circulation

The idea of tradition does not precipitate a need for crystal-ball gazing, since the future can be foreseen just by looking at the past. A given cultural object is valued insofar as it looks like valued cultural objects that have come before it. It is not that new objects never arise under tradition. Obviously, they do. It is that, when they do, they are accorded value retrospectively rather than prospectively. Their greatness is not trumpeted by metaculture upon their arrival, but is known, so to speak, after the fact, that is, after the appropriate circulations have taken place.

Emphasizing newness, however, generates a need for fortune-tellers—prospective evaluators of cultural worth, who foresee future circulations, even though the current object under scrutiny does not look, in its surface characteristics, exactly like ones that have come before it. The fortune-tellers are predictors of cultural circulation, and they accord cultural objects, such as films, their marks of distinction based on those predictions.

Why the need for fortune-tellers? After all, films and novels, as cultural objects, participate in pathways of capitalist circulation of culture that have their own built-in mechanism of evaluation: price as a reflection of demand. Demand—as reflected in price—is, indeed, a kind of metacultural statement. It indicates the relative pressure or force behind the lateral motion of culture elements that are produced. Accordingly, one form of ranking is a consequence or function of demand, regardless of the degree of perceived newness of the element that is in demand. So why should culture insist upon fortune-tellers and fortune-telling? What is the problem with relying solely on price for ranking, insofar as the motion of culture is concerned?

The problem for the motion of culture posed by ranking exclusively in terms of price or demand—which results in the stratification associated by Bourdieu ([1975] 1984) with economic capital—is that price has no regard for the content of the culture that is perpetuated. Its blind faith is in the fact of dissemination. But price ranking provides no way to assess the actual movement of culture over time as it finds its way out of an old object—for example, the book *Fail-Safe*—and into a new one—say, the film *Fail Safe*.

Demand is an index of the role an element plays in processes of local replication in the sites to which the element is disseminated. But with price alone, there is no way to assess the relationship between that expression and its predecessors as kinds of things-in-the-world. From the point of view of exchange value[4]—a given film has no more in common with its predecessors, nor, for that matter, with future films than it does with automobiles or loaves of bread. Nothing about the characteristics of the culture that is in motion seems to matter.

In an earlier discussion in chapter 2, I stressed the problem of making sure that the social learning embodied in mass-disseminated objects is actually reproduced. The reproduction of social learning embodied in an object occurs in fullest measure when another element like "it"—but obviously not "it"—is produced. Emphasizing newness means emphasizing the ability to reproduce the kind of object the object is.

Price provides no measure of the ability to reproduce the kind of object an object is. It measures only the demand the object generates within local processes of reproduction. The danger for culture is not only that the social learning will not be extracted from the object, but that the cultural genius that inspired the original object will actually be lost.

To be sure, this is not a perfect characterization of demand. In the case of printed books, I suggested that demand would occur only—or at least primarily—when the new book was actually in significant ways new. Unlike non-mass-mediated transmission of culture, such as that involved in the classical cases of myth, the problem is not trying to insure that one's own replica looks like older ones. Since the object one possesses—the book, in this case—can perpetuate itself in time and be carried through space without the aid of replication, there is no need to emphasize the accuracy or faithfulness of the copy. Demand for a new book would develop only if that book contained something new. So, in the case of printed discourse, at least, demand may correlate, in part, with innovation.

However, newness cannot be ascertained without contact with the objects in question, either direct contact or contact mediated through some third object. Newness is something that has to be discovered or made known. To appreciate the innovativeness of a specific cultural object, you have to compare that object with others. Thus, if a new object is produced, you as a demander have to, first, know of the existence of that object, and, second, compare that object to others that have come before it. But how can you know of that object? And how can you compare it without actually having it and, hence, exercising your expression of demand?

The former problem is solved by advertising—and, indeed, advertising is a form of metaculture continuous with the metaculture of film reviews. One role of the crystalline metaculture of reviews is simply to make known the existence of cultural objects to those who might potentially have a demand for them. In the case of films, seeing ads, watching previews,[5] or reading or listening to reviews are all ways of learning about new objects.

Demand lacks purity as a measure of newness because demand depends on making people know about the thing demanded. Hence, it is dependent on metaculture. In the case of films, this need not be only advertising or previews or reviews—mass-mediated forms—but can also be word-of-mouth metaculture. But the latter is still metaculture, and its movement is what insures the possibility of the demand for the new cultural object. Hence, demand can never be independent of metaculture, although it might be dependent in greater or lesser measure on mass-circulated metaculture.

How could demand be the only basis for ranking? If there were no advertising or crystalline metaculture—such as that of film reviews—demand would exist for what is already demanded, because that is what is known. You cannot know you want something if you do not know it is there to be wanted. Demand for the new exists only when there is knowledge that the new object exists. Small wonder that America—a country more under the sway of newness than any other—has become a culture of shopping. From the point of view of cultural motion, shopping is far more than the mundane and academically disparaged material activity it appears to be. Rather, it is something bound up with a quest for the new that is the spiritual force of modernity.

From the point of view of culture, advertising supplies knowledge of the new. But advertisements stem from the producer or, rather, reproducer of the cultural element. Hence, advertisements as metaculture provide no direct stimulus to the production of new culture. True, since status is a function of the price a producer can demand, there is an incentive for competing producers to come up with a better cultural object. But demand, as a measurement, provides no check on whether it is the cultural object or the metacultural object—the advertisement—that is the reason for the demand. That check comes only from someone who, like the demander, has actually tried out the two or more competitors.

Where to find someone on whom the demander can rely? That someone might be a friend or relative—indeed, in contemporary America, this kind of metaculture is a key component of demand. This is one reason that taste is lodged in the *habitus*—one learns about cultural objects from those around one. The form of motion of this kind of metaculture is no different from that of myth. Because dissemination of metaculture—in word-of-mouth transmission—depends directly on its replication, demand is tied to, and limited by, a traditional form of cultural motion.

For this reason, need develops for an independent form of metaculture, such as the metaculture of Habermas's ([1962] 1989) bourgeois public sphere, or of contemporary film reviews. This kind of metaculture mediates between the newness born of competition in the production or reproduction of culture, on the one side, and the newness of a possible future demand, a possible future trajectory for the motion of culture. Metaculture is what helps to bring those two together, to suture the gap between competition in the production of cultural objects and possible future demand for objects in processes of local cultural reproduction.

Any independent metaculture necessarily employs criteria of ranking in addition to demand. The criteria are based on the characteristics or content of the cultural objects themselves. Metaculture cannot use only demand as its gauge because the production of the metaculture precedes the existence of the demand—although some people may employ "bestseller" lists, for example, as metacultural guides to their own selections. Metaculture has to try to foresee or predict demand. But in so doing, it develops its own evaluative mechanisms. It looks at an object and tries to judge its innovativeness relative to other objects not based on the demand the new object generates, since the demand does not yet exist, but rather on the characteristics of the new object as thing-in-the-world. Do the characteristics suggest that the object is an innovation or improvement over what has come before, something that carries over the genius of prior objects in new and improved form?

There is a paradox here. If future demand could be easily foreseen such that any metaculture could predict demand for a new object based on the demand for prior ones, there would be no competition for price-based economic status. Producers would automatically know the future demand for their product relative to the demand for other products. Correspondingly, if the metaculture were simply based ex post facto on demand, it would have no raison d'être—other than scientific interest, perhaps. In such a world, knowledge would move instantaneously and unimpeded by friction. It would be the God-like knowledge of an omnipresent, omniscient being. But knowledge, in fact, makes its way through the world via signs or representations that are themselves material things. It slogs through the goo created by objects in physical space and time.

The existence of institutions for the production of metaculture such as film reviews attests to the fact that future demand is not transparent, that God-like instantaneous knowledge of the world for all individuals is not possible, that the standards of evaluation of cultural objects employed in institutionalized metaculture are in tension with the ranking system based on price. Evaluation through explicit metaculture is the basis for hierarchical order associated with Bourdieu's ([1975] 1984) "symbolic" capital,[6] which is, in turn, in tension with the economic capital associated with price and demand.

Metaculture as a Form of Retelling

How often has it struck me—and, no doubt, every other ethnographer of a distant culture—that people are farsighted, unable to see what is right before their eyes. Their own culture is just too close to them. The anthropologist Franz Boas is reputed to have said to one of his famous students, Edward Sapir—and this may be apocryphal—"So, you want to study Germanic languages. Fine, then you should begin by studying the Takelma Indian language of Oregon." The message is obvious: To understand your own culture, immerse yourself, for a time, at least, in another.

What struck me while living among Brazilian Indians, was how the same myths and stories were retold. No doubt because the pattern of retelling was unfamiliar to me, it was particularly salient. However, having studied that pattern and immersed myself in that culture, what strikes me about film in the contemporary United States is that people—at least those whom I interviewed for this research—tend to watch most films only once, though they have favorites like *Casablanca* or *Star Wars* that they watch periodically, including some they watch regularly, for example, *Miracle on Thirty-Fourth Street* at Christmastime, or the cult film *The Rocky Horror Picture Show*. There seems to be a restlessness when it comes to films; people are itchy to move on, constantly seeking something new.

Does this mean that the retelling of films—analogous to the retelling of myths—does not exist? In fact, in recommending movies they have seen to others, individuals regularly tell something about the movie. This ethnographic observation has led me to explore the ability of movie watchers to retell movies as orally transmitted stories. Based on recorded instances of such retellings, it appears that the ability to retell a film decays over time, tending towards zero or near-zero recall, in many cases.

Two days after watching a film, one individual was able to provide a detailed narrative of nearly a thousand words in length—this of a film that itself contained only eleven to twelve thousand spoken words. In many cases, this individual used actual words from the film, especially proper names, in the course of retelling. The retold narrative was nearly 10 percent as long as the original, and more detail on specific points could have been provided. The narrative was a form of retelling, like the retelling of myth. However, the very same individual had almost no recollection of the film *Dr. Strangelove*, despite the fact that he had watched the film approximately twelve years before (the interviewer happened to know this fact). Here is an excerpt of the conversation in which the film was discussed:

INTERVIEWER: Do you remember the movie *Dr. Strangelove?*
INTERVIEWEE 1: No, not really.
INTERVIEWER: Do you remember anything?
INTERVIEWEE 1: Was that the one where they dropped the bomb on Moscow *[pause]* or New York? Or was that *Fail Safe?* I don't remember anything about it.
INTERVIEWER: No, when they dropped the bomb on Moscow or New York, that was *Fail Safe.*
INTERVIEWEE 1: Have I ever seen *Fail Safe?* I don't know whether I've seen it or just heard you talk about it.
INTERVIEWER: Have you seen the movie *Dr. Strangelove?*
INTERVIEWEE 1: I don't know. It seems to me maybe I have, maybe years ago.
INTERVIEWER: Does *Dr. Strangelove* . . .
INTERVIEWEE 1: Isn't that the man with the arm?
INTERVIEWER: Yes, what do you remember about that?
INTERVIEWEE 1: Your enactment of it. That's all I know about the movie.

Notice the evidence here that the telling has a social life. The interviewee recalls a film through the retelling of it by another rather than through direct recollection of the experience of seeing the film.

The response of another interviewee confirms the inability to retell the film as narrative after a lapse of more than ten years since the last viewing.

INTERVIEWER: Do you remember what the movie *Dr. Strangelove* was about?
INTERVIEWEE 2: Why do you ask?
INTERVIEWER: I'll tell you later.
INTERVIEWEE 2: It was about this guy who was [the speaker grabs his throat] uh, uh [the speaker imitates choking sounds] choking himself. [Return to normal voice] I think there was some kind of doomsday machine.
INTERVIEWER: Do you remember anything else?
INTERVIEWEE 2: I think it has something to do with . . . uh . . . I can't remember.

INTERVIEWER: Did you ever see the movie *Fail Safe?*
INTERVIEWEE 2: Wait, am I getting this confused? I can't really remember. But I think Strangelove was the guy with his hand on his throat.

The half-life of the ability to retell the narrative probably differs little among Brazilian Indians—though I confess that I have not undertaken an analogous empirical study there. The key difference between the two situations, however, is that, because—as described in chapter 2—Brazilian Indian myths and other narratives are constantly retold within the household, the ability to renarrate a given myth is periodically reinforced. As a consequence, the myth is retained in memory and the ability to retell the narrative does not extinguish over time. This indicates that the holding environment for myths is not the individual memory—or, at least, not that alone—but memory aided by cultural patterns of retelling. The holding environment is the set of social interactions itself, which not only enable the transmission of the myths, as culture, in the first place, but also keep the myths—along with other culture—from fading out of collective memory.

One thing that intrigues me about film reviews in the contemporary United States is that they are also forms of retelling. Of the twenty-six reviews I sampled, twenty-three included sentences that I classified as plot renarrations. Indeed, as shown in Table 6, 11 percent of all the words in the reviews fall under the heading of plot renarrations.[7]

Some of these plot renarrations are minimal, barely more ample than the second retelling above, where more than a decade intervened between seeing and retelling. Here is an example from the *Chicago Sun-Times* review of *Dr. Strangelove:*

> The story (and incidentally, even the title makes sense to you once you have seen the film) describes the events that begin when an Air Force general dispatches a wing of bombers to attack targets located within Russia. He has his reasons, naturally; they have to do with the fact that the Russians never drink water but always drink vodka. (Keen 1964a, 58)

By my count, the dialogue in the film *Dr. Strangelove* contained some 11,882 words. This retelling contains sixty words, or just over one-half of one percent of the original. Since the reviewer had very recently seen the film, she could have, undoubtedly, given a more ample plot narration, probably of greater than one thousand words or 10 percent of the original, judging from the above-mentioned study—although, curiously, some

Table 6. Percentage of Space Devoted to Plot Renarration in Reviews of Two Films in Select Publications

BOTH FILMS		DR. STRANGELOVE		FAIL SAFE	
Life	18	Chicago Tribune	22	Life	31
New York Herald Tribune	18	Variety	18	New York Post	28
Chicago Tribune	17	New York Herald Tribune	17	New York Herald Tribune	19
Variety	14	Films in Review	14	The New Republic	17
The New Republic	14	The New Republic	12	New York Times	16
New York Post	12	Sight and Sound	11	Chicago Tribune	12
New York Times	12	Commonweal	9	Commonweal	12
Commonweal	11	Life	9	Variety	12
Films in Review	10	New York Times	8	Chicago Sun-Times	9
Sight and Sound	7	Newsweek	7	Newsweek	6
Chicago Sun-Times	7	Chicago Sun-Times	7	Films in Review	5
Newsweek	7	New York Post	0	Sight and Sound	0
Village Voice	0	Village Voice	0	Village Voice	0
Combined	11%		10%		14%

of the reviews get the plot wrong. True, some reviewers give more detail. Here is an example from *Life* magazine:

> An insane U.S. Air Force general, without the knowledge of the President, who is a nice boob, instructs his airborne nuclear bombers to attack their Russian targets. It turns out that the Russians have a "Doomsday Device" which will go off automatically when the U.S.S.R. is hit, and that this super-super deterrent, whose radioactive ingredients have a killing "half-life" of 93 years, will then wipe out humanity. Suspense builds through a crescendo of nightmare jokes, and the long and short of the plot is that one plane gets through, drops its bombs and the Doomsday Device begins its chain of world-ending explosions. (Wainwright 1964, 15)

But reviews, as metaculture, generally involve only the most minimal retelling.

The social functions of metacultural retellings are different from those of the Amerindian myths. Both are designed to entertain, but the film reviews, as metaculture, are designed also to synopsize, to give the essence of the story—like what might remain in memory perhaps a year after seeing a film. They are retellings that serve the purpose of advertisement, but also dissect the film into its constituent parts so that newness and quality relative to earlier culture may be assessed. The synoptic retelling is one way of making the "story" or plot of the film known to the reader or listener without the reader or listener having to spend the time and money to see it. It is thus part of the movement of the film, as culture, through the world.

The review, as retelling, is evidence of the movement of culture; it is evidence that something has gotten out of the film and into the reviewer. The reviewer demonstrates this internalization—as in classical cultural transmission—by means of renarration. By putting the film into their own words, reviewers give you—as reader or listener—the opportunity to see how they—as more-or-less impartial viewers, like you—responded to the film. The renarration is evidence for you of the effect of the film, as culture, on them.

There is considerable uniformity in what elements of plot get renarrated. In the case of Dr. Strangelove, the one aspect of plot that is most widely recounted—eleven out of thirteen reviews—is the American bomber attack on Russia initiated by a U.S. general variously described as a "crank," "wacky," "psychotic," "insane," "a right-winger," or a "madman." Fail Safe reviews are similar in this regard, reconstructing the story as about an accidental attack by U.S. nuclear bombers on Russia. Eight of the thirteen reviews mention this.

Other similarities appear, as well. Four of thirteen reviews of Dr. Strangelove—like the two interviewees quoted above—remark on Dr. Strangelove's uncontrollable arm (see Figure 18), and three mention the "doomsday machine." My conclusion is that a faithful carryover of culture has taken place from cultural object (the film projected onto a screen) to metacultural representation (the describing of the film), even though a conversion occurs between sensible film images and their conscious formulation in circulating words.

Indeed, there is not so much disagreement about the storylines as disparate pluckings of this or that feature for mention: In the case of Dr. Strangelove, for example, British officer Mandrake's attempt to elicit a recall code from the insane general, the general's suicide, Mandrake's puzzling out of the recall code, Mandrake's telephoning of information to the U.S. president, and the scientist Dr. Strangelove proposing a plan for post-nuclear survival. Evidently, the metaculture is—as plot retelling, at least—a faithful copy of the culture, much the way one telling of a myth is a copy of other tellings.

Perhaps you are wondering about the three reviews that did not mention

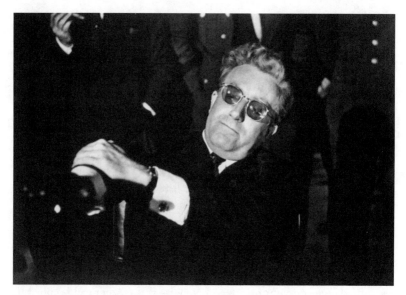

Figure 18. The arm of Dr. Strangelove, a sensible image that lives on. The culture contained in the image moves through space and time by acts of secondary replication—subsequent imitative behavioral reperformances and subsequent narrations of the image—in which sensible experience undergoes conversion into intelligible meaning. Such secondary replications may be remembered long after the plot of the film has faded from viewers' memories. From *Dr. Strangelove* (Columbia Pictures, 1964).

plot. If plot retelling is important, and if one key purpose of reviews, as metaculture, is to move the culture they are about through the world—to disclose that culture to others—then why should three reviews make no explicit mention of plot at all? The answer is that plot treats film as if it were, in essence, no different from literature. Stanley Kauffmann's reviews in the *New Republic* are typically of this sort. Some reviewers, in contrast, disclose the film to their audiences not by renarrating plot, but by putting into narrative form specific scenes and shots. In other words, they treat the film in terms of its uniquely filmic properties. Here is a small example from Judith Crist's review of *Dr. Strangelove* in the *New York Herald Tribune:*

> "[T]he sheer insanity of it all bubbles forth as Ripper babbles on about the purity of life fluids, a gum chewing Turgidson grapples with the camera-clicking Russian ambassador ("Please—gentlemen—you can't fight here—this is the war room," the President protests), an officer who has blasted his

way into an Air Force base questions the propriety of breaking open a soft-drink machine and Kong's crew cheerfully checks survival kits, from pep pills to tranquilizers to combination Russian phrase book and Holy Bible. (Crist 1964a, 8)

The correlation between plot and scene renarration is not perfectly inverse, but this is the tendency, as shown in Table 7. The three reviews that did no plot renarration—two in the *Village Voice* and one in *Sight and Sound*—rank high in terms of scene renarration.

Table 7. Percentage of Space Devoted to Scene Renarration in Reviews of Two Films in Select Publications

BOTH FILMS		DR. STRANGELOVE		FAIL SAFE	
Sight and Sound	25	New York Herald Tribune	40	Village Voice	52
New York Herald Tribune	24	Sight and Sound	26	Sight and Sound	22
Village Voice	22	Newsweek	19	New York Post	18
Newsweek	16	Village Voice	19	Newsweek	12
New York Post	15	Films in Review	17	Variety	8
Films in Review	10	New York Post	13	New York Herald Tribune	7
Variety	7	Chicago Tribune	11	Commonweal	2
Chicago Tribune	6	The New Republic	9	Chicago Tribune	0
The New Republic	6	New York Times	6	Films in Review	0
New York Times	3	Variety	5	Chicago Sun-Times	0
Commonweal	2	Chicago Sun-Times	0	Life	0
Chicago Sun-Times	0	Commonweal	0	The New Republic	0
Life	0	Life	0	New York Times	0
Combined	11%		15%		7%

Taken together, the retelling of plot and of scenes accounts for 22 percent of the words in these reviews. From this it is evident that the reviews, as metaculture, are in part retellings of the films as culture. They transmute the films into a distinct medium. In doing so, they also liberate the culture that is in the films and move it through space and time. They disclose the films, make them known, and hence render them possible objects of demand within a process of circulation based on demand. Insofar as what is known through the reviews excites or dampens demand, the reviews, as metaculture, serve to accelerate culture—to enhance the movement of culture through the world (by getting people to see films) or to retard movement (by discouraging potential viewers).

Tracking the Trajectory of Culture

Disclosing or making known is not all that reviews do. In addition, they situate a cultural expression in time—the time of culture's motion through the world. Simultaneously, the reviews evaluate the degree of newness of the objects. Is this one a stale reworking of familiar themes? Or is it ignited by a "true spark of creative genius"? With an emphasis on newness, a given expression achieves greatness only if it appears as an ω expression—something genuinely new, with prior culture as mere prelude. Correspondingly, the expression falls short of greatness—good as it may be adjudged—if it appears to be a "faithful copy," a replica of what has come before.

Stanley Kubrick, director of the 1964 film *Dr. Strangelove*, explained that he was working on a film adaptation of the 1958 novel, *Red Alert*, by Peter Bryant George. George's novel was a serious thriller about a world on the brink of nuclear annihilation, "but the 34-year-old Kubrick found that each time he tried to create a scene, it came up funny. 'How the hell could the President ever tell the Russian Premier to shoot down American planes?' he asked, with a broad wave of his hand. 'Good Lord, it sounds ridiculous'" ("Direct Hit" 1964, 79–80). Then it gradually dawned on him: He should portray the thriller as a "nightmare comedy." In that transformation emerged what one critic (Kauffmann 1964a, 26) called the "best American picture . . . since Chaplin's *Monsieur Verdoux* and Huston's *Treasure of the Sierra Madre* (both 1947)." Kubrick distinguished himself as possessing the "authentic touch of genius" (Winsten 1964a, 16). Conceptualized in terms of the movement of culture across time, Kubrick's film was great, however, not because it was totally new; were that the case, it would be unintelligible to metaculture. No, it achieved greatness because it was a *response to* rather than a *replica of* cultural objects that had come before it. Specifically, it was a response to the novel on which it was based.[8] It did not try to faithfully render the novel on the screen.

That very same year, 1964, the film version of Eugene Burdick and Harvey Wheeler's novel *Fail-Safe* appeared: The film's "producers weren't gambling in making this film. It is a faithful copy of last year's absurd, exciting and hugely successful book" (Oulahan 1964, 12). Although the movement of culture occurred across media—from book to film—the metacultural perception was that the film duplicated or copied the novel, and the author of this bit of metaculture recognized (correctly) the reason for that replication—the "huge" success of the book. If the book achieved wide circulation—tapped a nerve of interest in the American public, thereby creating a demand for itself—then a film replica of that book might tap the same nerve, becoming itself "hugely successful." What does the author of this bit of metaculture conclude from all of this? Well, not that *Fail Safe* was a great movie. No, the conclusion is that the "director, Sidney Lumet, does a credible job with his incredible material and the actors sometimes rise above their ridiculous roles and lines. The blame really falls on Burdick and Wheeler. Well, to be fair, perhaps not all the blame" (Oulahan 1964, 12). That author is by no means alone in his assessment. Stanley Kauffmann, in dismissing the film, notes that "an added irony is that *Fail-Safe* is Sidney Lumet's best piece of direction so far" (Kauffmann 1964b, 26).

It is not that replication itself is bad, insofar as the metaculture of film reviews is concerned. It is rather that the replica—in being recognized as such—is understood as carrying over too many attributes of the original. Distinction cannot accrue to the producer of a replica. Where replication is concerned, value accrues to the prior cultural object, which takes responsibility, so to speak, for the good or bad qualities of the copy. Thus, Oulahan's quip that "blame really falls on Burdick and Wheeler" (1964, 12).

At the same time, *Variety* magazine notes, approvingly, that *Fail Safe* "faithfully translates on the screen the power and seething drama of the Eugene Burdick-Harvey Wheeler book" ("*Fail Safe*" 1964, 6), and Winsten notes that the film is "taken with stunning accuracy from the Eugene Burdick-Harvey Wheeler best seller" (1964b, 29). Still, *Fail Safe*, because it is a "faithful copy" of the book, fails to bring the distinction to its director, Sidney Lumet, or to others associated with it, that Kubrick et al. earned for *Dr. Strangelove.*

Correspondingly, it is not that response to a prior cultural object is all it takes to achieve distinction. The worth of a new object depends on the nature of the response, not just on the fact that it is a response rather than a replica. But if a cultural object is recognized metaculturally as obviously linked to or derived from a prior object, then the new object can be construed as "brilliant," a work of "genius," only if it is understood, metaculturally, as a response to rather than a replica of that prior object.

Kubrick's film was unquestionably construed as "derived from George's novel *Red Alert*" (Kauffmann 1964a, 26), the latter being "the source book" (Winsten 1964a, 16) for the screenplay—the book "on which *Strangelove* was based" (Oulahan 1964), although one author qualifies this as "allegedly based" (Hart 1964, 113). Still, despite this recognition, the film achieved "distinction"—and here I refer to Pierre Bourdieu's ([1975] 1984) concept— because it was understood as a response to that earlier work. Not a single critic regarded the film as a "faithful copy."

This is despite the fact that *Dr. Strangelove*, in some cases, uses exactly the same words as *Red Alert*. I observed in chapter 2 that the novel *Dr. Strangelove*, purportedly by Peter George, bears no overall statistical relationship— insofar as choice of words is concerned—to the earlier book *Red Alert* by Peter George. But there are passages in the film that are word-for-word copies of the earlier book. One example can be found in the report of the psychotic general's explanation of his conduct in ordering a nuclear attack on the Soviet Union (see Figure 19). You can imagine the alchemical transmutation described earlier, as Kubrick struggled to create a film scene out of the book—the serious words of a madman transmute into fodder for parody.

Under a metaculture of modernity, the new cultural object—in this case, *Fail Safe* or *Dr. Strangelove*—is understood to be within the force field of prior cultural objects. It is suspended, initially at least, between α and ω. The metacultural judgment concerns whether the new element falls back into α, as a copy, or whether it breaks free of that force field, coming to appear as a new ω object in its own right—a response to earlier culture, to be sure, but an original response. The modern flow of culture over time—insofar as that flow is construed in terms of whole objects as copies of other prior whole objects—depends on a dialogical model of statement (prior object) and response (copy). A produces a cultural object; B produces a new object, understood as a response to A's; C produces a new object, understood as a response to B's; and so on.

Fourteen percent of all the words in the reviews investigated here were dedicated to relating the films in question to specific prior films or other works of art. This is more than is devoted to all other categories except— as I will discuss later—the effects of the films. The specific breakdown is given in Table 8: Eighteen of twenty-three reviews contain some discussion of the relationship of these films to specific prior cultural expressions. And all thirteen of the periodicals mention intertextuality in relationship to at least one of the two films.

There is widespread reference to the connection between the films and the novels on which they are based. Metaculture maps the movement of culture across time and space between novel and film, and also between the films themselves. A major focus of attention is the relationship between

Red Alert	Dr. Strangelove
DEPUTY COMMANDER'S REPORT ON GENERAL QUINTEN:	GENERAL TURGIDSON'S REPORT ON GENERAL RIPPER:
Sure, the orders came from me.	Yes gentlemen,
They're on their way in,	*they are on their way in* and no one can bring them back. For the sake of our country and our way of life,
and I advise you to get the rest of SAC in after them.	*I suggest you get the rest of SAC in after them,* otherwise we will be totally destroyed by red retaliation.
My boys will give you the best kind of start.	*My boys will give you the best kind of start,* fourteen hundred megatons worth,
And you sure as hell won't stop them now.	*and you sure as hell won't stop them now.* So let's get going. There's no other choice. God willing, we will prevail in peace and freedom from fear and in true health through the purity and essence of our natural fluids. God bless you all.

Figure 19. Comparison of one passage from *Red Alert* with one from *Dr. Strangelove.*

Fail Safe and *Dr. Strangelove.* Since *Dr. Strangelove* came out earlier, none of its reviewers mentions *Fail Safe,* but eleven of thirteen *Fail Safe* reviewers mention *Dr. Strangelove,* with several noting that *Fail Safe* "suffers considerably by being the second film . . ." (Keen 1964b, 55). Similarity to a prior film appears most harmful if the films are also temporally contiguous—indeed, *Fail Safe* was released only months after *Strangelove.*

These temporal linkages, however, by no means exhaust metacultural commentary. Interestingly, with a few exceptions—for example, Keen's observation that the Washington socialite in *Fail Safe* is "obviously borrowed from *La Dolce Vita*" (1964b, 55)—*Fail Safe* is not connected to specific prior objects other than *Dr. Strangelove* and the book on which it was based. In

Table 8. Percentage of Space Devoted to Intertextual Linkage in Reviews of Two Films in Select Publications

BOTH FILMS		DR. STRANGELOVE		FAIL SAFE	
Commonweal	26	Commonweal	20	Life	32
The New Republic	21	Village Voice	18	The New Republic	31
Village Voice	16	The New Republic	16	Chicago Sun-Times	29
New York Herald Tribune	14	Newsweek	10	Commonweal	29
Life	13	Sight and Sound	9	New York Herald Tribune	28
Variety	13	Films in Review	9	Sight and Sound	17
New York Times	12	New York Times	7	Variety	17
Sight and Sound	12	New York Post	5	New York Times	17
Chicago Sun-Times	12	Variety	3	Newsweek	15
Newsweek	12	Chicago Sun-Times	3	Films in Review	12
Films in Review	10	Chicago Tribune	0	Chicago Tribune	8
Chicago Tribune	4	Life	0	New York Post	0
New York Post	3	New York Herald Tribune	0	Village Voice	0
Combined	14%		14%		15%

the case of *Dr. Strangelove*, however, reviewers make a concerted effort to tie it to a past. Kauffmann (1964a, 26–27), as discussed earlier, refers to Chaplin's *Monsieur Verdoux* and Huston's *Treasure of the Sierra Madre*, but also to Kubrick's earlier films, which several other critics mention, as well: *Paths of Glory*, *Spartacus*, and *Lolita*. He also relates *Dr. Strangelove* to American novels, specifically, those by Terry Southern (scriptwriter for *Dr. Strangelove*), Joseph Heller, J. P. Donleavy, and Elliott Baker, who, he claims, "are creating a kind of modern Swiftian tradition" (Kauffmann 1964a, 27). Bosley Crowther links the film to "sick jokes" and to "cartoons . . . by Charles Addams and some . . . in *Mad Magazine*" (1964a, 24). Andrew Sarris, writing for the *Village Voice*, mentions the Kurosawa film *Rashomon*, the director D. W. Griffith, Josef von Sternberg's *Jet Pilot*, the films of Stan Vanderbeek, and Terry Southern's "underground classics," *Flash and Filigree* and *Candy* (1964a, 13–14). It is as if *Dr. Strangelove*, precisely because of its ω character, both taps into many different prior cultural expressions— thereby making prior culture appear to be an organized whole—and also demands that reviewers search out antecedents for its apparent "newness."

References to specific prior cultural expressions are not the only way that film reviews, as metaculture, track the flow of culture. The reviews also make use of "genre," to which, indeed, they devote on average 7 percent of their space, as shown in Table 9.

A surprising amount of consensus occurs in generic labeling, perhaps most so in the case of *Strangelove*, where it is called a "satire," a "comedy," a "farce," "burlesque," a "caricature," "slapstick," and a "sick joke," though it is also dubbed a "cliff hanger," a "fantasy," "melodrama," and a "suspense thriller." Virtually every reviewer recognizes in it the design features of something intended to be funny or to produce laughter, though they disagree on whether it succeeds and whether, if it does, that is a good thing.

The film *Fail Safe* is dubbed a "melodrama," a "drama," or a "suspenseful thriller," but it is also called "science fiction," a "mystery" (in a ruminating passage in *Newsweek*), a "doomsday film," a "war film," and one simulating the "style of a documentary." Reviewers recognize its serious intent, though they disagree as to the appropriateness of that intent—"pseudo-documentary realism is not the most effective way of presenting [the

Table 9. Percentage of Space Devoted to Genre in Reviews of Two Films in Select Publications

BOTH FILMS		DR. STRANGELOVE		FAIL SAFE	
Films in Review	16	New York Times	16	Films in Review	22
New York Times	15	Chicago Sun-Times	16	New York Herald Tribune	17
Chicago Sun-Times	11	The New Republic	14	New York Times	13
New York Herald Tribune	10	New York Post	14	Newsweek	12
The New Republic	9	Variety	13	Life	9
New York Post	8	Films in Review	11	Sight and Sound	5
Newsweek	7	Commonweal	9	Commonweal	4
Commonweal	5	Chicago Tribune	6	Chicago Sun-Times	1
Life	4	Newsweek	4	New York Post	0
Variety	4	New York Herald Tribune	4	Village Voice	0
Chicago Tribune	3	Sight and Sound	2	Variety	0
Sight and Sound	3	Village Voice	2	The New Republic	0
Village Voice	2	Life	1	Chicago Tribune	0
Combined	7%		8%		7%

dangers of nuclear annihilation]" (Davis 1964, 506)—and the film's actual effects—"some scenes are funnier unintentionally than *Dr. Strangelove* ever gets intentionally" (Sarris 1964b, 17).

The agreement, however, is not perfect. Ten of thirteen periodicals use the word "satire" to describe *Strangelove*, but Stanley Kauffmann, in the *New Republic*, makes a distinction that the other reviewers do not:

> This film is a comedy. A comedy, not a satire. Satire, in Fowler's good definition, is aimed at amendment. It is written by men about men for the improvement of their world. *Dr. Strangelove* has been made, quintessentially, from the viewpoint of another race on another planet or in another universe, observing how mankind, its reflexes scored in its nervous system and its mind entangled in orthodoxies, insisted on destroying itself. The film, therefore, does not hope to alter men; it is simply a (distant?) future report on what happened. . . . (1964a, 26)

Kauffmann's position differs from that of *Newsweek*, whose reviewer calls it both a "comedy" and "a biting bitter satire," and *Commonweal*, where Philip Hartung refers to it as a "satirical comedy."

From the point of view of cultural motion, genre appears as a device for tracking cross-temporal connections without referencing specific prior works on which a current cultural expression is based or to which it is related. A hypothesis suggests itself in this regard: Insofar as a given cultural expression is understood as a replica of others that have come before it— that is, insofar as a metaculture of tradition operates—in that measure is it unnecessary to trace temporal linkages metaculturally. Why puzzle out the past of something, when that something is so obviously a product of its past, and purports to be nothing other than the past's manifestation in a present? Correspondingly, the more cultural objects are represented as "new"—as under a metaculture of newness—the more importance genre assumes as a device for linking cultural objects to their past. Genre appears, in this way, as background "culture" for the emergence of new objects, obviating the need for reference to specific prior objects.

At the same time, metaculture, in tracking cross-temporal connection, also offers something "new" to the reader. Unlike plot summaries or scene narrations, linkage to prior cultural objects and to genres is not a task many viewers of a film automatically undertake on their own. The film review supplements the experience of seeing a film, rather than just recreating that experience in miniature. This is a point to which I propose to return. For film reviews, although themselves metacultural, act like culture subject to the influence of a metaculture of newness. To be praiseworthy, the metacultural object—like the culture it reflects and judges—must offer something new. Linkage of the cultural expression under review to a past is one—but only one—of the new things it adds.

Why should a public want a metaculture that furnishes this kind of temporal tracking? Reviews contribute to the operation of a public eye, more all-seeing than the private eyes of individual viewers. Under the culture of dissemination, individuals want reviews, in part, in order to determine whether they will, in the future, wish to see a film. Unless they have the leisure to take in the numerous films that come out every year—or unless they rely solely on producer advertisements—it is useful for them to understand where a given film is coming from, what its antecedents are. They are able to place a film—or, for that matter, almost any cultural object—in relation to other objects with which they are already familiar. Alternatively, if the review is read after viewing—as is also common among those interviewed for this study—the metaculture serves as a guide or road map to other cultural objects the potential viewer might wish to seek out or avoid.

If this explains why individuals want temporal tracking, it remains for us to learn what is in it for culture. Why should culture want to have its objects tracked across time? My contention is that it does so to assure the public that something from the past carries over in the present and on into a future—that is, to insure that culture is, indeed, moving through time. Under a metaculture of tradition, this assurance is given by the act of replication. When B repeats what A has said or done, there is public assurance of the movement of culture in the sensible form of the cultural object—whether a word, a gesture, or a ceramic pot. However, the relative severing of replication from dissemination means giving up on replication as a test of cultural motion. The test was replaced by faith in the material form of the disseminated thing. If A and B both want that thing, then some of the culture from that thing will find its way into each of them, different though their appropriations of the thing may be.

Where faith might be reasonably accorded to the material thing as a bearer of culture in this way, it is another matter altogether when it comes to the temporal passage of the immaterial culture contained in that object into another thing—especially when the new thing does not seem, to the senses, to resemble the older one. Faith in this kind of cross-temporal motion of culture is misplaced.

For this reason, it is in the interest of culture—as something abstract and immaterial moving through time as well as across space—to find a test of trans-temporal motion. The metaculture of film reviews, through temporal tracking, provides such a test. However, it substitutes the intelligibility of motion—as formulated explicitly in statements about trajectory—for its sensibility in replication. Culture finds in temporal tracking, therefore, a substitute for the traditional test of replication. Simultaneously, it singles out for commendation those new cultural objects that are not mere mechanical translations of older ones, but rather inspired creations that carry over into the future the genius of prior culture.

Supplying Additional Information about Production

Films—like the metal pots and knives discussed in chapter 2—are cultural objects in which replication (the making of new films or new pots) is relatively uncoupled from dissemination. The objects contain within themselves huge quantities of accumulated learning—the know-how to manufacture celluloid tape or photographic or projection equipment, the skills possessed by directors, actors, stage designers, makeup artists, stunt people, electricians, set builders, and on and on. Little of that know-how is made public when an average viewer takes in a film. How did they do that? The ordinary filmgoer has little or no idea.

Yet a viewer can extract something from the cultural object just by virtue of viewing. The viewer may be able to retell the story, reuse key lines, copy hair or clothing or speech styles, or act out scenarios from the film in their own interpersonal relations. This uncoupling of the uptake of the object (secondary replication) from the ability to reproduce the object (primary replication) is—as discussed in chapter 2—the essence of the division of labor described by Durkheim and countless others. The more cultural learning that goes into the production of a given kind of object—such as a film or a metal pot—the less likely is someone who merely uses the object to be able to reproduce the object. A considerable amount of culture remains locked up in the object, inaccessible to its beholder or user.

From this point of view, how fascinating that the metaculture surrounding films attempts to transmit some of the otherwise inaccessible cultural learning contained in the object. *Newsweek's* review of *Dr. Strangelove*, for example, goes on at considerable length about the production process: "Naturally, the picture was made without Pentagon help. The instrument-jammed B-52 cockpit was built from a picture in a British magazine. It cost $100,000. And each shot of the B-52 in flight, made with a 10 foot model and moving matte, cost more than $6,000" ("Direct Hit" 1964, 79–80).

This is an extreme example, involving as it does true journalism—digging up new information by interviewing—but such talk about production is also found, in lesser measure, in other reviews. Here is an example from *Films in Review*: Sidney Lumet's "technique, formed in television, is the limited one of close-ups and conservative cutting, and the careful avoidance of anything that is visually exciting. In *Fail Safe* he seemed unmindful, as tv directors often are, of script and editing flaws. Several sequences are inexplicable per se and unnecessary to the film as a whole" (Davis 1964, 506). Judith Crist, writing in the *New York Herald Tribune*, observes: "Lumet's quick, jolting directorial pace . . . make[s] for a relatively absorbing melodrama" (1964b, 17) These are characteristics of production of which ordinary viewers are unaware. As shown in Table 10, on average 5 percent of each review is devoted to unlocking the culture of production techniques embodied in films. The disclosing of production secrets is, evidently, a more specialized aspect of film reviews, since fully ten of twenty-six reviews made no mention of it.

Table 10. Percentage of Space Devoted to Production Techniques in Reviews of Two Films in Select Publications

BOTH FILMS		*DR. STRANGELOVE*		*FAIL SAFE*	
Newsweek	20	*Newsweek*	30	*Village Voice*	14
Variety	7	*Sight and Sound*	7	*Chicago Tribune*	11
Chicago Tribune	5	*Chicago Sun-Times*	5	*Variety*	9
Sight and Sound	5	*New York Herald Tribune*	4	*Films in Review*	9
Chicago Sun-Times	4	*Variety*	3	*Chicago Sun-Times*	4
Films in Review	4	*The New Republic*	2	*Life*	4
New York Herald Tribune	3	*New York Post*	0	*New York Herald Tribune*	3
Life	2	*Commonweal*	0	*Commonweal*	2
The New Republic	2	*Films in Review*	0	*New York Post*	2
Commonweal	2	*Life*	0	*The New Republic*	1
Village Voice	1	*Village Voice*	0	*Sight and Sound*	0
New York Post	1	*Chicago Tribune*	0	*Newsweek*	0
New York Times	0	*New York Times*	0	*New York Times*	0
Combined	5%		5%		4%

Many film reviewers are themselves just viewers, who—like their readers or listeners—have little direct acquaintance with production specifics surrounding a given film. What they have, rather, is knowledge derived from watching numerous films, coupled with an understanding of the principles of filmmaking. This understanding enables them to extract from a viewing aspects of the production process that are anything but obvious to ordinary viewers.

Settings could probably be amalgamated with production techniques, given that discussion of them similarly answers the question: How did the filmmakers do that? What is interesting about settings in specific, however, is that they are backdrops for the action in a film. Unlike storyline, they are not there to be noticed or remarked upon by a viewer so much as to create a consistent world or atmosphere in which filmic action takes place.

In Amerindian Brazil, domestically transmitted myths involve no distinctive settings, although myth-tellers map story space to the here and now of the immediate surround through body gestures. One narrator, for example, in telling a story about a man who dons feathers and flies to a land above the sky, pointed his right index finger skyward and moved it in a spiral gradually upwards, thereby portraying the upward spiraling motion of the winged man in the story. This kind of "setting" for a narrative could be readily transmitted to anyone present at the time of narration—indeed, I myself picked it up immediately, and use it to this day in my own retellings. A listener need only observe, as well as listen to, the narrator. This production technique can be passed on simply through participation in the dissemination (that is, the telling) itself.

In the case of film, however—as a form of culture whose dissemination, unlike that of myth, is relatively uncoupled from its replication—the typical viewer would have no opportunity—indeed, would not want—to recreate the settings in which a film takes place. Yet, as Table 11 indicates, nine of the thirteen periodicals studied here make at least some mention of them in connection with one of the two films.

In a few cases, settings are discussed at some length, often as part of plot renarration. This is especially true for *Fail Safe*, where the sets impressed reviewers:

> Interestingly enough, most of the exciting action, staged so effectively by Lumet from Walter Bernstein's screenplay, takes place indoors in three well-built sets: the Pentagon War Room, where Top Brass and some civilians are gathered to concentrate on the next steps after our bomber plane, through a failure in mechanism, gets the wrong signal and aims for Moscow with its deadly load; the SAC War Room in Omaha where the complicated fail-safe mechanisms and computers are and where officers are unable to signal the bomber plane to return because of Russian jamming of apparatus; and most important, the bomb shelter beneath the White House where

Table 11. Percentage of Space Devoted to Settings in Reviews of Two Films in Select Publications

BOTH FILMS		DR. STRANGELOVE		FAIL SAFE	
Commonweal	8	The New Republic	7	Commonweal	11
The New Republic	5	Variety	5	Sight and Sound	8
New York Times	3	New York Herald Tribune	0	Films in Review	7
Films in Review	3	Sight and Sound	0	New York Times	6
Sight and Sound	3	Newsweek	0	Chicago Sun-Times	5
Variety	3	Village Voice	0	Newsweek	4
Chicago Sun-Times	2	Films in Review	0	New York Herald Tribune	2
Newsweek	1	New York Post	0	Variety	1
New York Herald Tribune	1	Chicago Tribune	0	Village Voice	0
Chicago Tribune	0	New York Times	0	New York Post	0
Life	0	Chicago Sun-Times	0	Chicago Tribune	0
Village Voice	0	Commonweal	0	Life	0
New York Post	0	Life	0	The New Republic	0
Combined	3%		1%		4%

the President, who must make all final decisions, sits with the young man who is his translator. (Hartung 1964a, 72)

Newsweek singles out the person responsible for the sets: "Between him [Fonda] and the Albert Brenner sets with electronic maps on which drama and chase and life and death are reduced to little blips, there is a kind of surface tension to the film" ("Unthinkable Unthought" 1964, 114). And *Variety* follows suit: "Art direction by Albert Brenner is outstanding as he atmospherically registers with the Omaha War Room, the Pentagon, the White House and other sets . . ." ("*Fail Safe*" 1964, 6).

Here, as with production techniques more generally, the reviews—as metaculture—are performing a kind of extraction, pulling out of the films—as cultural objects—more of the culture that is carried along in them than can be retrieved by the ordinary viewer. The metaculture digs and scratches beneath the surface of the thing, as it is presented to the senses, and reveals a distinct kind of entity: one that is intelligible. Metaculture reveals the thing as accumulated plus innovated know-how.

Why should metaculture disclose artifice? Evidently, the review is not merely replicating or reprising the film. It is disclosing something about the film that the object itself does not automatically make available to its casual viewer. Why? It is understandable that some individuals might hunger for this information. If they have not yet seen the film, it gives them a better idea of what they will see visually. It is a way of describing the kind of experience they can expect, as in the case of genre and relations to prior cultural expressions. If they have seen the film, information about production supplements their experience, adding something new to it. In this sense, the movement between planes of circulation (culture to metaculture) involves more than replication. The metaculture vis-à-vis its antecedent culture (the film) is "new," as we should expect in the case of cultural motion under a metaculture of newness.

Yet why should culture want to circulate information about production? Why not rely on the object itself to carry the culture to its consumers? My contention is that, in this way, the metaculture guides—or, at any rate, endeavors to guide—the future movement of culture. It facilitates the extraction of the culture that goes into making a given object by focusing on the innovations in order to enable the movement of those innovations into new objects that will be produced in the future. It guides the sensibility of viewers to objects that are yet to come. And it guides potential makers of new objects by pointing out how they might re-embody existing culture in new material forms—showing what will count as a good carryover of culture.

Revealing the Homunculus within the Object

What a peculiar thing the modern cultural object is. It suffices as the bearer of a certain amount of culture, and it is capable of carrying that culture to faraway places; each object is also a time capsule, able to transport something of the present into a later time, where it can be reopened by a gawking future generation. Yet at the same time, unlike traditional cultural objects, the modern object itself cannot be fully replicated. For it to be replicated, for the immaterial culture contained in it to be liberated, so to speak, sent on its way into a future, the old object must be taken apart, dismantled. This allows us to glimpse the generative core or principle inside—the homunculus that makes it work, like the Wizard of Oz, manipulating the whistles and smoke that appear to the senses of ordinary people. Cultural motion, in this way, demands the death of an old object in order that a new object may be born from it, in a kind of splendid metamorphosis.

For this reason, the metaculture of film reviews is not content with the surface of things. It wants to chip away at the surface, hoping to break the thing open in order to reveal the cultural genius inside. And the genius is ultimately an individual—a director, an actor, an actress. These individuals connect the current object to its past—the earlier films which they directed or in which they acted. They also orient us to the future, as we try to understand what their genius has wrought. Table 12 shows that all but five of the twenty-three reviews discuss directors and directing, and, on average, 6 percent of the space in these reviews was devoted to that topic. Discussion of actors, acting, and casting accounts, on average, for 12 percent of the space in a given review, and all but three of the twenty-six reviews devote attention to these topics—making the discussion of actors slightly more prominent than plot retellings (see Table 13).

Table 12. Percentage of Space Devoted to Directors and Directing in Reviews of Two Films in Select Publications

BOTH FILMS		DR. STRANGELOVE		FAIL SAFE	
Chicago Sun-Times	20	New York Post	32	Chicago Sun-Times	20
New York Post	20	Chicago Sun-Times	20	Films in Review	9
Films in Review	11	Commonweal	15	The New Republic	8
Village Voice	7	Films in Review	12	Sight and Sound	5
Life	7	Life	10	New York Post	3
Commonweal	6	Variety	9	Commonweal	3
Sight and Sound	5	Village Voice	8	Newsweek	3
Variety	4	Sight and Sound	4	New York Herald Tribune	3
The New Republic	4	New York Herald Tribune	3	New York Times	2
New York Herald Tribune	3	The New Republic	2	Life	2
New York Times	1	Chicago Tribune	0	Variety	2
Newsweek	1	New York Times	0	Chicago Tribune	0
Chicago Tribune	0	Newsweek	0	Village Voice	0
Combined	6%		8%		5%

The focus on directors and directing draws the reader's attention to the faint presence of an individual otherwise undetectable behind the scenes—someone who controls the final shape of the object: "Sidney Lumet has directed it in a fast-paced, nervous fashion that gives it

Table 13. Percentage of Space Devoted to Actors, Acting, and Casting in Reviews of Two Films in Select Publications

BOTH FILMS		DR. STRANGELOVE		FAIL SAFE	
Chicago Tribune	26	Chicago Tribune	35	The New Republic	21
New York Times	20	New York Times	28	Sight and Sound	19
Films in Review	17	Variety	24	Chicago Tribune	17
Chicago Sun-Times	17	Films in Review	23	Newsweek	16
Sight and Sound	14	Chicago Sun-Times	22	Commonweal	15
The New Republic	14	New York Post	15	New York Times	11
Village Voice	13	Village Voice	14	New York Herald	11
				Tribune	
New York Post	12	Sight and Sound	11	Films in Review	9
Commonweal	12	The New Republic	10	New York Post	8
Variety	11	New York Herald	9	Chicago Sun-Times	6
		Tribune			
New York Herald	10	Commonweal	5	Life	6
Tribune					
Newsweek	5	Life	0	Variety	5
Life	2	Newsweek	0	Village Voice	0
Combined	12%		13%		12%

momentum and suspense" (Crowther 1964b, 36); "Lumet's quick, jolting directorial pace . . ." (Crist 1964b, 17); "Stanley Kubrick . . . puts a comic spin on the whole ghastly business" (Wainwright 1964, 15); "Kubrick tells his story with such control that, although one knows the inevitable conclusion, one has no idea how it will happen, and each episode comes not only as another nail in the coffin, but as a frightening demonstration of how power politics have become a Frankenstein monster which one little error can send out of control" (Milne 1964, 38). It is almost as if, adjusting our lens, we were able to bring into progressively crisper focus an image of the behind-the-scenes individual who had been but a blur in the background.

In the case of actors, the matter only appears to be different. The average viewer sees people on the screen. It is necessary to peel away this surface image of peopleness in order to reveal the true individuals, blood bubbling through their veins, who lie behind the image: "Peter Sellers in another multiple role as President, R.A.F. Officer, and Strangelove. What might so easily have been a trick is, in fact, completely successful, partly because only Strangelove is played for full Goon extravagance, with the

R.A.F. officer an affectionately gentle caricature, and the mild, balding, affable President played almost straight" (Milne 1964, 38); "Fritz Weaver lends his distinction to the role of a colonel who simply cannot break years of habit to tell the Russians a secret" (Kauffmann 1964b, 26); "Fritz Weaver is his usual overwrought embodiment of tenseness" (Davis 1964, 506–7). Why peel away the character to reveal the actor?

As I have argued, part of what film reviews—as metaculture—are doing is transmitting extra information about the production process, and, hence, more of the culture that is in the object than can be extracted by a simple encounter with the object. The focus on directors and acting is part of that transmission process. We, as readers of or listeners to film reviews, get more of an idea of how such a cultural object might be produced— how we ourselves might reproduce or replicate it. We learn what a director does and can do. We learn what an actor does and how a character is brought into existence by an actor. We come, in short, to appreciate the artifice of the object.

But does appreciating the artifice of a film mean focusing in on the artificer—the individual biological organism as producer and reproducer of culture? Are not films collective products, the result of a complex interaction among the different strands of culture flowing through many different individuals? Why focus on the biological individual as the artificer?

My answer, again: the logic of newness. Culture is socially learned by individuals from other individuals, directly or indirectly. In its pathways through the world, it finds a transient home in biological organisms. The logic of tradition is this: What comes out of the organism must be equal to what goes in. But clearly, as in the case of myth, changes do or, at least, can take place when culture flows through an individual. Yet this is not something on which the logic of tradition dwells—indeed, the logic of tradition is to overlook or even deny the new.

The new, however, is something on which the logic of modernity fixates. The changes that take place in culture as it flows through an individual must be the result of some agency, some will that the individual possesses. How else to account for the emergence of new objects out of the debris of old ones? And, if individuals change culture—if they fabricate or manufacture or produce new culture—then the logic of newness naturally downplays or overlooks or even denies the oldness of the object produced. The individual comes to seem the grand artificer, the wizard, able to create ex nihilo.

Yet Oz is not so easily demystified. We have not explained the great contraption by exposing the individual within. Indeed, there is irony here.

As discussed in chapter 3, a new type of novel emerged in the eighteenth century in Europe, in which the "I's" of characters and narrators came to seem more like the "I's" of flesh-and-blood individual human beings and less like the superhuman, hyperanimate beings of myth and legend. As the "I" of characters approaches that of actual individuals, however, it becomes necessary, in the metaculture, to remark the artifice. Why?

In some sense, it is obvious in the case of myth that the flesh-and-blood individual narrator is not identical to the prior mythical character whose deeds the myth recounts. Nor does the metaculture of tradition claim such an identity. Rather, it claims that something (the myth) is flowing through the narrator, and that the myth, as culture, is in a real sense in charge of the narrator—at least during the course of the narration. The narrator may tinker with or change the narrative, but that is not the ideal, and it is not something on which the metaculture focuses. The metaculture is interested in that larger superhuman force—the force of culture—that is flowing through individuals. Characters themselves merely embody that larger force or power in the universe.

When it comes to contemporary films, however, at least those that aspire to a peculiarly modern sort of realism, characters are often too close to actual individuals—so close that it becomes necessary for the metaculture to peel off the character's mask and reveal the individual beneath. At the same time, that individual comes to seem to be the producer or manufacturer of the character or image. Hence, it is often a derogation on the part of a reviewer to note the continuity, rather than disjunction, between the individual actor and the character. The lack of disjuncture is problematic even when the reviewer likes the character: "Fonda plays himself—as an old-time star always does, anyway—and gets away with it" ("Unthinkable Unthought" 1964, 114). Why should he have to "get away with it?" Evidently, "playing oneself" indicates that one is something less than a true agent or artificer or manufacturer of new culture.

At the same time, it is not that film reviewers, or the metaculture of films more generally, ignore the character of a film as a collective product. On the contrary, film reviews comment upon several actors, the director, even the producer or screenplay writer or photographer or editor. Yet the collectivity that emerges from this metaculture is a collection of individuals, not a superorganic entity—to use a now discarded term—that has a life of its own apart from any individual. The latter type of collectivity is one that might be imagined under an idea of tradition. In contrast, the metaculture of film reviews produces a collectivity analogous to the "we's" discussed in chapter 3, in which each individual articulator of that "we"—

each signer of the Declaration of Independence, for example—is, in some sense, the controller of that "we," the artificer behind it.[9]

It may seem curious that culture—as the immaterial stuff flowing between people across space and time—should develop a metaculture of newness that downplays that motion in favor of individual creativity. It is curious, however, only if you neglect the specific way culture moves under an idea of newness. It moves by leaving the old object behind—shedding it, so to speak—as the new, metamorphosed object appears. To dwell on surface motion is to miss the ethereal motion of the underlying generative principle of the object—its genius or homunculus within. The latter type of motion is the true hallmark of culture under an idea of newness. And what better place to find the genius or core than in the flesh-and-blood individual?

Assessing the Intention behind Cultural Objects

Under an idea of tradition, the cultural objects that are automatically accepted within a community are those that are replicas of prior objects—objects that have already circulated in that community. A telling of a myth can be immediately taken up because it is a replica, in some sense, of prior tellings. Any new telling has its place already marked out by the cultural element—the myth—that has passed through the community. Acceptability, in short, results from prior circulation.

This means that a cultural object need not be scrutinized for the intention behind it. Since the object expresses the intention of no single individual or subset of individuals, why should the intention behind it become an issue? Wide circulation is achieved by replication, by passing the cultural element through individual after individual. Receptivity to any new telling is thus a byproduct of prior reception, prior replication throughout a community. The cultural object in this way appears as a collective expression, the intention of no one artificer.

In contrast, when the cultural object appears to be new—that is, when there is an imaginable homunculus responsible for its surface characteristics—intention comes to the fore.[10] Such is the situation under a metaculture of newness or modernity. The relative separation of dissemination from replication means that it is possible to disseminate cultural objects—films or books, for example—without replicating them at each step along the way.[11] Therefore, the object created by a single individual or subset of individuals can reach a wide audience—perhaps an entire community—without the need of intervening replication. Consequently, the audience that has not been involved in the replication might well be curious about the object, if not suspicious of it. What is the intention behind its production? In this way, intention—as something explicitly remarked or noted at the metacultural plane—is a function of newness.

If intention is a byproduct of newness, do we find it in the metaculture hovering above culture, that is, in the film reviews that circulate independently of the films they are about? Indeed, we do. It is present in film reviews—and in literary-critical and hermeneutic metaculture more generally—in the form of interpretation: the uncovering of hidden meanings that the object encodes. Here is one example from a review in the *Chicago Sun-Times*:

> [I]t seems to me that Kubrick is describing—in addition to our predicament—man's inability to foresee the consequences of his own actions; and his habit of detaching himself from all facts except those he chooses to recognize.
>
> Man has always devised the means of extinction against his fellow man; but the world changed after Hiroshima, just as it did in Galileo's time. It is no longer man, but mankind, that is threatened. (Keen 1964b, 58)

You may not agree with the reviewer's rendition of the film's intention—namely, "man's inability to foresee the consequences of his own actions." However, you can appreciate that this interpretation captures a kind of authorial or homuncular intent. Indeed, the interpretation does not come out of the blue. The culture (the film, in this case) provides motivation for the metaculture that is produced (the film review), even if the culture does not determine the metaculture.

It is as if the review were itself a new cultural object inspired by the film. The metacultural object, in this regard, is like a cultural object—say, a new film—that has been inspired by an older one. The film review is not simply a replica of the original, although it contains plot and scene renarration. Instead, it grows out of the original object as a response to it, in much the way *Dr. Strangelove* was a response to—rather than a replica of—*Red Alert*. The reviewer chips away at the surface of the film, breaking it open to reveal the intention that informs its design. That intention is part of the genius of the original, part of the immaterial culture that can slip out of it and into new objects.

Table 14 shows the relative amount of each review dedicated to such uncovering of intention. Only 4 percent of each review, on average, is devoted to interpretation of hidden meanings. Not all reviewers are motivated by the films to attempt to disclose the secret purpose of the film's artificer.

Table 14. Percentage of Space Devoted to Interpretation in Reviews of Two Films in Select Publications

BOTH FILMS		DR. STRANGELOVE		FAIL SAFE	
Sight and Sound	11	Sight and Sound	16	Newsweek	21
Chicago Sun-Times	9	Chicago Sun-Times	14	The New Republic	17
Newsweek	8	Chicago Tribune	11	Commonweal	3
The New Republic	7	Life	7	Sight and Sound	0
Chicago Tribune	6	Village Voice	3	Variety	0
Life	4	New York Herald Tribune	2	Films in Review	0
Village Voice	3	Newsweek	2	New York Times	0
Commonweal	2	The New Republic	1	Chicago Sun-Times	0
New York Herald Tribune	1	Films in Review	0	New York Herald Tribune	0
Films in Review	0	Variety	0	Village Voice	0
Variety	0	New York Times	0	New York Post	0
New York Times	0	Commonweal	0	Chicago Tribune	0
New York Post	0	New York Post	0	Life	0
Combined	4%		5%		4%

There is a striking difference between *Fail Safe* and *Strangelove* in this regard: only three of thirteen reviews of the former contained interpretation, whereas eight of thirteen in the latter case did. *Strangelove* stimulated more interpretation than *Fail Safe*—or, at least, it stimulated more of its reviewers to interpret it. Since *Dr. Strangelove* is, evidently, the more highly regarded of the two films, we might wonder: Are those expressions that are most highly valued also those that, in general, stimulate or require or demand more response? Does better culture mean culture that elicits more response?

If a film does elicit stronger response, of course, it is more likely to become known, at least through the informal networks of family and friends. In the case of *Dr. Strangelove*, many of the people interviewed for this project knew of the film by repute, even though they had not themselves seen it.

At the same time, greater response from film critics—as cognoscenti—does not ineluctably translate into greater response among average viewers, even if it predicts the heightened importance of the film for future films—the greater influence that the film, as a piece of culture, will have over subsequent films. This suggests that, as regards films, at least, hierarchical ordering by metaculture may be a function not of breadth of circulation—something that is measured instead by price and demand—but rather of the role that the cultural object plays in the replication of the abstract culture embodied in it. The more a film stimulates people to produce new objects—whether interpretations or new films or other forms of expression—the more highly it is regarded.

Assessing the Truth of Cultural Objects

If interpretation or disclosure of intention is one kind of response stimulated by the cultural object under a metaculture of newness, assessment of "truth" of the object—that is, of the object's relationship to "reality"—is another. You can perhaps already see why truth is associated with circulation under modernity. Where tradition is operative, the truth-bearing cultural object is not new. It is only a replica of what has gone before. Each individual who produces a replica is simultaneously rearticulating a time-honored truth. There is no need for metacultural assessment of truth, because the truth-bearing object is not new and presumably contains no new truth that needs to be assessed.

Correspondingly, where the production of new objects is required for the replication of culture, the truth of those objects is in question. Since the objects might carry new claims about the world, such claims need to be assessed. A metacultural orientation to truth is thus a byproduct of circulation under modernity. We can expect such an orientation even in the case of films, which are not overtly about reality, and hence not designed to overtly capture truth. Assessments of truth or of relation to reality do not form a large component of the reviews examined here, but they are detectable, as indicated in Table 15.

The central question posed in the film reviews—eight of twenty-six—is: What is the relationship between the world, as portrayed in the film, and the "real world," as it is known by other means to the reviewer? This question is continuous with that associated with interpretation. However, whereas interpretation takes the meaning of the cultural expression to be cryptic, as something needing to be deciphered, truth assumes that the meaning of the film—or, rather, the world as represented in the film—is already accessible to the viewer. The question is not what to make of that world, but rather whether that world is an accurate reflection of the world that the reviewer—and, presumably, the reviewer's audience—knows.

The reviews pose the question in general terms, as in this discussion of *Fail Safe*, which appeared in *Life* magazine:

Now I am not an ostrich, and recognize that the world stands in peril of nuclear annihilation. I acknowledge, too, that the amen button may some day be pressed by some idiot official or through some unthinkable mechanical error. But I can't agree that anything could become quite so botched up as it is in *Fail Safe*. Or that any U.S. President would propose nuclear genocide in order to buy off Russia or any other potential enemy. (Oulahan 1964, 12)

Or, again, in this one of *Dr. Strangelove*:

To those who claim that its content is too ridiculous for credibility, I recommend the newspapers. In the same week in which the US takes economic action against nations who trade with Cuba because Castro is spreading Soviet Communism, we also sell a huge lot of wheat to Soviet Russia. Were those actions determined by Stanley Kubrick and Terry Southern or Johnson and Rusk? (Kauffmann 1964, 28)

Occasionally, the reviews focus on specifics of plausibility, as in Bosley Crowther's review in the *New York Times*: "I would not say that the solution of the dilemma seems to me a sensible or likely one . . ." (1964b, 36).

Table 15. Percentage of Space Devoted to Relation to Reality in Reviews of Two Films in Select Publications

BOTH FILMS		DR. STRANGELOVE		FAIL SAFE	
Chicago Tribune	13	Newsweek	14	Chicago Tribune	28
Newsweek	9	The New Republic	5	New York Times	9
New York Times	5	Sight and Sound	0	Life	9
Life	4	Chicago Sun-Times	0	Chicago Sun-Times	5
The New Republic	3	Chicago Tribune	0	New York Post	4
New York Post	2	Life	0	Commonweal	1
Chicago Sun-Times	2	Village Voice	0	Newsweek	0
Commonweal	1	New York Herald Tribune	0	The New Republic	0
Sight and Sound	0	Films in Review	0	Sight and Sound	0
Village Voice	0	Variety	0	Variety	0
New York Herald Tribune	0	New York Times	0	Films in Review	0
Films in Review	0	Commonweal	0	New York Herald Tribune	0
Variety	0	New York Post	0	Village Voice	0
Combined	2%		2%		3%

Interestingly, *Fail Safe* receives more attention to truth value than does *Dr. Strangelove*, while *Dr. Strangelove* calls forth more interpretation or disclosure of intention. The less obscure the intention, perhaps, the more subject to questioning the truth value. A corollary of this is that types of cultural object for which the questioning of truth is most prominent are those types in which meaning is most patent—for example, declarative prose that makes claims to documentary accuracy.

Assessing the Contextual Appropriateness of Cultural Objects

Are cultural objects appropriate for their contexts of circulation? This kind of question surfaces under a metaculture of newness.[12] Where the object is traditional, merely a replica of what has come before it, acceptability is established by prior circulation. The contexts in which the replicated objects appear are, presumably, themselves replicas of the contexts in which the prior objects appeared. Appropriateness, therefore, has been proven by prior circulation. It need not be assessed by metaculture.

New objects, by contrast, demand a response as to their contextual appropriateness. Since the pathways of dissemination are relatively distinct from the processes of replication of the objects that travel along them, new objects find their way into new contexts. What is the relationship between those objects and their new contexts of circulation? Are they appropriate for those contexts? As Table 16 indicates, 4 percent on average of a film review is devoted to these questions.

Discussions of contextual appropriateness shade into discussions of truth value. In the case of context, however, the correspondence (or lack of correspondence) between the world built up in the film and that in which we live is not at issue. The reviewers are interested, rather, in temporally defined social contexts, in relationship to which their concern is with effects—something I will discuss in more detail later. There are three types of context discussed in the reviews: the broad sociopolitical context of the contemporary United States, the context in which the film was shown or viewed, and the film industry context in which the movie was made.

For the most part, discussions of context are really responses to the film: "[T]he topical significance of [*Fail Safe*] endows it with a special urgency . . ." (Crowther 1964b, 36); "Any New Yorker, especially any Manhattanite, who can see *Fail Safe*, at Loew's State and Showcase theaters without a strong sensation of becoming a shadow on some scorched sidewalk, is unusually immune to very strong suggestion" (Winsten 1964b, 29); "Yet aside from questions of critical perspective, I think the whole

Table 16. Percentage of Space Devoted to Assessments of Contextual Appropriateness in Reviews of Two Films in Select Publications

BOTH FILMS		DR. STRANGELOVE		FAIL SAFE	
Village Voice	17	Village Voice	17	New York Post	18
Variety	9	New York Herald Tribune	4	New York Times	17
New York Times	9	Newsweek	3	Village Voice	15
New York Post	8	New York Times	1	Variety	14
Commonweal	6	The New Republic	0	Commonweal	8
Newsweek	2	Chicago Tribune	0	Sight and Sound	5
New York Herald Tribune	2	Chicago Sun-Times	0	The New Republic	0
Sight and Sound	2	New York Post	0	Chicago Tribune	0
Chicago Tribune	0	Commonweal	0	Chicago Sun-Times	0
Films in Review	0	Life	0	Life	0
Chicago Sun-Times	0	Films in Review	0	Newsweek	0
The New Republic	0	Variety	0	New York Herald Tribune	0
Life	0	Sight and Sound	0	Films in Review	0
Combined	4%		3%		7%

subject [of *Dr. Strangelove*] is about a year out of date. It is just Kubrick's bad luck that he instituted this project before the signing of the test-ban treaty and the Kennedy assassination" (Sarris 1964a, 14); "But the odd thing about *Fail Safe*, in its way rather encouraging, is how dated it looks. The mood is that of two years ago, of Kennedy and Khruschev, the Cuba crisis, the lonely intimacies of power. We are no longer, somehow, quite in that world" (Houston 1965, 97).

Like intention and truth, contextual appropriateness need not be assessed for the traditional object, since its appropriateness is preestablished. Because objects like the present one have circulated in contexts like the present one, and the earlier objects were contextually appropriate—a fact ascertainable retrospectively, through their circulation—a present traditional object is also necessarily appropriate. It is the continuation of established practice. But an object understood as new poses a question to viewer or previewer: Is it suitable for the present context? If it is not, then perhaps it should not—as a recommendation to others—achieve wide circulation.

Predicting the Effects of Cultural Objects

In Herodotus's fifth century B.C. history, the Lydian king Croesus consults the oracles of Delphi and Amphiaraus as to whether he should wage war against the Persian king Cyrus. The cryptic response comes back that if he "attacked the Persians, he would destroy a mighty empire" (1942, 27). When he is later defeated, and complains to the Delphic oracle about the prophecy, he is chided that "he ought, if he had been wise, to have sent again and inquired which empire was meant, that of Cyrus or his own" (1942, 51). Herodotus's long history is replete with similar accounts: Ill-starred rulers consult shadowy soothsayers who furnish them with inscrutable prophecies, the true meanings of which become discernible only after the fact, when it is already too late. There is an analogy here to the metaculture of tradition, which "foresees," so to speak—but only retrospectively—based only on prior acceptance.

How different the situation is from the metaculture of newness. An oracular function is present there also—for example, in the predictions found in film reviews about the effects of films—but the prophecy is anything but inscrutable: "Even children will find the scenic flights [in *Dr. Strangelove*] entrancing, imaginative" (Winsten 1964a, 16); "That [*Fail Safe*] will create much word of mouth comment, perhaps even attract certain possible Governmental attention, there can be no doubt" (*"Fail Safe"* 1964, 6). No mistaking these predictions. If anyone cared to do so, he or she could check these predictions for scientific accuracy.

Sometimes the prophecy is formulated as the reviewer's personal response: "I found myself at the edge of tears as I watched a series of nuclear explosions fill the screen and heard a sweet female voice singing, 'We'll meet again, don't know where, don't know when, but I know we'll meet again some sunny day'" (Wainright 1964, 15). Even here, though, the implication is that others will react similarly. The oracular response is an indicator of future public response.

Film reviews, as metaculture, are in this regard not only forward-looking, but also explicit regarding the future to which they look forward. They peer through what is to average viewers the impenetrable fog of time, glimpsing disseminations and replications that are yet to come, mapping trajectories for objects—in this case, films—beyond the present, as those objects become accessible to a broader public. Such metaculture is predictive, prophesying future pathways of motion.

Some reviews construe effects as categorical or absolute, without regard for distinctions among kinds of audiences: "[*Dr. Strangelove*] makes one think, laugh and weep in equal proportions" (Milne 1964, 37); "Seeing the President talking on the 'hot line' to the Soviet Premier, a Joint Chiefs of Staff meeting, the Omaha War Room, SAC bombers in the air, becomes pruriently exciting in much the way war films, which show combat action, raise the blood pressure rather than induce disgust of war" (Davis 1964, 506); "Some scenes [in *Fail Safe*] are funnier unintentionally than *Dr. Strangelove* ever gets intentionally" (Sarris 1964b, 17).

Other reviews show a sensitivity to different audiences, and hence to different possible reactions to the film: "Reactions to this taut, suspenseful, and acidly amusing film [*Dr. Strangelove*] will be highly individual. Professional military men may consider it a snide sneer at their dedicated efforts; others may just see the funny side of the story. Still others, after the laughter, may find it thought-provoking or even frightening. I'm afraid some of us haven't learned to stop worrying" (Tinee 1964b, 8); "This is not a film to please Peace Marchers or Nuclear Disarmers. It does not tell us what we must do to be saved. Nor is it a comfort for those who find smug superiority in irony: from the juvenile insipidities of Carl Foreman on film to the obscenity-decked liberal platitudes of Lenny Bruce in nightclubs. This film says, 'Ban the bomb and they'll find another way. The Doomsday Machine is men'" (Kauffmann 1964a, 26).

Whatever the case, the oracular function of predicting effects occupies a central position in the film reviews investigated here. As Table 17 shows, on average 16 percent of each review is devoted to it. In my study, this proved to be the single largest category. Indeed, no review failed to include at least some discussion of effects, and, in the case of some reviews, discussion of effects dominated the text.

Why accord such a prominent place to effects in film reviews? What does this fact reveal about film reviews as culture and metaculture? If my hunch is correct, it reveals something crucial about the nature of motion under a metaculture of newness and it provides a glimpse into the inner workings of acceleration. For the assessment of effects is simultaneously a response to the cultural object (the film) and the formulation of that response as an intelligible statement about the motion of culture.

Recall that the reviews of *Dr. Strangelove* valued it because it was not a "faithful copy" of what had come before—namely, the novel *Red Alert*. Had it been a copy or a replica, its stature would have been diminished. And this would have been so not simply because the original was not highly esteemed, but also because the act of copying itself—under a metaculture of newness—is not highly esteemed.

No, what made *Dr. Strangelove* great, in part, at least, was that it was not

Table 17. Percentage of Space Devoted to Discussions of Effects in Reviews of Two Films in Select Publications

BOTH FILMS		DR. STRANGELOVE		FAIL SAFE	
Life	45	Life	72	Variety	30
Variety	24	Commonweal	38	Films in Review	27
New York Post	20	New York Times	28	Chicago Tribune	24
Chicago Tribune	20	New York Post	21	Chicago Sun-Times	20
New York Times	18	New York Herald Tribune	17	Village Voice	19
Commonweal	16	Chicago Tribune	16	New York Post	19
New York Herald Tribune	14	Variety	11	Sight and Sound	13
Films in Review	13	The New Republic	11	New York Herald Tribune	11
Sight and Sound	10	Sight and Sound	9	Life	9
Chicago Sun-Times	10	Village Voice	8	Commonweal	8
The New Republic	9	Newsweek	6	New York Times	8
Village Voice	9	Chicago Sun-Times	5	Newsweek	7
Newsweek	7	Films in Review	2	The New Republic	6
Combined	16%		17%		16%

a copy of some prior original, but rather a response to one—a response that went vastly beyond the original. By means of response, the culture that is locked up in an object wiggles its way out of that object and into new ones, in the absence of knee-jerk replication. Just so does the formulation of effects contained in film reviews, as metaculture, represent a response to cultural objects. From this point of view, the metacultural object (the film review) is to the cultural object (the film) what a new cultural object (the film) is to an old one (the prior novel on which the film is based).

Indeed, so important is response to the motion of culture under a metaculture of newness that one might rightly regard it as a third aspect or moment of circulation, alongside replication and dissemination. In response, something from the original carries over. There is movement of immaterial culture, despite the fact that the immaterial culture transmogrifies—or perhaps transmigrates, like a soul undergoing metempsychosis—in the course of its motion. A great work of art is one that induces others to respond to it by creating their own new works of art, which carry over something of the original despite their different appearance.

The film reviews studied here not only acknowledge response as a key to cultural motion; they are also (as culture) themselves responses. Hence, they embody the motion of culture under an idea of newness, even as they comment upon that motion. They respond to the films rather than just replicating them through renarration, but they also formulate that response as an intelligible effect the film has (or will have) on others: "[*Fail Safe*] is a film that clutches you in its grip of annihilation" (Winsten 1964b, 29); "[*Fail Safe*] is so stylishly produced, so well acted and so loaded with suspense that millions of moviegoers will probably believe it all could happen this way" (Oulahan 1964, 12); "The extreme tastelessness of *Strangelove* may drive many people away from the movie" (Hartung 1964b, 633); "A tough film, then, [*Dr. Strangelove*] makes one think, laugh and weep in equal proportions, and . . . ends on an image which makes every other film about The Bomb look like a pretty game: mushroom clouds billow over the vast, unpeopled surface of the earth, and Vera Lynn's voice croons consolingly from a mysterious limbo beyond the soundtrack, 'We'll meet again . . . some sunny day'" (Milne 1964, 37).

A metaculture of tradition imparts an accelerative force to culture that is designed to overcome entropic deceleration. It stresses the need for accurately reproducing the past, and positively values a cultural object that is a replica of earlier ones. A metaculture of newness, by contrast, encourages innovation. It does so by its positive valuation of cultural objects that are themselves interestingly new.

At the same time, for a metaculture of newness to impart an accelerative force to cultural objects, the metacultural objects themselves must attract attention. The film reviews, for example, must kindle interest on the part of potential viewers in the films. Insofar as the film review itself is an interesting response to the film—insofar as it attracts the attention of its readers or listeners or viewers—it transfers that interest to the object it is about: the film. Therefore, the review, as metacultural object, embodies the very principle—motion through response—that it itself articulates. This is the secret of its efficacy.

What is crucial about the prophecies formulated by the oracles of Herodotus is that they captured the attention, and they did so, in part, by dint of their poetic inscrutability. Croesus asks the Delphic oracle: "Whether his kingdom would be of long duration." The reply comes back:

Wait till the time shall come when a mule is monarch of Media;
Then, thou delicate Lydian, away to the pebbles of Hermus;
Haste, oh! haste thee away, nor blush to behave like a coward. (1942, 28)

The prophecies had staying power because of their aesthetic design. They were sure to be remembered and replicated. But their "true" meanings became apparent only subsequently, when events occurred that made sense of them. Who could have foreseen that the "mule" of Delphic prophecy was, in fact, the Median king Cyrus: "For the parents of Cyrus were of different races, and of different conditions, his mother a Median princess . . . and his father a Persian and a subject, who, though so far beneath her in all respects, had married his royal mistress" (1942, 52).

Explicit metaculture shares in the attention-getting ability of oracular prophecy, but, to be effective, it must formulate its predictions explicitly and clearly. It directs the attention of a potential audience (or of potential users) to the cultural objects whose future it foresees, and it thereby also helps to bring about that future. The explicit prophecies of contemporary metaculture are self-fulfilling: If they are readily understood and if they are subscribed to, then in that measure will they orchestrate the outcomes they portend.

The Second Layer and Postmodernity

A central mystery of culture is this: How does it move through the world? I have argued in this book that a key to understanding culture as motion is inertia, and, moreover, inertia of two types: existential, where one acquires culture simply because it is there to be acquired, as in the mother tongue; and habitual, where any new object is processed, evaluated, and reproduced through existing schemata, as in the phenomenon of accent. However, inertia is inadequate as a complete explanation of cultural motion, as I have also argued throughout this book. It is necessary for us, as students of cultural motion, to comprehend the phenomenon of acceleration, where the existing cultural element is given extra impetus for its motion through the world, or deflected from its course, or actually deformed or reformed. Because of entropic deceleration, where culture is deformed in the course of its replication, something else—some additional accelerative input—is necessary even to maintain existentially received tradition at a steady state.

Enter metaculture—a set of cultural elements and objects, such as discourse, with the ability to represent or portray or refer to cultural elements and objects. Metaculture carries an idea about culture—for example, the idea that it is good, something to be striven for, to carry on or reproduce the cultural objects to which one has been exposed. That idea, which infuses consciousness, can—insofar as the cultural objects in which it is carried themselves circulate—affect the motion of culture. It can help to maintain the physical shapes of immaterial culture as it is reproduced over time. The idea imparts a force to the culture it is about.

The force of the idea, of course, derives in part from the cultural objects (or metacultural objects) in which it is contained. What is the source of that force? It can be, in part, the intrinsic interest people have in the metacultural objects as things in the world in their own right. As in the case of cultural objects more generally, those with certain design features—for example, poetic structuring—tend to seize our attention. Insofar as the metaculture is intrinsically interesting in this way, it redirects that interest to the cultural objects it is about. If a friend tells you about a film he or she has seen and you find the description intriguing, you are motivated to see the film. Similarly, if a published or broadcast film review attracts your attention, that interest is redirected to the film that the review is about. What a wondrous phenomenon: The meaning of an object rechannels the interest in that object to another one, which it happens to be about!

However, interest in a metacultural object derives not only from the intrinsic properties of the object itself. It derives also from the objects it is about. In the case of a metaculture of tradition, this is obvious. When the metaculture gets me to reproduce a prior object, part of the charge of the metaculture is my interest in that prior object—for example, a specific performance of a ritual I have already experienced. Metaculture is like a system of mirrors—on analogy with the 1980s nuclear deterrent concept known as "Star Wars"—able to deflect a beam from its course and redirect it to another target. A metaculture of tradition redirects interest in prior objects—such as ritual performances—to new ones that are yet to come—future ritual performances, for instance.

The phenomenon of redirection is obvious in the case of tradition. But it is present also under a metaculture of newness, albeit in novel ways. Since the cultural object, a specific film, for example, is construed as distinct from prior objects so, too, must the metaculture that champions it be new and distinct from prior metaculture. Hence, the metacultural object cannot straightforwardly redirect the interest I had in an old object to a new one, because the new object lacks physical identity with the earlier one. My experience of the object must be distinct in some ways. A wedge is inserted between cultural thing and metacultural response that makes the latter partially independent of the former—a more transparently separate or second layer of circulation, superimposed on the first. How can the process of redirection occur in this case?

The answer I propose is that such redirection depends upon response as one means by which culture passes between objects. The metacultural object—for example, the film review—responds to the cultural object—the film—and, in the course of that response, some of the immaterial culture locked up in the object carries over into the metaculture, where it can then circulate. Of course, the metacultural object also benefits from habitual inertia, since such objects—film reviews in periodicals, for instance—are often produced by the same person time and again. A reader of the periodical comes to depend on particular reviewers for orientation to the plethora of new films available. The cultural object is the beneficiary of that inertia, as well as any added intrinsic interest the film review may have.

However, and crucially, the metacultural object also carries over something from the cultural plane. A movement occurs which allows a part of the intrinsic interest in the cultural object to be disseminated through the metaculture in the absence of a direct encounter with the cultural object itself. The interest of that culture that has carried over—an interest, to be sure, that has become a property of the metacultural thing—can then be redirected to the cultural object as people seek it out (or avoid it, as the case may be).

What this means is that the metacultural plane of circulation becomes a plane in which culture itself circulates. Moreover, it is a layer that is partially independent of the layer of the cultural objects themselves. Under the idea of newness, because redirection of interest depends upon response, the separation of layers increases and more and more of the motion of culture itself takes place at the metacultural plane—hence the knowledge many people have of the film *Dr. Strangelove*, despite having never seen it themselves.

A parallel exists between the development of this second layer of circulation, especially during the twentieth century in Europe and America, and the ideas about culture associated with poststructuralism and postmodernism. The growing importance of the second layer leads students of language and culture to imagine that the second layer is itself the motive force behind the first, that representation determines, so to speak, the thing represented. Cultural objects appear to be less the source of their own intrinsic self-definition and more the product of meanings emanating from the second layer of circulation. Such an idea is present in Ferdinand de Saussure's concept of the arbitrariness of linguistic signs, but it is apparent especially in poststructural self-doubt about representation—the ability of signs to make contact with an outside world—a self-doubt turned into method by Jacques Derrida, among others. The slippage that exists between the layers of metacultural and cultural circulation gets read as a lack of connection between representation and thing-in-the-world. The slippage is present, to be sure, but that should not hinder recognition of the contact and commerce that does occur between these planes, the movement of immaterial culture from a primary layer of circulation (culture) to a secondary one (metaculture) and back again.

At the same time, the second layer of circulation places a premium on speed, and hence gives rise to the phenomenon of time compression discussed by David Harvey (1989) as a hallmark of postmodernity. In order for a metacultural object to disseminate information about or experience of the cultural object, it must itself be less massive, and move more speedily through the world than the cultural object. I scan page after page of short film reviews; I read blurbs on numerous boxes of videos, all in less than the time it takes to actually view the film to which my attention has been directed. To be in a position to disclose the cultural plane to individuals, metacultural objects must be small and quick. Indeed, the phenomena that Harvey associates with post-Fordism and late capitalism are products of the form of cultural motion occurring in this second layer of circulation—the layer of metaculture that hypertrophies under the idea of newness.

The second layer of circulation, to be sure, is not independent of the first—or, at least, is not wholly independent of it. Movement takes place between planes, between things in the world (cultural objects) and things (metacultural objects) that carry meanings about those things in the world. It is unthinkable that such movement would not take place. How else would culture—operating in accord with a principle of newness—make its way through the world? We, as analysts of culture, would be forced to subscribe to the absurdity of a rationalism in which every cultural object appears as the product of a systematic individual creation, with no dependence on prior creations—earlier cultural objects—that have paved the way for it, made it possible. At the same time, we would miss altogether the phenomenon of acceleration if we tried to deny the role of such creations, and to attribute everything to the inertia of received traditions.

6

Inability to Foresee

There is a tide in the affairs of men, a nick of time.
We perceive it now before us.
To hesitate is to consent to our own slavery.
> —John Witherspoon, Signer of the Declaration of Independence
> (1776), quoted in David Walker Woods, *John Witherspoon* (1906)

There is a tide in the affairs of women,
Which, taken at the flood, leads—God knows where.
> —Lord Byron, *Don Juan*, canto 6, stanza 2 (1819–24)

There is a tide in the affairs of every people when the moment strikes
for political action. . . . This is our chance.
> —Kwame Nkrumah, *I Speak of Freedom* (1961)

The Ebb and Flow of Newness

It was Shakespeare who, depicting a dialogue between Brutus and Cassius
on the occasion of their assassination of Julius Caesar, wrote: "[T]here is
a tide in the affairs of men . . ." (act 4, scene 3, line 218). The words themselves participated in their own tidal swell, augmented in prominence
through secondary replications, lapping up onto the shorelines of received

culture, reaching people previously untouched by them. To be sure, the imagery contained in the words is that of newness and change: a tide, "which, taken at the flood, leads on to fortune; omitted, all the voyage of their life is bound in shallows and in miseries." Here is quintessential acceleration, the stuff of narrative—the valorization of decisive, agentive conduct that leads to something new and reconfigures the social landscape. But the tide is also one of words, as things in the world, metacultural things, undergoing successive replications, increasing their presence in the daily lives of people. It is such a metacultural tide that leads to an expansion in the influence of ideas of newness—a surge of imagery valorizing novelty.

At the same time, what is curious about the imagery of tides in relationship to newness is that tides are cyclical. To be sure, the tide, as known to physics, is variable depending on the relative alignments of the earth, moon, and sun as well as, in details of its effects, upon the winds that produce waves of varying periodicities and magnitudes. But the basic fact is that tides flow and ebb, surge and subside. Can this be true also of the rise of metacultural ideas of newness? Do such ideas rise in popularity, achieve a certain circulation, and then fall back again, giving way to tradition?

If my suspicion is correct, ideas of newness and tradition have been co-present everywhere and at all times, with one set achieving dominance now, another then. The distinction I have drawn, throughout this book, between the inner logics of two types of metaculture does not map neatly onto distinct types of society—for example, "hot" and "cold," or "traditional" and "modern."[1] Indeed, the movement of innovation through the world—where the new thing is recognized as "new," and not as something "old" that has been tinkered with in minor ways—is actually unthinkable without the evaluation of the new as better—that is, without a metaculture of newness. The Uru-eu-wau-wau case demonstrates this. But our remarking of the empirical copresence of the two kinds of metaculture should not leave us with mouths opened, gawking, too stunned to respond to the possibility—nay, the probability, even certainty—that one type spreads more widely, becomes more dominant at one time than another.

For the two metacultural ideas carry different weights at different times and in relation to different aspects of culture. A rapid increase in what archaeologists call "complexity"—that is, the division of labor, with its attendant relative severing of dissemination from replication, and the refiguring of politically and administratively distinct classes—is probably accompanied, in some measure, by a tide of newness subscribed to by some of the individuals involved. How else could anything "new" take hold?

If newness arises to refigure cultural elements, to reshape social land-scapes, must it not also retreat, with innovations absorbed into patterns of replication? Surely newness has made major advances in the past—I have singled out ancient Greece as one likely place where it achieved a wide currency. But there have also been retreats. Symptoms of the ebbing of newness can be detected today—the claims of identity politics to intrinsic cultural worth, the resurgence of religious authoritarianism, even con-sumer complaints of exhaustion at too many choices, too much change. Has the metaculture of newness begun a major cyclical ebbing, or are these but minor ripples in a longer-term advance?

While I am unable to foresee the immediate future of this metacultural tide, the idea of cultural motion developed here suggests a way of ex-ploring macrocyclicity from a conceptual point of view. For individual cultural objects are impelled, in part, by analogous forces operating at the micromotional plane. In order to participate fully in traditional culture, to serve as carriers of it, sensible objects must—curious though this seems—die and be reborn. The objects participate in a kind of microcyclicity, as the absence of the prior thing provides motivation to reproduce it. Can there be a relationship between this microcyclicity and the macrocycles of metaculture?

The sphinxes of Egypt or the giant granite heads of Mount Rushmore are too durable, too monumental for this type of cultural motion, which finds its natural home rather in the ephemeron of a spoken word, a word that lives for but a flickering moment—unless electronically captured—and then vanishes, only to rematerialize in another thing that looks like it. The death of the ephemeron, as sensible object, consists in the denial of sensory access to it. Its rebirth consists in the production of a new object that, to the senses, appears as identical or nearly identical to it. Rebirth fills the need created by the death—by sensory deprivation—and it be-comes, thereby, the core mechanism of cultural motion.

Paradoxically, the durable object—a stone sphinx, the granite heads of Mount Rushmore, even a book or a reel of celluloid tape—is a less perfect embodiment of traditional culture because its very durability relieves the individuals interested in it of the need to reproduce it—at least, to repro-duce it as a whole object in an act of primary replication. True, the fifty-foot high Mount Rushmore heads are reproduced in other forms—in miniature models, in photographs and paintings, and in narrations of the experience of them. However, the durability of the objects, coupled with their monumental size, saps individuals of the motivation to make these things again. Consequently, the learning bound up in their original making fails to find its way out of them and into new ones.

In contrast with the ephemeron, the durable monument results in sensory saturation or satiation. Individuals grow bored with the new thing, able as they are to satisfy their interests in it without producing a new one just like it. The Mount Rushmore heads—blasted and chiseled into a mountainside in the sun-bleached hills of South Dakota—are not refashioned again and again, pace the example of Pierre Menard, who aspired, you will recall, to "write" *Don Quixote*, not simply to copy it. Paradoxically, therefore, durability impedes traditional cultural motion—where motion results from the stabilization of the sensible object through its continuous reproduction. No wonder a metaculture of newness comes to the rescue—imparting an accelerative force, keeping culture alive, in these cases.

Newness itself depends on microcyclicity, as the old durable object loses it value. That value—if culture is to move through the world—must be carried over into a new object, one that does not look exactly like the old one. Mount Rushmore has inspired the construction of a new mountain sculpture, the Crazy Horse Monument, whose size will dwarf the presidential heads and whose physical appearance to the senses is wholly distinct. But the techniques of production employed in this new creation carry on the culture locked up in the existing Mount Rushmore heads—the careful use of dynamite for sculpting, the erection of a "pointing machine" to scale up locations on the mountainside from a small model, even the routines of placing charges, then clearing the area for blasting at day's end.

Though culture moves through such production of newness, the spread of the metacultural idea can result in the destabilization of sensible objects. If new things appear in too quick a succession, if they come to form a feverish phantasmagoria, the idea of newness gives rise to the sense that, as in the case of the ephemeron, there is nothing to hold onto. A prior stable sensible object cannot be recaptured from the stream of apparently new objects that bombard the senses—even though strands of immaterial culture pass through them and become intelligible, like those infrared beams used to guard against burglary, which themselves can be "seen" with the aid of detecting lenses.

Even the durable cultural object immediately recedes into the past, slips from us, because it is so rapidly replaced by new ones, which, to be sure, carry over the cultural learning embodied in the earlier object, but which also leave the senses—if not the intellect—unable to grasp the motion of culture through the continuous recreation of palpably similar objects. Hence, curiously, a too pervasive metaculture of newness calls up feelings of object loss that motivate a desire to stabilize the sensible world, give it an air of permanence, through traditional replication such as gives rise to the motion of traditional culture in the first place.

Herewith can one grasp the tide-like cyclicity of metaculture. The idea of newness, while stimulating the motion of immaterial, intangible culture in the ways I have described throughout this book, simultaneously produces a phantasmagorical succession of sensible objects that lacks the feel of continuity and stability of a solid, orderly world. Consequently, its widespread proliferation as metaculture calls up a force that counteracts it—the feeling of instability that engenders a desire for tradition in the form of replication. Such a world of cascading newness has already taken shape in the core areas of North America and Europe. Does this account for the discontent that is bred in the very heartland of newness, rather than (or in addition to) the periphery?

At the same time, if the dominance of newness results in the feeling of emphemerality and instability of sensible objects, thereby calling forth a desire for tradition that counteracts the spread of newness, the opposite happens when tradition becomes too pervasive, too successful. The solidity of sensible objects makes them seem—like the monumental object itself—too durable, too boring. The senses are satiated by the cultural objects themselves, and this calls forth the itch for the new, the quest for the exotic. This itchiness, so closely allied with capitalist dissemination of culture and with the entrepreneur, in turn serves to counteract the spread and dominance of ideas of oldness and tradition.

That much said, if there is a tide-like quality to the spread of metacultures of newness and oldness, modernity and tradition, is there a larger trend in the movement of culture that cannot be fully reversed by the next ebbing? Has the world itself experienced a flood of epochal (or even biblical) proportions, a flood that has carried along human culture in its powerful currents to a point beyond which the full reconstruction of traditional cultural objects—including traditional, kinship-based classes—is no longer possible? Or are we simply accumulating, quantitatively, more culture that can just as well be traditionalized as passed through the creation of the new? Perhaps we are now able, thanks to economics and the other social sciences, to tinker with the rates of production of newness and hence, to modulate the great metacultural tides. Or perhaps we are entering a darkly atavistic era in which social groupings—like castes or clans, as ethnicities might become—re-emerge as strictly determined by rules of parentage and marriage, rather than being the probabilistic outcome of interactions among different forms of cultural motion.

I am no Delphic oracle. I am unable to foresee the future of our present tide, and unwilling to cloak a cryptic surmise in deniable inscrutability. Yet, in light of its possible cyclicity, it seems appropriate to reassess contemporary forms of social space, such as those described by Pierre Bourdieu for France. My proposal is that the contemporary forms are not simply objectively given, but rather the product of a cultural motion that has taken shape under the high tide of newness.

Classification Classifies the Classifiers

Bourdieu's ([1975] 1984) dictum, while cryptic, articulates a well-known truth: People get complimented for good taste, criticized for bad taste—in clothing, food, wine, and yes, even films. Their own classification of the world—what they like and what they dislike—simultaneously classifies them in the eyes of others. A hierarchy of people as well as things results.

Such a system for classifying and ranking people is closely bound up with mass-disseminated culture and, especially, with demand (reflected in price) as a key measure of cultural motion. Consequently, it is closely bound up with a metaculture of newness. Under tradition there is no need to classify people according to their tastes, because their classification as kinds of people is given by tradition, typically by rules of descent. Taste reflects ascribed social status.

What changes with a metaculture of newness is that social position is not determined by descent—or, at least, not by descent alone. If taste correlates with parentage, this is because taste is carried along, in part, by inertial culture, and the key locus of inertial cultural motion is the family. However, there is a crucial difference. Under a metaculture of newness, you can strive—like Eliza Doolittle—to change your received dispositions, to define your social persona through your tastes rather than to have your tastes defined for you by your ascribed persona. This is made possible by the restlessness of a culture that seeks constantly to find new pathways of motion through the world, that daringly jumps from one physical object to another apparently different one. As a result, individuals get bombarded with choices about which cultural objects they will take up. Those choices, in turn, define who they are, what position in society they occupy.

Of course, mass dissemination creates another basis for classification: the extent of your contribution to dissemination in the first place. Contribution to dissemination has a ready-made measure: your accumulated wealth, insofar as you earned that wealth rather than simply inheriting it. Consequently, a metaculture of newness spawns two competing and complexly interconnected means for classifying people. One organizes people by their tastes, and the other arrays them according to their accumulated wealth.

The two means for classifying people can be interpreted as forming the axes of a space—mappable onto Bourdieuian space—within which individuals are situated. Bourdieu takes as his two axes "total volume of capital" (a function of the combined positions on both the wealth and taste axes I have proposed) and "composition of capital" (a function of the relative contributions of taste versus wealth to position on the axis of total volume). It is thus possible to derive Bourdieuian space from the principles of cultural motion under a metaculture of newness.

A problem for the Bourdieuian approach, however—and one that a theory of cultural motion solves—is this: What is the basis for the classification of people according to their tastes? If different people classify the world differently—if they don't in fact agree upon what they like—then aren't there just so many disparate classifications, rather than one single axis along which all tastes can be ranged? The question does not arise regarding accumulated wealth, for there it is a matter of more versus less. In the case of taste, however, it is a question of this one versus that one. Do you prefer the *Well-Tempered Clavier* or the *Blue Danube*? Which do you like to eat more, fish or pork? Which do you read, *Le Monde* or *Le Figaro*? Do you say "either" [eether] or "either" [ayther]? The researcher can differentiate people according to their tastes, but who is to say which tastes are higher in social status?

One possible solution can be immediately discarded, namely, that tastes are scaled solely according to income. You demand what you can afford to demand. To be sure, the point is made by Bourdieu that the lower classes in France, at the time of his research, acquired tastes they could afford—the "taste for necessity" ([1975] 1984, 372 ff.). At the same time, the starting point for Bourdieu's research was the empirical observation that people at the same income level had different tastes. They deployed their available cash differently. This differential deployment is what, in the first instance, renders plausible the notion of a "space" through which people move. How can differential deployment be explained? Bourdieu argued that it could be explained by the existence of forms of noneconomic capital, which he termed cultural capital. Certain purchases were designed to enhance cultural or symbolic or social worth.

But how can you know which tastes have greater cultural worth, if you cannot use economics as a guide?

The problem led Bourdieu to posit an objective hierarchy, or, at least, an objective principle for discrimination, namely, aesthetic distance. But what is the status of that objective principle, if different members of society disagree as to what is better? The answer is to be found in the dissemination of metaculture, and, in particular, in the rise of metacultural expertise.

Every expression of taste is, in some sense, metacultural. It represents a response to a cultural object, and hence is about that cultural object, even if the response is only to buy it or not to buy it. However, as I have been arguing, not all metacultural responses are equal. When an idea of newness dominates, it becomes imperative that a public eye develop. To insure that new items really are new, to insure that culture is, indeed, carried over from one object to another, there is a need for metacultural experts, people who make it their business to become intimately familiar with classes of cultural objects, such as films or automobiles. Unlike ordinary judgments of taste, which may never make their way into words, or which may get expressed in words but communicated only to family or friends, much the way myths are, the judgments of experts get encoded in mass-disseminated forms such as magazine or journal articles, or television or radio commentary. These mass-disseminated metacultural judgments organize the plethora of different ordinary responses into a hierarchy, however loose or tight that hierarchy may be.

But it is not simply their wide distribution, with its attendant secondary replication, that makes expert opinions the arbiters of taste. There is also the fact that these responses are produced by people who possess greater familiarity with the class of objects that is undergoing evaluation. Such people claim to know the cultural object more intimately than those with only a passing acquaintance of them. They acquire authority as arbiters of taste by virtue of their closer proximity to truths about the object.

This much said, I want to back away—albeit not too far—from Bourdieu's claim that the axis of evaluation is objective, fixed, and stable. Through the circulation of metaculture, and in proportion as that metaculture gets taken up locally—in that measure there is agreement on a hierarchy of taste. But—and this is a big "but"—there are even important differences of opinion among the producers of mass-disseminated metaculture, that is, among the people who are supposed to know. Hence, the hierarchy that does emerge is necessarily statistical or probabilistic, not categorical. Correspondingly, it is one in which cultural objects make a difference. The hierarchy is not produced independently of the objects that are evaluated, but rather in response to them. The principles of evaluation are not disconnected from the things that are evaluated. If something necessarily carries over in the course of response—from the cultural object to the expression of response—then new objects can shift the very hierarchy itself.

In some sense, this is obvious. The new cultural object—as the previous chapter demonstrates—can only be fully evaluated in relationship to objects that have come before it. Hence, the new object will become, in its turn, part of the past against which some subsequent object will be judged. It is a once and future thing, predicting or foreseeing future objects, and contributing to the metacultural framework—the precipitated past—through which those future objects will be judged.

The shifting nature of the hierarchy of taste does not mean that taste is arbitrary. Nor does it mean that some cultural objects are not intrinsically better than others for some purpose. Presumably, the reason that the Uru-eu-wau-wau Indians decided to take up the metal pots and knives left for them by the government contact team in the early 1980s was that those objects performed existing cultural tasks better than the analogous cultural objects that the Uru-eu-wau-wau were producing. However, the cultural object does not, thereby, take on an absolute value. Its value is relative to contemporary local processes of cultural replication.

The hierarchy of taste described by Bourdieu—with the additional flexibility I am trying here to give it—is a product of a metaculture of newness. Taste itself depends upon the constant production of new cultural objects such that choices will always have to be made, such that taste will always have to be exercised. Suppose we froze the production of objects at a given moment. Suppose further that, at that moment, we replaced the metaculture of modernity with a metaculture of tradition. What would be the effect on social space? What kind of world might this transformation produce? Here, again, is the question of tidal cyclicity. What does the social world come to look like when newness ebbs?

At the moment we have fast-frozen our social space. There are differences as regards tastes, and there is a widely, albeit not uniformly, understood hierarchy of taste. There is also a hierarchy of income measuring the differential contributions of individuals to cultural dissemination. When we unfreeze the system so produced, what happens? Taste passes on inertially within families. Why? Because families are the locus of the kinds of close social relations through which inertial culture is transmitted, just as they are in Bourdieuian social space. In this new social space generated by changing over to a metaculture of tradition, the next generation has incentive not to change its tastes over time, but rather to maintain its existing ones. Hence, clearly circumscribed social groupings take shape, each defined by descent—since traditional taste passes down primarily through the family—and each the bearer of a distinctive set of tastes. In short, the transformation produces a society based on hereditary classes or estates or clans.

The metacultural ranking at the time this change takes place would itself have to become part of tradition rather than the subject of constantly new production. Hence, individuals would come to see themselves as having "places" in society, rather than, as Bourdieu dubs them, "trajectories" through social space ([1975] 1984, 109 ff.). For those opposed to modernity, this is an important conclusion to keep in mind. Is it possible to imagine a metaculture that is alternative to modernity, but that does not result in retraditionalization and the loss of flexibility for individuals to redefine themselves and their positions within a social world?

I have painted the distinction with a broad brush, and I do so to bring out the significance of metaculture not only for the kind of cultural motion that occurs, but also for the kind of social world—so replete with possibilities and alternative futures—in which we live. I am aware that contemporary metaculture contains emphases on both newness and oldness. Indeed, as I have proposed, probably every metaculture involves some mixture in emphasis. But I also believe that the metaculture of newness has assumed unprecedented significance in the West during the past five hundred years—we are at the flood stage. The flood is a factor—perhaps even the key factor—in the organization of social space in the United States, western Europe, and elsewhere. A retreat from this organization would involve a major tidal shift in the history of cultural motion.

Response Is a Form of Cultural Motion

In her review of Dr. Strangelove in the Chicago Sun-Times on February 20, 1964, Eleanor Keen wrote: "[I]t seems to me that Kubrick is describing—in addition to our predicament—man's inability to foresee the consequences of his own actions; and his habit of detaching himself from all facts except those he chooses to recognize" (1964a, 58). This is an example of one kind of response to a cultural object—the response in which one interprets it. The response, as this example shows, is distinct from straightforward replication such as is attempted in myth-telling, and even that which underlies the pattern of command and inept compliance found in the Cherokee Indian myth discussed in chapter 4. In those cases, we find replication of many of the same words.

It is not that replication of words from the films is absent in film reviews. On the contrary, especially in connection with scene narration and plot renarration, we find traces of the exact words from the film, as, for example, in Judith Crist's review of *Dr. Strangelove* in the *New York Herald Tribune*:

> And so a well intentioned President Muffley copes with a besotted Premier Kissoff on the hot line ("Now then, Dimitri, you know how we've always talked about the possibility of something going wrong with the bomb— the bomb, Dmitri, the Hydrogen bomb. . . ."). General "Buck" Turgidson urges a follow-up on Ripper's attack ("It is necessary to choose between two admittedly regrettable but nevertheless distinguishable post-war environments: one, where you've got 20 million people killed and the other where you've got 150 million people killed"). . . . (Crist 1964a, 8)

This is only a sampling of the quotes in her review. Here is a side-by-side comparison of the quotes with the film transcript:

TRANSCRIPT	CRIST REVIEW
it is necessary *now [to] make a choice,*	It is necessary [. . .]
to choose between two admittedly	to choose between two admittedly
regrettable, but nevertheless,	regrettable but nevertheless
distinguishable post-war environments:	distinguishable post-war environments:
one where *you got* twenty million people	one, where *you've got* 20 million people
killed, and the other where *you got a*	killed and the other where *you've got*
hundred and fifty million people killed.	150 million people killed
Now then Dimitri. You know how	Now then, Dimitri, you know how
we've always talked about the possibility	we've always talked about the possibility
of something going wrong with the bomb.	of something going wrong with the bomb—
The bomb, Dimitri. The hydrogen bomb.	the bomb, Dmitri, the Hydrogen bomb . . .

The differences are minor, indeed, as indicated by the highlighted portions of text. The important point is not that these are minor differences,[2] but the fact that Crist's review carries over—in word-for-word fashion—material from the original film. And Crist is not alone. About a third of the reviews employ direct quotes from the film to some significant degree. However, the reviewers do not always recall the words correctly, as, for example, in *Newsweek*'s review of *Dr. Strangelove* ("Direct Hit" 1964, 79). While discussing George C. Scott's portrayal of General Buck Turgidson, the reviewer writes: "Their retaliatory force, [Turgidson] says, will be reduced so that the U.S. will suffer 'only acceptable casualties—ten to twenty megadeaths,' and he adds with a sporting shrug, 'depending on the breaks.'" (79). The quoted material is actually drawn from two separate passages that have been run together. Both are misquoted, as shown in this side-by-side comparison:

TRANSCRIPT	NEWSWEEK
only [modest and] acceptable [civilian] casualties	only acceptable casualties
ten to twenty *million killed* [, tops. Uh . . .] depending on the breaks.	ten to twenty *megadeaths* depending on the breaks

The level of misquotation is consistent with that of someone retelling words they have heard from another, so that the review looks much like the replication found in myth-telling. How many of us have heard someone quote and misquote from a film in this way? This is prima facie evidence of cultural transmission—secondary replication.

But while it is prima facie evidence of cultural transmission, it is not the norm in film reviews. The reviews as metaculture are less replications of actual words and more the transmission of the kinds of meanings contained in or carried by the cultural object, as in Keen's interpretation: "Kubrick is describing . . . man's inability to foresee the consequences of his own actions." But are such interpretations a form of cultural motion? If so, what is moving? And do responses more generally effect or result in the movement of culture?

In the case of direct quotation, as observed by Voloshinov ([1929] 1973), the purpose is to carry over the actual physical shape of the original utterance.[3] One strives for a representation of the words as physical things-in-the-world, so that, even in the movement from auditory experience to graphic representation, the point is to capture the actual linear unfolding of the audible sound. However, in this regard, the misquotation noted earlier is intriguing. The reviewer gets the meaning right but the words wrong ("million killed" > "megadeaths"). Meaning is carried over in some measure in spite of the mutation of the physical things—the words as objects.

Even in the case of direct quotation, therefore, there is replication of the meaning extracted from the sensible material (the sounds uttered by actors in a film) in addition to replication of the sensible material itself. In other words, replication, in the form of not quite exact but nevertheless equivalent wording, involves a conversion of the original perceptible or sensible cultural object into another form—the meaning carried by that sensible form. And if this is true in the case of the words themselves, it is all the more true in the case of other aspects of the cultural object. The metaculture (the film review, in this case) reproduces the cultural object (the film) by converting sensible experiences—experiences that the reviewers themselves have of the film—into intelligible meanings. It is the intelligible meanings that are then circulated in the new (meta)cultural object: the film review.

Perhaps this suggests a way of thinking about the motion of culture under a metaculture of modernity. If something about the cultural object—both its sensible form and its intelligible meaning—is working its way out of the object and into the response, which also ranks that something relative to prior cultural objects, then that response, that metaculture, is carrying the culture of the object forward in time.

It is not just carrying it forward for its own sake, but also for the sake of foreshadowing responses to new cultural objects that will be produced in the future, as well as to the presently circulating one. The culture of the object moves into the response, which in turn determines—if the response is that of the filmmakers, for example, or is circulated and taken up by them—what new objects will be produced. Culture here travels from the original object to the new one via the response. In other words, the pathway of the motion is: cultural object → metacultural response → new cultural object.

Under a metaculture of tradition or oldness, by contrast, a cultural object such as a particular telling of a myth is construed as a replica of what has come before it. The underlying cultural element—the myth—passes from one object to another object in a direct, not a circuitous, way. Its motion is not mediated by response. Of course, one might respond to a myth by not telling it to someone else, or, perhaps, by modifying it or tinkering with it in some way. But metaculture directs one's attention to the "it"— to the abstract culture that is passing through the world in a consistent material form rather than to the individual as responder or to the specific response.

In the contemporary United States, the matter is quite different. Since the emphasis—in the case of films or novels, for example—is on producing a new cultural object, that object must look physically different from objects that have preceded it. Hence, the movement of culture cannot be based on the replication of sensible, physical form. But this does not mean that culture is failing to pass in the course of production of new objects. On the contrary, as I hope I have now made clear, it is merely that the pathway of motion is distinct.

Under modernity, underlying culture passes from old objects into new ones via responses. The responses, as metaculture, carry over something from the object responded to, just as they carry over something from prior responses to other objects—in keeping with metaculture as a somewhat separate layer or plane of circulation. At the same time, responses are also forward looking. The production of new cultural objects is guided by responses to them, even as they are being produced. Those responses—the result, in part, of inertial habituation, but also of mass-circulated metaculture that has been taken up—allow the passage of culture extracted from earlier objects into new ones.

It is evident—is it not?— that the culture transported in this way cannot be too bound up with the sensible, perceptible shape of the thing. The world, so to speak, cannot be too much with it. Since an idea of newness requires that the thing appear new, it cannot look or sound or taste or smell or feel too much like something that has come before it. It cannot be identifiable as a "faithful copy" of that earlier thing. Yet it must be an object that produces the same kind of response. What is crucial to the continuity of culture, in this regard, is the response.

Recall, in this light, *Dr. Strangelove* reviewer Eleanor Keen (1964a, 58). She responded to the film (the cultural object) with an interpretation (the metacultural object): "[I]t seems to me that Kubrick is describing . . . man's inability to foresee the consequences of his own actions. . . ." Perhaps you can appreciate how such an interpretation grows out of—and is extractable from—the object (the film *Dr. Strangelove*), how it carries over some of the culture contained in the object—even if you, and certainly I, might not consider the interpretation adequate or illuminating.[4] Major King Kong and the B-52 bomber crew fly blithely on, unaware that their dogged efforts might (indeed, do) trigger an earth-destroying doomsday device; in fending off a would-be caller, a secretary, engaged moments before in hanky panky with General Buck Turgidson, hasn't a clue that she is wasting precious minutes, minutes that might be deployed for saving humanity; the Russian premier, in authorizing a "doomsday machine," never imagined that it might be triggered accidentally. Little people go about their business, each in their own way, unthinkingly, unwittingly,

hammering nails into the collective coffin, each contributing to perma-
nent, steely-cold global death.

Yes, unintended consequences abound here. Keen is right. Yet the interest in them—in the inability to foresee—is not unique to this cultural
object. A great number of objects play upon such interest. Slapstick
comedies—Abbott and Costello, the Marx Brothers, and others—exploit
it regularly. You and I watching as one character, while walking next to
his partner, transports on his shoulder a long wooden board. Never stop-
ping to contemplate the consequence, the character turns swiftly to one
side, simultaneously rotating the board, and, in so doing, whacking his
partner in back of the head. You and I, as audience, foresee the consequence, but the character does not. How often is this interest in human
folly played for comic or tragic effect?

The response—as a form of metaculture—is something that can be reproduced by an endless string of cultural objects, much the way a myth
can be retold countless times. Put into explicit metaculture—as it surely
was long before Keen scribed these words—the response itself becomes
mass-disseminable, able to guide the self-conscious production of new
cultural objects: "If that's what the folks out there want, then, by golly,
that's what we'll give them!"

That continuity of response—that carrying over of something from
prior objects—insures that the production of newness will not result in
fragmentation, disconnection from the past, and complete rupture. Rather,
the past appears—thanks to response—as forward-looking, as a past that is
prelude to a future. How else to reconcile the production of newness with
continuity, the demand for difference with the idea that "If you liked the
book, you'll like the movie"? How else to comprehend the proliferation of
movies such as *Die Hard, Rocky, Star Wars,* or even *Thin Man*? How else to
fathom the popularity of genre productions, such as the recent spate of disaster movies involving volcanoes, fires, meteors, earthquakes, even sinking
ships? Evidently, continuity is sought here in metacultural response rather
than in surface identity.

*The Public Sphere Results from the Mediation of Cultural Motion
by Metaculture*

The logic of newness demands the development of methods of assessment
that are prospective and predictive, that allow people to foresee, to gaze
into the crystal ball, to fathom, from its hazy images, what is not yet but

will be. Because of the need for prospective assessment, local taste—whether that of the consumer of cultural objects or that of the producer—can never supply the test of quality. Yes, demand measures that quality. It is an index similar to the ones provided by tradition, although the time depth is probably shorter. Evidence of demand is retrospective. The best culture is that which achieves widespread or long-lasting demand. But this kind of test is not prospective. There is no oracular function here, no judgment as to whether a putatively "new" object is better than preceding ones.

Consequently, something like a public sphere emerges as an inescapable byproduct of a metaculture of newness. The logic of such a metaculture is to find ways to assess whether new objects are, indeed, better. Assessment requires a critical orientation to culture, an orientation that attempts to articulate response. Is this a good piece of literature? What is good about it? Is this a good automobile or stainless steel pot? What is good about it?

The earliest manifestations of the bourgeois public sphere in Europe in the latter 1600s—the salon tradition in France, as described by Habermas ([1962] 1989)—took shape out of a felt need, produced by the logic of a new type of cultural motion, for critical assessment of culture. This development, from the very start, organized disparate local tastes into a hierarchy—albeit a loose and contested one—a hierarchy of the sort required by Bourdieu's ([1975] 1984) version of social space in contemporary France. The development of a taste hierarchy depended upon the rise of a public sphere, where critical judgments could get articulated and circulated.

In the early phase of development, "ordinary citizens" came together to discuss and debate matters of culture. The citizens made no claims to superior judgments based on special knowledge or skills. They were, in this sense, ordinary (extraordinary though they may have been as regards wealth). As a consequence, their judgments appeared to reflect the "voice of the people." They appeared to be collectively shared judgments.

In Habermas's ([1962] 1989) scenario, critiques of literature spilled over into the critical discussion of politics. Laws or decrees or actions affecting the public are also, of course, pieces of culture. They move like other pieces through space and time via social pathways. They should, therefore, come under the aegis of metacultural scrutiny in the same way as works of literature and art. If the basis for assessment of a law is no longer its past history and dissemination—that is, its status as traditional—then to judge it as better or worse requires prospective assessment. Hence, laws and decrees require the same kind of metacultural scrutiny as literature or other cultural objects or elements.

I must admit that, as an anthropologist who has spent much time in remote corners of the earth studying persistent local traditions to whose right to survive I remain committed, I am nevertheless awestruck by the culture that has emerged in the West. So much of contemporary anthropology has been critical of western culture, viewing it at something that helps to stamp out local traditions. I value that gadfly quality of anthropological critique—and, indeed, now understand it more clearly as part of the critical functions that the metaculture of newness has engendered. The voices of anthropology are part and parcel of public sphere processes.

At the same time, having now trained my lens on the culture of the West and especially of the contemporary United States, how could I not but marvel at it? Is it not an astonishing and ingenious creation? I take each clever little piece, look at it, scratch my head, and think: So *this* is how it fits together. True, the currently dominant metaculture of newness has antecedents, not only in the historical processes of dissemination at work for thousands of years, but also in the proselytizing religions of the last two millennia. Still, the implications of the current metaculture of newness—with its intrepid valuation of the production of novel cultural objects over the perpetuation of old ones—are staggering. As the tide of newness spreads, as it enters the flood stage, it reorganizes not only the motion of culture through the world—no mean feat—but also the social relations of the people among whom culture moves. In this regard, the idea is world-making.

Dissecting the Cultural Object

In Habermas's ([1962] 1989) rendition[5] of western history, the public sphere of the eighteenth century, which gave rise to democratic forms of government and the promise of rule by "the people," degenerated in the nineteenth and twentieth centuries. Public discussion and debate—critical metaculture—became subordinated to advertising and economic interests. The people came to be consumers of public opinion rather than producers. Rational dialogue and debate were distorted by power and money.

Viewed through the lens of cultural motion, however, the fate of the public sphere takes on a distinct coloration. If I am correct, the public sphere—as critical reflection on culture by ordinary people—came into existence as the result of a felt need arising from the displacement of a metaculture of tradition by a metaculture of newness. Since the metaculture of tradition provided a method for making judgments about culture—a retrospective method wherein one assessed worth through durability and historical spread—rejecting a metaculture of tradition meant finding a new method of assessment. That method had to be forward-looking. Demand alone could not suffice, since evidence of demand is had only after the fact.

Looking forward from qualities of the cultural object or element meant scrutinizing the object. In what ways could this new object be judged better than ones that had come before it? Ordinary individuals, debating amongst themselves, reached their own conclusions. But a metaculture of tradition had the benefit of automatic publicity. One piece of culture was obviously better than the others because it, rather than the others, was carried on. Just look around. You can see the acceptance it has already achieved.

Individual opinions about worth lack the benefit of publicity unless those opinions circulate and emerge as consensus. Everyone—or almost everyone, or at least most people—agrees that this cultural object is superior to that one. For such an agreement to become known, the metaculture itself must circulate. Having circulated, the "voice of the people" goes public. This model reflects an ideal of democracy that Habermas and others valued in the earlier public sphere.

From the perspective of cultural motion, however, there are problems with the model. For metacultural judgments to circulate and achieve consensus, everyone, or most people, would have to have experienced the object already. The test of metacultural consensus would not be prospective at all, not as regards dissemination, but, like demand, would only be retrospective. True, a consensual metaculture might judge the object differently than demand judges it. The object might be highly esteemed, but in low demand, or vice versa. Still, the test would not be prospective, would not allow the object and its qualities to be made known to people before they encountered it.[6] Yet newness requires evaluation that is predictive, that looks towards the future of cultural circulation.

Consequently—and though this step is lamented by Habermas— metacultural production itself becomes specialized. Some individuals, because of their relative expertise regarding kinds of cultural objects, come to have opinions that carry more weight. Rational debate over culture among a public at large comes to be replaced by the pronouncements of specialists, who deliberate matters among themselves. The public turns over responsibility for judging cultural objects to people who are familiar with those objects. In this way, the public becomes consumers rather than producers of metaculture.

In the area of science and understanding of the natural world, a social hierarchy of opinion-making had been developing at least since the seventeenth century, with its oft-cited clash between metacultures of tradition and newness—the one, that is, involving Galileo and his confrontation with the Catholic Church over the Copernican view of the solar system. Traditional authority continued to be important for scientific authority through the eighteenth century. Indeed, it still is! We in the United States have fights to this day over the teaching of evolution versus special creation in the classroom. Even as I write these words, I have learned that the Kansas Board of Education, astonishing though it seems, voted on August 11, 1999, "to embrace new standards for science curricula that eliminate evolution as an underlying principle of biology and other sciences" ("Kansas Rejects Evolution" 1999). Are we on our way back to the seventeenth century, or even earlier?

Specialists, arrayed in social hierarchies, are essential to the production of metacultural assessments of new cultural objects—whether movies or laws or scientific theories—because culture needs prospective assessment if the metacultural emphasis on newness is to be maintained. Of course, there is no guarantee that an emphasis on newness can be maintained. Kansas Board of Education members, in fact, rejected "pleas by educators and most scientists" ("Kansas Rejects Evolution" 1999). Is this a darker side of the democratic ideal touted by Habermas, in which ordinary citizens decide matters of science?

> "It's a step forward. We're going to improve rather than detract from science education in Kansas," said Scott Hill, a farmer and board member who helped write the new standards. "There's a liberal agenda to build up or glorify evolution in our schools," Hill said, adding that evolution had been pushed on students as a "dogmatic fact." ("Kansas Rejects Evolution" 1999)

Evolution is, of course, still "new" relative to biblical accounts of special creation, despite its more than century-old existence. And its circulation through the world remains incomplete. Can the claim for its superiority as explanation—a claim emanating from specialists, from those most familiar with the subject matter—be upheld in the face of substantial nonspecialist support for the traditional alternative?

If the emphasis on newness is to be maintained—and granting the uncertainties which hang on that "if"—the future of cultural objects needs to be foreseen, or, at least, foretold. Who better to foresee or foretell the future than those with the most intimate and long-term familiarity with the object: communities of metacultural specialists?

Cultural objects must also get segmented by metaculture in consistent ways. This is because the new object—being "new"—is not a replica of some whole prior object, but rather has links to a host of earlier objects. For example, the various actors in a film link it to prior films in which those actors performed. The plot links it to others, the director to still others, and so forth. Consequently, metaculture needs to establish the respects in which a new object might be linked to older ones, might be judged in relation to them. The respects define segments or facets of the object, and, simultaneously, the strands through which culture flows into the object.

I have shown how this dissection takes place in the case of film reviews, where overall assessments of a film are backed up by assessments of its aspects—plot, scenes, direction, acting, settings, relations to previous films, relations to social context, and so forth. Those partial assessments are used to gauge the whole. Widespread, albeit not unanimous, agreement exists regarding the dissection process, that is, regarding what aspects need to be examined.

A new cultural object must, in turn, be designed with an eye to the responses given to the various aspects. Consequently, metaculture produces a set of guidelines for the production of new cultural objects, strands through which culture flows. It says, in effect: If you want to make a new object, bring together these strands. The bringing together of the prescribed strands insures that the new object bears sufficient resemblance to older ones to make it intelligible to metaculture. A social hierarchy of opinion, coupled with a method of dissection, supplies the basis for insuring a continuity of culture—a continuity that takes shape in the absence of a metaculture of tradition.

In the case of traditional myth, an identity exists between cultural object and cultural element—the object (the particular telling) is an exemplar or instance of the element (the myth). In the case of film and literature, produced under a metaculture of newness, the new object does not approach, in all of its respects, identity with a prior object. It is not an exemplar of any single underlying element. Rather, it is assembled from parts or strands, which are the form that elements take under newness.

Those parts or strands are not random pieces of the cultural object. Rather, they reflect consistent, shared segmentations, deriving from the interaction between the attempt to produce a new object and the metacultural method through which new objects are assessed. Metacultural segmentation accurately reflects the structure of the object, in part, because the object is built up with that segmentation in mind. Hence, metacultural segmentation—insofar as newness is concerned—carries and defines the continuity of culture.

Is the Truth Out There?

In Habermas's (1984 and 1987) view, rational dialogue and debate—such as occurs in an ideal public sphere—leads humans closer to the truth, and, also, to the best ways of doing things, the best culture. If the public spheres of eighteenth-century Europe seemed to suggest that culture was moving toward mass rational dialogue and debate and destined to sift out truth, the nineteenth and twentieth centuries appeared as a disappointing recession from that utopia. Instead, specialization set in, and the opinions of the few—those at the top of developing social hierarchies of assessment—carried the day. But has specialization increased the distance between western culture and the "truth" or the best ways of doing things? Is western culture more spurious, as a result?

In traditional truth claims—for example, that God made the heavens and the earth, Adam and Eve, and all of the animals in a seven-day act of creation—truthfulness is vouchsafed by prior circulation. Truthfulness can be assessed by determining whether an utterance corresponds to utterances that are already accepted, that have already circulated. Is this truth claim one that has withstood the test of time? If so, then one need ask no more.

However, if you accept that new truth claims—for example, that humans evolved gradually over five or ten million years from ape-like ancestors—may be superior to old ones—that is, if you subscribe to a metaculture of newness—then the new truth claim must be evaluated as to its suitability for future dissemination by some means. But who is to evaluate? To wait for total acceptance by a population is to revert to a traditional test of truth. Consequently, for new truth claims to be prospectively assessed, a population must—mustn't it?—rely on groups of metacultural specialists.

The claim to authoritativeness that metacultural specialists make is not that their arguments are accepted by everyone in society after an all-inclusive public debate. It is rather that they have an intimate familiarity with the kinds of truth claims most closely related to the new ones under assessment, and that they have long-term involvement in the community that produces and/or assesses such truth claims. The argument is: If you devoted as much of your time to this as I have, you would agree with me. How could it be otherwise, once the quantity of knowledge in a population exceeds the capacity of any one individual? The accumulated knowledge necessary for producing truth claims is, in this regard, like the accumulated learning necessary to produce nondiscursive objects—ceramic pots, for instance. No one individual is capable of acquiring all the know-how for producing all of the kinds of objects that get produced in the contemporary United States.

Still, if a metaculture of newness cannot rely on the acceptance of truth claims by a whole population as its test—that is, if it cannot rely on universal public debate—nevertheless it demands that the community of producers and/or evaluators of truth claims be open to all who would participate in it. Descent—as a pathway of inertial culture—cannot, in principle, intervene. This is not Habermasian openness of truth claims, as cultural objects, to broader democratic scrutiny and debate—as if decisions about scientific or scholarly merit could be had by taking radio show popularity polls. Rather, this kind of openness is a challenge to the broader society—indeed, to broader humanity. It says: "Scott Hill, join this community and convince us that special creation is superior to evolution, or, alternatively, be convinced by us that evolution is superior."

Status within a metacultural community is achieved by producing something—a new cultural object, a new metacultural assessment—that wins approval by members of that community, that circulates widely within it. Such is the status of Darwin and the theory of evolution within biology and neighboring metacultural communities.

Simultaneously, however, to participate in a metacultural community, to be able to fashion new objects, one must be socialized into the community. One must master what is, in effect, its traditional culture. Scott Hill would have to become a stealth biologist, thoroughly conversant with evolution, but working from within it to discredit it, to show other biologists why special creation is superior. Only in this way could he be in a position to have his new truth claims win approval. The specialized communities supply the foundation of continuity of culture that is more widely disseminated.[7]

If Hill[8] did adopt a metaculture of newness so as to work within the evolutionary framework, he would presumably become convinced of it. In spy jargon, he would be "turned," becoming a "double agent" for evolution. In fact, however, if Hill subscribes to a metaculture of tradition, then he could respond to biologists by saying: "It is not I who need convince you, but rather the other way around. For my acceptance of special creation is grounded in tradition, that is, in the prior history of circulation of special creation in Western culture. And that prior circulation should be obvious to all of you."

But, of course, were Hill a thoroughgoing traditionalist, scientists could not convince him, anyway, since the only persuasive argument for a true traditionalist is one concerned with prior circulation. The qualities of the object are subordinated to the object's replication over time. To be converted, to be "turned," Hill would already have to accept that something new might be superior: that a novel idea (like evolution) might be better than an old one (like special creation).

Metacultures of oldness and newness, tradition and modernity, seem at loggerheads, hopelessly in conflict, over this crucial question—how to judge a cultural object as superior. The one argues from prior circulation, the other from possible future circulation. The one takes account of qualities of the object that attest to a historical time-depth of acceptance, the other ignores time-depth, focusing instead on qualities indicative of intrinsic worth. How to get beyond this point?

The matter would be hopeless, the way permanently blocked, were metaculture the only force affecting culture, the only thing causing it to move. True, the two (modernity and tradition) are—from the point of view of contestation—a Scylla and Charybdis, the one a six-headed monster, the other a great, swirling whirlpool threatening to pull our weary traveler asunder. But our traveler has also his own internal momentum—not only inertia that carries him along, but also intrinsic usefulness. Metacultures are not arbitrary. They do not push this or that bit of culture along for reasons having nothing to do with the culture itself. No, metaculture in some measure taps into the culture, captures a truth about it. It is able to dip into the sensible—for the cultural object is always made known through the senses—and retrieve something of the world from it.

Culture moves thanks to both inertia (hence its understanding through tradition) and usefulness (hence its understanding through modernity). Any item of culture—for example, special creation or evolution as explanations for the origins of humans—spreads because it is already in motion, and because of its intrinsic worth. If one of two objects in contestation wins out, it is because the forces impelling it exceed those opposing it. [And, yes, this does suggest that Scott Hill has a point; there are reasons why special creation has lasted so long.]

Yet this provides us with little help concerning our initial question: Is culture more spurious if metacultural specialization sets in? Does generality of acceptance produce better assessments of cultural objects than the judgments of specialists? Here it is worth noting that metacultural specialization parallels the cultural specialization (division of labor) underlying the original valuation of dissemination over replication, such as proliferated in

Europe half a millennium ago. The forms of culture arising out of cultural specialization, thanks to the quantitative concentration of culture in the bodies and minds of producers, are, arguably, better, more convincing, more truthful as a result—in regard to the whole spectrum of objects for which there are specialized cultural communities of production. Is metacultural specialization, with its attendant concentration of accumulated learning in the bodies and minds of assessors, any different?

To be sure, there are limits to specialization, insofar as the motion of culture is concerned. Were cultural objects chopped up into so many pieces that each individual member of the assessment community appeared as master of one and only one piece—for example, by having separate evolutionary theories for each species, but no overall theory—little in the way of public checks would be placed on the metacultural assessments. In such a situation, individual judgments—lacking the oversight of a broader community—might become truly arbitrary with the resultant cultural objects, including assertions of truth, possessing a diminished claim to superiority.

The beauty of a metaculture of newness, with its attendant emphasis on dissemination over replication, however, is that such limits will never be reached. This is not only because metacultural evaluations must themselves circulate, but also because such evaluations are only one mechanism for the assessment of cultural objects—even if they are the only truly prospective mechanism. There is still evaluation based on demand for the object—the local uptake by other biologists, and, indeed, other scientists or nonscientists, of the research results produced by any one of them. Dissemination of the cultural object can be only partially influenced by assessments coming from this or that metacultural specialist. Demand for the cultural object—either broad but short-term, or narrow but long-term—counterbalances the assessments derived from prospective dissection. Since assessment through demand is closer to evaluation by means of a metaculture of tradition—what has worked best in the past is best—in fact, a metaculture of newness combines retrospective and prospective evaluation techniques.

There is, however, a key difference between demand and tradition as techniques for the evaluation of cultural objects and elements. Tradition is concerned with time depth within a population. Demand, in contrast, is designed principally to measure spatial spread, although it can be used to measure time depth as well—the evidence of continuing demand. Consequently, tradition tends towards isomorphism with a circumscribable population defined by geographical location and descent. While a traditional item can be passed to other populations—through diffusions or imposition via conquest or other coercive means—that passage is less significant than its persistence through time. Correspondingly, while demand can be used to measure temporal persistence, its primary purpose is to measure spread. As a consequence, demand is associated with the restless, global motion of culture across population boundaries, however those are defined.

Is the Nation Modern?

The nation, as distinct from traditional social groupings, is closely linked to the origin and spread of a metaculture of newness. It is unlike a clan or a caste because, unlike groupings in which membership is prescribed for individuals by rules outside of their control, individuals must want positively to belong to the nation. Their membership must be construed, according to the logic of newness, as voluntary—even if in fact it is constrained.

Why would individuals want to belong to one nation as opposed to any other? The answer must be that individuals subscribe to, or see as expressions of themselves, the statements (and other culture) surrounding and attached to the "we" of that nation: "We hold these truths to be self-evident, that all men are created equal. . . ." The nation, in effect, makes an appeal: "If you subscribe to these words, if you subscribe to this culture, then ally yourself with us; become part of this group." It demands an answer: "Yes, I will ally myself with you."[9]

To Benedict Anderson's ([1983] 1991) account of the origins of nations and nationalism, therefore, a theory of cultural motion requires that we add, crucially, something like an account of what Antonio Gramsci (1981, 1985: 196–211; see also Mouffe 1979) called hegemony. The nation is not only something that arises from the circulation of print; it is not just an imagined community thinkable because one can envision other readers or viewers like oneself reading and viewing the same thing. No, this is only part of the story, and perhaps not the most interesting part. The nation is also, and more importantly, something that comes to seem an expression of oneself, under one's control, insofar as acceptance or rejection is concerned. The slogan "America, love it or leave it," obnoxious as it is, underscores that element of choice. You and I are here because we want to be. The group so formed is a peculiarly voluntary group.

My argument is not based on empirical observation of what it means, in different nations around the globe today, to be a citizen. Empirical nations restrict the flow of individuals into and out of their borders; some restrictions are more sinister, more nefarious than others—the Soviet

Union from the 1940s to the 1980s, for example, which strangled or, in any case, severely restricted, migration to the West. Even the contemporary United States endeavors to keep out illegal aliens, especially those from Mexico, thereby limiting voluntary alignment with the United States and its principles.

My argument is not that borders are, in empirical nations today, uncontrolled. It is that a metaculture of newness demands that the nation be construed as voluntary. The logic of newness in relationship to cultural flow is this: Individuals are not mere conduits for culture; upon receiving culture, they seize control of it and make it their own. What they pass on to others bears their imprint or, minimally, their imprimatur. As a cultural entity received from a past generation by a present one, the nation is taken hold of by the current generation, which stamps its imprint on it and lends its approval to it. It is the individuals making up a nation who are the imagined controllers of it. The nation is an expression of them as a "people." The very idea of a "citizen" is linked to the idea of control over a nation.[10] And control is a logical consequence of the idea of cultural newness. Unconnected as the two—newness and citizenship—seem superficially, they are connected through the principles of cultural motion.

Hegemony, therefore, is a necessary concomitant of newness. If individuals are in control of the nation, if volition is ascribed to them, then the involvement of individuals in collective action must be won by persuasion, not exacted by coercion. Such is the logic of newness. Hegemony is a process whereby individuals are persuaded to subscribe to a particular "we" that is embedded in a particular matrix of discourse. It is the process whereby the participation of individuals in a collectivity is made to seem to them something toward which they—in the words of Durkheim ([1925] 1961, 96)—"spontaneously aspire."

I am aware that the term "hegemony" has been used by scholars to characterize prenational social configurations such as the colonial rule of the British over their South African subjects, as described by John and Jean Comaroff (1991). My point is not that symbolic devices were not used in that context to aid in the system of control that was put into effect. It is rather that the British were not predisposed to view colonial subjects as fellow citizens who were equal partners in Britain, whose voluntary cooperation had, therefore, to be enlisted. While the British undoubtedly did use symbolic means to effect control, as the Comaroffs suggest, those symbolic means supplemented social relationships understood first and foremost in terms of inequality, in terms of colonial domination by a ruling elite.

Yet there is something more to be said here. The idea of individual control over the group—the idea of citizenship—is implicit in the metacultural emphasis on newness. It spreads with that metaculture. And that metaculture did diffuse to South Africans, though its implicit promise may not have been realized until recently, and perhaps, for some or many, languishes unrealized even today.

A "we" understood as the expression of its individual members is a "we" that must persuade those members to articulate or subscribe to it. Such a "we" lays the seeds of its own historical transformation, as I have tried to show in the case of the United States. From Jefferson's initial phrase—"all men are created equal," or any of the variant expressions widespread at the time—to Elizabeth Cady Stanton's "all men and women," to Martin Luther King Jr.'s emphasis on the "all," the "we" who "hold these truths to be self-evident," inspires the participation not only of those to whom its original utterers intended it to refer, but also those who take it upon themselves to become its utterers. Such a "we" can be instrumentally used to demand rightful control.

Does Globalization Undermine the Nation?

If the nation is a peculiar species of social grouping that takes shape under a metaculture of newness, however haltingly, however much in fits and starts, and if it depends on persuasion to enlist participation—and hence depends on its members subscribing to, in some measure, a shared culture in the form of a shared set of statements—how does the nation square with an emphasis on dissemination, which knows no boundaries? For, as I have argued, a metaculture of newness grows into ascendancy over a metaculture of tradition hand in hand with the dominance of an idea of dissemination of culture over that of replication. Emphasis is placed on disseminating cultural objects regardless of the local purposes for which those objects are taken up. Such an emphasis dispenses with tests of replication, where one wants to see evidence—as in the catechism—that what is disseminated has been properly reproduced. If the nation is based on the persuasion of individuals to accept some statements as their own, isn't the nation grounded in replication, and therefore isn't it incompatible with a metacultural emphasis on dissemination?

I will state my conclusion up front: Peculiarities of the nation as a kind of social grouping—namely, as one in which individuals are understood to be in control of the group rather than the other way around, and in which they are thought, in some sense, to "choose" to belong in that group—

make it compatible not only with a metaculture of newness, but also with the emphasis on dissemination over replication which goes hand in hand with it. I have already argued that the peculiar form of "we" associated with the nation—"we, the people"—is a precipitate of newness. But what about dissemination itself? Is the nation not still a group dependent on shared culture?

Here it is important to recognize that not all shared culture is the same. Culture can be shared because it is passed on via replication in the context of intimate social relations, as in the case of myth-telling in the domestic group in Amerindian Brazil, or as in the case of taste—as understood by Bourdieu—in the West. But culture can also be shared because it is extracted from cultural objects involved in mass dissemination, where the dissemination is relatively uncoupled from replication. Extraction is a process of secondary replication. One sees a film, and one is able to pull culture out of it—to recite or employ lines from it, to model one's behavior or clothing or hair styles on characters in it, to script one's interaction with others according to the plot that organizes it.

Because of secondary replication, I find plausibility in Benedict Anderson's ([1983] 1991) association of the rise of nations and nationalisms with print mediation, though pressure for dissemination preceded the technological breakthroughs. Print[11] is a form of culture which, by its very nature, moves through space and time via mass dissemination coupled with secondary replication. It is not the kind of culture that passes through primary replication.[12] A group built up around such disseminated culture, shared by virtue of secondary replication, is only apparently similar to a group built up out of primary replication, such as occurs in the case of myth transmission.

The larger point is that persuasion comes to the fore in the case of mass-disseminated cultural objects in a way that it does not in the case of traditional culture. A nation is a social group grounded in the persuasiveness of a set of disseminated cultural objects—such as the Constitution, Declaration of Independence, laws, and even canonical literature. Should an individual dislike any given "shared" cultural object that is part of the nation, he or she is free to challenge it, or to try to change it. Should the individual dislike all the cultural objects making up the nation's core definitional kit, he or she is free to leave the group in favor of another. The shared cultural objects forming the definitional kit act as magnets in relation to which individuals align like so many iron filings. The stronger the magnet, the more it pulls filings away from weaker ones. The strong magnet—that is, the strong collection of cultural objects in the definitional kit—is, in this sense, better than the weak magnet.

To be incompatible with an emphasis on dissemination over replication, the nation would have to completely and permanently seal off its borders from dissemination from outside, including migration and even travel. Again, my argument is not that various groupings around the world that are called "nations" have not sealed their borders at certain points in their histories and in relationship to certain kinds of cultural motion or classes of cultural objects. Indeed, probably all nations effect some kinds of control on motion in the present, and some may endeavor to shut their borders completely for certain periods of time. One reason for this is obvious, and has been remarked by Immanuel Wallerstein (1974), although from an economic point of view and not with a sensitivity to cultural motion per se. Shutting down borders allows a population to stimulate the production of disseminable cultural objects within those borders in order that the developing nation—that is, the individuals making up that nation—may be able to compete with individuals from other nations in the future.

Similarly, one can appreciate the motivation a nation—understood as individuals volitionally attached to a set of cultural objects—has to endeavor to resist out-migration of its members, and to resist secession of some of its members who lay claim to parts of the national territory, as in the "Republic of Texas" or other contemporary secessionist movements in the United States. A reduction of numbers within the nation, or a reduction of physical space occupied by the nation, along with that space's inhabitants, detracts from the apparent success of the core set of cultural objects—such as its constitution—in the nation's kit. Those objects, which some members wish to maintain, become the basis for resisting attempts by others to secede or leave.

Cultural objects are successful in perpetuating themselves over time insofar as they engender loyalty, insofar as they kindle strong positive feelings. This persuasive or rhetorical power of objects propels them through space along existing pathways of dissemination. It also helps them to penetrate uncharted territory, where they must cut their own new paths, being, in this sense, world-making. Persuasive power also secures the persistence in time of the objects, which become venerated. The objects instill in individuals a desire to preserve them—recall the placement in 1952 of the founding documents of the United States into helium-filled thermopane cases—and also to insure their continued high esteem. Diminution in the numbers of individuals esteeming those objects, as in the case of out-migration or secession, is an assault on the objects themselves, and, therefore, on their survival through time.

The curious quality of the "we" of the nation—a "we, the people"—is that, unlike other kinds of culture, "we" refers to the very collection of individuals whose individual volitions are understood, metaculturally, to give rise to it. It refers to the population in which it is designed to circulate. In this regard, it is unlike a stainless steel pot or even a film that is disseminated and taken up into local processes of cultural reproduction because of its utility in those local processes. The collection of individuals insuring the dissemination in space of the culture contained in pots and in films, and insuring their perpetuation through time, is a collection that is not overtly referred to by the cultural objects themselves. Yes, those objects are designed for a certain target group of individuals. But it is possible for those objects to survive, and even flourish, even if some or all of the target population rejects them. All that is required is that other non-target individuals take them up. However, if a "we, the people of the United States" is rejected by those to whom it refers, it cannot be taken up in local processes of cultural reproduction elsewhere. It must succeed in kindling the loyalty of its target population or die out.

You can perhaps understand how nations take shape under a metaculture of newness, with its attendant emphasis on restless dissemination and on ever-expanding markets. Still, wouldn't the movement of culture defined by those two principles—newness and globalization—be better off without that particular, pesky form of disseminated culture built up around "we, the people"? After all, the boundaries erected by nations from time to time inhibit the global dissemination of cultural objects. They deflect the flow of culture outwards from its centers of production and reproduction. Is it in the interests of cultural motion through space and time to have social entities like nations that disturb its outward flow?

Nations are actually useful for the motion of culture in at least one regard: They prevent the pathways of culture from becoming too narrowly circumscribed. If the far-flung journeys of culture are rendered seemingly more arduous by nations, the pathways for motion are also smoothed out by them. Nations strive to overcome the eccentricities of local cultural difference within their borders that might make even the shortest journey difficult, if not impossible.

The problem is foreseen in Sir Thomas Malory's Le Morte d'Arthur—a fifteenth-century work, one of a number setting down on paper the legend of King Arthur and the Knights of the Roundtable. Malory's Arthurian paladins travel the world, spreading a single rule of right. On their journeys, they encounter strange and inauspicious customs and all manner of wickedness, which they struggle to overcome. So Sir Galahad stumbles upon the accursed "Castle of the Maidens" (Malory [1470] 1982, 539–40), where "all pity is lacking," and "all hardness and mischief is therein." He is told to turn back:

> "Sir knight, ye ride here in great folly, for ye have the river to pass over."
> "Why should I not be able to pass over the water?" said Sir Galahad . . .
> "Knight, those knights in the castle defy thee and prohibit you to go farther till they know what ye want."
> "Fair sir," said Sir Galahad, "I come to destroy the wicked customs of this castle."

As the Knights of the Roundtable discover again and again, differentiation of local cultures is constantly at work, and, without a centripetal force to pull the local out of its localness, the pathways of dissemination might actually break down, thereby thwarting the expansive aspirations of culture.

Viewed as part of a system, in which nations have carved up all the living space on planet earth, any particular nation resembles a taste-based status group, in Bourdieu's sense. Insofar as culture continues to move through time and space locally, via processes of transmission in which dissemination and replication are inextricably linked—as they are in the case of myth-telling in Amerindian Brazil or in Bourdieu's idea of taste—some culture must continue to be transmitted through intimate contact and face-to-face interaction, and hence to spread via propinquity. In the course of its motion, culture passing in this way always undergoes micromodification so that differences inevitably emerge.[13]

Part of the differences emerging through local replication involves taste for disseminated cultural objects. Since this kind of replication is based on spatial and temporal contiguity of the participants in the transmission process, there is always an incipient spatial organization of taste, reflected within nations in the cultural distinctions between geographical regions, within cities in the differences between neighborhoods. Therefore, there are always also incipient spatial distinctions in the prominence of disseminated cultural objects.

An obvious example is the movement of language itself, which takes place, in part, through intimate interactions such as occur because of spatial propinquity. The movement of mass-disseminated printed material is affected by the spread of language through processes of replication. Certain cultural objects—books, magazines, newspapers, and films, for example— circulate more readily within the space established by language spread, as

Anderson ([1983] 1991) has observed of literature. It is not that such objects could not be more widely disseminated through translation—some of them, obviously, are. It is that the statistical prominence of them is greater within the boundaries established by the spread of the language in which they are written or produced.

Nor does mechanical translation solve the problem. If language spreads in significant measure through intimate interaction, that is, through processes of transmission in which dissemination is inextricably tied to replication, then this is all the more true of style, topic, plot, and the like. Such locally defined tastes keep alive or facilitate the circulation of certain kinds of cultural objects. They benefit that circulation.

Looked at from another point of view, the nation is a way of broadening circulation that might otherwise become more and more narrowly circumscribed—as when Sir Galahad destroys the local wickedness that renders other culture unpassable through that region. My concern has been with the nation as a smaller-level spatial grouping than the globe—the target for mass-disseminated cultural objects. From this perspective, the nation undercuts global flow. However, from the point of view of the local replication of taste, a distinct kind of problem arises for mass-disseminated culture, namely, that local tastes become too diverse to allow for global movement. The local motion of culture fosters secessionist movements that narrow the flow of mass-disseminated cultural items by carving up existing territory into ever smaller units based upon locally replicated culture. From this perspective, nations broaden the circulation of disseminated culture, preventing it from being sucked back into the local. Nations ensure that locally replicated cultures of taste do not undermine the broader dissemination of culture.

Between the global aspirations of mass-disseminated culture and the constantly differentiating property of local replication, the nation appears as an equilibrium formation. Under a metaculture of newness, with its attendant emphasis on dissemination over replication, culture is impelled to find ever more far-flung destinations for its local uptake. Owing to the forces of local replication, and of culture perpetuated through intimate interaction, however, cultures of taste tend to diverge from one another, as microchanges occur in the course of replication. Such local differentiation runs counter to global motion. From this perspective, the nation simultaneously broadens the sphere of the local and narrows the sphere of the global. Nations in this way become status groups, and the status hierarchy among nations comes to resemble the status hierarchy among taste groups within Bourdieu's scheme.

What makes the global flow of culture possible, despite the local motion associated with primary replication, is the distinctively modern character of the nation. Its "we" is not understood metaculturally as traditional,
that is, as defined by its past—or, at least, as defined alone by its past.
Rather, the nation is understood as a product of the active consent of the individuals to whom it refers. That is, it is understood in terms of Gramscian
hegemony—a form of domination based on elicitation of active compliance through persuasion. Individuals move physically from one nation to
the next when their attractions to the new nation outweigh their attractions to the old one—or, alternatively, when new cultural objects and elements arise within the old nation that engender a repulsion that can only
be overcome by out-migration.

The Acceleration of Culture

The spread, in the West, of a metacultural emphasis on newness makes
possible and necessary the configuration of social space outlined by Bourdieu for modern society. It is what enabled the development of public-
sphere processes of criticism, including the progressive specialization of
knowledge. It is what, indeed, is the prime mover behind the development
of the modern nation as a peculiar social formation. Ideas of newness have
been present in cultures around the globe, more often than not, and have
been more prominent at some times than at others. They may have surfaced to dominate tradition at different historical periods—notably, in ancient Greece. But their development in the West, especially during the
past five hundred years, has produced a new kind of culture, one with remarkable ability to move laterally through space, allowing it to ensnare
the globe within its net.

A metacultural emphasis on newness has resulted in the incorporation
of acceleration into the very mechanism of cultural reproduction. For culture to be transmitted over time, it must, by design, change shape, like a
trickster figure out of mythology, appearing here in one guise, there in another. But unlike the traditional trickster, who resumes his original shape,
the modern trickster never returns fully to the original, never closes the
circle. Just when one thinks one has discovered its true nature, it slips off
into the future as something else again. No wonder modern thought has
been de-essentializing. The very culture on which you and I might reflect
to find essences is itself continuously changing shape. Its mercuriality and
ephemerality defy essentialization.

True, culture has never been the palpable, material thing one imagines under an idea of tradition—which stabilizes the sensible world through replication of traditional objects. It has never been truly identifiable with its surface appearance in this or that ritual or in this or that myth. No, these have always been mere surface manifestations of something vastly more mysterious, more profoundly unsettling. That something is immaterial, and yet it transitorily inhabits objects in this sensible world. It is a powerful immaterial thing, as Durkheim ([1912] 1969) observed, one that has control over individuals, that shapes the material world, leaving its imprint on perceptible things, that is the propulsive force behind physical motion of some objects, notably, those that move through dissemination networks. Yet it itself is not a thing in the perceptible realm.

The brilliance of a metaculture of tradition is that it converts the immaterial into the material, the ineffable into the uttered, the ghost into the flesh-and-blood person. It fixes and maintains the shape of cultural objects in which it becomes lodged as it makes its way through individuals, and, hence, through time and space. No, culture cannot do without things—stainless steel pots and knives as well as words, whole myths, or ritual performances. Those things are its manifestations in the material realm. By fixing its manifestations, culture converts itself into consistent material shapes; it becomes recognizable to the senses and to the intellect. Yet culture is only moving through those material shapes, invisibly, silently. It is only disclosing itself to us, giving us an inkling of its awesome force.

With an emphasis on tradition, culture has been hugely successful. No doubt about it. Its circulation is assured by the recognizability of the objects in which it circulates. What is traditional is known, and hence acceptable, by virtue of being known. It is seemingly risky for culture to make the move to newness, where it must leap, somehow, from shape to shape, thing to different thing. Such leaps are susceptible to failure. Might not the new object be unrecognizable as the bearer of the culture embodied in it and carried forth from older objects? Might it not be rejected by those very people who cherished its predecessor? Yes, there is risk here.

But if there is risk, there is also potential reward—reward not as readily achieved by traditional culture. In etching the restless pursuit of acceleration into the very center of its brain, culture embarked on an experiment that led to its unprecedented ability to move through space. Cultures that rely on specific, fixed traditional forms—whether communism, or Islamic or Christian fundamentalism—find it difficult to achieve the degree of lateral spread associated with a metaculture of newness, tenacious as they may be for those for whom they have become tradition. The amazing flexibility of culture under a metaculture of newness—a culture that is constantly prodded to embody itself in new things—makes it ideally suited for adapting to new places and to changing circumstances. Will it also be ideally suited, once it has completely encircled the globe, for perpetuating itself through time?

At the heart of this new kind of culture lies a fundamental discovery: The similarities between objects through which culture is carried can be displaced onto a more abstract plane, one less accessible to the immediate sensation. In the case of novels and films, similarities are displaced onto plots or "structures" manifested through different words, different characters, different settings. To "see" the similarities—and hence to "see" the motion of culture—requires analysis precisely because those similarities cannot be seen in the usual sense of the term. They are not directly accessible to the perceptual faculties. To "see" them requires the intervention of thought and reason. They must be rendered intelligible.

There is a different dependence on perception here than in the case of traditional culture. Under tradition, the possibility of circulation rests upon the perceptual recognizability of the cultural object—it looks like what has come before it; ergo, it must be the same. But the continuity of culture, in the case of a metaculture of newness, is based on recognizability not to the senses but, instead, to the intellect. Or, alternatively, continuity is based on the concealment of that continuity from the senses. Under an idea of newness, the motion of intelligible meanings depends on the continual interconversion between the senses and intellect, as new cultural objects demand to be deciphered or read. A heightened consciousness of culture goes along with the attempt to perpetuate culture in the world.

True, continuity also occurs through taste, which need not be rendered transparent to consciousness. One might sense that a cultural object is similar to ones that have come before it by virtue of one's feelings or responses to it, without articulating what about the object has produced those feelings or responses.

While one can imagine the continuity in taste, at a local level, without consciousness of the underlying cultural forms to which that taste responds, it is vastly more difficult to imagine the production of new objects without the intervention of consciousness and reason. New objects must be crafted out of an idea of some sort, so that the continuity of culture is displaced onto the level of intelligibility. It is a higher level of intelligibility that makes possible the shaping of different objects after a single image. Habermas's (1984, 1987) insight about the ever-expanding role of reason in the evolution of society can be translated into an insight about the role of consciousness in relation to cultural continuity: The culture that has developed in the West reflects a greater consciousness of culture on the part of its producers. It also reflects greater agency—a taking of control over destiny through self-consciousness or understanding—insofar as it requires the continual fashioning of new cultural objects out of older, underlying ideas and abstract patterns.

I am left wondering, and perhaps you are wondering as well: What is this mysterious underlying entity or stuff that is moving through the world, through people, through space and time, and yet is not itself a material thing? What is its role in the universe? Does it have goals or purposes other than its own survival and propagation? The journey on which I have taken you in this book is but a preliminary reconnaissance of the terrain surrounding these questions.

Throughout, I have been interested in what are unquestionably little, even microscopic, things, the minutiae of the world: the linear organization of words into stories, the pronoun "we," the role of imperatives within narrative. How much less significant for decision makers can these things be? I am not asking, or trying to answer, the grand social questions they pose: Will there be a labor strike? Will we go to war? What language will we teach our children? No, my quest is after something quite different.

My object of study—culture—has its closest analog in the concept of spiritual forces, such as the Judeo-Christian God. Like spiritual forces, culture is profoundly immaterial, though it shapes matter. Like spiritual forces, it brings sustenance to people, though it itself cannot be tasted. Indeed, like them, it has power of life and death over individuals, motivating human actions, making possible executions for crimes and justifying war; yet it itself is not a person, at least not any of a sort with which we humans are familiar.

Emile Durkheim, in his *Elementary Forms of the Religious Life* ([1912] 1969), attributed these god-like powers to the "collectivity." The present study of cultural motion suggests a refinement of his claim. Even the collectivity—whether the clan or the caste or the nation—is a product of culture. The motion of culture leaves social groupings and social relations, in its wake. But Durkheim was close enough. Accumulated social learning, ways of acting, talking, and thinking socially transmitted over time and between people—these are processes that go beyond the individual, that cannot be adequately explained in terms of the material world, even if they can only be studied through material manifestations in the world.

My principal concern in the present book has been to explore the peculiar type of motion associated with a metaculture of newness, in which, apparently, less emphasis, rather than more, is placed on making immaterial patterns of motion detectable in perceptible manifestations. Material continuity diminishes in favor of novelty—the scriptwriter substitutes new characters, new settings into old formulae, and the director adds new actors, thereby concealing the abstract continuity of the formulae from the senses of the audience. The fact of cultural motion in the world—in which each of us understands that something profoundly immaterial is moving through us, that we are but its momentary bearers—has been concealed from us beneath a surface of perceptual novelty and innovation, the phantasmagoria of the material.

Simultaneously, however, the focus on novelty in material manifestations makes it necessary to render the profoundly immaterial character of the underlying formulae intelligible to the intellect. For those who have mastered the formulae behind successful films, the possibility arises of using that mastery to move culture, to change the culture through conscious design, no matter how minor the detail. Those who control the secret to success—those who are masters of the invisible, immaterial culture that is manifested time and again in putatively new films—have the possibility of reshaping the formulae, experimenting with them, and thereby accelerating culture. Consciousness assumes greater control over the motion of culture just because consciousness is indispensable to that motion.

At the same time, what an enormous inertia there is in the movement of that abstract, ideal culture. The inertia makes it, paradoxically, less rather than more changeable than traditional culture. Though consciousness of underlying principles is essential to movement—to the reproduction of abstract forms in material objects—it is not the case that consciousness readily redirects motion. To be a success, to achieve comparatively wide circulation, new cultural objects forged out of consciousness must experience demand from sites of local cultural reproduction. The shape of the object brought into existence by consciousness must fit into local patterns. It must appear as desirable to local tastes. Therefore, its properties as object must conform to historical patterns that are, in considerable measure, independent of its producers.

This is the flip side of the problem of conscious control. If the concentration of cultural reproduction in the case of mass-disseminated objects is localized in centers of cultural production—most importantly, in the contemporary world, corporations—then control seems to lie in the hands—or, rather, the minds—of the producers of that culture. However, since success as a producer is measured, in part, by demand, control is also lodged in the local cultures that receive the mass-produced items. Consequently, despite the necessity of a consciousness of culture movement, control over the abstract patterns or formulae is limited. Yes, the producer controls the shapes of the disseminated object, but the receiver controls the demand for that object's dissemination.

The result is that the conscious accelerative force that could be used to change the direction of cultural motion is typically used to maintain it. Because they are constantly forced to put the abstract patterns into new physical objects, producers of objects get better and better acquainted with the patterns themselves. The patterns become more clearly defined, more luminous to consciousness, and, ultimately, more reproducible. Ironically, therefore, a metacultural emphasis on newness—an emphasis that causes seemingly perpetual change in the material manifestations of culture—results in continuity in the abstract patterns underlying it. Culture harnesses consciousness for the purposes of reproducing itself as abstract, immaterial form by insisting on changes in its sensible appearance.

Thinking Reeds

If something is cultural—that is, if it is socially learned, socially transmitted—then it must get lodged in concrete, publicly accessible things at key points. This is a rock-bottom requirement (so to speak). For something cultural to get from A to B, it must be deposited by A in a physical form that B can grasp through the senses. If the physical form itself is not reproduced—as it is not, as least not in all of its rich detail, under a metaculture of newness—then how can it be culture?

Here is a seeming conundrum. Because of it, the solution opted for by some disciplines—economics, for example, or linguistics—appears to make sense. They propose that what is involved in the creation of a new cultural object is not culture at all, but something prior to it—rationality or reason, for instance, in the case of economics, or innate brain structures, in the case of formal linguistics. These are biologically inherited capabilities of individuals, not socially transmitted achievements of populations. The solutions bypass culture.

If we can pull ourselves back from the intellectual thicket, however, if we can catch even a brief glimpse of the forest, the solutions appear. At best, they are only partially adequate; at worst, they are ludicrous. Imagine a science, for example, that is not based on socially transmitted learning—learning passed across the generations—but only on biologically acquired wit and innate intelligence. How preposterous to think that a single brain, confronting the universe, could come up with anything so grand as the collective efforts of generations of scientists, building on the work of their predecessors and augmenting collective insights and received understandings, as I hope I am in the present book.

Is it any easier to imagine our economy, or even a single corporation, producing material objects—whether cars or computers, or cupcakes or ketchup—without cumulated learning? Could an isolated individual (Pascal's thinking reed) unequipped with prior socially transmitted learning, possessing only a brain and reason, and thrust into a physical world— could such a thinking reed in one lifetime come up with the remarkable accumulation of clever techniques and ideas that have gone into the making of modern things? Could such a reed invent even one empirical language, with all of its richness and diversity? Our theories of wit and savvy need to be brought back to their senses. The exclusion of culture—of cumulated social learning—from an understanding of the economy or language or science simply makes no sense, not in the grand sweep of things.

Yet, if the physical objects through which culture is carried are not replicated, how can the motion of culture take place? What are our thinking reeds up to? Such questions lead to doubt: Perhaps the assumption is wrong. Perhaps physical objects, even under a metaculture of newness, are replicated. Isn't traditional motion what accounts for domestically transmitted culture—mother tongues, for instance, or taste, as Bourdieu understands it? Must this not be the case with all culture? New objects can't really carry over culture from old ones, can they?

Your doubt might lead you to argue that the styles of mass-produced objects—cars, for instance—change but little from year to year. You might even trace the elements of automotive style over time, charting their transformation. Perhaps the newness of "new" cars is really no more new than a tinkered-with variant of an old myth.[14] Maybe, more generally, the striving after newness results in changes no greater in magnitude than those stemming from cultural drift.

A careful reading of the previous chapters, however, should help to assuage this doubt. For one thing, there is the motion of culture as found in new films or novels. As I hope I have shown, a startling difference exists between myths and novels. In the case of new novels, even where overall similarity is so close as to stir up accusations of plagiarism, lexical similarities between the two novels are not much greater—if they are greater at all— than between two obviously unrelated stories. In contrast, even maximally dissimilar versions of a single myth contain easily detectable lexical similarities. How to account for this disparity?

For a second thing, even in the case of automotive styles, you can zero in on a key difference. While the year 2000 Volvo appears—to the outside observer—only slightly different from the 1999 Volvo, this difference is the product of design. The makers of the new Volvo vouchsafe a desire to be different; they flaunt the differences. Change here is not a result of random drift—although graphs can make it appear that way. Rather, it is the result of an idea held by a thinking reed—an idea about newness, about improvement, about perfection. Even our thinking reeds—in the contemporary United States, at least—think of what they are doing as something other than passing on time-honored tradition.

Still you are tempted by alternative explanations: If automotive styles change over time—despite a technology able to insure exact replication—perhaps this is due to cultural drift in the realm of taste. If Bourdieu is right—as I think he is, in part—about taste being transmitted through close interaction, such as occurs in the family, then taste changes the way myth does: incrementally, in the course of its movement through people. Therefore, wouldn't change occur in exactly analogous ways in Amerindian myth and in the contemporary United States? Why bother with the problem of metaculturally induced newness?

The skeptics' argument is plausible and, no doubt, partially valid. Perhaps microchanges in local tastes over time account for the stylistic changes in mass-disseminated objects. However, the skeptics fail to tell the full story. For if local tastes diverge from one another over time—as a result of drift or entropic deceleration—they cannot guide the motion of mass-produced objects. They will, rather, go their own separate ways. Consequently, the coordination of local tastes into a social space itself depends on the mass dissemination of culture and metaculture. How else can producers hold onto a market that otherwise fragments over time as local tastes diverge?

It is intriguing that new novels, new films are designed to appear to untutored sensibilities as "new," as different from what has come before them. The incremental movement of culture is, in part, disguised. Old objects—disaster movies with romance embedded in them, for example—are recycled. A tutored observer can fathom the continuity, see the infrared trails connecting new objects to older ones, recognize this film as a copy of that one, place one object into a group consisting of instances of a type. Something in the material form of the film facilitates that recognition, no doubt about it.

Yet the indices most salient to consciousness as markers of traditional objects—words, phrases, and sentences—change. Substitution is the name of the game here. Producers of culture direct the focus of attention away from continuity—even though continuity as incremental change is there. They reshape the tastes of consumers, in however small a way.

The motion of culture under an idea of newness is made possible by a kind of trick. No amount of random chiseling away at the perceptible surface of cultural things will crack them open, reveal their true essence. The chisel has to be guided by ideas, and those ideas are part of metaculture. Metaculture looks down upon cultural motion, seeing in the face of the deep its own mysterious shape—a shape that corresponds also to its reflected image of other objects.

It is metaculture, not just the thinking reeds that carry it, that makes contact with cultural objects. In the course of its own motion, it extracts something from the world. A dynamic interchange takes place. The movement of metaculture produces a tracking of the movement of culture, and it produces a cumulative understanding of it. For this reason, the metacultural experts—film reviewers, for example, or scientists—are not just isolated reeds with thinking caps on. Were they only that, they would have no more privileged access to cultural objects than anyone else, including local consumers. In fact, they would be nothing other than local consumers with megaphones.

What allows such experts greater access to things, what accounts for their more accurate tracking of motion, is the greater quantity of cumulated metaculture they possess, the greater quantity that flows through them by virtue of their position relative to the pathways of metacultural motion. It is that restless metaculture itself that makes contact with objects, that directs attention to their discrete facets, that reveals their truth, their continuities and discontinuities with the past.

The motion of culture—as manifested in films and novels, for sure, but elsewhere, as well—is made intelligible by metaculture, yes. But how is continuity manufactured, in the first place? Evidently, taste plays a role in the production process. Creators of putatively new cultural objects fashion those objects, in part, out of their own responses—that is, according to what Bourdieu calls their *habitus*, their internalized set of predispositions to respond. Yet new object creation requires more than response guided by habitual inertia. It requires the putting forth of something that can be responded to. That putting forth is the realization of an idea of the object, an idea that, to be sure, can be amorphous, one whose shape in the material world of things evolves over time in the course of its realization—but an idea nonetheless.

The idea, however, is not free-floating. If the object it produces is to embody the motion of culture, the idea must participate in the motion of culture. It must be an idea that has been passed on, either extracted from prior cultural objects through responses to them, or directly carried by metacultural commentary—itself a form of response. In the case of mass-disseminated items, metacultural commentary in the form of words looms large.

It is possible to identify a key locus for the transmission of such meta-cultural words: the corporations that produce the objects to which those words refer. The motion of mass-disseminated culture—understood as the movement of abstract forms or ideas through people—is to be found first and foremost inside corporate walls. And this is what makes the corporation something more than just another locale, another collection of local tastes.

As dense nodes of social connectivity, corporations are the product of cumulative cultural learning—learning suffusing the minds and bodies of its employees. Corporations are also the pathways through which that learning flows across time into a future. And such learning does not flow through all local arenas. The individuals who make mass-disseminated objects—films, for example—constitute but a small portion of those who will actually use or take up the objects. The producers have mastered, like no one else, the art of getting old culture into new objects, even if they lose control of what culture is extracted from those objects by local users.

True, some of the metaculture within a corporation—the know-how for making objects—is transmitted outside corporate walls, within colleges and universities, especially. But the academy does not carry the exquisite detail of knowledge—as in a Jan van Eyck painting, where even the smallest gem appears with hyperclarity—that is requisite for the production of just this specific kind of cultural object.

Corporations—and the people in them—are closest to the nuts and bolts of cultural object production, to the artifice that brings objects into being. They are the bearers of often proprietary knowledge, but also of knowledge more generally—however seemingly insignificant—that passes in large measure, if not primarily, within their walls. Indeed, a corporation, as a distinctive social entity, is definable by the metaculture transmitted within it, carried by it.

Here we come finally to how the motion of culture is possible despite the apparent differences in surface shapes through which it is manifested. We come to the seemingly magical motion of ideal forms, whose movement takes place apparently without the help of traditional culture's replication processes. This motion cannot be understood by reference to continuity in the perceptible shapes of cultural objects alone. It cannot be understood by local tastes alone. Any adequate understanding must take into account the metacultural talk or writing or other communication (including nonverbal communication) within the corporation that produces the new object. The corporation carries the metaculture for making the object and for foreseeing how well it will work at the cultural plane.

A key component of that metaculture is the idea of newness itself. It is newness, however, tempered always by talk about what has worked in the past, especially if the corporation has a substantial time depth. It is, therefore, newness tempered by an idea of underlying continuity, despite surface difference. Does this film script fit the formula for success? Does this musical "sound" resonate with other "sounds" that have achieved currency? Will this automotive "look" have the appeal that previous "looks" have had?

This is talk about continuity. But it is continuity of an unusual sort, one that theories of culture have yet to fully grasp. It is continuity grounded in an idea that difference matters, that change or betterment is important. Change has to occur in the obvious appearance of things, even as the detectable, but less readily apparent, idea behind the things remains the same or itself changes only incrementally. A split opens between the thing as it appears to the senses and the thing as it can be made known to the intellect. This split is rendered possible because the idea of the thing can be carried in metaculture rather than (or in addition to) the superficial appearance. The discerning eye, directed by metaculture, picks out the similarity. Simultaneously, metaculture makes it possible to "foresee," in the mind's eye, a shape that local tastes will recognize, even if the thing itself appears to local eyes and ears—as well as noses and tongues and hands—to be different.

Such a split is feasible where there is a chasm between the locus of cultural production and the local sites of cultural uptake of the objects, that is, where dissemination has become relatively uncoupled from replication. It takes a producer who is not simultaneously the recipient of the cultural object produced to want to disguise the continuity of the idea that is carried in the object from the physical appearance of the object itself. Such a producer wants to maximize simultaneously the sense of familiarity surrounding a cultural object and the intrigue of its apparent or obvious newness.

Conclusion

The Answer and the Question

The riddle has proven subtler than it at first seemed: What moves through space and time, yet has no Newtonian mass? The answer is culture, to be sure. But the riddle turns out to be wrapped inside a mystery: How can something move at all if it has no Newtonian mass? Our initial response: by traditional means, that is, by manifesting itself always in consistent material shapes, so that its sensible form becomes replicable. The abstract idea of the thing approaches, or even merges with, the thing's perceptible, kinesthetically reproducible outline. Culture moves—like the biological information deposited so delicately in a gossamer strand of DNA—by a process of replication. What moves is abstract, but the process of movement is this-worldly.

Yet the mystery lies inside an enigma: Culture moves also, sometimes, in saltatory fashion, leaping from object to object, without the apparent conservation of perceptible shape. The same culture inhabits objects that look different from one another. How can this be? Too much of contemporary social science, taking its cue from economics, has reckoned: Well, what you see in these objects is not really culture at all, but something else—in particular, it is rationality. New objects take shape through a confrontation between individual brains and the world.

There is truth here, but a brain installed in a reed, out of touch with its fellow reeds, adds but little to its strength, to its foresight. To transcend itself, the reed needs contact with other reeds, such that social learning can accumulate over time. But how can such accumulation take place? And how can the accumulation result in the production of what appear, to the senses, to be new and different objects? Until we answer these questions, our way out of the postmodern doldrums remains blocked.

But now the answers have begun to take shape, as if a fog were lifting from our brains. Culture consists of two parts: one cuts pathways through the cloud chamber of sensuous experience (the cultural part); the other etches an image of those objects and pathways onto the diaphanous membrane of intelligible understanding (the metacultural part). Between the two, between the palpable realm of things and the numinous realm of meanings, an improbable passage takes place. Culture rarefies, and then, suddenly, as if riding some great electrical arc into the heavens, ascends from object to reflection, and then back again. In the process, matter gets converted into meaning, meaning back into matter.

Here, at last, is the answer the sphinx wanted, and not just for disinterested reasons. It has a stake in all this. How else might the learning locked up inside it—or even in the ancient Egyptian stone images[1] that bear its name—find its way out of it and move forward through time and space? For is the questioner (the sphinx) not itself also culture, asking its questions through us, through me, even as I write this sentence? Yes, I add my insights to the understanding I have received—brain-equipped reed that I am—but that understanding has accumulated over centuries, millennia. My thought would amount to little were it not for those reeds who have gone before me, who are here with me now.

Though our answer to the riddle has killed the beast—as ancient mythology says it surely must—yet it is out there still, haunting the here-and-now. From its stony surface, something escaped. A wraith-like idea of it wiggled free. The idea hovers above us, like some numen. And, as if whispering in our ears, it guides us as we fashion new objects in this empirical world. We can sense its presence, however lightly. It is sending us clues—clues to the way out of here. Shall we follow those clues? Is this the adventure for which we have been preparing?

Notes

1 THE ONCE AND FUTURE THING

1 Dan Sperber (1996) is notable, among anthropologists, for taking an epidemiological view of culture, that is, for seeing culture as something that spreads through the world the way disease does. I will be arguing, in what follows, that an epidemiological model—based on face-to-face interaction—accounts for part of the movement of culture. However, crucially missing from this epidemiological conception is an understanding of cultural movement under modernity. Such motion involves mass dissemination through media rather than face-to-face interaction. And the movement is saltatory in character, the "old" culture making its way (because of an idea of newness) into seemingly "new" objects. It is able to do so because of the crucial role played by metaculture.

   The general idea of culture as epidemic has gained a hold on the popular imagination ever since Richard Dawkins published *The Selfish Gene* (1989), in which he proposed a counterpart to the gene which he called the "meme," a self-reproducing idea. The concept has been elaborated by parapsychologist Susan Blackmore in her book *The Meme Machine* (1999) and by Richard Brodie in *Virus of the Mind* (1996). None of these authors, however, develops the epidemiological model as explicitly as Sperber. Perhaps the most recent installment of this epidemiological series is Malcom Gladwell's *The Tipping Point* (2000).

2 However, "mechanical reproduction," as Walter Benjamin (1969) called it in his justly celebrated essay, has made possible the production of identical or nearly identical copies, such that α appears to be nonunique. The interchangeability of the mechanically reproduced copies merely gives more people access to the object, which also achieves a greater temporal longevity. It is a way of making α elastic, stretchable in both time and space. Hence, it becomes a way of facilitating, what will be called, in chapter 2, the "dissemination" of culture without insuring its

"replication," that is, without requiring that the social learning embodied in the production of the objects be passed onto others, who then produce them again.

3 It was, of course, Max Weber, who, responding to materialist interpretations of Marx, stressed the causal role of ideas in human action. This is a central theme in *The Protestant Ethic and the Spirit of Capitalism* and in the abstract theory of social action charted in *Economy and Society*: "We shall speak of 'action' insofar as the acting individual attaches a subjective meaning to his behavior" (Weber [1925] 1968, 4). Weber's insights were central to the sociology of Talcott Parsons (1968).

4 Asif Agha, in his forthcoming work *Honorific Language*, has begun to elaborate what promises to be a valuable way to study complex circulatory processes involving discourse. Building on the speaker-hearer dyadic model, Agha develops the notion of a "speech chain," where the requirement for this chain is that the speaker of the n+1th speech event was a hearer for the nth event. The chain involves the carrying over of something (culture, obviously, but precisely what and how must be determined) from the nth to the n+1th event.

See also the analyses of entextualization and recontextualization processes in Silverstein and Urban (1996).

I am concerned in this book with an understanding of cultural motion more generally, but discourse will figure centrally. The notion of speech chains, in particular, requires that we go beyond the idea of motion as replication. I will be attempting to do so throughout this book as I first distinguish "dissemination" from replication (see, especially, chapter 2), and then develop a notion of "response" in relation to replication (see, especially, chapter 5).

5 These α's are to be distinguished from mechanically reproduced copies (Benjamin 1969)—the sum of which make only one α—because each α is evidence that socially learned knowledge and skill to produce something like α has been passed on. In this sense, α is evidence for the motion of culture. In the case of mechanically reproduced items, the individual item provides no evidence that the ability to produce the item has been passed on socially. One individual may have designed the cookie cutter and produced all of the seemingly identical cookies that one finds distributed around.

6 This process strongly resembles—probably not coincidentally—the process of scientific article writing, as described in the fascinating piece by George Markus (1987). The scientist brings together an area of research through citation, making it appear as if the area had existed all along. This provides a ready-made set of pathways along which the new article should flow. An analogous process is at work with ω culture more generally. See the forthcoming book by Dan Segal for an account of the inertial and accelerative aspects of the production of "Western civilization" textbooks in the United States.

7 Proof that this story has long stood out in my mind is that I narrated it at a 1987 conference at the University of Chicago (Singer 1988).

8 Because I did this at the time without the aid of a computer, I know I have undercounted the document. At the same time, I believe that, were a new study to be undertaken, the patterns would still hold.

9 These results were published in 1988 in an article entitled "The Pronominal Pragmatics of Nuclear War Discourse."

10 The idea of motion is already present in the late nineteenth- and early twentieth-

century notions of "diffusion"—that a cultural invention (the spinning wheel, the bow and arrow, the Orpheus myth) occurring in a specific place and time passes not only through the pathways of familial transmission, but also through contacts between neighboring lines.

The idea of diffusion is based on the principle that imitation is easier than creation. This led the European diffusionists—Fritz Graebner (1911) and Wilhelm Schmidt (1912–55) in Germany, for example, and Grafton Eliot Smith (1911, 1927) and William J. Perry (1924) in Britain—to view creation as rare, occurring only at certain centers. A culture complex, or *kulturkreis*, develops at one location and then diffuses over an area through processes of imitation based on contact. The extreme limit of such concentration of creativity is found in Smith and Perry's "heliocentric" theory; for them, virtually all major cultural inventions had their source in a single location (ancient Egypt) from which they then diffused.

While an idea of inertia—that it is easier to imitate than to create—seems to undergird classical diffusionism, the view is out of accord with the framework developed in this book in one key respect. I will be arguing that the primary pathways of inertial motion—at least of the existential variety—are familial, since it is in the context of the family and related institutions of socialization that children pick up and replicate culture simply because it is there to be replicated. In the view of diffusion, by contrast, the motion of culture is lateral. But if my claim is correct, that lateral motion cannot in fact be inertial. Rather, it must be accelerative.

Diffusion requires that new culture be picked up by people who already have culture that the new culture must displace—they have the culture they received through the family and related socialization institutions. Because the new culture encounters old culture that is already flowing, diffusion—rather than finding its foundations in the lethargy of people, for whom it is easier to imitate than to create—requires an understanding of acceleration. To diffuse, the new culture has to displace, in some measure, something that is already there. Hence, to understand diffusion—pace the early diffusionists themselves—we need to incorporate an idea of acceleration into the theory of motion.

The American "culture history" school, associated with Franz Boas, Alfred Kroeber, Clark Wissler, and others, was less inclined to dichotomize the centers of creation and peripheries of diffusion. What took the place of centers of creativity and peripheries of imitation was the notion of a "culture area"—for example, the eastern woodlands of North America—where a series of cultural elements diffused, resulting in broad similarities across geographical regions with inventions taking place, possibly, at multiple sites.

It is important to distinguish diffusion per se from the kind of cultural motion associated with the contemporary processes of globalization and circulation of commodities (Appadurai 1986, 1996; Hannerz 1992, 1996). Diffusion is based on replication. The recipients of a cultural object—a spinning wheel, for example—themselves learn to produce that object.

As I hope to show in chapter 2, the motion of culture under capitalism is of a distinct sort. Cultural objects get disseminated without primary replication—that is, without the production of new objects that are more than simple copies of previous ones. Hence, there continues to be a locus for the production of new objects that is distinct from the sites of uptake of those objects. In the case of capitalism, the disseminated object (a spinning wheel, for example) is taken up in local processes of replication, but is not itself reproduced in its entirety (that is, by making a new spinning wheel). While the disseminated object gives rise to certain kinds of replication, the replication is of a secondary sort, part of the uptake of the object into ongoing activities.

It is all too easy to confuse the cultural object with the cultural element, as in many contemporary archaeological discussions, and hence to conflate diffusion and globalization. Take, for example, the statement that "amber from the Baltic region diffused to the Mediterranean coast." The motion of material stuff is here conflated with the motion of underlying culture. The displacement of the object through space per se is not evidence of diffusion of culture—understood as something that is socially learned and transmitted. Rather, evidence for diffusion depends on finding new objects produced locally that resemble in significant ways those produced elsewhere—that is, it depends on finding proof of replication.

In the case of global commodities, as will become clear in chapter 2, there is a test for whether a cultural object has been taken up in local processes of replication. That test is demand, associated with price. But an isolated object found archaeologically cannot provide an adequate basis for inferring the motion of culture.

11 Actually, the linguist Roman Jakobson ([1960b] 1971), in a celebrated article, argues that [mama] and [p^hap^ha] are the result of elementary sound oppositions. They tend to develop first because children are able to make the phonetic discriminations necessary for their production before they can make others. But my point is not which phonetic discriminations can be made first. It concerns, rather, the particular phonetic combinations that children learn for referring to the world. Children learn those phonetic combinations that are spoken by others around them. If the words for "mother" and "father" are [ñõ] and [yug^n], as in one of the Brazilian Indian languages with which I am familiar, children learn to reproduce those words, not [mama] and [p^hap^ha].

12 This is a problem that plagued British social anthropology. Radcliffe-Brown ([1952] 1965) was certainly prescient enough as regards his insights about the maintenance of continuity. While emphasizing the continuity of social organization—the maintenance of the collectivity—Radcliffe-Brown failed to see that the collectivity itself was a product of the motion of culture; it was in fact a key habitual inertial pathway or set of pathways that had been laid down by culture in the past.

13 This is an aspect of the problem Webb Keane addresses in his book *Signs of Recognition* (1997)—the problem of semiotic "risk."

14 The concept is discussed at length in Herskovits (1949, 1955; see also Eggan 1941, 1963). Apparently, the notion of cultural drift was modeled on the well-known phenomenon of linguistic drift, attributable to Edward Sapir (1921), wherein a language tends over time to change. However, my colleague Igor Kopytoff (personal communication), an eminent former student of Herskovits, informs me that the two notions differ somewhat, since Herskovits's drift is "directed."

In the case of language, vocabulary is gradually replaced, and the sound shapes of contemporary words diverge more and more from those of their ancestors. Within one thousand to two thousand years, the ancestral language ceases to be intelligible to the present generation of speakers. The older language has, in essence, given rise to a new one. This phenomenon is responsible—through the isolation of populations speaking the same language—for the origins of diversity. After one thousand or two thousand years of relative isolation from one another, two distinct populations carrying on the original common language can no longer understand one another. For a brief contemporary discussion of one example of linguistic drift, see Slobin (1992).

There is, of course, a parallel in the biological concept of genetic drift, as developed by Sewall Wright (1951). The biological concept was developed after the linguistic one, perhaps under influence from it—Wright was a professor at the University of Chicago at a time (1926–54) when Sapir and Fred Eggan were also there.

15 In chapter 2, I will make a crucial distinction between dissemination and replication. Here I am trying to be consistent in my usage with that latter distinction. Dissemination and replication are aspects of the larger process I call "circulation."

16 See Gal's (1979) study of language shift in Austria, Milroy's (1980) work on Northern Ireland, and the general discussion in Gumperz (1982, 40–48). Gumperz notes that "whenever networks of relationships reflect long-term, interpersonal cooperation in the performance of regular tasks and the pursuit of shared goals, they favor the creation of behavioral routines and communicative conventions that become conventionally associated with and serve to mark component activities" (1982, 42). This seems to privilege social relations over interest in semiotic forms as a basis for language spread. But the point here, again, is the need for communication that could otherwise take place only through translation as a basis for language spread. Since social relations develop around the need for communication, it is to the basis of that need—the movement of that need, so to speak—that one must look ultimately for reasons behind the development of the social relations themselves. The desire to make sense of semiotic objects, or, alternatively, to produce semiotic objects that others can make sense of, is what motivates language spread.

17 This notion has a contemporary resonance with the concept of "hybridity" as used by Deborah Kapchan (1996) and others.

18 He subsequently authored *Fighting For Peace: Seven Critical Years in the Pentagon*, and (with Peter Schweizer) *The Next War*, among other works.

19 Actually, in Schell's case, the adoption of a human species "we" seems to have involved something of a detour in his journalistic career, as such "we's" do not come so hot and heavy in his later writing, such as the 1997 book *Writing in Time*. Nor are they prominent in his earlier work on Watergate, *The Time of Illusion*, published in 1976. *The Fate of the Earth* seems to have reflected a peculiarly accelerative moment in Schell's own life that was not fully maintained or consolidated.

At the same time, neither does a "we" of the United States, and, in particular, of the U.S. government, play a particularly prominent role in Schell's habituated patterns. A random sampling of his early and late "we's"—I confess that I have not done a systematic study—suggests a "we" of those looking in from the outside, with suspicion, at government. See, for example, Schell "Customarily, *we* think of Washington as the land of illusion and the country at large as the place where reality appears. The politicians 'inside the Beltway,' *we* like to think, are constantly at risk of losing contact with the rest of the country" (1997, 49; italics added).

Schell, however, also shows an awareness of the pronoun "we" in relationship to the government. Describing voter anger at the politicians they have elected, he notes, "It is a way of blaming 'them' for the country's travails without recognizing that all along they were obeying 'us'"(1997, 13). His trajectory with respect to "we" usage merits further study.

20 Radcliffe-Brown's ([1952] 1965) lasting contribution was to focus attention on the maintenance of continuity, although he never envisioned a principle of continuity that might apply to culture more generally. His structural-functional view emphasized the role of the piece of the collectivity in relation to maintenance of the whole. However, he is not entirely wrong even in this regard, since part of the mechanism through which cultural elements maintain themselves is by attaching themselves, or making themselves seem to be attached, to others. It is an empirical question in what measure every cultural element within a community has been made to fit together with others, but the tendency ought to be for culture—in isolated communities, at least—to become integrated. Integration is the product of the survival mechanisms used by the individual elements to maintain themselves.

21 The relationship of metalanguage to language and metadiscourse to discourse is a subject of intensive investigation in current anthropological research. See Lee (1997), Silverstein (1993), and other papers in Lucy (1993).

22 Ironic, perhaps, yes, but also fully understandable from the perspective of cultural motion. The discussions are part of the process whereby cultural learning (about how to manipulate DNA) passes into metacultural understanding (about what makes us who we are, about how we should behave, about what we value), which, in turn, interprets and regulates cultural learning (how we actually deploy the ability to manipulate DNA, for example).

2 IN MODERN TIME

1 The term "modernity" carries more philosophical baggage than is, perhaps, appropriate here, and I will more generally refer to an idea of "newness." However, it seems probable to me that the philosophical idea of modernity, which Habermas ([1985] 1987, 7 and passim) understands as having taken shape in the eighteenth century, is the result of a metacultural idea of newness or modernity that predates this development. The battle of the ancients and moderns itself begins in the seventeenth century, but the explicit formulation of these metacultural positions—if the theory presented in this book is correct—must have been preceded by the circulation of ideas of the "new" as better.

In The Philosophical Discourse of Modernity ([1985] 1987), Habermas provides an overview of the philosophical issues that is consonant with the metacultural orientation described in this book: "Because the new, the modern world is distinguished from the old by the fact that it opens itself to the future, the epochal new beginning is rendered constant with each moment that gives birth to the new" ([1985] 1987, 6). His concern is with the postmodern critique of modernity, especially as developed by Derrida and Foucault. He begins with Hegel and subject-centered views of modernity in order to show that the critiques of modernity from the perspectives of power and language focus precisely on the earlier subject-centrism. His hope is to recapture a space for modernity and rationality by adopting a communicative approach grounded in processes of agreement-seeking by a community.

For other overviews of modernity, see David Harvey's The Condition of Postmodernity (1989), which places postmodernism in the context of a neo-Marxist view of late capitalism, and Jean-François Lyotard's The Postmodern Condition (1984), which adopts the perspective of narrative. See also Arjun Appadurai's *Modernity at Large* (1996), which focuses on the problem of globalization, including the British colonization of India.

The term "postmodernity" itself seems to bespeak a hypermodernism. How, after all, if emphasis is on the new, can one get past modernity? At the same time, postmodernism has a neotraditionalist flavor, given its emphasis on the arbitrariness of systems of representation, which can only be justified by appeals to some factor extrinsic to representation per se—for example, power, as in the case of Foucault, or tradition itself.

From the point of view of cultural motion, however, it is apparent that the movement of culture takes place for reasons having to do with the material characteristics of cultural objects and with their representational characteristics as meaning. Inertia is one reason for the persistence of culture, but it alone cannot purport to explain all of culture, ignoring as it does the accelerative forces that are at work on it. The inertial culture had to become inertial. How did it do so? An appeal to power only displaces the problem—as Habermas correctly argues—without solving it. And I believe that there are solutions, as I will begin to show in this chapter, solutions having to do with the properties of culture as something that moves through the world, through space and time.

2 There is a substantial recent literature on first contact, including the debate between Marshall Sahlins (1981, 1995) and Gananath Obeyesekere (1994) over the encounters between Captain Cook and the Hawaiian islanders. Sahlins emphasizes the role of inertial culture (as structure) in determining this encounter (the Hawaiians thought Cook was the god Lono); Obeyesekere argues for individual rationality, politics, and contingency (the Hawaiians knew Cook was really just a man, and it is Sahlins and other scholars who have passed off the myth of Cook's apotheosis as part of the imperialist project of the West). See also the work by Stephen Greenblatt (1991) and Tzvetan Todorov (1992) on the New World and Edward Schieffelin and Robert Crittenden (1991) on first contacts in Papua New Guinea.

3 See the essays in Lamberg-Karlovsky and Sabloff (1975) for the connection between trade and the rise of ancient civilizations.

4 The vast literature on the subject of culture contact seems to divide into two parts: culture contact under conditions of relative peace and equality between populations (a presupposition in much of the diffusionist literature—see chapter 1, footnote 10), and culture contact under situations of asymmetry (the culture and conquest literature, as well as acculturation studies, whether acculturation is viewed as forced—as in the case of many Native American populations—or voluntary—as in the case of most European migration to the United States. Added to these literatures is the work on cultural syncretism and hybridity (on which see the discussion in Kapchan [1996, 6–18] and Hannerz [1987]; see also the classic work by Herskovits [1938]; Taussig's [1980, 1987] work is of interest in this regard as well). I will not say more about the idea of hybridity or creolization here except to say that the process of forming a new cultural element from two or more older ones has a link to modernity, where the new cultural object typically derives its newness from the merger of distinct strands of culture, as I have already argued, and as will become further apparent subsequently.

Here I am concerned with the problem of motion per se, how culture moves across the inertial lines constituted by familial pathways and those associated with socialization more generally. Discussion of this problem is an old one in anthropological literature, going back to the very conception of culture as socially transmitted, socially learned—that is, going back to the diffusionist literature (see ch. 1, note 10).

The kind of motion associated with classical diffusion (pace many of the diffusionists themselves, as discussed earlier) is grounded in an idea that accelerative qualities may be found in the actual objects through which culture is circulated. Thus, we find the idea that the bow and arrow is better suited for certain kinds of hunting tasks than the spear. For this reason, the idea of it spreads across inertial lines. Those who use spears or other hunting devices find the bow and arrow to be superior for certain purposes, and so they take it up. Because of its greater accelerative force, one cultural element displaces another with which it comes into competition.

The idea is distinct from that found in the literature on colonialism and conquest, where the concept of "directed diffusion" or "directed change" has been sometimes used. (See the essays in Turgeon, Delâge, and Ouellet [1996] for discussions of diffusions between America and Europe that run the gamut from the classical type to the power-laden.) In the case of directed diffusion, it appears that the accelerative qualities of the culture are not properties of the cultural objects per se as they pertain to local processes of cultural replication, but rather something the objects acquire by virtue of their association with a population understood to be in a position of superiority. Acceleration here is not a function of objects, but of social relations and power, the key term found in so many contemporary studies inspired by the work of Michel Foucault. This idea is central to most of his writing, really, but see especially the little book *Power/Knowledge* (1980).

At one end of this continuum is power as overtly coercive, where people are made to do things they do not want to do, and hence culture is made to flow across relations wherein there is resistance (see chapter 4). At the other end is power as a function of desire—the desire, for example, to be like the other, and to act and look like that other. Hence, culture is made to flow across relations by a desire to assimilate to or become like the other. The type-cases for directed diffusion along this continuum are colonial encounters, for example, between Europeans and New World Indians, Africans, or Australian Aborigines, on the one side, and voluntary immigration, for example, from Europe to the United States, on the other. The literature on Native American acculturation is especially large (see, to mention only a few examples, Driver and Driver [1963], Foster [1960], Oliveira [1960 and 1964], Schaden [1965], and Spindler [1962]). There is, at the same time, resistance to directed diffusion (see, for example, Farriss [1984] on the Maya under Spanish colonial rule or Comaroff and Comaroff [1991, 1992] on the Tswana of South Africa). Such resistance results from the presence of culture already flowing through the social pathways, which the new culture, propelled by directed diffusion, would have to displace.

But is it really the social relations, as something distinct from culture, that impart an accelerative force to cultural objects and elements in the case of directed diffusion? The answer I give in this chapter and throughout this book is: No. Some of the accelerative force propelling cultural objects and elements through the world does, indeed, come from outside those objects and elements themselves. However, it does not come from social relations per se—as distinct from culture. Rather, as you have undoubtedly already surmised, the force comes from metaculture (culture that is about culture) as a distinct plane or layer of circulation articulating in various ways with the cultural plane. If it seems to come from social relations, this is only because the latter are a precipitate of cultural motion, simultaneously as they are the conduits through which culture flows.

Even the threat or selective application of force, from this point of view, is metacultural. It is a way of communicating something about culture, namely, that the threatened individuals or groups must comport themselves in specific and definable ways—those ways being the culture that is transmitted to them by the threatener—if they are to avoid harm to themselves. The metaculture directs attention to the consequences for the individuals of this or that culture flowing through them.

There is a similarity here to the diffusion of the bow and arrow, since this, too, has consequences that users recognize, even though they might also be heralded by the bow and arrow's purveyor. But the consequences, in the latter case, are more evidently intrinsic to the pattern of conduct associated with the bow and arrow that constitutes the cultural element. In the case of a threatened use of force to motivate a pattern of conduct, the consequence of that pattern (or cultural element) is in considerable measure extrinsic to the pattern (or element) itself, depending as it does on the response of another to it.

5 However, the range of phenomena that can be captured through the village study is impressive, as even a cursory reading of the classical literature reveals. Warner's Yankee City series is monumental, documenting in detail the social life of a New England city, its status system, ethnic groups, factory organization, and symbolic life. My comments are not meant to discourage community-based studies, which, because of the spatial-locatedness of the ethnographic method, should continue to play a central role in ethnographic research. Rather, they are intended to deny that the community can directly stand—in a microcosm-macrocosm way—for the whole. In his survey of ethnographies of the contemporary United States, Michael Moffatt (1992, 214) notes the persistence of an essentialist idea of American culture, "associated with some sort of middle-class mainstream."

Anthony F. C. Wallace's (1978, 1987) historical ethnographic studies of Rockport and St. Clair, however, had already shifted the emphasis of the early community ethnographies from representative of the whole to a specific problem pertaining to the whole. A trend in some, if not much, recent ethnographic research on the United States has been to find field sites that make sense for the investigation of aspects of culture in America. See, for example, the research by Aaron Fox (1992, 1995) on country and western music, which finds its site in a specific town, and even a specific honky-tonk bar—although the research did become multisited. Fox purports to see that site (or those sites) not as directly extrapolatable to the American culture, but rather to aspects or facets of that larger culture—namely, sensibilities in working-class American culture that are linked to country and western music. This is true also of Susan Lepselter's (1994, 1997) research on UFO groups and believers and their relationship to experiences of the uncanny. The same can be said of Philippe Bourgois's (1996) work on drug addicts in New York City. Such research focuses on facets of American culture that are not representative of the whole, but are pieces of a bigger puzzle, and must often be multisited (Marcus 1995).

6 As examples, see Thomas Porcello (1996) and Louise Meintjes (1996).

7 The potentially enriching insights of the method, however, especially as regards the construction of cultural ideals, are major, as demonstrated by Robert N. Bellah (1996) and other contributors to the volume.

8 See Appadurai (1996, 48–65) on ethnoscapes, and also Conklin and Graham (1995) on the global circulation of images of Amazonian Indians, as well as Faudree (1999) on Western discourses—missionary and ecological activist—about a specific Amazonian people, the Waorani.

9 This is the conceit of "modernization theory" from the 1950s and 1960s—a well-founded one, even if metacultures of tradition rise up to counter it. For an overview of the modernization literature, see the articles by Daniel Lerner (1968), James Coleman (1968), and Ronald Dore (1968) in the much-forgotten *International Encyclopedia of the Social Sciences*, a repository of information that deserves to be consulted by the next generation of scholars (and also by those of us who once familiarized ourselves with this literature, but then subsequently forgot it). Indeed, "modernization" is one of those terms that has drifted sufficiently from memory, yet which retains enough recognizability to allow it to appear as cutting-edge for a new generation of scholars while simultaneously building on the inertia of prior circulation.

It is intriguing, from the point of view of cultural motion as understood in this book, that modernization was construed, in the 1950s and 1960s, as "the process of social change in which development is the economic component" (Lerner 1968, 387). That process, as I describe in this chapter, is part and parcel of replacing a metaculture of tradition with a metaculture of newness. Coleman actually describes "typological political modernization" as "the process of transmutation of a pre-modern 'traditional' polity into a posttraditional 'modern' polity" (1968, 395). Note the chronological sequencing here, which makes sense of the terminological unfolding of postmodernism by a process of analogy—traditional : posttraditional :: modern : X, where X is the absent signifier.

10 If demand measures the force associated with the movement of specific cultural objects, migration measures another kind of attractive force, namely, that associated with the people who produce the desired cultural objects and the place of production of those objects. A discussion of this topic is beyond the scope of the present book. The subject of migration is complex, in part because people may move for negative reasons—the desire to leave an existing place and people (see the discussion of the nation in chapter 6)—as well as positive ones. However, it is important here to note that the movement of people is linked to the attractive (and repulsive) forces associated with the dissemination of cultural objects themselves.

11 A large literature exists on the written/oral distinction, on which see the key works by Goody (1986, 1987) and Ong (1982). There is no question that writing aids dissemination. Writing renders the original object copiable in the absence of full replication, such as I discuss in the last section of this chapter. Full replication involves internalization of the original, followed by the recreation of that original. Copying is more mechanical, as when one writes down the words one sees, without thinking about them or what they mean. Of course, it is possible to copy spoken discourse in this way, as well, as when one memorizes and repeats words in a foreign language,

though not fully cognizant of what they mean. Such copying is a first step towards replication. As I will discuss, print does away with even that first step.

12 The distinction between price-setting or "open markets" and other types is discussed in Salisbury (1968). See also papers in the volume edited by Lamberg-Karlovsky and Sabloff (1974, 1975).

13 Marcel Thomas ([1958] 1976) describes the copying processes that were put into place during the thirteenth through fifteenth centuries: "To assure the reproduction of copies under the best conditions, so that the text would be unaltered and the copyists could not make unjustified profits, the universities devised an ingenious system. Manuscripts were loaned which had been carefully checked and revised. From them copies could be made and charged for according to a fixed tariff or 'tax.' The original text (the 'exemplar') was returned to the stationer after copying, and he could hire it out again. This method prevented the corruption of the text, which could otherwise become worse with every copy made, since by this method each copy was made from the same original. Anyone who has had to study the transmission of ancient texts will understand what a good idea this was" (21).

14 Of course, there are other reasons for demanding a book, such as those of modern book collectors, who want them for their future market value. My argument focuses on those aspects of demand that arise out of the interest in the discourse that the written documents carry.

15 See, for example, Dell Hymes's (1985) analysis of the difference between two tellings of the same story.

16 See the rapidly growing literature on "oral formulaics," originally spawned by the work of Milman Parry (1954, 1971) and Albert Bates Lord (1960 and 1991) and developed by Acker (1998), Amodio (1994), Foley (1991, 1995), Gellrich (1995), and Mackay (1999).

17 Reducing tokens to countable types is actually a complex task, since some words are linguistic variants of others—"jump" versus "jumped," for example. Where the similarity between words was obvious in the physical form of the words themselves—and, of course, this is a matter of metacultural judgment—I counted the two tokens as belonging to the same type. Where the similarity was not based on physical shape but on meaning—as in "I" versus "me"—I counted the items as distinct.

The method works very well here because neither English nor Xokleng (or Shokleng), as the Amerindian language is called, depend a great deal on morphology for building up words, unlike so-called "polysynthetic" languages, such as the Amerindian languages of the Northwest coast of North America. The method would have to be modified and adapted to work on other kinds of languages.

18 The longer the narrative, of course, the more likely that any given word will be repeated. The phenomenon will become clearer in the next section, where I discuss the ratios of tokens to types. If you hold that ratio constant, then your whole narrative has a maximum length that will be defined by the size of the vocabulary available. After the size limit is reached, the ratio has to go up. As I will show, there may be reasons why stories, under a metaculture of newness, must keep those ratios down.

19 For an introduction to this literature, see key works by Hymes (1981), Tedlock (1983), and Sherzer (1990).

20 One question I had was whether still vital Euro-American mythological traditions—

in particular, the Christian Bible—would show the same tendency as the Amerindian Brazilian myths towards repetition. I sampled the first chapter of Genesis, which, indeed, showed a 5.81 tokens:type rate of repetition, a figure remarkably close to the average (5.70) for the Brazilian myths. I then sampled the first chapter of one of the New Testament gospels (Luke); the rate turned out to be 4.01 tokens:type. To extend the sample somewhat, I analyzed the first two chapters of Exodus as a unit—the ratio was 3.77—and then the third and fourth chapters as a unit—the ratio was 5.31. The average for these samplings was 4.72, which fell between the novels (3.20) and the myths (5.70). I would not be surprised to find generally lower rates in the New Testament.

21 For an in-depth, sympathetic cultural account of tradition, see Laura Graham's excellent ethnography, *Performing Dreams: The Discourse of Immortality among the Xavante of Central Brazil* (1995).

3 THIS NATION WILL RISE UP

1 Actually, as my subsequent argument will reveal, there is reason to suspect that the "United States" had greater social reality, both before and after the Declaration, than did the "Republic of Texas" after the Official Call. The issue here is breadth of circulation of the idea within the relevant population. However, my point is that the Declaration was only one moment in that process of circulation of the idea of an independent United States of America.

2 I chose clauses, in this case, rather than sentences—as I used in some other cases, discussed later—because of the extremely variable nature of sentence length in this document. Clauses here seemed to give a better picture of the pacing of first-person pronouns over the duration of the text, but other forms of durational segmentation can be used as measures (such as number of words) with essentially the same results.

3 The phrase "We, the people of the United States" appears in the preamble to the Constitution. The Declaration's phrase is "We, therefore, the Representatives of the United States of America."

4 For the different senses of "we" as used in the American context, see Hollinger (1993). There is a substantial and growing literature on the first-person plural pronoun in relation to group membership, concerning which see Grimshaw (1994, 311–71) and Singer (1989).

5 This is a seemingly elementary idea. If one views a given narrative—or any other cultural object—as ω rather than α culture, then the source of its ω-ness must be sought in something outside of culture, at least in terms of culture construed as the replication of α's. Simple though the idea is, it has far-reaching implications which, I believe, conform to the insights about the modern self laid out in the masterful work by Charles Taylor, *Sources of the Self: The Making of the Modern Identity* (1989). Taylor's conclusions derive from a study of philosophical, political, and religious literature, but they are, or so it seems to me, compatible with those I have reached by studying microscopic aspects of discourse in relation to the macromovement of culture.

Particularly relevant to the transformations in narrative and in the use of the pronoun "I," discussed in this section, is Taylor's account of modern "inwardness." He sums up the difference, for example, between Augustinian and Cartesian inwardness by saying that "Descartes situates the moral sources within us" (1989,

143). Those sources, of course, are the basis for individual control necessary for the production of ω culture.

Indeed, Descartes' *cogito* can be rethought from the perspective of cultural motion under a metaculture of newness. If the specific utterance of the *cogito* is viewed as an ω object—that is, not as an α replica of something one has heard others say— then its utterance could be meaningfully interpreted as affirming the existence of an inner subjectivity. Ironically, however, for all of us who live in the shadow of Descartes's words, the cogito becomes ersatz ω culture—stale culture that has been handed down across the generations. Our present-day assertion of it might as well be the replication of some aspect of traditional culture—that is, unless we construe that assertion through the filter of a metaculture of newness, namely, as something unconditioned by its prior articulations, something that is a unique expression of ourselves.

6 Laura Graham (1995) has documented a similar pattern of projective "I" usage for another central Brazilian Indian group. And Alan Rumsey (2000) has analyzed the chiefly "I" in Polynesia, where a single individual speaks in the first person as a long-since-dead ancestor. The "I" of possession trance, where spirits inhabit the concrete body of the person entranced, falls into this class of "projective" "I's," as well.

7 A given translation (the King James Version, for example) may be taken as definitive by some people; and a literalist approach may locate the truth in the actual words of that translation (see Crapanzano 2000); but even in those cases, one copy of the translation is equal in value to another.

8 Of course, from an anthropological perspective, if the Declaration continues to have value eight hundred years from now, and if American English continues to evolve at the usual rate, the document will no longer be fully intelligible. Two thousand years from now it will appear to have been written in a different language.

9 See G. Markus (1987) on citation in scientific publications.

10 Here I make a distinction between an internal movement "we" and a secessionist "we." The latter is also a movement "we," but it does not pose the problems found in internal movement "we's," where acceptance of the "we" has to be imaginable among a larger grouping of individuals than those immediately aggrieved.

11 It is well known that both sides of the slavery controversy of the 1840s and 1850s drew on the Declaration of Independence for authority, as in the case of the Lincoln-Douglas debates of 1854 (Maier 1997, 203).

12 In discussing the Amerindian case, I want to head off a possible misunderstanding. My argument is not that the modern "we" is based on a living/dead opposition. It is rather that a modern "we" is viewed as under the control of its current articulators. Its relationship to "we's" that have come before it is rendered insignificant by the idea of control. Correspondingly, a traditional "we" can seize upon the living/dead distinction, as I argue here. What is crucial to its status as a traditional "we" is that its utterers see the utterance of it not as something they themselves have created, but rather as something that has been passed on to them by those who have come before.

Still, there is a fit between the modern "we" and the living/dead opposition precisely because the living are the ones in control of current utterances. Such a formulation makes sense from the perspective of newness. From the point of view of the utterer, it is harder to imagine a "we, the living" as having come from the ancestors because those ancestors are excluded from the referential scope of that "we." I say harder, but clearly not impossible. *We* could see ourselves as having received many things from *them*, including a pattern of "we" usage that excludes *them*.

13 Within the huge literature on nationalism (see Calhoun 1997, and Eley and Suny 1996, for an orientation), the connection between nations and modernity has long been recognized—see, for example, Kohn (1944), whose work foreshadows that of Benedict Anderson ([1983] 1991) in many ways. Gellner (1983), in particular, sees the modern form of nations as linked to the industrial revolution as people from diverse backgrounds migrated to industrial centers. A common culture or way of life had to emerge among them, despite differences as regards the inherited culture with which they came. Hence, a national identity came to take precedence over (and, in some cases, to dominate) other sources of identity, including the family and ethnic group (see, in this regard, Berlant [1997], Berlant and Warner [1998], Mosse [1985], and Ramaswamy [1997]).

I take this latter characteristic to be the defining feature of nationalism: the tendency of people to regard their national identity as their principal identity. And, of course, some people are more fervent in this regard than others, although at some points almost everyone must reckon with these ardent nationalists and their beliefs and actions. It is to this aspect of the nationalism literature that the present chapter, as well as other parts of this book, especially chapter 6, endeavors to contribute. I am concerned with the foundations of such identification in the orientation to pronouns, not just the first-person plural, as I have proposed, but also the singular. A distinctive orientation to "we" goes hand in hand with a distinctive orientation to "I."

At the same time, this microfocus on the motion of culture suggests that the rise of nationalism is not a function of economic transformation per se, as if the latter were an acultural infrastructure. Rather, the close-up inspection of pronominal identification suggests that the changes leading to nationalism are—like the rise of capitalism itself—part of the processes of cultural motion. In particular, they are part of the restless side of culture, as it is spurred on by a metacultural idea of newness, namely, that abstract underlying culture must move from an old object to a new one that is not a precise replica of it, and that it must seek out new people who would not otherwise acquire it through inertial motion.

From this perspective, the work of Charles Taylor (1989, 1998) appears most compatible with the present formulation. In his monumental study, *Sources of the Self* (1989), Taylor traces the rise of new subjectivities associated with modernism that are not simply a reflex of infrastructural transformations, but that make possible a Cartesian cogito, as contrasted with an Augustinian one, and that lay the groundwork for civil society and also for the nation and nationalism.

The view put forth here is that nationalism and capitalism both have the same root cause: the ascendance of a metaculture of newness. Hence, I am not inclined to subscribe to Gellner's formulation, in which nationalism is a consequence of capitalism per se, although the fact that both spring from the same cause indicates a close connection between them. For this reason, I am not entirely unsympathetic to some of the criticisms of the linkage between nationalism and modernity—for example, A. D. Smith's ([1986] 1998) contention that nations have an older time depth than modernity theory suggests; or Partha Chatterjee's (1993) claim that, while the material aspects of Indian nationalism were linked to the Indian response to colonialism, the spiritual aspects have deeper roots not tied to colonialism. From the point of view of the present formulation, however, nationalism—as a voluntary alignment with the nation, an alignment that takes precedence over other tradition-al ascriptions of identity—is clearly tied to modernity insofar as it (like capitalism itself) is grounded in a metaculture of newness. True, such a metaculture probably surged to the fore in other places at other times. But it has been especially promi-nent in the last five hundred years of European (and, from there, world) history. The modern form of nationalism grows out of it.

14 As I indicated in chapter 2, note 1, postmodernism can be construed either as hypermodernism, a way of being newer than new, or as a form of neotraditionalism. It is the latter construal to which I am referring here. Arguments that reduce truth to power reduce it, ultimately, to tradition.

15 It has been documented also by Hugh Mehan (1997) for the debate over illegal im-migration in California.

16 Even in the "Internationale," pronominal deployment appears to be that of a move-ment. Its point of view is activists telling the workers to rise up, not workers speak-ing to the world:

> Arise ye workers from your slumbers
> Arise ye prisoners of want
> For reason in revolt now thunders
> And at last ends the age of cant.
> Away with all your superstitions
> Servile masses arise, arise
> We'll change henceforth the old tradition
> And spurn the dust to win the prize.

In this regard, the hymn appears haughty and contemptuous, demanding of the workers that they cease being who they are and become what the communist movement wants them to be.

4 THIS IS RIDICULOUS

1 As Benjamin Lee notes: "According to logical positivists, truth-functional uses of language included statements, descriptions, and assertions. Among these, those which were empirically verifiable, and therefore which had specifiable truth condi-tions, were meaningful; all others were meaningless" (1997, 6).

2 I use the term "imperative" here to highlight linguistic form. Imperatives are gram-matically describable linguistic expressions that signal themselves as devices for telling someone to do something, rather than, for example, as devices for communi-cating information. The term "command," in contrast, draws attention to function, to what it is that A is trying to get B to do. Of course, imperatives may serve func-tions other than commanding, and commands may be expressed through linguistic forms other than imperatives (see Ervin-Tripp 1972, 1976). However, I am especial-ly concerned in this chapter with situations in which there is a confluence between the two, with what grammatically are imperatives being used functionally to express commands. Hence, my particular choice of the term "imperative" versus "command" at any given moment in this chapter is a matter of relative emphasis.

3 Even though inexact compliance with them, as you will see, is the source of irreversible change.

4 While the Cherokee text I analyze here is an English translation, similar micropatterns can be found in native language texts from other indigenous populations (see Urban 1991, 58–78, for an example).

5 This particular story was obtained by Mooney "in nearly the same form from Swimmer and John Ax (east) and from Wafford (west)" (Mooney 1900, 431), which suggests that Mooney may have compiled this version from several others. He could have been the source of the change, or the change could have been introduced by the translator(s), Chief N. J. Smith or someone in his family (see Mooney 1900, 13), or, again, by an editor.

6 The energy concentrated on replicating the myth was harnessed in part also by ritual; the myth was "held so sacred that in the old days one who wished to hear it from the priest of the tradition must first purify himself by 'going to water,' i.e., bathing in the running stream before daylight when still fasting, while the priest performed his mystic ceremonies upon the bank" (Mooney 1900, 431).

7 This kind of rationality is perhaps more akin to what Habermas (1984, 1987) calls "communicative rationality."

5 THE PUBLIC EYE

1 Strange in the abstract, yes, but the idea that consciousness may be lodged in discourse, and hence may circulate, has been present for some time. See, in this regard, especially Voloshinov's *Freudianism: A Marxist Critique* ([1927] 1976), where he focuses on the conscious/unconscious distinction in relationship to signs in social life.

2 We can understand with particular clarity, in connection with this problem of influence, why anthropologists sometimes focus on social relationships as if they were prior to the motion of culture through those relationships, though they are actually themselves, in considerable measure, a product of that flow. This perspective is associated especially with A. R. Radcliffe-Brown ([1952] 1965) and the British social anthropologists.

3 I actually studied many more reviews of these and other films and also of books, but I limited my sample size for this study in order to insure a pairing: the periodical had to contain reviews of both films.

4 Marx ([1867] 1970, 44 ff.) distinguished the "use value" an object might have from its value as something that might be exchanged for other objects also possessing use value. This latter "exchange value" thus reflected an interconvertibility among objects.

To relate this distinction to the present scheme, use value—although it has been interpreted in reductive ways from time to time—refers not to the satisfaction of biological needs, but to the motion of culture. Use value is the significance an object has in processes of local cultural reproduction. An object is useful insofar as it participates in or facilitates the replication of local culture. Mass-disseminated objects (or commodities) are useful in this way.

At the same time, the characteristic of the mass-disseminated object is that, while people find it useful for local replication, they themselves do not produce it. Rather, they get the object from elsewhere and then extract from it the culture they need. Exchange value measures how important the mass-disseminated object is for processes of local cultural reproduction.

Evidently, therefore, exchange value is a kind of metaculture. Indeed, in some respects it resembles the film reviews discussed in this chapter. It is a commentary about culture that tells just how great the demand for the thing (the mass-disseminated object) is, and hence how strong the force is that impels the culture carried in the object through the world.

5 It is intriguing that Fredric Jameson, in his book *The Cultural Turn* (1998), argues for previews or trailers as exemplars of quintessential "postmodern" culture that exhibit properties of compression and speed of circulation. This leads one to wonder about the connection between the rise of an idea of postmodernism and the ascendance of explicit metaculture as an accelerative force behind the circulation of culture, a force associated with a peculiar kind of cultural object and a peculiar form of circulation. I will return to this point at the end of this chapter.

6 Bourdieu wants to find an axis for cultural ranking of objects, which is associated with properties immanent in the objects themselves. In *Distinction* ([1975] 1984), these properties have to do with distance from necessity, and hence with detachment. The more distant from necessity, the higher-ranking the object in question is. The argument has plausibility for a given moment in the history of Euro-American cultural circulations, but I think it incorrectly turns what is a property of circulation into a fixed principle of an objective space.

7 The reviews for *Dr. Strangelove* include Crist (1964a), Crowther (1964a), Davis (1964), "Direct Hit" (1964), "Dr. Strangelove" (1964), Hart (1964), Hartung (1964a), Kauffmann (1964a), Keen (1964a), Milne (1964), Oulahan (1964), Sarris (1964a), Tinee (1964b), Wainwright (1964), and Winsten (1964a). For *Fail Safe*, they include Crist (1964b), Crowther (1964b), "Fail Safe" (1964), Hartung (1964b), Houston (1964), Kauffmann (1964b), Keen (1964b), Sarris (1964b), Tinee (1964a), "Unthinkable Unthought" (1964), and Winsten (1964b).

8 On the concept of response, see Goffman (1981) and Urban (1996a). The idea is essential to an understanding of culture as "dialogical" as opposed to "monological"— see the papers in Tedlock and Mannheim (1995) and Maranhão (1990), which build on Voloshinov ([1929] 1973) and Bakhtin (1981). At the same time, given the dependence of response, and hence of dialogicality itself, on a metaculture of newness, it is all too easy, from the vantage point of the contemporary United States, where the metaculture of newness has gained such currency, to read dialogicality back into discourse where its presence may not be recognizable to the producers.

9 You may recall from earlier discussions in chapters 1 and 3 that patterns of "we" usage can be replicated, under modernity, in part because they are less readily accessible to awareness, working their way through the world from A to B by getting into B's rhetorical unconscious, and then undergoing—unwittingly, as in my own case—replication in B's own cultural expressions. Were the patterns more accessible to consciousness, they could be more readily challenged as individual artifice, and hence responded to rather than replicated. This would suggest that metaculture— as a form of public consciousness—regularly overlooks "we" patterning. This does seem generally to be the case.

However, one review of Jonathan Schell's *Fate of the Earth*, Michael Kinsley's piece in *Harper's* (1982, 11), actually focuses in on that "we": "Schell is convinced, though, like the rest of the antinuclear movement, that the main task is education—convincing people of how bad a nuclear war would be. 'If we did acknowledge the full dimension of the peril . . . extinction would at that moment become not only "unthinkable" but also undoable.' The key word here is 'we.' But there is no 'we.' There are individual actors who cannot completely know or trust one another. That's life" (11). Kinsley zooms in on and dissolves the "we." Evidently, he would be disinclined to replicate that pattern—though his own usage is intriguing in this regard. For example, "That said, where do *we* stand? *We* stand where *we've* stood for three decades, with East and West in a nuclear stalemate that could turn at any moment into mutual annihilation" (Kinsley 1982, 11; italics mine). At various points throughout the essay, there is an ironic, raised-eyebrow replication of the Schell "we" which is, in fact, a kind of response.

What is intriguing, however, is neither Kinsley's rejection of the "we" nor his ironic usage of it, but the vision he puts in its place: ". . . there is no 'we.' There are individual actors. . . ." Kinsley here expresses, with uncanny clarity, the preoccupation with individuals that grows out of an idea of newness. Metaculture foregrounds individual bodies, individual brains as the locus of agency and creativity and artifice. "We" can only be a collection of individuals, each responsible for, and in some sense controlling, the production of a given "we."

Kinsley's view derives from a specific metacultural orientation to culture: Play up the extent to which individuals are artificers, play down their role as inheritors of a vast flow of culture that has come to them through time and space and with which they can tinker, at best, only minimally. In this sense, Kinsley is no different from the numerous film reviewers discussed here.

10 Are there implications here for the work on speech act theory originating with John L. Austin's 1962 book, *How To Do Things with Words,* and continuing through the work of Searle (1969, 1983) and others (see the discussions of intention in Lee [1997])? In what measure does philosophical discussion focus on intention not simply because it is out there, in some universal sense, in all speech, but rather because attention is drawn to it by a metacultural orientation to newness?

11 This is not to say, however, that there is not also secondary replication, in which individual readers of a book or watchers of a film replicate aspects of it—lines or plots or mannerisms, and so forth.

12 Writing as an anthropologist—not as a linguist—it strikes me that post-1950s formal linguistics grew up around an idea of newness and the attempt to account for newness. Among Chomsky's (1957) most persuasive arguments were those dealing with new utterances or sentences, ones that, while no one had ever uttered or written them before, were nevertheless interpretable. You can take a sentence and add to it a dependent clause, then take that new sentence and add to it another dependent clause, and so forth. You will eventually get to a sentence with more dependent clauses than you have ever seen. The sentence is, in this regard, new. Despite its newness, however, you will know what to do with it when you see it. Therefore, according to Chomsky, you must have some kind of mental rule that allows you to make the bridge to the new.

If I am correct, however, grammaticality is linked to circulation, which is a social phenomenon. What it means for a sentence to be grammatical is not that this or that isolated individual will judge it so. It means, rather, that the circulation of the sentence within a community—its replication or uptake—will not be hindered by its grammatical form. However, as every student of conversation in the contemporary United States knows, transcripts of naturally occurring speech are loaded with unintelligible, "ill-formed" discourse. Such sentences usually do not achieve wide circulation. Though they are produced by speakers, they are not formed in such a way as to be acceptable to a broader community.

What is interesting about myths, as parts of traditional culture and as bearers of "grammatical" discourse, is that, because they are already widely distributed, they often define what counts as grammatically acceptable. Myths are replicated again and again in part because they are known to be acceptable, and they are known to be acceptable because they have already circulated. In these cases, the standard of acceptability is prior circulation, and, hence, prior replication. What is important here is not a "judgment" of grammaticality made by a native speaker, but a judgment made, so to speak, by a community—a judgment inscribed in the facts of prior replication.

Here we come back to the modern case. Novels and films are also governed by circulation and acceptability. A novel or film is designed to reach a relatively wide audience. In this regard, novels and films are similar to myths. But there is a crucial difference. Circulation of novels and films is not dependent, at least not in so obvious a way, on prior replication. A novel or film is designed to be "novel," that is, new. Hence, unlike a myth, which achieves broader circulation over time via replication, a novel or film is disseminated through a population, and then either taken up or not. To be sure, many novels and films are failures; only some of them surface to achieve wide distribution. And the intelligibility of the discourse within them contributes to that circulation.

What this means is that a premium is placed on the ability to foresee—as if peering into a crystal ball—what discourse will be acceptable to a population. One aspect of this acceptability, is, of course, grammaticality. Hence, a premium is placed on the discernment of rules of language, such that given new instances of discourse can be foreseen, by means of those rules, to be grammatical. Along with this goes the development of soothsaying institutions, embodied in editors, dictionary makers, marketing specialists, and the like.

So there is a closer relationship between grammaticality and replication than might at first seem to be the case. Both are linked to the acceptability of discourse within a broader population. Replication achieves acceptability on the basis of the past. It means doing whatever has been done before. If the old thing that is being replicated was successful, then presumably the newer one will be, too. In contrast, formal grammar ascertains acceptability in advance, foreseeing that a new instance of discourse—which does not look exactly like one that has come before it—will nevertheless be able to circulate within a broader population.

Even one's understanding of what language is, therefore, may be linked to the dominant metaculture to which one subscribes. Where tradition is emphasized, the test of acceptability is oldness. Language can be construed in terms of replication of extant structures. Where emphasis is on modernity or newness, however, the test of acceptability has to be something else. How can one foresee what new discourse will circulate within a broader population? How can one know what will catch on except by seeing what discourse in fact circulates? The answer is that one has to internalize and employ a set of rules for the production of discourse. One has to cultivate a special branch of metaculture for this purpose. Grammaticality rules provide one means of foreseeing circulation or distribution in the absence of a test of time. They are, therefore, an essential ingredient of the modern motion of discourse through the world—through space and time.

6 INABILITY TO FORESEE

1 One possible criticism of the present book—one that, as should now be apparent, lacks cogency—is that it repeats the mistakes of the older distinction between "hot" and "cold" societies (see Lévi-Strauss 1966), a distinction that has been rightly criticized by Jonathan Hill (1988, 3–5) and Terence Turner (1988, 235–39), among others. In the first place, the metadiscourses of tradition and newness are, as I have repeatedly maintained, found side by side in all societies at all times, even though one comes to dominate over the other at different historical periods, and even if the last five centuries in Europe have witnessed an unprecedented surge in the metaculture of newness. The terms do not refer to distinct types of societies—one unchanging (the cold society) and the other incessantly changing (the hot society). Second, while the metacultures have efficacy—they do affect the motion of culture—my distinction refers first and foremost to the plane of metaculture, not to the plane of culture. The terms focus attention on how the motion of culture is represented or talked about or construed by those who are its bearers.

2 These could be a result of differences between the original script (to which reviewers sometimes have access) and the actual film version.

3 However, quotations are already forms of response, if only incipient ones, rather than pure replications. This is because they involve the interaction between voices, as Voloshinov ([1929] 1973, 115–23) pointed out, with the quote-framing voice in some measure—varying along a continuum from authoritative to relativistic, in Voloshinov's ([1929] 1973, 123) scheme—talking back to the quoted voice. For this reason, in the continuum between use and mention, use falls on the side of replication, while mention is closer to response; although authoritative mention is more replication-like, critical and relativistic mention is more response-like.

4 While unintended consequences abound in *Dr. Strangelove*, this is not, in my opinion, the film's principle message, if such there is. The unintended consequences theme is perhaps too prevalent—in films and related art forms—to capture the specific line of cultural learning in which *Dr. Strangelove* fits. A more specific characterization of *Dr. Strangelove* might be this: that it points to the almost purposive, lemming-like activity of humans as they pave the way to their own doom. To accidentally kill themselves as a species is one thing, to set out purposefully to make it possible for them to kill themselves is another. The death wish theme is older, too, but the collective, species-wide character of this death wish gives the older theme a novel twist.

5 See also the papers in Calhoun (1992).

6 Such a consensual, already circulated metaculture, however, may be prospective in gauging the influence that a current object will have on the production of future objects. Hence, it may be prospective in regard to replication, but it cannot be prospective as regards dissemination.

7 Such a system is what lends credence to Foucault's (1980) view that knowledge and power are intimately intertwined, although power here translates as influence over the circulation of discourse within a metacultural community. Scientific communities are simultaneously cultural and metacultural communities—they produce statements for broader circulation at the same time as they evaluate those statements for their circulability. The productive and evaluative moments are aligned. In this regard, they are different from the film industry. Filmmakers produce new objects, but those objects are evaluated by film reviewers, who form their own quasi-independent metacultural community.

8 I am, of course, not referring to the actual Scott Hill. I know nothing more about the real Mr. Hill than I have read in the Reuters article. My discussion here is of an imaginary Scott Hill who supports creationism over evolution for traditional reasons—that is, because the Bible tells him so.

9 In this regard, Michael Warner's *The Letters of the Republic: Publication and the Public Sphere in Eighteenth-Century America* (1990) is particularly intriguing, since he views both the "individual" (an ideological formulation read off of the new "I" of discourse) and the "people" (an ideological formulation read off of the new "we") as "local outcomes rather than origins" of a "broad change in social and cultural systems" (ix).

10 The point has been eloquently made by Charles Taylor (1990; and Taylor et al. 1992) and others that citizenship implies a stake in the nation, and hence responsibility for control over it. Related to this thesis is not only Gramsci's conception of hegemony, but also the literature on voluntary associations. Indeed, the nation—in the form it logically takes under a metaculture of newness—is nothing more than a voluntary association writ large.

You can perhaps see the links here also to the distinction between achieved and ascribed social status proffered by Ralph Linton (1936). Translated into present terminology, achieved status is a position you acquire by virtue of contributions to the motion of culture, especially in the contemporary United States, through its dissemination. Achievement, like voluntary alignment, is dependent on a metaculture of newness. Ascribed status, by contrast, is dependent upon the idea of tradition. The idea here is that you are somebody because of the culture that happens to be flowing into you—for example, as the child of certain parents—rather than out of you. Ascription is incompatible with the full functioning of the modern nation because the latter depends on an agentive conception of individuals as producers of culture rather than on a passive conception of them as recipients. Hence, the gradual demise of kingships and aristocracies with the spread of nationalism.

11 Here again I am careful to distinguish print from writing. The former is defined, in part, by mass dissemination. It is therefore defined in part by the motion of culture in situations where dissemination has become relatively uncoupled from replication. Writing per se, as I have argued, can be (and has been) put to the service of dissemination through replication.

12 This leads to an observation about the old "type/token" distinction. Within a theory of cultural motion, each "token"—each specific utterance of the underlying word "the," for example—is produced by an individual as part of a process of replication. Hence, each token furnishes evidence of the movement of underlying, abstract culture—that is, of the "type"—through people.

This is not true in the case of mechanical copies—as Walter Benjamin recognized, in his essay on "The Work of Art in the Age of Mechanical Reproduction" (1969). Mechanical copies, viewed in relation to one another, provide no evidence of the movement of culture. Each is, rather, interchangeable with the other. Mechanical copying is a way of amplifying the original cultural object. It is as if the voice of the myth-teller were connected to a loud speaker so that it could be heard by many more people. Mechanical copies are amplifications of cultural objects, which permit their greater dissemination without further replication. The token, in contrast, as a copy produced by an individual, reflects individual learning—the movement of culture through the world. Each token, in this sense, has its "aura." Benjamin saw mechanical reproduction as resulting in the loss of "aura." This is another way of getting at the distinction between replication and dissemination. Mechanical reproduction allows dissemination that does not depend entirely upon replication. Hence, a mechanical copy lacks the aura of an individually produced token.

13 Steve Feld (Feld and Keil 1994) has remarked that, for "world beat musics," the simultaneous processes of homogenization and heterogenization that are attendant upon what he calls "schizophonia"—that is, the severing of sound (for example, a CD recording) from its source (the musicians and instruments that produced it). As the schizophonic sound is appropriated into local processes of reproduction, it itself becomes transformed, and hence produces new material for dissemination.

14 In the case of myth, it is possible to develop a mechanics of spatial and temporal displacement reminiscent of Newtonian mechanics. The principle of cultural inertia— an only somewhat wry replica of the Newtonian original—holds that an element in motion through time (or space) ought to continue in motion, unless acted upon by some other force. In fact, the theory of "cultural drift" posits such an external force—dissipation and reshaping of the object as it is replicated in new objects.

In some cases, as proposed in chapter 2, it is actually possible to measure the dissipation or reshaping. I was able to record a number of tellings, over several years, of the origin myth in one Brazilian Indian community. The two different narrators—Nil of the *macuco* and Wãñëkï Patè—had learned the story as boys some sixty years earlier, and, while they had subsequent contact with one another, they were rivals at the time of my field work for the position of knowledgeable elder. As such, they never listened to one another, and actually disparaged the knowledge the other had, claiming that the other's rendition of the myth was muddled, even without merit. For this reason, I was astonished to discover that the segments I studied were nearly identical—word-for-word identical. They shared between 84 percent and 93 percent of their words. The differences were often accidental, resulting from slips of the tongue, corrected by the speakers themselves in the course of narration. I counted the slips and corrections in the totals. Excluding them, between 90 percent and 95 percent of the words were shared between the two versions. So, despite a few significant differences in word choice, replication over time was nearly perfect.

Nearly, but not wholly, perfect. Micromodifications result, even in this case, in a reshaping of the cultural element. Assuming that the two learned the same myth as youths—and I think that is probable, given their social proximity in early youth, though their lives later diverged from one another—and assuming that the differences between their versions reflect average rates of divergence over a sixty-year period—that is, 90–95 percent similarity—the myth would transform according to the trajectory mapped out in Figure N1. At the 90 percent rate, by the time 660 years had elapsed, the similarity between the stories, at least as reflected in word choice, would have plummeted to about 31 percent. That is, a story told now and a descendant of it told 660 years from now would show no more similarity as regards word choice than two unrelated stories, similar only by virtue of the language in which they were told. At the 95 percent rate, it would take 1,380 years to reach this level. If the rate could be pushed up to 97 percent, it would take 2,280 years; if up to 98 percent, 3,480 years, and so forth.

I should note, parenthetically, that empirical study of this macrotemporal problem is actually possible through comparison. A somewhat similar origin myth is found among the Kaingang peoples, who speak a closely related but distinct language, the two languages having separated, according to glottochronological estimates, between one thousand and two thousand years ago. Hence in theory, the myths themselves could be compared for their word-for-word similarity. Unfortunately, I have not yet been able to assemble the materials that would allow such a comparison, and hence I have not been able to calibrate these microtemporal processes.

In any case, to transmit the story with less modification requires the input of

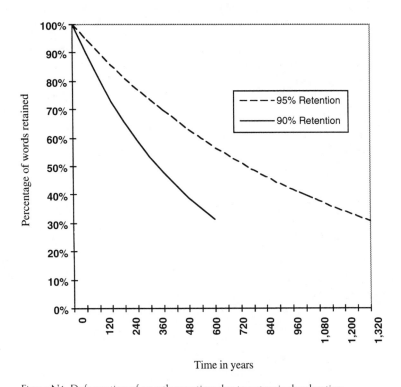

Figure N1. Deformation of a myth over time due to entropic deceleration.

accelerative force—stemming, of course, from a metaculture of tradition and taking the specific form of an even greater emphasis on memorization and regurgitation. Greater emphasis on transmission, in turn, means more time spent on the myth; time spent on the myth detracts from time that could be spent in acquiring and transmitting other traditional culture elements. Hence, in accord with a conservation principle, preserving one element means losing others, all elements being similarly subject to dissipation or reshaping over time.

It would be easy to add another axis to the diagram in Figure N1: mapping change in relation to physical displacement through space. Figuring in the physical movements of the individual bearers of the element, and the other peregrinations of the cultural objects themselves, a Newtonian mechanics of traditional cultural motion could be developed.

A graph analogous to that in Figure N1 could also be made for calculated stylistic changes—for example, in automobile design. The two graphs represent the operation of a constant force on culture in motion. But the forces in these two cases, as I argue below, are distinct. The myth is affected by "cultural drift," changing despite the best efforts of people to preserve it. The automobile is modified on purpose, despite the ease with which it could be preserved in its present form.

CONCLUSION

1 There is a difference between the Egyptian and Greek sphinxes. The Egyptian stone figures, dating from about 2500 B.C., are based on a mythological creature with the body of a lion and the head of a man (typically, a Pharaoh's head). In the story of Oedipus, the sphinx was a winged monster with the body of a lion but the head of a woman. Inhabiting the vicinity of Thebes, the sphinx posed riddles to people there and killed those who could not find the solutions. She offered to destroy herself, should anyone correctly solve the riddle:

> What goes on four feet, on two feet, and three,
> But the more feet it goes on the weaker it be?

Oedipus provided the answer: "Man."

References

Acker, Paul. 1998. *Revising oral theory: Formulaic composition in Old English and Old Icelandic verse.* New York: Garland.

Agha, Asif. Forthcoming *Honorific language.*

Amodio, Mark C., ed. 1994. *Oral poetics in Middle English poetry.* New York: Garland.

Anderson, Benedict. [1983] 1991. *Imagined communities: Reflections on the origin and spread of nationalism.* London: Verso.

Appadurai, Arjun. 1996. *Modernity at large: Cultural dimensions of globalization.* Minneapolis: University of Minnesota Press.

Appadurai, Arjun, ed. 1986. *The social life of things.* Cambridge: Cambridge University Press.

Austin, John L. 1962. *How to do things with words.* Cambridge: Harvard University Press.

Bakhtin, Mikhail. 1981. *The dialogic imagination.* Trans. C. Emerson and M. Holquist. Austin: University of Texas Press.

———. 1984. *Problems of Dostoevsky's poetics.* Trans. C. Emerson. Minneapolis: University of Minnesota Press.

Bellah, Robert N., ed. 1996. *Habits of the heart: Individualism and commitment in American life.* Berkeley: University of California Press.

Benjamin, Walter. 1969. The work of art in the age of mechanical reproduction. In *Illuminations*, ed. H. Arendt, trans. H. Zohn. 217–51. New York: Schocken Books.

Berlant, Lauren. 1997. *The queen of America goes to Washington City: Essays on sex and citizenship.* Durham, N.C.: Duke University Press.

Berlant, Lauren, and Michael Warner. 1998. Sex in public. *Critical Inquiry* 24(2): 547–66.

Blackmore, Susan J. 1999. *The meme machine.* Oxford: Oxford University Press.

Borges, Jorge Luis. [1944] 1962. Pierre Menard, author of the *Quixote.* In *Labryrinths: Selected stories and other writings*, ed. D. A. Yates and J. E. Irby. 36–44. New York: New Directions.

Bourdieu, Pierre. [1975] 1984. *Distinction: A social critique of the judgement of taste.* Trans. R. Nice. Cambridge: Harvard University Press.

Bourgois, Philippe. 1996. *In search of respect: Selling crack in el barrio.* Cambridge: Cambridge University Press.

Brodie, Richard. 1996. *Virus of the mind: The new science of the meme.* Seattle, Wash.: Integral Press.

Bryant, Peter (aka Peter Bryan George). 1958. *Red alert.* New York: Ace Books.

Burdick, Eugene, and Harvey Wheeler. 1962. *Fail-safe.* New York: Dell.

Butler, Octavia E. 1976. *Patternmaster.* New York: Warner Books.

Calhoun, Craig. 1997. *Nationalism.* Minneapolis: University of Minnesota Press.

Calhoun, Craig, ed. 1992. *Habermas and the public sphere.* Cambridge, Mass.: MIT Press.

Chagnon, Napoleon A. [1968] 1992. *Yanomamö.* New York: Harcourt Brace.

Chatterjee, Partha. 1993. *The nation and its fragments: Colonial and postcolonial histories.* Princeton, N.J.: Princeton University Press.

Chomsky, Noam. 1957. *Syntactic structures.* The Hague: Mouton.

Clancy, Tom. 1987. *Patriot games.* New York: Putnam.

Coleman, James S. 1968. Modernization: Political aspects. In *International Encyclopedia of the Social Sciences.* Vol. 10. 395–402. New York: Macmillan.

Comaroff, John, and Jean Comaroff. 1991. *Of revelation and revolution: Christianity, colonialism, and consciousness in South Africa.* Chicago: University of Chicago Press.

————. 1992. *Ethnography and the historical imagination.* Boulder: Westview Press.

Conklin, Beth A., and Laura R. Graham. 1995. The shifting middle ground: Amazonian Indians and eco-politics. *American Anthropologist* 97(4): 695–710.

Cott, Nancy F. 1987. *The grounding of modern feminism.* New Haven, Conn.: Yale University Press.

Crapanzano, Vincent. 2000. *Serving the word: Literalism in America from the pulpit to the bench.* New York: New Press.

Crist, Judith. 1964a. *Dr. Strangelove:* Comic, bitter, one of best. *New York Herald Tribune,* 30 January, 8.

————. 1964b. Fail-safe—Relatively absorbing melodrama. *New York Herald Tribune,* 8 October, 17.

Crowther, Bosley. 1964a. "Dr. Strangelove": A shattering sick joke. *New York Times,* 30 January, 24.

————. 1964b. Film festival: Fonda in Sidney Lumet's *Fail Safe. New York Times,* 16 September, 36.

Davis, Daniel S. 1964. Fail Safe. *Films in Review* 15(8): 506–7.

Dawkins, Richard. 1989. *The selfish gene.* Oxford: Oxford University Press.

Deloria, Vine. 1974. *Behind the trail of broken treaties: An Indian declaration of independence.* New York: Delacorte.

Derrida, Jacques. 1986. Declarations of independence. Trans. T. Keenan and T. Pepper. *New Political Science* 15: 7–15.

Dick, Hilary Parsons. 1999. Competing over immigrant families: The workshop of social reproduction in cosmopolitan anthropology. Master's thesis, Department of Anthropology, University of Pennsylvania.

Direct hit. 1964. *Newsweek,* 3 February, 79–80.

Dore, Ronald. 1968. Modernization: The bourgeoisie in modernizing societies. In *International Encyclopedia of the Social Sciences.* Vol. 10. 402–9. New York: Macmillan.

Dr. Strangelove, or, how I learned to stop worrying and love the bomb. 1964. *Variety,* 22 January, 6.

Driver, Harold Edson, and Wilhelmine Driver. 1963. *Ethnography and acculturation of the Chichimeca-Jonaz of northeast Mexico*. Bloomington, Ind.: Indiana University Press.

Durkheim, Emile. [1893] 1933. *The division of labor*. Trans. George Simpson. New York: Macmillan.

———. [1912] 1969. *The elementary forms of the religious life*. Trans. J. W. Swain. New York: The Free Press.

———. [1925] 1961. *Moral education*. Trans. E. K. Wilson and H. Schnurer. New York: The Free Press.

Eggan, Fred. 1941. Some aspects of culture change in the northern Philippines. *American Anthropologist* 43: 11–18.

———. 1963. Culture drift and social change. *Current Anthropology* 4: 347–55.

Eley, Geoff, and Ronald Grigor Suny, eds. 1996. *Becoming national: A reader*. Oxford: Oxford University Press.

Ervin-Tripp, Susan. 1972. On sociolinguistic rules: Alternation and co-occurrence. In *Directions in sociolinguistics: The ethnography of communication*, ed. J. J. Gumperz and D. Hymes. 213–50. New York: Henry Holt.

———. 1976. "Is Sybil there?" The structure of American English directives. *Language in Society* 5: 25–66.

Fail Safe. 1964. *Variety*, 16 September, 6.

Farriss, Nancy M. 1984. *Maya society under colonial rule: The collective enterprise of survival*. Princeton, N.J.: Princeton University Press.

Faudree, Paja. 1999. Barbaric, noble, civilized, free: The Waorani and the trope of the savage; or, Discourse and its discontents. Unpublished M.A. report, Department of Anthropology, University of Pennsylvania.

The Feast. 1970. Produced and directed by Timothy Asch and Napoleon Chagnon. 29 min. WPSX Media Sales (Pennsylvania State University). Videocassette.

Febvre, Lucien, and Henri-Jean Martin. [1958] 1976. *The coming of the book: The impact of printing, 1450–1800*. London: New Left Books.

Feld, Steven, and Charles Keil. 1994. *Music grooves*. Chicago: University of Chicago Press.

Foley, John Miles. 1991. *Immanent art: From structure to meaning in traditional oral epic*. Bloomington, Ind.: Indiana University Press.

———. 1995. *The singer of tales in performance*. Bloomington, Ind.: Indiana University Press.

Fortes, Meyer. 1969. Filiation reconsidered. In *Kinship and the Social Order*. 250–75. Chicago: Aldine.

Foster, George McClelland. 1960. *Culture and conquest: America's Spanish heritage*. New York: Wenner-Gren Foundation for Anthropological Research.

Foucault, Michel. 1980. *Power/knowledge*. New York: Pantheon Books.

Fox, Aaron. 1992. The jukebox of history: Narratives of loss and desire in the discourse of country music. *Popular Music* 11(1): 53–72.

———. 1995. Out the country: Language, music, feeling, and sociability in American working-class culture. Ph.D. dissertation, Department of Anthropology, University of Texas at Austin.

Gal, Susan. 1979. *Language shift: Social determinants of linguistic change in bilingual Austria*. New York: Academic Press.

Geertz, Clifford. 1973. *The interpretation of cultures*. New York: Basic Books.

Gellner, Ernest. 1983. *Nations and nationalism*. Ithaca, N.Y.: Cornell University Press.

Gellrich, Jesse M. 1995. *Discourse and dominion in the fourteenth century: Oral contexts of writing in philosophy, politics, and poetry.* Princeton, N.J.: Princeton University Press.

George, Peter. 1964. *Dr. Strangelove.* New York: Bantam Books.

Gilbert, W. S. 1871. *Pygmalion and Galatea: An entirely original mythological comedy in three acts.* London: S. French.

Gladwell, Malcom. 2000. *The tipping point: How little things can make a big difference.* Boston: Little, Brown.

Goffman, Erving. 1981. *Forms of talk.* Philadelphia: University of Pennsylvania Press.

Goody, Jack. 1986. *The logic of writing and the organization of society.* Cambridge: Cambridge University Press.

———. 1987. *The Interface between the written and the oral.* Cambridge: Cambridge University Press.

Graebner, Fritz. 1911. *Methode der ethnologie.* Heidelberg: C. Winter.

Graham, Laura R. 1995. *Performing dreams: The discourse of immortality among the Xavante of central Brazil.* Austin: University of Texas Press.

Gramsci, Antonio. 1981. Class, culture and hegemony. In *Culture, ideology and social process: A reader,* eds. T. Bennett et al. 191–218. London: Open University Press.

———. 1985. *Selections from cultural writings.* Ed. D. Forgacs and G. Nowell-Smith, trans. W. Boelhower. Cambridge, Mass.: Harvard University Press.

Greenblatt, Stephen. 1991. *Marvelous possessions: The wonder of the new world.* Chicago: University of Chicago Press.

Grimshaw, Allen D. 1994. *What's going on here? Complementary studies of professional talk.* Norwood, N.J.: Ablex.

Gumperz, John J. 1982. *Discourse strategies.* Cambridge: Cambridge University Press.

Habermas, Jürgen. [1962] 1989. *The structural transformation of the public sphere: An inquiry into a category of bourgeois society.* Trans. T. Burger. Cambridge, Mass.: MIT Press.

———. 1984. *The theory of communicative action.* Vol. 1, *Reason and the rationalization of society.* Trans. T. McCarthy. Boston: Beacon Press.

———. [1985] 1987. *The philosophical discourse of modernity: Twelve lectures.* Trans. F. Lawrence. Oxford: Basil Blackwell.

———. 1987. *The theory of communicative action.* Vol. 2, *Lifeworld and system: A critique of functionalist reasoning.* Trans. T. McCarthy. Boston: Beacon Press.

Hannerz, Ulf. 1987. The world in creolization. *Africa* 57(4): 546–59.

———. 1992. *Cultural complexity: Studies in the social organization of meaning.* New York: Columbia University Press.

———. 1996. *Transnational connections: Culture, people, places.* New York: Routledge.

Hart, Henry. 1964. Dr. Strangelove. *Films in Review* 15(2): 113–14.

Hartung, Philip T. 1964a. Dr. Strangelove, I presume? *Commonweal,* 9 October, 72–73.

———. 1964b. What five-sided building? *Commonweal,* 21 February, 632–33.

Harvey, David. 1989. *The condition of postmodernity.* Oxford: Blackwell.

Herodotus. 1942. *The Persian wars.* Trans. George Rawlinson. New York: Random House.

Herskovits, Melville J. 1938. *Acculturation: The study of culture contact.* New York: J. J. Augustin.

———. 1949. *Man and his works: The science of cultural anthropology.* New York: Knopf.

———. 1955. *Cultural anthropology.* New York: Knopf.

Hill, Jonathan. 1988. Myth and history. In *Rethinking history and myth*, ed. J. D. Hill. 1–17. Urbana: University of Illinois Press.

Hollinger, David. 1993. How wide the circle of the "we"? American intellectuals and the problem of the ethnos since World War II. *American Historical Review* 98(2): 317–37.

Houston, Penelope. 1964. Fail Safe. Sight and sound: The international film quarterly 34(2): 97.

Hymes, Dell. 1981. *"In vain I tried to tell you": Essays in Native American ethnopoetics.* Philadelphia: University of Pennsylvania Press.

———. 1985. Language, memory, and selective performance: Cultee's "salmon's myth" as twice told to Boas. *Journal of American Folklore* 98(390): 391–434.

Jakobson, Roman. 1960a. Linguistics and poetics. In *Style in language*, ed. T. Sebeok. 350–77. Cambridge, Mass.: MIT Press.

———. [1960b] 1971. Why "Mama" and "Papa"? In *Selected writings. Phonological Studies.* 2d ed., Vol. 1, 538–45. The Hague: Mouton.

Jakobson, Roman, and Linda R. Waugh. 1987. *The sound shape of language.* Berlin: Mouton de Gruyter.

Jameson, Fredric. 1998. *The cultural turn: Selected writings on the postmodern, 1983–1998.* London: Verso.

Jehlen, Myra, and Michael Warner, eds. 1997. *The English literatures of America, 1500–1800.* New York. Routledge.

Kansas rejects evolution in science classes. 1999. August 11 Internet release by Reuters News Agency.

Kapchan, Deborah. 1996. *Gender on the market: Moroccan women and the revoicing of tradition.* Philadelphia: University of Pennsylvania Press.

Kauffmann, Stanley. 1964a. Dean Swift in the twentieth century. *New Republic*, 1 February, 26–28.

———. 1964b. Less funny but less serious. *New Republic*, 12 September, 26–27.

Keane, Webb. 1997. *Signs of recognition: Powers and hazards of representation in an Indonesian society.* Berkeley: University of California Press.

Keen, Eleanor. 1964a. Dr. Strangelove. *Chicago Sun-Times*, 20 February, 58.

———. 1964b. Fail Safe. *Chicago Sun-Times*, 9 November, 55.

Kinsley, Michael. 1982. Nuclear holocaust in perspective. *Harper's*, 8–12 May.

Kirch, Patrick V., and Marshall D. Sahlins. 1995. *Anahulu: The anthropology of history in the kingdom of Hawaii*, Vol. 1. Chicago: University of Chicago Press.

Kohn, Hans. 1944. *The idea of nationalism: A study of its origins and background.* New York: Macmillan.

Laclau, Ernesto, and Chantal Mouffe. 1985. *Hegemony and socialist strategy: Towards a radical democratic politics.* London: Verso.

Lamberg-Karlovsky, C. C., and J. Sabloff. 1974. *The rise and fall of civilizations: Modern archaeological approaches to ancient cultures.* Menlo Park, Calif.: Cummings.

———. 1975. *Ancient civilization and trade.* Santa Fe: University of New Mexico Press.

Lee, Benjamin. 1997. *Talking heads: Languages, metalanguage, and the semiotics of subjectivity.* Durham, N.C.: Duke University Press.

Lepselter, Susan. 1994. UFO stories: The poetics of uncanny encounters in a counter public discourse. Master's thesis, Department of Anthropology, University of Texas at Austin.

————. 1997. From the earth native's point of view: Earth, the extraterrestrial, and the natural ground of home. *Public Culture* 9(2): 197–208.

Lerner, Daniel. 1968. Modernization: Social aspects. In *International Encyclopedia of the Social Sciences*. Vol. 10. 386–95. New York: Macmillan.

Lévi-Strauss, Claude. [1949] 1969. *The elementary structures of kinship*. Trans. J. H. Bell and J. R. von Sturmer. Boston: Beacon Press.

————. 1966. *The savage mind*. Chicago: University of Chicago Press.

Linton, Ralph. 1936. *The study of man: An introduction*. New York: D. Appleton-Century.

Lord, Albert Bates. 1960. *The singer of tales*. Cambridge: Harvard University Press.

————. 1991. *Epic singers and oral tradition*. Ithaca, N.Y.: Cornell University Press.

Lucy, John A., ed. 1993. *Reflexive language*. Cambridge: Cambridge University Press.

Lutz, Amanda. 1971. Elizabeth Cady Stanton. In *Notable American women 1607–1950: A biographical dictionary*. Vol. 3. Ed. E. T. James, J. W. James, and P. S. Boyer. 342–47. Cambridge: Belknap Press of Harvard University Press.

Lynd, Robert Staughton, and Helen Merrell Lynd. 1929. *Middletown: A study in contemporary American culture*. New York: Harcourt, Brace.

————. 1937. *Middletown in transition: A study in cultural conflicts*. New York: Harcourt, Brace.

Lyotard, Jean-François. 1984. *The postmodern condition: A report on knowledge*. Theory and History of Literature Series, vol. 10. Minneapolis: University of Minnesota Press.

Mackay, E. Anne, ed. 1999. *Signs of orality: The oral tradition and its influence in the Greek and Roman world*. Boston: Brill.

Maier, Pauline. 1997. *American scripture: Making the declaration of independence*. New York: Alfred A. Knopf.

Malinowski, Bronislaw. [1922] 1961. *Argonauts of the western Pacific: An account of native enterprise and adventure in the archipelagoes of Melanesian New Guinea*. New York: E. P. Dutton and Co.

Malory, Sir Thomas. [1470] 1982. *Le morte d'Arthur*. Ed. R. M. Lumiansky. New York: Macmillan.

Maranhão, Tullio, ed. 1990. *The interpretation of dialogue*. Chicago: University of Chicago Press.

Marcus, George E. 1995. Ethnography in/of the world system: The emergence of multi-sited ethnography. *Annual Review of Anthropology* 24: 95–117.

Markus, George. 1987. Why is there no hermeneutics of natural sciences? *Science in Context* 1(1): 5–51.

Marston, John. [1598] 1926. *Metamorphosis of Pigmalion's image*. Waltham-St. Lawrence, Berkshire, England: Golden Cockerel Press.

Marx, Karl. [1867] 1970. *Capital*. Vol. 1. London: Lawrence and Wishart.

Mauss, Marcel. 1967. *The gift: Forms and functions of exchange in archaic societies*. Trans. I. Cunison. New York: W. W. Norton.

————. 1979. Body techniques. In *Sociology and Psychology*. Trans. B. Brewster. 97–123. Boston: Routledge and Kegan Paul.

Mehan, Hugh. 1997. The discourse of the illegal immigration debate: A case study in the politics of representation. *Discourse and Society* 8(2): 249–70.

Meintjes, Louise. 1996. *Mediating difference: Producing Mbaqanga in a South Africa studio*. Ph.D. dissertation, Department of Anthropology, University of Texas at Austin.

Milne, Tom. 1964. *Dr. Strangelove. Sight and Sound: The International Film Quarterly.* 33(1): 37–38.

Milroy, L. 1980. *Language and social networks.* London: Basil Blackwell.

Moffatt, Michael. 1992. Ethnographic writing about American culture. *Annual Review of Anthropology* 21: 205–29.

Mooney, James. 1900. Myths of the Cherokee. In *Nineteenth Annual Report of the Bureau of American Ethnology.* Part 1. 1–576. Washington, D.C.: Government Printing Office.

Mosse, George L. 1985. *Nationalism and sexuality: Respectability and abnormality in modern Europe.* New York: Howard Fertig.

Mouffe, Chantal. 1979. Hegemony and ideology in Gramsci. In *Gramsci and Marxist theory,* ed. C. Mouffe. 168–204. New York: Routledge and Kegan Paul.

Nanda, Serena. 1994. *Cultural anthropology.* Belmont, Calif.: Wadsworth.

Obeyesekere, Gananath. 1994. *The apotheosis of Captain Cook.* Princeton, N.J.: Princeton University Press.

Oliveira, Roberto Cardoso de. 1960. *O processo de assimilação dos Terêna.* Rio de Janeiro: Museu Nacional.

———. 1964. *O indio e o mundo dos brancos: A situação dos Tukúna do alto Solimões.* São Paulo: Difusão Européia do Livro.

Ong, Walter J. 1982. *Orality and literacy: The technologizing of the word.* London: Methuen.

Oulahan, Richard. 1964. Doomsday is better as a farce. *Life* 57(30 Oct. 1964): 12.

Parry, Milman. 1954. *Serbo-Croatian heroic songs.* Ed. A. B. Lord. Cambridge: Harvard University Press.

———. 1971. *The making of Homeric verse: The collected papers of Milman Parry.* Ed. Adam Parry. Oxford: Clarendon Press.

Parsons, Talcott. 1968. *The structure of social action: A study in social theory and special reference to a group of recent European writers.* New York: The Free Press.

Perry, William James. 1924. *The growth of civilization.* London: Methuen.

Porcello, Thomas Gregory. 1996. *Sonic artistry: Music, discourse, and technology in the sound recording studio.* Ph.D. dissertation, Department of Anthropology, University of Texas at Austin.

Powers, Richard Gid. 1979. Introduction to *Dr. Strangelove,* by Peter George. v–xxiii. Boston: Gregg Press.

Radcliffe-Brown, A. R. [1952] 1965. *Structure and function in primitive society.* New York: The Free Press.

Ramaswamy, Sumathi. 1997. *Passions of the tongue: Language devotion in Tamil India, 1891–1970.* Berkeley: University of California Press.

Republic of Texas Web Site. 1996. Official call. URL: web.texramp.net/~rtxgov/. Consulted on 6 October 1998.

Rumsey, Alan. 2000. Agency, personhood, and the "I" of discourse in the Pacific and beyond. *Journal of the Royal Anthropological Institute* 6: 101–15.

Sahlins, Marshall D. 1976. *Culture and practical reason.* Chicago: University of Chicago Press.

———. 1981. *Historical metaphors and mythical realities: Structure in the early history of the Sandwich Islands kingdom.* Ann Arbor: University of Michigan Press.

———. 1985. *Islands of history.* Chicago: University of Chicago Press.

———. 1995. *How "natives" think: About Captain Cook, for example.* Chicago: University of Chicago Press.

Salisbury, Richard F. 1968. Trade and markets. In *International Encyclopedia of the Social Sciences*. Vol. 16. 395–402. New York: Macmillan.

Sapir, Edward. 1921. *Language: An introduction to the study of speech*. New York: Harcourt, Brace.

———. [1933] 1968. The psychological reality of phonemes. In *Selected writings in language, culture, and personality*. Ed. D. G. Mandelbaum. 46–61. Berkeley: University of California Press.

Sarris, Andrew. 1964a. Come, now, Dr. Strangelove. *Village Voice*, 13 February, 13–14.

———. 1964b. The Festival: II. *Village Voice*, 24 September, 16–17.

Schaden, Egon. 1965. *Aculturação indígena: Ensaio sôbre fatôres e tendencias da mudança cultural de tribos indias em contacto com o mundo dos brancos*. São Paulo: Associação Brasileira de Antropologia.

Schell, Jonathan. 1976. *The time of illusion*. New York: Vintage Books.

———. 1982. *The fate of the earth*. New York: Avon Books.

———. 1997. *Writing in time: A political chronicle*. Wakefield, R.I.: Moyer Bell.

Schieffelin, Edward L., and Robert Crittenden. 1991. *Like people you see in a dream: First contact in six Papuan societies*. Stanford, Calif.: Stanford University Press.

Schmidt, Wilhelm. 1912–55. *Der Ursprung der Gottesidee: Eine historisch-kritische und positive Studie*. 12 vols. Münster: Aschendorff.

Schneider, David M. 1980. *American kinship: A cultural account*. Chicago: University of Chicago Press.

Searle, John R. 1969. *Speech acts*. Cambridge: Cambridge University Press.

———. 1983. *Intentionality: An essay in the philosophy of mind*. Cambridge: Cambridge University Press.

Segal, Dan. n.d. Educated pasts: "Western civ" in American higher education in the twentieth century. Typescript.

Shaw, George Bernard. [1916] 1970. *Pygmalion: A romance in five acts*. Baltimore: Penguin Books.

Sherzer, Joel. 1983. *Kuna ways of speaking: An ethnographic perspective*. Austin: University of Texas Press.

———. 1990. *Verbal art in San Blas: Kuna culture through its discourse*. Cambridge: Cambridge University Press.

Silverstein, Michael. 1993. Metapragmatic discourse and metapragmatic function. In *Reflexive language*, ed. J. Lucy. 33–58. Cambridge: Cambridge University Press.

Silverstein, Michael, and Greg Urban, eds. 1996. *Natural histories of discourse*. Chicago: University of Chicago Press.

Singer, Milton. 1989. Pronouns, persons, and the semiotic self. In *Semiotics, self, and society*, eds. B. Lee and G. Urban. 229–96. Berlin: Mouton de Gruyter.

Singer, Milton, ed. 1988. *Nuclear policy, culture, and history: Report of a colloquium held at the University of Chicago*. Chicago: Center for International Studies.

Slobin, Dan. 1992. Drift in English/position in constructions. LINGUIST List 3.628. 13 August. Internet posting.

Smith, Anthony D. [1986] 1998. *The ethnic origins of nations*. Oxford: Blackwell Publishers.

Smith, Grafton Elliot, et al. 1911. *The ancient Egyptians and their influence upon the civilization of Europe*. New York: Harper and Bros.

———. 1927. *Culture: The diffusion controversy*. New York: W. W. Norton.

Sperber, Dan. 1996. *Explaining culture: A naturalistic approach*. Oxford: Blackwell.

Spindler, Louise S. 1962. *Menomini women and culture change*. Menasha, Wisc.: American Anthropological Association.

Taussig, Michael. 1980. *The devil and commodity fetishism in South America*. Chapel Hill: University of North Carolina Press.

———. 1987. *Shamanism, colonialism, and the wild man: A study in terror and healing*. Chicago: University of Chicago Press

Taylor, Charles. 1989. *Sources of the self: The making of the modern identity*. Cambridge: Harvard University Press.

———. 1990. *Invoking civil society*. In Working papers and proceedings of the Center for Psychosocial Studies, no. 31. Chicago: Center for Psychosocial Studies.

———. 1998. Nationalism and Modernity. In *The state of the nation: Ernest Gellner and the theory of nationalism*, ed. John A. Hall. 191–218. Cambridge: Cambridge University Press.

Taylor, Charles, et al. 1992. *Multiculturalism and "the politics of recognition."* Princeton, N.J.: Princeton University Press.

Tedlock, Dennis. 1983. *The spoken word and the work of interpretation*. Philadelphia: University of Pennsylvania Press.

Tedlock, Dennis, and Bruce Mannheim, eds. 1995. *The dialogic emergence of culture*. Urbana: University of Illinois Press.

Thomas, Marcel. [1958] 1976. Manuscript. In *The coming of the book: The impact of printing, 1450–1800*, ed. L. Febvre and H.-J. Martin. 15–28. London: New Left Books.

Tinee, Mae. 1964a. *Fail Safe* is chilling as film, too. *Chicago Tribune*, 9 November, section 2, page 9.

———. 1964b. *Red Alert* makes exciting, thought-provoking film. *Chicago Tribune*, 20 February, section 2, page 8.

Todorov, Tzvetan. 1992. *The conquest of America: The question of the other*. Trans. R. Howard. New York: Harper Perennial.

Turgeon, Laurier, Denys Delâge, and Réal Ouellet, eds. 1996. *Transferts culturels et métissages Amérique/Europe, XVIe–XXe siécle—Cultural Transfer, America and Europe: 500 Years of Interculturation*. Québec: Les Presses de l'Université.

Turner, Terence. 1988. Ethno-ethnohistory: Myth and history in native South American representations of contact with western society. In *Rethinking history and myth*, ed. J. D. Hill. 235–81. Urbana: University of Illinois Press.

Unthinkable unthought. 1964. *Newsweek*, 12 October, 114–15.

Urban, Greg. 1988. The pronominal pragmatics of nuclear war discourse. *Multilingua* 7(1–2): 67–93.

———. 1989. The "I" of discourse in Shokleng. In *Semiotics, self, and society*, ed. B. Lee and G. Urban. 27–51. Berlin: Mouton de Gruyter.

———. 1991. *A discourse-centered approach to culture: Native South American myths and rituals*. Austin: University of Texas Press.

———. 1996a. Entextualization, replication, and power. In *Natural histories of discourse*, ed. M. Silverstein and G. Urban. 21–44. Chicago: University of Chicago Press.

———. 1996b. *Metaphysical community: The interplay of the senses and the intellect*. Austin: University of Texas Press.

Verhovek, Sam Howe. 1997. Before his armed standoff, Texan waged war on neighbors in court. *New York Times*, 2 May, late edition, section A, page 12.

R e f e r e n c e s

Voloshinov, V. N. [1927] 1976. *Freudianism: A Marxist critique.* Trans. I. R. Titunik. New York: Academic Press.

———. [1929] 1973. *Marxism and the philosophy of language.* Trans. L. Matejka and I. R. Titunik. Cambridge: Harvard University Press.

Wainwright, Loudon. 1964. The strange case of Strangelove. *Life* 56(13 March): 15.

Wallace, Anthony F. C. 1978. *Rockdale: The growth of an American village in the early industrial revolution.* New York: Knopf.

———. 1987. *St. Clair: A nineteenth-century coal town's experience with a disaster-prone industry.* New York: Knopf.

Wallerstein, Immanuel Maurice. 1974. *The modern world-system: Capitalist agriculture and the origins of the European world-economy in the sixteenth century.* New York: Academic Press.

Warner, Michael. 1990. *The letters of the republic: Publication and the public sphere in eighteenth-century America.* Cambridge: Harvard University Press.

Warner, W. Lloyd. 1959. *The living and the dead: A study of the symbolic life of Americans.* Yankee City Series, vol. 5. New Haven, Conn.: Yale University Press.

Warner, W. Lloyd, and J. O. Low. 1947. *The social system of the modern factory: The strike: A social analysis.* Yankee City Series, vol. 4. New Haven, Conn.: Yale University Press.

Warner, W. Lloyd, and Paul S. Lunt. 1941. *The social life of a modern community.* Yankee City Series, vol. 1. New Haven, Conn.: Yale University Press.

———. 1942. *The status system of a modern community.* Yankee City Series, vol. 2. New Haven, Conn.: Yale University Press.

Warner, W. Lloyd, and Leo Srole. 1945. *The social systems of American ethnic groups.* Yankee City Series, vol. 3. New Haven, Conn.: Yale University Press.

Weber, Max. [1925] 1968. *Economy and society: An outline of interpretive sociology.* Ed. G. Roth and C. Wittich. Berkeley: University of California Press.

———. [1958] 1976. *The Protestant ethic and the spirit of capitalism.* New York: Scribner's.

Weinberger, Caspar W. 1986. U.S. defense strategy. *Foreign Affairs* 64(4): 675–97.

———. 1990. *Fighting for peace: Seven critical years in the pentagon.* New York: Warner Books.

Weinberger, Caspar W., and Peter Schweizer. 1996. *The next war.* Washington, D.C.: Regnery.

Winsten, Archer. 1964a. Dr. Strangelove at two theaters. *New York Post,* 30 January, 16.

———. 1964b. Fail Safe opens at Loew's State. *New York Post,* 8 October, 29.

Wissler, Clark. 1938. *The American Indian: An introduction to the anthropology of the New World.* Oxford: Oxford University Press.

Woods, David Walker. 1906. *John Witherspoon.* New York: Flemin H. Revell Co.

Wright, Sewall. 1951. Fisher and Ford on "The Sewall Wright Effect." *American Scientist* 39: 452–58.

Index

Borges, Jorge Luis, 15–16, 90–91, 176
boundaries, cultural, 27, 30, 69
Bourdieu, Pierre: on capital, 185, 189, 233–37, 289 n. 6; on inertial culture, 23–24, 28, 266–68; on social space, 183, 233–37, 243, 258–60; on taste (distinction), 23–24, 198, 233–37, 243, 255, 258–60, 266–68, 289 n. 6
Bourgois, Philippe, 281 n. 5
Brazil, 10–12, 49–54, 56–57. See also Brazilian Indians; nuclear war, Brazilian views on; Posto Indígena Ibirama; Uru-eu-wau-wau
Brazilian Indians: circulation of myths, 43, 63, 73–77, 189, 191, 206; narratorial style of, 109; use of imperatives, 149. See also Posto Indígena Ibirama; Uru-eu-wau-wau; Yanomamö
bricolage, 127–28
Brodie, Richard, 273 n. 1
Burdick, Eugene, 81, 196–97

capitalism: and dissemination, 63, 74; and newness, 286 n. 13; religious origins of, 56
Chagnon, Napoleon, 149, 151–52
charisma, 173
Chatterjee, Partha, 286 n. 13
Cherokee Indians. See myth, Cherokee
Chomsky, Noam, 290 n. 12
circulation. See consciousness and motion; motion, culture as
citizenship, 253–54
Clinton, Bill, 121
Comaroff, John and Jean, 253
Commander-1 (novel), 82, 84
commands. See imperatives
communism, 144, 287 n. 16
comparison. See metaculture, and comparison
complaint. See litany of complaint
configuration of social space, 44–48, 73–75, 263, 288 n. 2; and metaculture, 183, 234; and omega culture, 30–32, 229–30; in theory of Anderson, 20–22; in theory of Bourdieu, 23–24; in theory

of Gramsci, 24–26. See also metaculture of newness
consciousness and motion, 92, 181–85, 224–25, 264–65, 288 n. 1. See also metaculture, and consciousness; motion, culture as
Constitution, U.S., 29, 98
conversion religion. See dissemination, and conversion religion
Cook, Captain James, 279 n. 2
corporations, 55, 264, 269–70
Cowell, Adrian, 49–54, 58, 63
Croesus, 220, 223
cultural capital. See symbolic capital
cultural drift, 19, 267, 276 n. 14, 294 n. 14
cultural objects, 38–40, 65, 78, 85, 185, 208, 250; and contextual appropriateness, 218–19, 247; durability of, 230–32, 256; and intention, 213–16; and metacultural segmentation, 247–48; and motion, 240–42; and prediction of effects (see newness, and prediction); as response (see response and culture); and taste, 235–36; and truth, 216–18, 248–52. See also film; material culture; motion, culture as; myth
culture: acceleration of (see acceleration of culture); American, 55–56; anthropology's traditional conceptions of, 2, 12, 19, 25, 42–43; area, 69, 274 n. 10; boundaries of (see boundaries, cultural); and centralized authority (see tradition, and centralized authority); competition of elements, 20, 74, 152–53, 177–78, 188; and configuration of social space (see configuration of social space); contact, 279 n. 2, 279 n. 4; and deceleration (see deceleration and culture); defined, 2; and discourse, 64, 73–74, 98–99, 117, 224, 274 n. 4; dissemination of (see dissemination, of culture); and entropy (see deceleration and culture); and futurity (see futurity and culture); and immateriality, 2–5, 37, 40, 42–54, 62–65, 78–80 (see also meaning); and imperatives (see imperatives); iner-

taste, 233; and truth claims, 248–52; Weberian, 173; and writing, 73. *See also* language, and metaculture of tradition; transubstantiation of culture, and tradition

transubstantiation of culture, 146–55, 157–60, 175, 263–72; and modernity, 262; motion between layers of circulation, 184–85; and narrative, 160, 162–63; and replication, 159–61, 239–40; and tradition, 261

truth. *See* cultural objects, and truth type, 78, 283 n. 17, 283 n. 18, 293 n. 12

Uru-eu-wau-wau, 49–58, 62, 67–68, 71–74, 229, 236
"us." *See* "we"
use value. *See* exchange value

value, 62–63
Van Kirk, John C., 95
Virginia Declaration of Rights, 137
voice, 183–84
Voloshinov, V. N., 175, 239, 288 n. 1, 292 n. 3

Wallace, Anthony F. C., 281 n. 5
Wallerstein, Immanuel, 256
Warner, Michael, 293 n. 9
Warner, W. Lloyd, 55, 281 n. 5
wars of conquest. *See* dissemination, and wars of conquest

"we," 10–14, 16–18, 26–31, 92, 95–96, 99, 112–13, 284 n. 4; of African Americans, 121–22, 139–40; aggrieved, 121–22, 128, 285 n. 10 (*see also* litany of complaint); of the American colonies, 96–105; and authorship. 141–43; of communism, 144; of Declaration of Independence signers, 103; and discourse of danger, 142–43; and futurity, 135–44; of the human species, 11–14, 17–18, 27, 29–31, 96, 99, 103, 106–7, 144–43 277 n. 19; limits on use, 131–36, 139; of the living, 138–40, 285 n. 12; and modernity, 111–13, 121, 139, 144 (*see also* "we," and futurity); of the nation, 12–14, 27–31, 95–97, 99–108, 135–36, 140–44, 252–55, 257, 260, 277 n. 19; of politicians, etc., 106; telos of, 141–44; of the women's movement, 133, 135

Weber, Max, 56, 60, 173–74, 181, 274 n. 3
Weinberger, Caspar, 26–31, 106
Wheeler, Harvey, 81, 196–97
Wissler, Clark, 274 n. 10
Wright, Sewall, 276 n. 14
writing. *See* dissemination, and writing; newness, and writing; replication, and writing; tradition, and writing

Yankee City, 55, 281 n. 5
Yanomamö, 149–53, 157

GREG URBAN is professor of anthropology at the University of Penn-sylvania. His books include *A Discourse-Centered Approach to Culture: Native South American Myths and Rituals* and *Metaphysical Community: The Interplay of the Senses and the Intellect.*